T0305555

Accelerating Sustainability in Fashion, Clothing and Textiles

The issue of sustainability is characterised as a 'Wicked Problem' in the fashion, clothing and textiles sector and is now coming into increased focus due to growing consumer, business and policy pressures. This in-depth volume presents a comprehensive overview of the challenges and emerging opportunities faced by the sector, and provides strategic solutions as to how the sector can substantially accelerate sustainability.

This book collates research and industry best practice to provide a 'one-stop shop' exploring the complex and interconnected issues surrounding sustainability in fashion, clothing and textiles. The practical and digestible chapters include innovative examples and perspectives from different regions of the globe, addressing topics from policies to supply chain issues and materials innovation. Five unique case studies of sustainable businesses provide detailed examples of pioneering practice. Edited by three professionals with long-standing knowledge and expertise, the book takes a global perspective with examples that illustrate the scale and breadth of topics and regions in the scope of sustainability. This holistic approach brings together both academic and industry perspectives on the critical areas that require immediate action to move towards a more sustainable fashion, clothing and textile sector.

This is an invaluable resource for those working in the industry, policymakers and for those in business or academia with an interest in sustainability in fashion, clothing, textiles and related sectors worldwide. It is also relevant to professionals and students in the areas of sustainability, innovation, supply chains, design and development, consultancy, education and training.

Martin Charter is Professor of Innovation and Sustainability and Director at the University for the Creative Arts. He has worked on sustainability and innovation issues for 35 years and is the author/editor of numerous publications. Martin is a fellow of the Royal Society of Arts and Clean Leadership Growth Network.

Bernice Pan is an award-winning design entrepreneur, speaker and author, combining vision, theory and practice. She founded DEPLOY in 2006 to reform fashion sector; in 2022, the company received B Corp status.

Sandy Black is Research Professor and design educator in the Centre for Sustainable Fashion, London College of Fashion, University of the Arts London. As a pioneering author of numerous book titles on fashion and sustainability, Sandy works to catalyse sustainable fashion and textiles practices and sustainable prosperity.

"To change the impact of the fashion industry on people and nature, we must revolutionise all that we consider to be normal. This book scopes ideas for immediate action to tackle this wicked problem with creativity and commitment, so we can wear clothes that fit our principles."

Orsola de Castro, *Author and Co-Founder,*
Fashion Revolution

"A thought-provoking collection combining academic research and industry experiences, this is a valuable resource for a wide range of stakeholders with insights, ideas, and key questions, highlighting the complex issues facing a sector that urgently seeks a sustainable future."

Andrew Martin, *Executive Vice President,*
Sustainable Apparel Coalition

Accelerating Sustainability in Fashion, Clothing and Textiles

Edited by
Martin Charter, Bernice Pan and
Sandy Black

Routledge
Taylor & Francis Group

LONDON AND NEW YORK

Cover design: Bernice Pan
Front cover image: DEPLOY | Matthieu Spohn
Back cover image: MUD Jeans

First published 2024
by Routledge
4 Park Square, Milton Park, Abingdon, Oxon OX14 4RN

and by Routledge
605 Third Avenue, New York, NY 10158

Routledge is an imprint of the Taylor & Francis Group, an informa business

© 2024 selection and editorial matter, Martin Charter, Bernice Pan and Sandy Black;
individual chapters, the contributors

British Library Cataloguing-in-Publication Data
A catalogue record for this book is available from the British Library

Library of Congress Cataloging-in-Publication Data
Names: Charter, Martin, editor. | Pan, Bernice, editor. | Black, Sandy, editor.
Title: Accelerating sustainability in fashion, clothing and textiles /
edited by Martin Charter, Bernice Pan and Sandy Black.
Description: Abingdon, Oxon; New York, NY: Routledge, 2024.
Identifiers: LCCN 2023015121 (print) | LCCN 2023015122 (ebook) |
ISBN 9781032225197 (hardback) | ISBN 9781032225173 (paperback) |
ISBN 9781003272878 (ebook)
Subjects: LCSH: Clothing trade–Environmental aspects. | Textile
industry—Environmental aspects. | Fashion
merchandising—Environmental aspects.
Classification: LCC HD9940.A2 A23 2024 (print) | LCC HD9940.A2 (ebook) |
DDC 338.4/7687—dc23/eng/20230414
LC record available at https://lccn.loc.gov/2023015121
LC ebook record available at https://lccn.loc.gov/2023015122

ISBN: 978-1-032-22519-7 (hbk)
ISBN: 978-1-032-22517-3 (pbk)
ISBN: 978-1-003-27287-8 (ebk)

DOI: 10.4324/9781003272878

Typeset in Baskerville
by codeMantra

Contents

About the editors

Martin Charter, Professor and Director, The Centre for Sustainable Design, University for the Creative Arts, UK

Martin Charter is Director of The Centre for Sustainable Design® at the University for the Creative Arts (UCA) that was established in 1995. He is a former Visiting Professor in Sustainable Product Design and presently Professor of Innovation & Sustainability at UCA. Martin has 30 years' experience in sustainable innovation, product sustainability and circular economy. Martin has sat on many international expert committees and advisory boards including P&G, InterfaceFlor, World Resources Forum, DEFRA and Global Ghost Gear Initiative. He is the organiser of the Sustainable Innovation series of international conferences (1995–2023). He has also been active in standardisation: the convenor of ISO14006:2011 and ISO14006:2020 (eco-design), UK expert to both ISO TR 14062:2002 (eco-design) and IEC/ISO 62959:2019 (eco-design), ISO TC 323 (circular economy) and core team member of BS8001:2017 (circular economy). Martin founded and is the chair of the charity Farnham Repair Café. Martin is an author and editor of many publications including *Sustainable Solutions, Greener Marketing I & II* and *Designing for the Circular Economy* and is a regular speaker in conferences worldwide.

Bernice Pan, Design Entrepreneur, Founder and Creative Director, DEPLOY, UK

Bernice Pan is a creative entrepreneur combining vision, theory and practice. She identified early on the endemic social-environmental issues of overconsumption and the pressing need for structural change, thus set her mission to problem-solve using design thinking, gaining her PhD in design management for The Fashion System, after architectural training at University of Cambridge and Royal College of Art. Bernice founded direct-to-consumer brand DEPLOY in 2006 (certified B Corp) as a strategic action plan to reform fashion with 360° sustainability. Its novel circular business model of multi-functional product, service-experience customisation, zero-waste supply chain, on-demand production, agile retail operation, bespoke after-sale service and humanitarian partnerships increases human benefit while reducing environmental wastage, fulfilling 12 of 17 UN SDGs. This exceptional approach won international accolades and is widely featured in the media including BBC and *Vogue*. Her speaking engagements span from Harvard and London Business Schools, to The Royal College of Art and Beijing Institute of Fashion & Technology, to The Institute of Directors. She has taught in Brunel and Kingston Universities, consults for apparel businesses in UK, US and Asia and is a contributing writer to several books.

Sandy Black, Research Professor, Centre for Sustainable Fashion, London College of Fashion, University of the Arts London, UK

Sandy Black is Professor of Fashion and Textile Design and Technology and Key Researcher at the Centre for Sustainable Fashion, a University of the Arts London research centre based at London College of Fashion. Having previously run her Sandy Black Original Knits fashion knitwear label for many years, Sandy works at the intersections of fashion and textile practice, design for sustainability, business, technology and culture. She has published pioneering texts on sustainable fashion and design (*Eco Chic: The Fashion Paradox*, 2008; *The Sustainable Fashion Handbook*, 2012) and on knitwear design, history and technology (*Knitwear in Fashion*, 2002; *Knitting: Fashion, Industry, Craft*, 2012; *Classic Knits of the 1980s*, 2021). Recent work brings together academic research with the designer fashion sector (especially inventive micro and small businesses) through dialogue and collaborative projects, focusing on the role of creative entrepreneurship, design, new business models and innovative technology application in addressing issues of sustainability in fashion. Sandy is founder and Editor-in-Chief of the academic journal *Fashion Practice: Design, Creative Process and the Fashion Industry*, published since 2009.

About the contributors

Helga Ahrens-Wels, Researcher, Institute of Textile Technology, RWTH Aachen University, Germany

Helga Ahrens-Wels is Researcher in the field of "Additive and Joining Technologies" at the Institute of Textile Technology at RWTH Aachen University, Germany, supervised by Professor Thomas Gries. Helga Ahrens-Wels holds a diploma in Fashion Design from HAW Hamburg. Helga Ahrens-Wels has been gathering expert knowledge in the field of pattern making, grading and fit analysis for more than 30 years in national and international projects. She has been the owner of COMCUT Patternmaker for 27 years. Her research focuses on 2- and 3-dimensional pattern construction with regard to sustainability in the textile process chain.

Mathilde Asseman, PhD Candidate, Partner, Institut Français de la Mode, France

Mathilde Asseman obtained a Master's degree in Public Policy and Sustainability from Sciences Po Paris and studied Fashion Design and Marketing at Parsons New York. She is currently a PhD candidate in Management at the Sustainability IFM-KERING Research Chair (Institut Français de la Mode) and at the Arts et Métiers Institute within the LIRSA research laboratory. She focuses her research on the link and dynamics between positive social impact and value creation for businesses integrating CSR within their strategy. Her work on the creation of a positive social impact measurement, evaluation and visualisation management tool is supported by the fashion luxury brand Chloé.

Christine Baeza, Drexel University, US

Christine Baeza has had an extensive 20+ year career as an accomplished design and merchandising executive. She has multi-tier capabilities in men's, women's, accessories and children with particular emphasis on brand strategy for different channels of distribution. Her positions in the industry allowed her work with top brands such as Tommy Hilfiger, Hugo Boss, Adidas, Dockers and Nautica. Her background in branding, textiles, design, product development and merchandising bring real-world experience to the classroom. Chris has a passion for design, ethics and purpose-driven businesses. Her research seeks to explore and answer the following overarching question: are students who study design and merchandising better prepared after graduation when ethics and social entrepreneurship are an integral part of their curricula? She holds a Bachelor's degree in Fashion Design and Textile Design from Philadelphia College of Textiles & Science and a Master's degree in Leadership Development from Pennsylvania State University.

Jen Ballie, Researcher, DJCAD University of Dundee, Scotland

Jen Ballie is a PhD graduate from UAL's Centre for Circular Design whose research explores social innovation within fashion and textiles to re-think future practices. She is now Research Manager at V&A Dundee – a Design Museum in Scotland. Jen's journey began within textile design but has organically become more interdisciplinary over time, drawing upon the fields of design strategy, innovation and service design. Within a world proliferated with too much stuff, Jen's passionate about the role and responsibilities of the design professional and seeks to explore how we can add value to our everyday lives through design.

Oliver Bealby-Wright, Sustainable Consumption Project Specialist, Consumers International, UK

Oliver Bealby-Wright is Sustainable Consumption Project Specialist at Consumers International, where he has worked on the contribution of consumption to climate action and food and energy systems transformation. He is currently leading research on the role of consumer protection in the energy transition, and on the policy, frameworks needed to drive sustainability in e-commerce. Previously, he sat on the Coordination Desk of the UN One Planet network's Consumer Information Programme for Sustainable Consumption and Production. His interest in sustainability grew out of an interdisciplinary academic background in the humanities.

Elizabeth Bigger, Computational Fashion Practitioner and Researcher, Spain

Elizabeth Bigger is a computational fashion practitioner, artist and researcher exploring algorithmic systems for ecological data integration within fashion and on-body dynamics to optimise garment sustainability goals. She has an active curiosity for data and actualising evolutionary design methods for climate action. Elizabeth has spent the past decade implementing advanced computational tools for bespoke digital fashion design, fashion analytics systems, generative fashion systems, 3D body databases, wearable computing projects and interactive art installations. In 2019, Elizabeth co-created the educational curriculum for the award-winning master's studio programme, *Augmented Senses*. She began research into circular initiatives, garment waste output and fashion workflows in 2013. Elizabeth has been awarded several international design awards in wearable computing, has published numerous research papers and lectures and exhibits globally. Elizabeth began her career as a traditional tailor crafting bespoke garments for 15 years before including computational programming, parametric design and electronic hardware into her practice.

Natasha Bonnelame, Director, Digital Learning, London College of Fashion, University of the Arts London, UK

Natasha Bonnelame is the Programme Director: Digital Learning at London College of Fashion, University of the Arts London. She holds a PhD from the Centre for Caribbean and Diaspora Studies, Goldsmiths, University of London where she has taught on Black British Literature and Theatre, and Caribbean Women's Writing. With a specialism in digital learning, she has delivered projects for the Royal National Theatre as the Project Manager for the National's Black Plays Archive (2011–2014). Establishing the first digital platform documenting the first production of every African, Caribbean and Black British play produced in the UK. She worked as the Project Manager (2014–2016) on Tate Gallery's partnership with Khan Academy and Smarthistory, to explore the affordances of digital platforms and their capacity to reach users with little or no knowledge of art and engage them with Tate's collections.

Mila Burcikova, Researcher, Centre for Sustainable Fashion, London College of Fashion, University of the Arts London, UK

Mila Burcikova's research interests encompass the human dimension of fashion. At the Centre, she works across a range of research and knowledge exchange projects, with an emphasis on micro and small fashion businesses that offer alternatives to the current fashion system. Her research interrogates the connections between fashion and everyday life within the context of climate emergency. Mila's PhD 'Mundane Fashion: Women, Clothes and Emotional Durability' investigated emotional durability of clothing through the lens of a designer-maker practice. In 2018, she guest-edited the special issue of the journal *Utopian Studies* entitled Utopia and Fashion.

Elizabeth Bye, Professor, Apparel Studies, College of Design, University of Minnesota, US

Elizabeth Bye (she/her) is Professor in Apparel Studies in the College of Design at the University of Minnesota. Her scholarship balances published research and creative works with a focus on the relationship between design/manufacturing/sustainability, socially responsible design and apparel technology including human factors, sizing and fit of wearable products. Recent projects include Racial Equity in Sustainable Apparel and work with Native American designers around Gratitude & Reciprocity as Foundational Values for a Sustainable Apparel Future. Dr Bye is an International Textile and Apparel Association (ITAA) Fellow, Distinguished Scholar, and has received the ITAA Lectra Innovation award for faculty research twice. She received the College of Design Outstanding Teaching Award and the Tekne Award for Collaboration for Community Impact. Dr Bye was the department head of Design, Housing and Apparel from 2011 to 2020 and past ITAA president.

Jesús Rosales Carreón, Assistant Professor, Copernicus Institute of Sustainable Development, Utrecht University, The Netherlands

Jesús Rosales Carreón studied Chemical Engineering at the National University of Mexico. He has worked for leading companies such as "Lyonnaise des eaux" and "Owens Corning." He obtained a Master of Science degree in Energy and Environmental Sciences. He received his PhD from Groningen University in the field of Knowledge Management in Sustainable Agriculture. Currently, Jesús is Assistant Professor at the Copernicus Institute of Sustainable Development, Utrecht University. He is interested in understanding the environmental and social implications associated with the implementation of the concept of circular economy and living labs. Current projects are embedded in the fashion, construction and education sectors. Furthermore, he coordinates the Master's Programme in Energy Science in Utrecht University.

Sara Cavagnero, IP Lawyer, PhD Researcher: IP Law for Sustainability in the Fashion Industry, Italy

Sara Cavagnero is a PhD researcher at Northumbria University and qualified IP lawyer admitted at the Italian Bar. Sara's work is devoted to the use of IP assets as private sustainability governance tools and the legal implications arising thereof. Her analysis is framed within the under-considered SMEs' perspective and focused on suppliers along the value chain. Sara is involved as an expert at UN/CEFACT "Enhancing Traceability and Transparency for Sustainable Value Chains in Garment and Footwear" project. She is the Law & Sustainability Specialist and one of the co-founders of the NGO *rén collective*, a platform providing sustainable fashion SMEs with network opportunities and viable options for an industry reset.

Ichin Cheng, Co-Founder and Director, Sustainable Innovation Lab, UK

Ichin Cheng is Director and Co-Founder of Sustainable Innovation Lab and Fellow of RSA and has more than 25 years professional experience in the field of green business, circular economy, sustainable innovation, climate change policy, low carbon and green technology, sustainable materials and products. The work includes social-economic aspects, environmental impact, international environmental policies and management, environmental assessment techniques in many countries in Europe, US and Asia. Ichin is involved in many international expert committees and advisory boards. She is currently independent technical advisory panel of The Sustainable Manufacturing and Environmental Pollution (SMEP). SMEP programme supported by an UK The Department for International Development (DFID) investment of GBP 25 million over five years (2019–2024). DFID has partnered with the United Nations Conference on Trade and Development (UNCTAD). Ichin was the advisory board expert of EC Horizon 2020 of Industrial Technologies and for international cooperation. She is also innovation expert for Climate-KIC and final jury of Reinventing Paris. She is presently leading a team of international experts focused on the global commercialisation of Taiwan circular solar photovoltaic technology.

Yoon Jung Choi, Assistant Professor, Virginia Polytechnic Institute and State University, US

Yoon Jung Choi is Assistant Professor in Industrial Design at Virginia Tech. Her research interests focus on the application of design to social, environmental and humanitarian innovation in creating products, interactions and systems and sustainable innovation through impactful industry/public collaboration. Yoon completed her PhD at the Royal College of Arts. Her thesis focuses on design for owner–object detachment through care practice, for object longevity and environmental benefit. Yoon has a MA in Communication Design at Kingston University. She has ten years' experience in industry, as a senior/middle-level designer at various brand design consultancies in London and then as an independent designer at Samsung Design Europe, Lewis Moberly and SiebertHead for clients such as Coca-Cola, Cadbury, Cussons, GSK,

Carlsberg, McDonald's, Werther's Original and Sainsbury's. She has previously taught in Central Saint Martins and Royal College of Art.

Philippa Crommentuijn-Marsh, Post-Doctoral researcher, Open University, UK

Philippa Crommentuijn-Marsh's PhD focused on clothing purchasing and consumption by ordinary women and studied their awareness of sustainability and the sustainability of their behaviour. Philippa's ethnographically inspired research took the form of case studies to study the participants' behaviour in detail. Interests include all aspects of sustainable fashion but particularly the consumer viewpoint and clothing consumption.

Samantha Corcoran, Lecturer Printed Textiles, Textile and Surface Design, National College of Art and Design, Republic of Ireland

Samantha Corcoran is a designer and lecturer in Printed Textile and Surface Design in the National College of Art and Design, Dublin, with 25 years of lecturing and experiential workshop practice across screen and digital print, dyeing and material innovation. She is passionate about, future thinking, material, colour, surface, collaborative knowledge sharing and the emotive power of materials and making, with an interest in environmental ethics and restorative design principles. She is an award-winning urban allotmenteer with a healthy obsession for hands in the earth, organic growing, environmental awareness and natural living. With an education that spans textile design, history of art and design and fine art media, Samantha has worked in the fashion industry as a print designer for John Rocha and in collaboration with architects and public bodies on Per Cent for Art site-specific installations, with work produced, exhibited and shown in both an art and design context.

Jacqueline Cramer, Chair, Dutch Circular Textile Valley, The Netherlands

Jacqueline Cramer is chair of the national Dutch Circular Textile Valley and the Circular Textile Hub of the Amsterdam Metropolitan Area, supervisory board chair of Holland Circular Hotspot and a professor of sustainable innovation at Utrecht University. She has also been actively engaged in circular economy initiatives for eight years as a member of the Amsterdam Economic Board. From 2007 to 2010, she was the Minister of Housing, Spatial Planning and the Environment for the Dutch Labour Party. Since 1990, Jacqueline has been a consultant, advising over 200 companies and many partners cooperating in product chains and at a regional level on implementation of sustainable entrepreneurship, corporate social responsibility and the circular economy. To this day, she is a member of various governmental, industry and non-profit advisory boards. Some of her other current roles include chair of the Dutch Concrete Agreement and the Dutch Building Agreement Steel.

Joanna Czutkowna, Director, I Went Shopping Today, UK

Joanna Czutkowna has over 20 years of international experience, based in China for ten years, and has managed global sourcing strategy for a range of UK fashion brands before starting up innovation departments for some of the world's largest brands. She has worked across China, Bangladesh, Indonesia, India, Turkey, Japan, Korea and the UK, developing suppliers and supporting brands with innovation, materials and business strategy. Working across every part of the product development process, from ideation to sampling, manufacture and buying, she has hands-on extensive industry insight and experience. She now consults as a subject matter expert on circular design, leadership collaboration, digital transformation, supply chain partnerships and inclusive design practices. She is completing her PhD focusing on circularity while continuing to drive innovation through Research and development within the sector.

Angela Davies, Senior Lecturer Textile and Garment Technology, School of Fashion and Textiles, De Montfort University, UK

Angela Davies is Senior Lecturer in Textile and Garment Technology, with a PhD in Technical Textiles. Her PhD focused on sustainable incontinence product development for residential and hospital use, providing her with expertise in the medical textile development and testing. Angela has been principal and co-investigator on numerous regionally and European-funded products, working with technical textile and pharmaceutical SMEs and larger enterprises to support the development of new products and processes. This has involved the development of undertaking of product performance and textile testing of fibres, years, fabrics and end-products. Her research interests include healthcare textiles, sustainable performance textiles, wearable technologies and product performance. Programme leader for MSc in Textile Design, Technology and Innovation, Angela teaches across four programmes at both undergraduate and postgraduate levels including dissertation and PhD supervision. Key areas of teaching include product performance and quality control – textile testing, textile innovation and textile sustainability.

Sage Davis, Researcher, University of Minnesota, US

Sage Davis is a PhD student and DOVE fellow at the University of Minnesota. Her focus in the Apparel Studies Programme is on the history and culture of dress with an emphasis in Indigenous Studies. Her research interests include sustainability, design activism and social justice in the textile and apparel industry. Sage has been working in education since 2011, primarily with Native American students. Sage received her undergraduate degree in Communication, Media, and Rhetoric in 2011 and a Master of Education degree in 2018. Upon completion of her PhD, Sage plans to become a Professor of Design to continue to research social justice, equity and sustainability in the fashion industry, while teaching through the lens of Indigeneity.

Trevor Davis, Managing Director, Trevor Davis & Associates Ltd, UK

Trevor Davis is a consumer industry futurist, a Fellow of the Royal Society of the Arts and former IBM Distinguished Engineer. He is also an expert on good practices for developing and launching sustainable brands and products. With over 30 years of international business experience working with leading consumer brands, Trevor brings deep industry insight and a distinctive point of view on digital technologies such as Artificial Intelligence (AI) and Industry 4.0. Trevor has been a pioneer in development and application of cognitive computing and big data techniques. In the food, beverage and fashion industries, Trevor is a leader in using AI techniques for market research and predicting trends. Trevor's most recent research and practice has focused on ethical application of the latest digital technologies to consumer-brand relationships, sensory science and sustainability. Among others, Advertising Age, the *New York Times* and Forbes have covered his innovative techniques for consumer insight.

Marte Cázarez Duarte, Co-Founder and Co-CEO, Adriano Di Marti S.A. de C.V., Mexico

Marte Cázarez Duarte is Co-Founder and Co-CEO of Adriano Di Marti S.A. de C.V (with Adrián López Velarde), the Mexican company behind the development of Desserto®, a plant-based bio material made of cactus, aiming to replace animal leather and the high contamination of polyvinyl chloride (PVC) as an alternative for the fashion industry, and Deserttex®, it's variant for the automotive industry. Before working full time on the development of Desserto, Marte served as an international sales representative for a company producing Aloe Vera products for the home care industry, and as commercial director for Cloe Time, a national fast-fashion Mexican brand. Marte and Adrián are committed to creating new sustainable solutions and promoting ethical practices in the fashion industry in order to help build a better green world through the same fashion industry. Adriano Di Marti and their products won several awards including a Green Product Award, Monte Carlo Fashion Week Sustainable Fashion Award, Innovation Award by Samsung, PETA Compassionate Business Award, Good Design Award, Adolf Horn Award, and also received a special mention as second runner up and favourite in the materials category at the LVMH Innovation Award.

Lucy E. Dunne, Professor, University of Minnesota, US

Lucy E. Dunne is Professor at the University of Minnesota, where she directs the Apparel Design programme and is the Founder and Co-director of the Wearable Technology Lab. She is co-author (with Susan Watkins) of *Functional Apparel Design: From Sportswear to Space Suits* (2015), and her academic background includes degrees in Apparel Design (Cornell University, BS and MA), Electronic Engineering (Tompkins-Cortland Community College, AAS), and Computer Science (University College Dublin, PhD). Her research is focused on pursuing the vision of scalable, wearable garment-integrated technology, and explores new functionality in apparel, human-device interface, production and manufacture and human factors of wearable products. Dr Dunne has received the National Science Foundation's CAREER award and the NASA Silver Achievement Medal for her work with functional clothing and wearable technology.

Rebecca Earley, Professor and Co-Founder, Centre for Circular Design, Chelsea College of Arts and Design, University of the Arts London, UK

Rebecca Earley is a practice researcher and sustainable/circular textile designer. Since the late 1990s, her work has focused on using design to explore sustainable strategies, with different applications from small- to large-scale industry contexts. Her most recent work looks at circular fashion through a social design lens, directly meeting the needs of users and enhancing the lives of women around the supply chain. These products last a long time, are supported by different business models in local geographic loops and change function at key stages. Rebecca is currently leading the circular, local and bio-design guidelines research for the Herewear project (H2020, 2020–2024). She also advises on She Makes, another EU project that supports the advancement of girls and women in the industry. In October 2020, she co-founded World Circular Textiles Day 2050 with a team of like-minded collaborators who all want to co-create new, interconnected textile roadmaps for circular futures.

Claudia Eckert, Professor of Design, Open University, UK

Claudia Eckert spent ten years in the Engineering Design Centre at the University of Cambridge, where she was a senior research associate and associate director, leading the design process improvement group, which developed tools and methods to support the development of complex engineering products working with companies manufacturing helicopters, jet engines, cars and diesel engines. In 2013, she became Professor of Design after returning to the Open University from the University of Cambridge in 2008. She is interested in understanding and supporting the design processes of complex systems in this interplay between creative freedom and the need to reuse and work around existing solutions.

Patrick Elf, Research Fellow, Social and Sustainable Business, Middlesex University, UK

Patrick Elf is a research fellow focused on Social and Sustainable Business at the Centre for Enterprise and Economic Development Research (Middlesex University) and Co-Investigator at the ESRC-funded Centre for the Understanding of Sustainable Prosperity (CUSP) at the University of Surrey. His research focuses on investigating sustainable business models, how to advance the circular economy, issues around sustainable finance and entrepreneurship ecosystems, and avenues for behaviour change approaches towards the adoption of more sustainable lifestyles. Recent research projects examine the potential of sustainable small and medium fashion enterprises to foster sustainable practices, and research exploring the mechanisms of the sustainable innovation ecosystem in Brazil and the UK.

Ahmed Fardin, Co-Founder, Circular Cradle and Manufacturing and Operations Lead at SXD, UK/Canada

Ahmed Fardin is a sustainable manufacturing and operations expert with project management, engineering and consulting experience in multiple industries across Europe, Asia, North America and Australia. Fardin holds a postgraduate degree from St John's College, Cambridge, and an undergraduate degree from the National University of Singapore. His thesis at Cambridge assessed fabric waste in garment factories and quantified its economic and environmental worldwide. His research now focuses on developing an efficient material utilisation algorithm for zero-waste designs focusing on universally worn garments. He is the Co-Founder of Circular Cradle, a sustainable clothing company manufacturing and has recently partnered SXD from Harvard Business School to develop a zero-waste denim jacket. Fardin was the recipient of the Singapore MIT Alliance Innovation Grant and the NUS Innovation and Research Award. He is a member of the Project Management Institute and the American Society of Quality.

Miguel Ángel Gardetti, Founder and Director, Sustainable Textile Centre and the Centre for Study of Sustainable Luxury, Argentina
Miguel Ángel Gardetti holds two Master's degrees before obtaining his doctoral degree: one in Business Administration from the IAE Business School (Universidad Austral, Argentina), and the other one in Environmental Studies and Sustainable Development from the Universidad de Ciencias Empresariales y Sociales (Argentina). He is currently pursuing his third Master's degree in Latin American studies at the Universidad Nacional de General San Martín. He founded on one hand, the Sustainable Textile Centre and the Centre for Studies on Sustainable Luxury. He was guest co-editor for several publications in journals and books. Moreover, he was a renowned professor at different Latin American universities and participated both as trainer and instructor in projects of the Inter-American Development Bank. Between 2012 and 2015, he was also a member of the Consulting Board of the "Future Fashion" Project of MISTRA (a Swedish government foundation that conducts research into environmental topics). He participated in the activity "Changing the World through Fashion," organised by the United Nations for the 4th Conference on Sustainable Development (Rio+20).

Gözde Göncü-Berk, Associate Professor, Department of Design, University of California-Davis, US
Gözde Göncü-Berk is Associate Professor at the University of California-Davis, Department of Design. She directs her research group under WearLab (https://wearlab.ucdavis.edu), focusing on human-centred design of textile-based wearable products for people with special needs. Dr Göncü-Berk's research has received over US$1 million funding and explores the possibilities of electronic textiles and smart clothing including new material and digital fabrication technologies to facilitate design for a variety of body types, environmental and activity-based

contexts. Her academic background merges product design and tex-tiles with a PhD degree in Design (University of Minnesota), MA degree in Textiles and Clothing Design (Mimar Sinan University of Fine Arts) and BSc degree in Industrial Design (Istanbul Technical University). Dr Göncü-Berk is the author of numerous articles in high-impact jour-nals and international conference proceedings.

Kadian Gosler, Researcher, Fashion, Textile and Design, University of Arts London, UK

Kadian Gosler is a theory- and practice-based PhD candidate in Fash-ion, Textile and Design at the University of Arts London and a New Scholars Fellow with the Bristol & Bath Creative Research and devel-opment. Her PhD explores experience through a multi-perspective ap-proach in the design and development of Bra Wearables – a subsection of smart bras. She employs an interdisciplinary methodology layering Feminists HCI, Black Feminists Thought and Deweyan Pragmatism to extend a woman-centred approach. Current research interests include the bra's patent history, advanced technology within the bra and mar-ginalised bra wearers' multifaceted garment experience. Kadian has over 12 years as a professional lingerie designer and merchandiser; completing a Master's degree in Merchandising and Management cen-tred on lingerie entrepreneurship and innovation from the Academy of Art University, San Francisco; and a Bachelors and Associates, Magna Cum Laude in Intimate Apparel Design from the Fashion Institute of Technology, New York.

Christine Goulay, Founder, Sustainabelle Advisory Services, France

Christine Goulay has over 20 years of professional experience at the intersection of sustainability, entrepreneurship and innovation, with a specialisation in fashion. She recently launched Sustainabelle Advisory Services, focusing on innovation as the key to driving positive environ-mental and social impact. Previously, Christine was the Global Director of PANGAIA Science, the B2B arm of the direct-to-consumer brand, PANGAIA. Additionally, Christine was Head of Sustainable Innovation at Kering where she worked to fast-track circular and impact-driven in-novations across the group. She also spent several years at INSEAD in the Centre for Entrepreneurship, where she focused on business model innovation for double and triple bottom line companies. Before that, she launched the B2B business, Edun Live, part of the ethical fash-ion brand, Edun Apparel, founded by Ali Hewson and Bono. She also practiced as a corporate lawyer specialising in venture capital and private equity law. Christine attended Harvard University, holds a law degree from Boston College Law School and has an MBA from INSEAD.

Shalini Gupta, Associate Dean, Styling and Beauty, Pearl Academy, Mumbai, India

Shalini Gupta holds a Bachelor of Design degree from the National Institute of Fashion Technology, New Delhi and Master's degree in Fashion and Textiles. Shalini also holds a Post Graduate Certificate in Academic Practice. She started her career as Co-founder and Head of Design at 'What's Pink' a successful Fashion Accessories label retailing across India, Europe and the Middle East from 2000 to 2015. Over 23 years, she has designed and styled for magazines, television and celebrities before making the switch to education when she joined Pearl Academy in 2014. As an academic, she works on curriculum design and delivery, faculty training curriculum validity and assessment. As a teacher, she is actively involved in subjects that deal with image, identity, visual literacy and innovative creative practice. Her research practice revolves around embedding sustainable ways of thinking in design curricula, fashion as an embodiment of activism and image making. She has been the principal investigator on a project funded by the British Council under their Crafting Futures India Scheme in collaboration with Manchester Metropolitan University. She is currently pursuing her PhD in the area or neuroesthetics.

Karen Marie Hasling, Associate Professor, Lab for Sustainability and Design, Design School Kolding, Denmark

Karen Marie Hasling works as Associate Professor and Co-Lead at Lab for Sustainability and Design at Design School Kolding, Denmark. With backgrounds in textile technology and design engineering, her research centres on material understandings and bridging perspectives on design education. In the last ten years, her research has specialised in investigating the role of materials in design for sustainability and methods use as an active means for curriculum development. Examples of her work include the two decks *Sustainable Design Cards* (2016) and *Material Pathways* (2020) that offer respectively approaches to sustainable design and positions to take if wanting to engage with materials in design for sustainability as well as being the editor of the *Learning Activity Tool* (2021) and the *Book of Lectures* (2021). As well as having widespread experience with teaching in design programmes with emphasis on arts, engineering and management, Karen Marie has been involved in developing the MA programme Design for Planet that she is now the programme manager for.

Frankie Hewitson, CEO and Founder, The Frank Impact Company Ltd, UK

Frankie Hewitson began her career as a fashion supplier designer in London. While working with the UK high street by day, Frankie also worked on her own luxury brand, showing at London Fashion Week for four years. In 2014, Frankie then moved to Southeast Asia, and it was here she saw first-hand the devastating effects fashion has on the environment. She became passionate about human rights and transparency within fashion and began working with supply chains to become more ethically responsible. As her efforts were originally rejected by the big brands, Frankie began working on her TOBEFRANK brand while creating a framework designed to track and improve the impact fashion has on the environment and people. Frankie then launched a fashion supplier 'The Rubbish Fashion Company' to implement the framework at a larger scale. Today Frankie is the founder of The Frank Impact Company, a manufacturing consultancy working with companies to actively reduce their negative impact.

Veronika Kapsali, Research Professor, Materials Technology and Design, London College of Fashion, University of the Arts London, UK

Veronika Kapsali is Professor of Materials Technology and Design at the London College of Fashion, University of the Arts London (UAL). Veronika is a leader in the newly emerging field of bio-inspired textiles and has worked for 15+ years on a range of industry-focused applications that include the invention and development of biomimetic active fibres and textiles. Within this role at UAL, Veronika established the Active Material Systems Research Group and has attracted over £1 million in funding (UKRI/AHRC, Innovate UK, H2020, industry) including an AHRC Leadership Fellow to advance biologically informed design within the context of sustainable/circular textile practice. In November 2014, she received the ITMA Future Materials award for INNOVATOR OF THE YEAR for her work in biomimetic fibre innovation.

Hannah C. Kelbel, Researcher, Institute for Textile Technology at RWTH Aachen, Germany

Hannah C. Kelbel is a researcher and PhD student in the field of "Additive and Joining Technologies" at the Institute for Textile Technology at RWTH Aachen, Germany supervised by Professor Thomas Gries. She is Research Associate at the excellence cluster 'Internet of Production' at RWTH Aachen. Hannah Koch holds a Master of Science degree in Mechanical Engineering from RWTH Aachen and is a graduate from the School for Design Thinking at Hasso-Plattner-Institute in Potsdam, Germany. She has published two peer-reviewed papers and four conference submissions. In her research, she is developing active textile structures and identifies strategies to reduce material use in the textile industry.

Andrée-Anne Lemieux, Head of the IFM-KERING Sustainability Chair, Institut Français de la Mode, France

Andrée-Anne Lemieux has a doctorate in Industrial Engineering from ENSAM, with a PhD from Polytechnique Montreal. Andrée-Anne has studied transformation and innovation through lean management and agility in the fashion and luxury sector. After 15 years of experience in operational management positions in product development, purchasing, marketing and retail sales in the fashion industry, Andrée-Anne is now dedicated to higher education and research at the Institut Français de la Mode in Paris, where she is head of the Sustainability IFM-KERING Research Chair. Her research areas are transformation, sustainability, fashion and luxury, agility, environmental and social impacts.

Claire Lerpiniere, Associate Professor, Sustainable Textiles, School of Fashion and Textiles, De Montfort University, UK

Claire Lerpiniere is Associate Professor of Sustainable Textiles, with an MA in Design and Manufacture, and a PhD in Design Theory. Her PhD focused on consumer experience of textiles and garments as symbolic locations of family and personal stories. This understanding of the relationship we have with textiles and clothing feeds into her current research on how emotional connections impact garment longevity and durability in the context of the sustainable fashion and textiles. As Senior Fellow of the Higher Education Academy, Claire's research focuses on complex systems, understanding leverage points and working for systemic paradigm change within the fashion and textiles industry from within. As a member of De Montfort University's Textiles Engineering and Materials Research Group, her research and PhD supervision are centred on the human and ecological impacts of the fashion and textiles industry, circular textile economies and shifting the paradigm of the industry towards responsible design.

Sabine Lettmann, Senior Lecturer, Institute of Jewellery, Fashion and Textiles, Birmingham City University, UK

Sabine Lettmann works as part-time Senior Lecturer at the Institute of Jewellery, Fashion and Textiles at Birmingham City University. She holds fellowships of the Royal Society for Arts, Manufactures and Commerce as well as the Higher Education Academy, UK. She has international teaching experience in fashion design, circular design systems and in costume design. Since her degree in 2001, she also works as a freelance fashion designer and creative consultant. Both fields shape her research in which she explores the subjects of design, consumption, the social dimension of circular design and circular fashion education. Sabine uses her research to define learning tools for the contexts of higher education and consulting. Amongst others, this led to the development of the Circular Design Matrix framework and the Circular Design Cards, a physical hands-on learning experience addressing the creation of circular fashion concepts for learners at a beginner level.

Helena Leurent, Director General, Consumers International, Switzerland

Helena Leurent is Director General of Consumers International, the membership organisation for 200+ consumer advocacy groups around the world in more than 100 countries. Consumers International works with members and partners to empower consumers, to ensure consumers are treated safely, fairly and honestly worldwide, and to drive change in the marketplace on global consumer issues including digital access and rights, product safety and sustainability. Prior to joining Consumers International, Helena worked for the World Economic Forum developing global partnerships and programmes with government, business, civil society and academia on issues such as advanced manufacturing, sustainable agriculture and humanitarian assistance. Helena has also worked for Tesco Stores Plc, Unilever, McKinsey & Co and The LEK Partnership. Helena holds an MA from the University of Oxford and an MBA from the Kellogg School of Management.

Fergus Lyon, Director, CEEDR, Professor, Enterprise and Organisations, Middlesex University, Deputy Director, ESRC Centre for the Understanding of Sustainable Prosperity, UK

Fergus Lyon is Director of the Centre for Enterprise and Economic Development Research, Middlesex University in London and Deputy Director of the ESRC Centre for the Understanding of Sustainable Prosperity. His research interests include social and sustainable enterprises and enterprise support policy. He has carried out research in Bhutan, Ghana, India, Nepal, Nigeria, Pakistan and UK. Recent work has included a study of sustainable fashion design entrepreneurs. He has been a trustee/director of a number of social enterprises/B Corp.

Jan Mahy, Professor, Sustainable and Functional Textiles, Saxion University of Applied Sciences, Chair of TexPlus Foundation, The Netherlands

Jan Mahy is Professor Sustainable and Functional Textiles at Saxion University of Applied Sciences and Chair of the TexPlus Foundation, actively engaged in the transition to a circular textile economy in the Netherlands. As co-founder of the NETFAS Association, a network of European UAS with textile and fashion in 12 countries, he is board member of the ETP textile organisation at the heart of the European Textile Strategy and related programmes. He leads the research group on textile recycling, functional textile design and innovative textile processes and works with his team closely with the Fashion and Textile Technology programme as part of the bachelor's and the Innovative Textile Development programme as part of master's education.

Rawan Maki, Researcher, London College of Fashion, University of the Arts London, UK

Rawan Maki is a PhD Researcher in design for Sustainability and fashion designer of an eponymous label. Rawan's PhD research, at the London College of Fashion, explores social, material and behavioural transitions required to move towards sustainability in the Gulf and Arab world, using Bahrain as a case study. In particular, she is interested in differing ontologies of design, and how non-Western ontologies may be disruptive for sustainability. The Rawan Maki fashion line is a London-based avant-garde brand, dubbed "reminiscent of Balenciaga" by Blanc Magazine, and has been featured in *Vogue* Arabia, British *Vogue*, *Mojeh Magazine* and *JDEED*. Rawan has displayed her collections on runways and events in New York, London, Berlin, Beirut, Dubai and Riyadh. Rawan is also a founding member of the "Fashion and Ethnicity" interest group at UAL, reviewer for the *Fashion Practice* journal published by Routledge, and coordinator for Fashion Revolution.

Andrew Martin, Vice President, Membership and Stakeholder Engagement, Sustainable Apparel Coalition, US

Andrew Martin is currently Vice President, Membership and Stakeholder Engagement at the Sustainable Apparel Coalition. After 20 years in global textile manufacturing, he spent ten years working in the education/non-profit sectors. From 2015 to 2019 at Amfori, a leading sustainable trade association, his achievements included launching a pioneering audit integrity programme, and the largest capacity building programme of its kind for social and environmental performance in global supply chains. He has a BA (Philosophy and Theology, Kings College London), is an Associate of the University of Exeter, where he completed his MBA in 2012 and in 2015, he obtained a postgraduate certification in team coaching (UWE, Bristol), while leading a Masters in Entrepreneurship (Falmouth University). He is inspired by Bhutan's philosophy of Gross National Happiness, an alternative values-based model for measuring and guiding economic, societal and personal wellbeing.

Lisa Nel, Researcher, Art and Design, Fashion Sustainability, University of Johannesburg (UJ), South Africa

Lisa Nel is a lecturer, fashion designer and creative. Her research focuses on sustainable design paradigms in education and fashion systems. Nel received a Master's degree in Design in 2019. She is a member of 'The Union of Concerned Researchers in Fashion.' Her focus in teaching is social design and design citizenship. Nel is passionate about the teaching pedagogy of service-learning (SL) as an effective experiential learning approach. SL enables art and design students to integrate their 'different knowledges' and experiences for application to real-world problems in community contexts. Furthermore, SL approaches foster graduates' human abilities by integrating human values and capital paradigms towards nurturing a sustainability-oriented ethic. As a result of her SL field efforts, she has received the 'Vice Chancellor's Award of Excellence for Community Engagement.' She is currently registered for a PhD in Art and Design (philosophy) in fashion sustainability at the University of Johannesburg (UJ).

Ann Marie Newton, Founder, Creative Orange Studio, UK

Ann Marie Newton has a career spanning 30 years in the fields of textiles and colour. This includes roles as a scientist, designer, technologist and trend forecaster; both in the UK and US. Experience at all levels of textile supply chains while working at companies such as Interface, Target and Marks & Spencer give Ann Marie a rounded perspective. Having been awarded a distinction in her MA Innovation Management degree at Central Saint Martins, Ann Marie went on to establish Creative Orange Studio. Working with clients globally, this innovation consultancy collaborates with teams and individuals to elevate creativity and innovation skills; all with a view to shifting people's relationship with our world for the better. Based in London, UK Ann Marie enjoys periodically lecturing at Ravensbourne, NBU and UCA. She also delights in supervising postgraduates with Hyper Island. Ann Marie is a member of the Textile Institute and a fellow of the RSA.

Jens Oelerich, Associate Professor, Sustainable Textiles, Saxion University of Applied Sciences, The Netherlands

Jens Oelerich is Associate Professor Sustainable Textiles at Saxion and coordinates several projects with a focus on mechanical and chemical recycling of (poly)cotton, circular design concepts, transparency in the textile value chain and the optimisation of yarns for circular textile products. Since 2021, these activities are accommodated in the Circular Textile Lab of the research group Sustainable & Functional Textiles. Oelerich is particularly interested in material recycling with a focus on value retention. Oelerich is co-founder of SaXcell B.V., a chemical recycling company for cotton, as well as founder and director of Impartex B.V., which is a consulting company for textile recycling and the circular economy of textiles.

Carolina Roberte de Oliveira, Assistant, Multincubadora, Technological Innovation Center, University of Brasília, Brazil

Carolina Roberte de Oliveira is a Brazilian biotechnologist and entrepreneur seeking to promote new ventures' financial and socioenvironmental sustainability. Currently working at the Technological Innovation Center of the University of Brasília as an Assistant at Multincubadora, a Technological Business Incubator, Carolina has experience with new ventures, intellectual property, bioeconomy, economic and social-environmental impact, ESG, research and development and innovation, and market research on the circular economy. Her Master's thesis involved a great understanding of the circular economy and research and development in biotechnology. She studied current bio-fabrication projects and companies promoting innovation in the market. Carolina focused her research on the textile value chain and the possibilities that the biotechnology renewables can offer. She is thrilled by the market evolution on climate change subsidies and it is her passion to leverage sustainable projects.

Robyn Owen, Associate Professor, Entrepreneurial Finance, Centre for Enterprise and Economic Development Research (CEEDR), Middlesex University, UK

Robyn Owen is Associate Professor of Entrepreneurial Finance at the Centre for Enterprise and Economic Development Research (CEEDR)

Middlesex University. Robyn's research focuses on business finance and support policy and local economic development. She recently completed an ESRC-funded grant research project investigating SME productivity and measurements for a low carbon economy. She is also a Fellow of the Centre for the Understanding of Sustainable Prosperity (CUSP) with research on financing early-stage green innovation businesses.

Alka Puri, Founder, Fashion Rethink, Thailand

Alka Puri is an entrepreneur, activist, educator and self-appointed 'Sustainable Fashion Futurist.' With a multifaceted career in the Fashion Industry spanning over 35 years, she has come to be recognised as one of the most prominent Asian voices advocating for transformational change to regenerate the Fashion Industry. Alka contributes well-informed, real-world perspectives to address the numerous challenges facing the Fashion Industry, both in her capacity as Senior Lecturer in Fashion Marketing and Management at Raffles Design College, Bangkok, Thailand and as a Researcher focusing on consumer culture. Coining the term 'Sustainable Newness' as a collaborative consumption solution, meeting consumers' fashion needs through clothing swaps, Alka's research provides a baseline for understanding consumers' attitudes in the Thai context. Alka has launched 'Fashion Rethink,' a platform for building awareness about the global state of fashion in terms of production and consumption to change mindsets and has recently completed her MBA with distinction from Stamford International University, Bangkok.

Elizabeth S. Quinn, Assistant Professor, Fashion Design, Albright College, US

Elizabeth S. Quinn is a designer with over 20 years of industry experience as both a merchant and design executive and five years of academic experience as a university instructor. Her intersectional approach to design and industry knowledge come together in the courses she teaches, including global issues and responsible practice in design, textile science and material innovations. Elizabeth is passionate about disrupting fashion industry norms through partnering with and consulting for small businesses with strong ethical and environmental values and a commitment to social responsibility. Materiality and circularity are the foundations of Elizabeth's research, which focuses on the longevity and impact of the textile and fashion industries. Challenging students and businesses to lead the change, Elizabeth aims to answer these questions: "What is our responsibility as designers, makers, and artists to planet Earth and each other?" and "How can we continue to create newness while doing no harm?"

Ulla Ræbild, Associate Professor, Lab for Sustainability and Design, Design School Kolding, Denmark

Ulla Ræbild is Researcher and Co-Lead at Lab for Sustainability & Design at Design School Kolding, where she supervises and teaches at BA, MA and PhD levels. She has a background in fashion design and holds a PhD in fashion design method practice. Her research sits between design for sustainability, curriculum development, design pedagogics and fashion design practice with a strong focus on new roles and engagements for designers in society. She was leading the development of Design for Planet, a multi-disciplinary MA programme in design and sustainability at Design School Kolding launched 2018. As part of her research, Ræbild has co-authored two open-source tools, Sustainable Design Cards and Material Pathways and contributed to multiple tools on the FashionSEEDS resources for tutor's platforms such as the Learning Activity Tool and the FashionSEEDS cards.

Joséphine Riemens, PhD candidate, Institut Français de la Mode, France

Joséphine Riemens has an academic background in Health and Social Law, after which she graduated with the specialised Mastère® in Fashion and Luxury Management at the Institut Français de la Mode. She is currently a PhD candidate researching on traceability within the Sustainability IFM-KERING Research Chair at the Institut Français de la Mode and the LAMIH research laboratory at the Arts et Métiers Institute of Technologies. Supported by the Federation de la Haute Couture et de la Mode (FHCM), her PhD thesis focuses on the implementation of multi-tier traceability towards sustainable value chains in the fashion industry.

Agnès Rocamora, Professor, Social and Cultural Studies, London College of Fashion, University of the Arts London, UK

Agnès Rocamora is the author of *Fashioning the City: Paris, Fashion and the Media.* Her writing on the field of fashion and on the fashion media has appeared in various journals, including *Fashion Theory, Journalism Practice, Sociology, Sociétés* and the *Journal of Consumer Culture.* She is co-editor of *Thinking Through Fashion: A Guide to Key Theorists, The Handbook of Fashion Studies* and *Fashion Media: Past and Present* and a contributor to *Fashion as Photograph, Critical Luxury Studies* and *Fashioning*

Professionals. Agnès is also a co-founder of the *International Journal of Fashion Studies* and is on the editorial board of Cultural Sociology, dObras, and Fashion Studies. She is currently developing her work on digital fashion media.

Lilian Sanchez-Moreno, Researcher, Circular Economy, The Centre for Sustainable Design®, University for the Creative Arts, UK

Lilian Sanchez-Moreno is a design practitioner and researcher in circular economy at The Centre for Sustainable Design® at the University for the Creative Arts. She was awarded a PhD from the School of Architecture and Design at the University of Brighton where she explored the professionalisation of social design in discourse and practice from the mid-1970s to contemporary design. Prior to completing her doctoral studies, Lilian worked in the private sector as an industrial designer. She has also lectured on design methods and design studies and history, with a focus on the intersection between development, humanitarianism and design.

Carra Santos, Educator and Adviser, Carra Santos Sustainable Futures, UK

Carra Santos is a sustainable futures educator and adviser with a special focus on enabling creativity through business, design and the built environment. She combines an interdisciplinary MSc with 20 years in creativity and design to develop strategic knowledge and learning tools supporting visionary leaders to shape a thriving future. Carra's career has evolved from internationally acclaimed product innovation and 'future concept' design features for world-class events, to futures skills and foresight for leading design schools, top ten UK architecture firms and award-winning design studios. She offers an uplifting and robust perspective on the sustainable futures transition, blending academic and industry insights with the creative energy to connect unexpected dots. Carra holds an MSc in Sustainable Development in Practice with Distinction from UWE, and a BA (Hons) in Fashion Promotion & Illustration from Surrey Institute of Art and Design (now UCA). She is a Design Council Specialist Expert and a fellow of the RSA.

Emily Rosa Shahaj, Designer/Founder, Gravity the Studio, UK

Emily Rosa Shahaj, MA, is an early theorist and practitioner within the virtual fashion movement, advocating for digital production and consumption as a means of reducing physical fashion waste in a society which largely expresses itself digitally. She earned a BFA in

Communications Design from Syracuse University and worked on digital advertising for global brands. She then pursued an MA in Printed Textiles for Fashion and Interiors from the University for the Creative Arts, where she worked collaboratively between the Fashion and Gaming departments. In 2020, she founded the virtual fashion interoperability infrastructure startup Gravity Layer. Her past research focused on cross-platform interoperability of digital identity assets using blockchain and open-source 3D formats, framing the implications of technologically mediated human interactions, and the decentralised Metaverse. She is currently ethnographically researching self-expression amongst virtual communities in massively multiplayer online game (MMOGs). She advises numerous startups and is often engaged to lecture.

Nina Stevenson, Head of Education, Centre for Sustainable Fashion, London College of Fashion, University of the Arts London, UK
Nina Stevenson is an educator who enjoys collaborating with others to develop complex sustainability ideas into creative and measurable learning in online and offline spaces. Nina is leading Fashion Design for Sustainability as curricula through co-creation with partners from higher education, research and industry to find new experimental spaces for learning both in the classroom and online. The delivery of these models informs the research work of CSF and enhances our understanding of the essential skills and capabilities for practitioners and creative thinkers of future fashion systems. Nina holds an MA in Transnational Studies from Southampton University and a Certificate in Education for Sustainable Development from the Earth Charter Initiative.

Claudia Stuckrath, Researcher and Consultant, Copernicus Institute of Sustainable Development, Utrecht University, The Netherlands
Claudia Stuckrath is a consultant and a doctoral researcher at the Copernicus Institute of Sustainable Development on living labs for Sustainable Development, focusing on Circular Economy. She also is a specialist for UULabs. Exploring living labs as a transformative approach to sustainable transitions, she facilitates transdisciplinary teams to co-create towards a common goal. Claudia's experience in the intersection of academia and industry closes the gap between the two worlds finding innovative solutions to complex problems. Claudia graduated

as a Civil Engineer with an interdisciplinary MSc from the Pontificia Universidad Católica de Chile and with an MSc in Sustainable Business and Innovation from Utrecht University. Her ongoing research is about living labs for sustainable transitions with a focus on circularity, climate action and restoring biodiversity. She participates in living lab projects related to circular fashion, nature-positive energy and monitoring of air quality, among others.

Lis Suarez-Visbal, Ashoka Fellow, Consultant and Researcher, Copernicus Institute of Sustainable Development, Utrecht University, The Netherlands

Lis Suarez-Visbal is an Ashoka fellow, a system-thinker, consultant and a doctoral researcher at the Copernicus Institute of Sustainable Development, Utrecht University. She has a MSc in Sustainable Business and Innovation and specialises in the intersection of Circular Economy and social impact with a gender lens. She has over 16 years of experience leading initiatives connecting producers and consumers, governments and academic institutions to co-create more sustainable industries. She has work in various countries including Canada, the Netherlands, Spain, Colombia, Bolivia, Ecuador, Mali, Thailand and India. She founded and directed for over 13 years FEM International and ETHIK Eco-Design Hub, two pioneer organisations established in Montreal, that contributed to build a more sustainable and conscious fashion culture with high-school students, academic institutions, businesses and consumers alike.

Paige Tomfohrde, Researcher, University of Minnesota, US

Paige Tomfohrde (she/her) is a graduate student researcher and DOVE Fellow at the University of Minnesota. She is a diasporic settler of colour living on the ancestral homelands of the Dakota people. She received an MA in Apparel Studies: Dress, History, and Culture and will be studying at Cornell University for her PhD. Her research interests include environmental justice, intersectionality and sustainability. She received undergraduate degrees from the Fashion Institute of Technology (AAS: Fashion Design) and Purdue University (BS: Apparel Design and Technology). She has over seven years of design industry experience focused on textiles and trend research. After completing her PhD, Paige intends to become a professor focused on using decolonising and intersectional pedagogies to incorporate a social justice lens to fashion education.

Bert van Son, Founder and CEO, MUD Jeans International B.V., The Netherlands

Bert van Son is founder and CEO of MUD Jeans, a fast-growing sustainable jeans company from the Netherlands. The company allows customers to shop guilt-free and do good for the environment, while looking fashionable and modern. As a 23-year-old, he moved to China to work for a trading company in the clothing industry. His 30 years of experience has enabled Bert to see the impact fast fashion has on the environment and made him believe that there is an alternative way. In 2012, he started the idea – "Lease A Jeans" – a concept that makes it possible for customers to use jeans and give them back after use. The approach allows customers to regularly renew their wardrobe, while MUD Jeans makes sure the materials will be recycled after use. Bert van Son knows about the challenges in today's (fast) fashion industry and how he and his team try to implement the circular economy in the fashion industry.

Adrián López Velarde, Co-Founder and Co-CEO of Adriano Di Marti S.A. de C.V., Mexico

Adrián López Velarde is Co-Founder and Co-CEO of Adriano Di Marti S.A. de C.V. (together with Marte Cázarez Duarte), the Mexican company behind the development of Desserto®, a cactus-based sustainable biomaterial as an alternative to leather for the fashion industry, and Deserttex®, its variant for the automotive industry. Before devoting his full time to Adriano Di Marti S.A. de C.V., Adrián was involved in the research and development of biomaterials and served as a key account manager in the automotive industry. Adriano Di Marti is committed to create new sustainable solutions and promoting ethical practices in the fashion industry in order to help build a better green world through the same fashion industry.

Ian Vickers, Senior Research Fellow, Centre for Enterprise and Economic Development Research (CEEDR), Middlesex University, UK

Ian Vickers has over 20 years' experience of researching small- and medium-sized enterprises and economic development policy and has authored many academic papers and published policy reports. His research interests relate to entrepreneurship and innovation; business sustainability, resilience and supportive ecosystems; 'good work' in small enterprises; and alternative business models for inclusive and sustainable growth.

Andrea Werner, Associate Professor, Business Ethics, Middlesex University Business School, UK

Andrea Werner is an Associate Professor of Business Ethics at Middlesex University Business School. Her main research interest is in ethics in small and medium-sized enterprises (SMEs), on which she has published widely in leading business ethics journals. Recent projects have focused on the motivations, strategies and practices of sustainable fashion design entrepreneurs, and on the implementation of the Living Wage in SMEs.

Dilys Williams, Professor, Founder and Director, Centre for Sustainable Fashion, London College of Fashion, University of the Arts, UK

Dilys Williams' practice explores fashion as a conduit for living well together as humans in a more than human world. This is applied to education, business, public and political spheres. As special adviser to a UK House of Lords All Party Parliamentary Group, and via the UNFCCC Fashion Charter Advisory Panel, she brings climate and social justice considerations into key discourses. Drawing on extensive experience as a practicing designer, she publishes in international academic journals, books and media outlets. Dilys is a keen contributor to explorations that sit at the tension between where we are and where we might be.

Foreword

As we move beyond the global pandemic and navigate a changing geopolitical world, we must not lose our collective knowledge and enthusiasm for change that brings a more sustainable future. We know we are running out of time to hit net zero targets but there are also other global imperatives to solve, like the growing loss of global biodiversity and rising inequality in most countries. Accelerating our actions to solve these problems will deliver benefits that are not just seen and felt in the natural world but by all of us, in terms of improved livelihoods, health and wellbeing.

To make these changes, we need to work on all aspects of our economic systems – and a useful lens is to consider the environmental costs of the value chains of different business sectors. I was surprised to learn that Apparel and Textiles is the fifth largest global industry sector – outranking finance, energy and automotive.[1] The sector formally employs nearly ten million people worldwide, not including the countless informal workers in the broader supply chain. As a result of fast, cheap fashion, the sector's growth rate outstripped that of the tech industry in the two decades leading up to the pandemic in 2020. This growth came with a high environmental price, however. Estimated carbon emissions are higher than that of the shipping and aviation industries combined, while an often-unregulated supply chain conceals poor working conditions and low wages.

This isn't a fashionable place to be, and we owe the world a lot better.

There are changes on the horizon: with the European Green Deal and a Textiles Strategy planned for the coming years, companies will be expected to prepare for carbon reduction, removal and radical disclosure within their own operations, and to engage with their supply chains to improve up- and downstream activities. We will move from targets and plans to accountability and action as sustainability moves from niche to mainstream. Making that shift will be tough ... So where to begin?

Accelerating Sustainability in Fashion, Clothing and Textiles brings together the factors required to move the great 'Fashion System' towards a more circular, low carbon and inclusive approach. Through a unique combination of leading academic research, pioneering business pilots and community case studies, it combines updated, balanced and wide-ranging perspectives from the UK, Europe, Asia and the Americas; while breaking down the complexities of the issues into digestible chapters that share strategic knowhow and practical learnings with clarity and comprehensiveness.

Martin, Bernice, Sandy and all the contributing authors of *Accelerating Sustainability* have come up with a powerful call-to-action for business leaders to commit to: strengthening the **resilience** of activity all along the supply chain; increasing **regeneration** to improve innovation, and driving **reinvention** of "capitalist consumerism" in order for us to get to a more equitable future that every fashion, clothing and textile consumer, including you and I, should aspire to reach.

Claire Perry O'Neill, Co-Chair of the Advisory Board, World Business Council for Sustainable Development, Former UK Minister of Energy & Clean Growth. Claire Perry O'Neill had a 20-year career in consultancy and finance before entering UK politics where she was Minister of State for Energy and Clean Growth in the UK Cabinet. She led the UK's winning bid to host COP26 and was appointed COP26 President-Designate until she left politics in 2020 to join the World Business Council for Sustainable Development, where she now co-chairs their Global Advisory Board.

NOTE

1 https://www.ibisworld.com/global/industry-trends/biggest-industries-by-employment/.

1 Introduction

Martin Charter, Bernice Pan and Sandy Black

BACKGROUND

Sustainable development emerged as a core concept from the Brundt-land Commission in 1987 (Brundtland Report, 1987). This was followed five years later by the Earth Summit in 1992, where global stakeholders – particularly from NGOs – came together in Rio de Janeiro to discuss sustainability. Following Rio, major companies started to engage more seriously in discussions surrounding the 'triple bottom line', and the World Business Council for Sustainable Development (WBCSD) was formed. In the 30 years since Rio, climate change has emerged as the centre stage, global concern. However, over the years, there have been ebbs and flows in interest and concerns over environmental and social issues across economies and societies, and amongst policymakers, business and civil society.

In 2023, we sit in a fifth green wave. The first wave was in the late 1960s with the publication of Rachel Carson's *Silent Spring* (Carson, 1962) with interest in low-impact societies and the counterculture. The second wave was in the late 1980s with the discovery of the hole in the ozone layer and the publication of the global bestseller *The Green Consumer Guide*. The third wave emerged in the 2000s with the growing climate change concern where the discussion of 'personal carbon footprints' came to the fore. The fourth wave was driven by youth, with the 'future generation' expressing concerns over climate change culminating in global street protests. The fifth wave that we are in now includes a mix of ongoing youth anxiety over climate change and increased engagement with nature and community accelerated by remote and home working during the pandemic. Many companies have suddenly discovered or rediscovered a sense of responsibility, but greenwashing is rife. Will this wave trickle away or grow in scale and velocity? One thing is clear, environmental degradation, alongside technological acceleration

DOI: 10.4324/9781003272878-1

and globalisation, has now been recognised by a range of global experts as one of the three mega trends. The World Economic Forum consistently places climate change at the top of the table in its annual analysis of risks to business. However, the pandemic and the Russia–Ukraine war have exposed the cracks in the globalised supply chain model, and glocalisation may start to replace the old model – working simultaneously globally and locally.

How has this impacted on the fashion, clothing and textile sector? Positive progress has included the setting up of the UK Sustainable Clothing Action Plan, the Sustainable Apparel Coalition, the Global Fashion Agenda, the EU Strategy for Sustainable and Circular Textiles, and the United Nations Fashion Industry Charter for Climate Action (UN-FICCA). Yet, despite industry and government establishing sustainability initiatives in Europe and the United States over the last 15 years, the sector as a major global economic player has been slow to engage with the agenda. There are early signs of shifts in concern, where climate change has emerged as a risk to asset investments and global supply chains. However, the 'Wicked Problem' of overproduction, overconsumption and waste in the sector is a pervasive issue throughout global marketplace and value chains. Initiatives to date have been voluntary, and there remains little policy and regulatory development related to sustainability in the sector worldwide. Europe is now taking the lead and is driving the green agenda, and some US states are proposing regulatory change, but there is little activity in the Asia-Pacific region or elsewhere. In Europe, policymakers have now signalled that the sector is coming under the spotlight. Extended Producer Responsibility (EPR) may be implemented across the sector over the next five years with national legislation now in place or emerging in several European countries. Such legislative change in Europe may well lead other countries to follow suit. However, the development of policy in the sector lags well behind the packaging, electronics and automotive sectors where EPR was implemented in the 1990s and mid-2000s. In addition, due to a lack of external and internal drivers, the infrastructure to enable textiles recycling is immature at present, and a considerable volume of clothing is being incinerated and landfilled often in Africa, Asia or South America. New sustainable brands and material innovation are starting to move from the margins to the mainstream market, and sustainability is emerging as a consumer concern with reuse models and buying second-life clothing becoming more common and acceptable, driven by new online platforms and models.

Issues related to greenwashing and the lack of transparency loom high in the sector and are gaining increased policy, media and NGO attention. Recent examples include Bloomberg's November 2022 exposé of garments entering the United States that have been made from cotton using forced labour from the Xinjiang region of China, banned under US law (Prasso, 2022).

The fashion, clothing and textiles sector is at a 'turning point' with increased stakeholder pressures now building. Legislative change related to net zero and waste in Europe may trigger a global policy response in other countries. Fast fashion alongside built-in product obsolescence has moved above the parapet as an issue for both policymakers and consumers. However, sustainability initiatives in the sector are fragmented with a lack of clear leadership, implementation programme and timings. Lack of standards, data, information and measurement continues to hold back change and control held by particular interest groups in the sector that have been reluctant to change. So, will there be an acceleration of sustainability urgently required in the fashion, clothing and textile sector? And, is the sector ready and able to respond?

CONCEPT

The issue of sustainability confronted by the fashion, clothing and textiles sector can be characterised as a 'Wicked Problem' and is now coming into increased scrutiny due to growing consumer, business and policy pressures. The power of this near US$3 trillion global industry (Fashion United, 2016, Business of Fashion & McKinsey, 2017) is significant, and its impact is wide-reaching. Its complex and fragmented ecosystem presents many challenges as well as emerging opportunities.

Accelerating Sustainability in Fashion, Clothing and Textiles is an in-depth volume presenting a comprehensive overview with strategic solutions as to how to substantially speed up sustainability in the fashion, clothing and textiles sector. Based on a collation of cutting-edge research and leading practice, this book uniquely brings together thought leaders, changemakers, researchers and practitioners – tackling the multifaceted topic and its interconnected aspects. This book explores the critical question of *how* to accelerate sustainability within the fast-changing environmental, social and economic landscapes of the 21st century. *Accelerating Sustainability in Fashion, Clothing and Textiles* has been completed by three editors with long-standing knowledge, expertise and published research related to the topic. This book takes a global perspective with examples that illustrate the scale and breadth of topics and regions in the scope of sustainability.

Accelerating Sustainability in Fashion, Clothing and Textiles is structured into eight parts incorporating 32 chapters and five case studies on industry pioneers. Each chapter builds on selected papers and key learnings from the Sustainable Innovation 2021 international conference, as well as invited authors with a combination of individually and collaboratively written chapters. The seven parts include Fashion System Landscape; Policy and Standards; Case Studies; Consumers, Culture and Ecosystems; Circular Economy; Education; and Future and Technology. This holistic approach brings together both academic and industry perspectives on the critical areas that require immediate action to move towards a more sustainable fashion, clothing and textile sector. Finally, a concluding chapter draws together the diverse strands of the book and presents critical recommendations and urgent actions for the immediate future.

To provide an overview of the book, an abstract for each chapter is outlined as follows. Reading the abstracts will provide a 'helicopter view' of the book and allows readers to 'dip in' and 'dip out' of chapters that are of particular interest.

PART I: FASHION SYSTEM LANDSCAPE

Chapter 2 Overview

Charter provides an overview of issues related to accelerating sustainability in fashion, clothing and textiles backed up by a range of examples. This includes discussion over the complexity of the sustainability challenges faced by the global sector that is dominated by major brands but also includes a high number of SME manufacturers in South and Southeast Asia. The significant challenges related to high levels of carbon emissions, water pollution and waste produced by the sector are highlighted alongside new circular solutions related to product life extension, biomaterial and fibre development. New policy developments, fast fashion, greenwashing, increasing demands for transparency, and traceability of supply chains related to social and environmental considerations are discussed. Issues surrounding the interplay of culture and regions related to fashion, clothing and textiles are also considered. The emergence of digital and online technologies in the sector is evaluated for their pros and cons in relation to sustainability. The emergence of sustainable entrepreneurs in the sector is discussed alongside new approaches being taken by large companies, followed by the importance of education and training. Finally, future issues, opportunities and challenges related to accelerating sustainability in the sector are explored.

Chapter 3 The Wicked Problem

Pan dissects the 'Wicked Problem' confronting the highly successful yet controversial contemporary Fashion System. The root causes of over-production and over-consumption of the fashion industry's dominant cradle-to-grave model are discussed alongside its associated value distortion and destructive activities. Illustrating where the sector has been and is heading, the chapter explains why the sustainability agenda will continue to fall perilously short from the net zero targets set by the United Nations (UN) Fashion Industry Charter for Climate Action (FICCA) in the current 'growth' trajectory. The chapter urges systemic change where cooperative and quantifiable action must be taken in five areas: 1) definition and implementation guidelines for transition to sustainable practice; 2) regulation for measuring standards and mandatory disclosures from pre-supply chain resource provenance to post-consumer waste disposal; 3) sustainable investments informed by societal and environmental risk assessment of over-production; 4) commercialisable innovation that utilises renewable materials, and carbon neutral and zero-toxin processes (as an alternative to the fossil fuel-dependent and chemical-intense system); and 5) citizen education programmes to adapt the principles of sustainable living and unlearn the habits of disposable consumerism. These actions will require multi-lateral accountability and scalable solutions to mitigate the ultimate consequences of fashion's 'Wicked Problem' and in turn enable the sector to reach the 2050 climate goals.

PART II: POLICY AND STANDARDS

Chapter 4 Global policy covering sustainability in fashion and clothing: a review and implications

Charter and Sanchez-Moreno highlight the lack of industry-wide policies to regulate the fashion and clothing industry. The clothing industry has a significant environmental and social footprint, e.g., accounting for 10% of global carbon dioxide (CO_2) emissions, but it is surprising that efforts towards decarbonisation and the reduction of global greenhouse gas (GHG) emissions remain voluntary. The chapter provides an overview with insights into key emerging policies related to sustainability in the sector. It highlights developments across Europe, North America and Asia-Pacific regions related to climate and net-zero, waste management, eco-design, transparency and marketing claims. Europe is shown to be leading the way, primarily through the European

Commission, with initiatives such as the EU Strategy for Sustainable and Circular Textiles published, along with other national initiatives such as textile-specific EPR schemes emerging in France, the Netherlands and Sweden. The chapter concludes that global policy on waste management, transparency and social sustainability for industry is limited, but there are now indications that policymakers in Europe and in some states in North America have put fashion, clothing and textiles on their sustainability agendas.

Chapter 5 Traceability, transparency and greenwashing: highlighting growing drivers for traceability and transparency in the sector, and emerging challenges surrounding greenwashing of garments

Riemens, Asseman and Lemieux discuss the issues of traceability, transparency and greenwashing in the fashion industry. Due to the globalisation and the fragmentation of supply chains, the industry has been exposed to several environmental and social scandals in the recent decades, raising traceability as a crucial priority to address and mitigate the sector's impact. Pressure for accountability and transparency has accelerated with forthcoming policies announced to address greenwashing in the sector. While traceability acts as the cornerstone of transparency and sustainability, its implementation is still facing considerable barriers in practice. Beyond issues of information accessibility and reliability, traceability requires the use of innovative digital tools to improve data collection and analysis for sustainability management. In addition, communication to consumers must be provided in a clear and consistent way to enable informed decision-making, raising the topic of disclosure standardisation. In summary, key drivers and current challenges to improve traceability and transparency towards sustainability in the sector are reviewed.

Chapter 6 Using textile testing information to ensure garment quality, longevity and transparency

Lerpiniere and Davies highlight that the fashion and textiles industry of the 21st century is driven by unparalleled expansion, particularly in terms of the consumption of low-quality, low-durability garments. While some retailers have already paved the way towards a circular textile economy through improved material use and longevity, new accreditation and legislation such as the new European Commission Strategy for Sustainable and Circular Textiles, the upcoming EPR legislation and Green Claims Code regulations in the UK will start to force the large brands and retailers into reducing their environmental impacts. Guidelines exist to benchmark product durability in relation to material use, quality, maintenance and end-of-life options. However, this is lost in translation to the average consumer due to the low level of accountable and comprehensive information on garment-textiles sourcing and production provided by the brands and retailers, hidden amongst the myriad greenwashing tactics adopted by many companies as part of their marketing strategies. It is proposed that industry standards and guidelines should not only be mandatory for the retailers but also be translated into easy-to-interpret advice for consumers on purchasing criteria, garment maintenance and post-use disposal. Increased transparency and consumer knowledge can encourage informed purchasing decisions with a greater level of consumer and retailer responsibility for climate and resource preservation collectively.

PART III: BUSINESS AND INNOVATION

Chapter 7 Finance and funding for upscaling sustainable fashion

Lyon, Elf, Owen and Werner explore the issues related to financing early-stage sustainable fashion businesses. As these businesses grow, the demand for finance to support their scaling grows. Examining a sample of fashion businesses that have sought external finance, the authors identified the common scenario of early-stage businesses reliant on entrepreneurs' own investment and that of family and friends, complemented by grant finance. As businesses grow and mature, they seek other types of finance but may be excluded from conventional sources of bank and institutional investment because of their 'liability of newness and smallness' and their focus on sustainability. Therefore, businesses are seeking alternative forms of borrowing and equity investment from social investors and business angels who are better aligned with their sustainability goals. The authors also show that many businesses decide not to take on external finance as their business models show limited potential to generate a surplus for repayment, or they prioritise their sustainability goals over financial growth.

Chapter 8 Managing sustainable innovation

Goulay discusses how many brands today are putting in place ambitious impact-related targets as a response to the looming climate crisis, new environmental regulations and in search of market differentiation. These targets are centred around topics such as the need to stay within the 1.5 degree temperature rise, to become carbon neutral and to adopt practices in line with circular economy. While it is positive to publicly declare such ambitions, the underlying strategy often remains ill-defined. One thing is clear: a step-change is needed, and 'business as usual' will not cut it. A rush towards finding new sustainable technologies to replace today's existing, often archaic means of working in the apparel sector is therefore emerging. Historically under-invested as a sector, the opportunity for improvement is substantial. However, numerous hurdles exist to meaningfully implement solutions at scale. By walking through the apparel value chain from raw material sourcing to a product's end of life, this chapter identifies both challenges and opportunities facing brands in adopting innovations in the apparel space. Keys to success will include analysing impact hotspots, focusing on implementation feasibility, incentivising stakeholders properly and forming meaningful partnerships to iterate efficiently.

Chapter 9 Fostering sustainable practices: the case of micro and small designer fashion enterprises

Black et al. highlight that the UK designer fashion sector is largely made up of micro and small enterprises (MSEs) and represents a significant part of the UK's creative industries, widely recognised for its fashion influence globally. In addition to its cultural and economic distinction, the sector is acknowledged for its pioneering sustainability-led practices. This chapter presents findings from the 'Rethinking Fashion Design Entrepreneurship: Fostering Sustainable Practices' project, working with 48 innovative fashion MSEs in the UK. With their strong sense of values and purpose, contributing to community while maintaining viability, such MSEs provide best-practice examples of innovation to foster sustainability in fashion. More fashion design enterprises are gaining the internationally recognised B-Corp certification, demonstrating that social justice and environmental stewardship are equally as important as financial success. Values-based fashion design entrepreneurs pursue growth organically to increase their positive social and environmental impact and develop strong customer relationships through direct communication, transparency and engagement activities. Despite the severe effects of COVID-19, the investigation revealed the exceptional resilience of some fashion design entrepreneurs. Such agile, purpose-led enterprises exemplify a redefinition of what fashion business can be, presenting viable pathways to recovery and building towards a sustainable prosperity that transforms how fashion is done.

PART IV: CASE STUDIES: VALUES-BASED ENTREPRENEURS

Chapter 10 Desserto®: cactus fibre as leather substitute

Black discusses Desserto, the brand name for an innovative leather substitute bio-material, created using cactus fibre as a key component. The case study discusses the research and development challenges and opportunities, and the partnership and startup company behind this innovative fabric. The business – Adriano di Marti S.A. de C.V – was formed in Guadalajara in Mexico in 2017 by co-founders Adrián López Velarde and Marte Cázarez Duarte. Both founders previously worked within industries that utilise high volumes of leather products: Adrián in the automotive industry and Marte in the fast fashion sector. Recognising the environmental issues associated with bovine leathers or synthetic leather substitutes, the pair spent two years developing Desserto fabric (first launched in October 2019), and they now collaborate with many fashion brands making accessories and clothing. Adriano di Marti has also developed an automotive upholstery fabric branded Desserttex and has key partners in the automotive industry. All their customers seek a sustainable alternative to the use of animal leathers in a wide range of products, and demand for the fabrics is growing, as is the business.

Chapter 11 DePloy: customisation for 360° sustainability

Black discusses DePloy, a fashion house based in London, producing high-quality womenswear that has operated from an ethos of '360° Sustainability' since its inception in 2006. Bernice Pan is DePloy's entrepreneurial founder and Chief Creative Officer who set up the business to provide well-fitting, fine-tailored designer clothing to women of all ages. The B-Corp-certified business is consumer-driven, foregrounding personal service (especially with regard to clothing fit and customisation). With its unique, often multifunctional and versatile designs and attention to developing strong personal customer relations, DePloy creates long-term loyalty from its clients. The case study focuses on Bernice Pan's innovative way of doing fashion, addressing all aspects of the supply chain using her 360° Sustainability Compass starting from the creative direction and design processes. This holistically represents DePloy's circular fashion brand ethos, business model, supply chain processes and product-service-experience offering. DePloy operates internationally taking its products and service directly to the customer in several countries. It extends its impacts through corporate, philanthropic and educational partnerships while contributing towards 12 of UN's 17 Sustainable Development Goals (SDGs).

Chapter 12 TOBEFRANK: transparency in practice

Charter discusses TOBEFRANK and The Rubbish Fashion company that were established by Frankie Hewitson with the purpose of increasing transparency and reducing environmental impact in the fashion sector. The case study illustrates numerous issues faced by the companies including the challenges of meeting investor demands, balancing pressure for orders versus personal sustainability values, the impact of COVID-19 on supply chains and payment of 'living wages'. In addition, the endemic problem of greenwashing and lack of quality and consistent supply chain data is illustrated. The case study highlights that there is growing sustainability awareness amongst consumers that is now driving some leading retailers to start to change their supply chain practices, but significant change will take time. Finally, four key issues that need to change in the sector are highlighted: 1) ensuring the payment of 'living wages' amongst production workers; 2) reducing water usage, particularly at the textiles manufacturing stages; 3) identifying the sources and authenticity of raw materials; and 4) managing product 'end of life' stages of the value chain.

Chapter 13 MUD Jeans: denim with circularity

Black discusses MUD Jeans, a pioneering B-Corp-certified denim jeans brand, founded by Bert von Son who established its business model from the outset on circular materials principles. The business aims to transform the way jeans are made and used and has been trading for ten years. MUD Jeans became a leader in sustainable denim by 'doing jeans differently'. Based on circularity and transparency, it focuses on one main product in a small number of styles that remains mostly constant in its range – a truly slow fashion model. The case study examines the innovative business model operated by MUD Jeans. By offering a non-season-based product range, taking back used jeans and encouraging a leasing model of consumption, the business has provided an alternative to fast fashion, with consideration for people and planet at the heart of its operations. MUD Jeans continues its materials journey with an ambition to develop jeans with 100% recycled post-consumer content and collaborates with its small number of supplier partners to continuously develop more sustainable dyeing, manufacturing and finishing processes. Through its website, MUD Jeans publishes life cycle assessment data for its jeans, and reports annually on its sustainability progress to fulfil its transparency promise.

Chapter 14 SXD: working with climate refugees

Charter discusses the evolution of an upcycled jacket brand that was set up by Ahmed Fardin – from idea to commercialisation. The case study highlights the identification of a business opportunity to produce an upcycled jacket using offcuts from jeans manufacturers in Bangladesh that resulted from a research field trip, which then led to a pilot project to test the product. Fardin's connection to SXD – a zero-waste brand – during the test marketing phase and the subsequent merging of Fardin's activities into SXD is illustrated. The engagement of 'climate change refugees' to produce the jacket and the actions taken to pay 'fair wages' are also discussed. Finally, four key issues that the sector needs to tackle are highlighted based on experience from this case study: 1) the paramount importance of improving working conditions and the payment of 'fair wages'; 2) the problems of over-production and over-consumption; 3) the critical need to reduce waste through the value chain; and 4) the priority for 'designing for circularity' to become mainstream industry practice.

PART V: CONSUMERS, CULTURE AND ECOSYSTEMS

Chapter 15 Clothing 2050: garment scenarios to drive circular material systems

Earley looks ahead to 2050, through the eyes of consumers, at a range of garments and explores how they might be created, purchased, used, recirculated, recreated and regenerated. Drawing on insights from projects and events that the author led or participated in – with fashion brands, students, material scientists, museum curators and industry leaders – new future scenarios are formulated, presented and discussed. A range of research projects in the last five years have explored circular fashion textile design strategies, through future scenario-building

techniques executed in workshops. These findings resulted in garment
concepts that incorporate user's needs and desires as the first consideration in the product life cycle and forecast that fashion for future users is
circular, connected, local, regenerative, fair and fun. Fashion users are
increasingly aware of the need for the industry to address climate justice
and climate change. However, for the industry to meet this expectation and reach the net zero goal, investment at scale must take place
and stakeholders will need to realign interests for the substantial and
effective changes required. And while the technologies and strategies
to facilitate change are becoming available, challenges lay ahead in defining and agreeing on the industry-wide changes that are needed and
the measures required to put plans into action. The currently differing
and at times opposing priorities – in the commercial context – suggest
solutions that work for some stakeholders may not work for others or
may even conflict with the immediate interests of their counterparts.

Chapter 16 Shifting the needle: can we build the next generation of consumer activism and advocacy for sustainable fashion?

Bealby-Wright and Laurent ask whether a new wave of consumer activism and advocacy can create change in the modern fashion and clothing system. The chapter highlights the changing attitude of consumers
towards sustainable fashion and the systemic barriers that prevent individuals from shifting behaviours in practice. The authors suggest how
the principles of consumer rights, such as the right to adequate information and the right to safe products, can help to shape a vision of a
fair and sustainable fashion industry. Three detailed case studies from
Consumers International members illustrate the tools that consumer
advocates use to drive change, including national and international
consumer awareness campaigns, consumer interest research, product
testing and labelling, practice guidelines and pledges, policy and standards recommendations, and collective buying schemes. Finally, the
authors compare the consumer advocacy movement of yesterday and
today to assess where innovative technologies and non-conventional
partnerships are needed to achieve impact at scale.

Chapter 17 Crafting connections with clothing: values, influence and relationships

Santos, Gosler and Newton highlight that one aspect of the current
'Wicked Problem' the clothing industry faces is the disconnect between

customers and production. This disconnection decreases the value placed on clothes, with today's customers often buying, wearing, then discarding them without much regard. Exacerbated by an increasingly trends-driven fashion system, this unsustainable behaviour has become a social norm, which customers cannot easily break by themselves. Innovative brands can empower customers to exchange this social norm for more sustainable behaviours by restoring connections to the materials, competences and meaning of clothing. Craft is shown as one route to reconnection, showcasing the making process as a way to deepen relationships with materials and resources. Social media is highlighted as another tool for engagement and community building. Insights from five lingerie brands' strategies to connect with and educate their followers are illustrated. Both methods illustrate opportunities to involve customers in the production process, supporting them to evolve from passive 'consumers' into active 'participants'. Overall, it is suggested that a sustainable future of fashion requires restoring value and meaning throughout the product life cycle – a systemic transformation that will require ongoing collaborative relationships between brands and their customers, forged on principles of education, transparency, resource preservation, repurpose and repair.

Chapter 18 Unheard voices: reclaiming fashion sustainability

Bye, Tomfohrde, Nel and Davis suggest that a lack of ethics and agency in the fashion industry contributes to the depletion of earth's resources. Globally, black, indigenous and people of colour (BIPOC) who have been oppressed by colonialism and capitalism are not free to act or exert the power needed for change in the fashion industry, yet they provide labour and resources that prolong unsustainable growth. The experiences of these individuals are marginalised, but solutions to this crisis require diverse voices. Consumerism and reduced or unequal opportunity for individual and cultural expression are core to the lack of agency. The wisdom and practices of indigenous peoples survive over time and offer strategies to realign our relationship with the earth. Considering the barriers that individuals in under-represented BIPOC groups face in supporting sustainable fashion can enable a deeper understanding of how to address challenges such as lack of visual representation and cultural integration. A problem–solution model is used to illustrate how an ethics of care approach can address the oppression of under-represented groups and emphasise relationships, connection and community to support environmental, human and economic flourishing and sustainability through more inclusively ethical approaches.

Chapter 19 Regions, communities and localism

Gardetti, Maki, Gupta and Cavagnero highlight the slow and simplified advances in sustainability of the fashion, clothing and textiles system, which mean that growth continues to be prioritised with sustainability remaining a peripheral concern. Essentially, industry is adapting to sustainability around its current needs and operations, rather than hardwiring change into the system. How can we change this standpoint? One approach is to initiate in-depth interaction with multidisciplinary groups and skills at all levels, opening conversations and hearing the un-represented voices in fashion (e.g., indigenous communities, artisan groups and people living under vulnerable conditions, amongst others). Another approach takes account of regionalism and localism that favour the use of nearby, local resources, place-specific knowledge and community self-reliance. Both approaches give expression to practices shaped by traditions, necessity, geography, climate and imagination. Experiences and learnings from indigenous people of Argentina, artisans from India and communities in Bahrain and the Arab Gulf are presented with regard to issues surrounding the sustainability of fashion. Finally, as fashion products are often characterised by a reputational link to the place of manufacture, this chapter further explores the drivers and obstacles of harnessing the use of geographical indicators (GIs) as a potential incentive and measure to accelerate sustainability.

PART VI: CIRCULAR ECONOMY

Chapter 20 Circular economy in the textile and apparel sector: an overview of global trends, challenges and opportunities

Suarez-Visbal, Stuckrath and Rosales Carreón highlight that the fashion, clothing and textile value chain – by and large – represents a linear business system that is spread throughout different geographical locations, often characterised by the take-make-waste model. The concept of circular economy has increasingly gained currency around the world, as it addresses concerns over rising global pressure on resources while reconciling the objectives between economic growth and environmental sustainability. This chapter presents prominent strategies used in the fashion, clothing and textiles sector to implement circular economy principles operationally, with concrete examples presented. An overview of trends, policy, challenges and opportunities focuses not only on global perspectives but also on regional initiatives and international networks. Learnings and action points from the adaptation of circular strategies are highlighted to aid and improve the sector's transition to circular economy and accelerate sustainability.

Chapter 21 New forms of governance to accelerate circular textiles in the Netherlands

Cramer highlights that circular textiles are one of the key priorities of the Dutch circular economy policies. The big challenge is how to transform the current Dutch clothing and fashion industry, which is highly globalised and competitive, fully focused on producing fashion speedily and cheaply. Restructuring this complex and fragmented business sector into a circular system cannot rely only upon the conventional public governance and goodwill, as meaningful change requires the upgrade and migration of the whole system in which the clothing and fashion industry operates. Therefore, complementary network governance mechanisms need to be devised and installed. The Netherlands aims to pilot the change by coupling these two forms of governance, utilising insights gained from transition management. Analysing the way in which the Dutch government has integrated public and network governance with a variety of stakeholders, this chapter assesses the merits and interaction between national policies and regional initiatives taken by networks of partners. It concludes that while public governance remains crucial in facilitating and incentivising a circular clothing and fashion industry, goal-oriented network governance powers the circular economy.

Chapter 22 Accelerating circularity in textiles: lessons learned from a regional perspective

Mahy and Oelerich highlight that a closed-loop 'textile-to-textile' recycling is a prerequisite not only for meeting the 2030 sustainability goal but also for the regulatory objectives in the transition to a circular economy towards 2050. The regional utilisation of textiles beyond their first use-phase requires a systemic view of circularity incorporating all relevant value chain actors including textile collectors and sorters, and mechanical and possibly chemical recyclers, before yarns and fabrics can be made into circular-designed garments. Close collaboration between new value chain actors is required to develop new, innovative technology (e.g. sorting) and processes to implement circular business models and accelerate scale-up. A triple-helix (government, industry and academia) partnership in the Netherlands is presented in this chapter, highlighting strengths, risks, threats, challenges and opportunities on operational, regional and systemic levels. This partnership is founded in TexPlus, combining academic and applied research and education institutions, municipal organisations, thrift shops, startups and established manufacturers of the textiles industry. This initiative was selected as 'Best Practice' by the EU Committee of the Regions as a demonstration of the 'Green Deal going Local'. The collaboration between similar but complementary regional initiatives in the Netherlands is coordinated through the 'Dutch Circular Textile Valley' and is discussed in Chapter 21.

Chapter 23 Biomimicry, biomaterials and textiles

Kapsali discusses how models such as Circular Economy and Cradle-to-Cradle draw on biology as a paradigm to reimagine the linear, take-make-waste model. Emerging from the intersection of ecology and systems thinking, these top-down views provide a framework for alternative ways of sustainable production and consumption. Novel, bottom-up approaches that have emerged from the intersection of biotechnology and the textile sector challenge the status quo and stimulate new narratives around sustainability and conventional industry practice. This chapter maps current innovations in the biotechnology and textile space and outlines the key challenges and obstacles that prevent new materials from being fully commercialised. Opportunities for research and development are also highlighted that would accelerate market-ready biotechnology innovations and biomaterials for the use of fashion and textile industry at scale.

Chapter 24 Reincarnation: waste, reuse, repair and upcycling

Choi, Ballie and Puri discuss how clothing might be designed, used and cared for in the future, where consumers can be part of the circular system to reuse more clothing. The aim of this chapter is threefold: 1) to understand consumer's barriers to bringing clothing back to life at the end-of-use stage; 2) to acknowledge that design-oriented education and raising public awareness are promising interventions to change behaviour; and 3) to propose design strategies that encourage consumers to take proactive roles in reducing their own fashion waste. Through a participatory research method used within a live research project 'Sewing Box for the Future', four practical design strategies were established to contribute towards empowering the consumer to reuse items. Under the themes of care, repair and customisation, this chapter discusses how hands-on design opportunities might encourage the business to rethink clothing reuse in the future. It urges business leaders, designers and researchers to develop business models that support clothing's future reuse as part of the circular system by reconsidering the consumer's role as an 'active user'.

PART VII: EDUCATION

Chapter 25 Curriculum: challenges, opportunities, and approaches to increasing sustainability content in fashion and textiles education

Baeza, Corcoran and Quinn highlight that one of the main challenges for fashion and textiles education is having the courage to explore different ways of thinking and making beyond the currently irresponsible industrial systems. As design practices shift, awareness of ethical and ecological implications has become a necessity and responsibility not only for design professionals but also for educators who are teaching the next generation. Truly sustainable collections must carefully analyse the design phase in the product life cycle for positive impacts. Design and merchandising curricula may skim the surface of ethical practices that consider a high level of care and awareness for the creation and making process. However, they often fall short of aligning ethical decision-making with design processes and business practices. Prioritising a protective and holistic material strategy could help develop a collective pathway towards a sustainable system beneficial to all. Curriculum needs to be agile and have the ability and resources to recognise and protect good design practice, skill and knowledge, while incubating future design thinking, experiential making and new business models, with ethics and sustainability at the core. Redefining our value system in relation to design, creation and production by integrating ethics, entrepreneurship and restorative design into curricula will create more transformative, sustainable and adaptive industry professionals.

Chapter 26 Methodologies and tools: incorporating sustainability content in fashion, apparel and textiles educational curriculum through facilitating materials

Ræbild, Lettmann and Hasling address the notion of tools and methodologies advancing design for sustainability in fashion, clothing and textiles educational curricula. As the need for incorporating design-led sustainability in industry and subsequent educational content has increased, the question of how to inform the change has risen with it. This has led to a growing interest in facilitating teaching and learning materials that bridge the gap between sustainability knowledge and industry know-how for fashion education, design practitioners and industry stakeholders. The aim of the chapter is to contribute to the understanding of the need for strategic design education support through the use of new tools and why they must be continuously developed in order to build sustainability competencies. The chapter introduces chronological overview of tools with two cases that exemplify and contextualise different types of tools for specific purposes. Firstly, *Material Pathways* targets learning through reflection, awareness and dialogue. Secondly, *Let's Play Fashion: Circular Design Cards and the Circular Design Matrix* facilitates hands-on action-based learning in practice for non-traditionally educated designers. While the tools do not provide quick fixes, they are very useful in helping to transform knowledge into understanding and can be shared and applied in both education and industry to help support increased understanding of sustainability in the sector.

Chapter 27 The use of digital pedagogies for accessible and equitable teaching and learning of fashion design for sustainability: a case study

Bonnelame and Stevenson highlight that online learning facilitates the creation of massive cohorts of learners in diverse demographics and global locations. This enables a wide range of learning modes including continuing professional development and lifelong learning. Fashion design for sustainability involves conceiving, realising and communicating multiple ways in which fashion activities can help create prosperity at micro and macro scales while consuming less of the earth's finite resources. The merits, opportunities and limitations of digital learning are considered in this chapter as a means to further the pursuit of accessible and equitable fashion education and lifelong learning that puts planetary health and human equity first. Curriculum co-created between Centre for Sustainable Fashion (a research centre at the University of the Arts London) and luxury fashion group Kering that was delivered in three formats is discussed: a 12-week postgraduate taught course for 40 learners, a 6-week MOOC (Massive Open Online Course) with a community of more than 80,000 learners, and a blended postgraduate unit for 15 learners. Both qualitative and quantitative data were collated from a range of participants including learners, tutors, researchers, digital learning experts and industry partners- to present and opportunities for the improvement of fashion education.

PART VIII: FUTURE AND TECHNOLOGY

Chapter 28 A pathway towards to future sustainable fashion in 2030

Cheng and Charter highlight that fashion, clothing and textiles, clothing are a fundamental part of everyday life and an important sector in the global economy but has a significant environmental impact. Therefore, fashion industry will increasingly need to implement design and development (D&D) strategies to enable disassembly and the separation of fibres at the 'end of first life' stage to reduce waste and enable product and materials life extension. This chapter explores how the major technological acceleration and sustainability challenges will impact the fashion industry in the coming decade, for example, wearable technology, digital fashion, circularity and bio-based materials. In addition, there is discussion over how leaders in the sector are starting to move in a more sustainable and circular direction. For example, new developments in bio-based materials and a selected list of future-ready bio-based fabrics are highlighted.

Chapter 29 Risky business: sustainable fashion through new technologies

Davis, Dunne and Bigger assess how advanced digital technologies and applied innovation such as artificial intelligence (AI) can improve sustainability in fashion. This chapter illustrates this through original research on new-generation technologies and their associated barriers. Case studies on generative design analysis, predictive modelling and the implications of machine-supported decision models in fashion illustrate the importance of human creativity in successful adoption. The chapter also proposes a schema for the evolution of technology in fashion to create alternative sources of value, reduce waste reduction and counter overproduction. Sustainability in the fashion industry is multi-faceted, spanning the full-product life cycles. The industry requires solutions that balance environmental concerns, social justice and value creation where changes are needed on both supply side and demand side. As illustrated through the book, the fashion industry faces a 'Wicked Problem' with no neat specific solution. Instead, multiple whole system approaches are need to exploit the most promising technologies. Starting from Industry 4.0, this chapter outlines pathways for technological innovation in the fashion sector and puts forward a framework for overcoming barriers to change, e.g., technology risks, prevailing organisational culture and lack of a common language for technology.

Chapter 30 Wearable tech, virtual fashion and immersive technologies

Göncü-Berk and Shahaj discuss the rapid expansion of advancements in three emerging areas of digital innovation as they relate to fashion and textiles, namely, wearable technology, virtual fashion and immersive technologies. As the fashion industry undergoes discussion over transformation related to sustainability, the introduction of digital textiles may further exacerbate the sector's existing problems of built-in product obsolescence, non-recyclability and over-consumption. Wearable technology products – which include clothing and textiles with embedded electronic functions – have grown in popularity and are expected to become more ubiquitous. However, this growth does not come without a considerable cost: approaching wearable technology with the existing models of the fashion system which promote rapid change in styles could further threaten sustainability. Virtual fashion (VF) can be defined as a 3D visualisation of clothing overlaid on a 2D image of a person – either manually manipulated, applied using machine learning techniques, or body-tracked in real-time. Meanwhile, the historically disparate fields of fashion and gaming are intertwining with the growth of immersive virtual reality (VR) metaverses. While sustainable in its premise of replacing physical garments and their impact, consumer taste for virtual substitutions eg VF, VR and gaming, and associated environmental impacts must be evaluated.

Chapter 31 Fashion ex machina: human–machine collaboration to support sustainability through customized design and production

Bigger, Ahren-Wels and Kelbel highlight that Industry 5.0 production strategies offer the potential to strike a balance between the needs of consumers and planetary environmental concerns. To enable this, garment production *values* need to increase, while garment production *volumes* must decrease to sustain the fashion industry in the long haul. Data-informed fashion design and production strategies challenge the status quo of wasteful mass production methodologies and make it possible to eliminate overstock production. The chapter discusses emerging production technologies of Web 3.0, human and machine collaboration and interoperability of systems for transitioning towards sustainable and bespoke local fashion production. Furthermore, factory transitions of nearshoring to localism are opportunities for decreasing production volumes and thus fashion's environmental footprint. Finally, practical solutions for generative garment design for sustainable analysis and adaptive pattern design for agile digital production systems and their respective iterative workflows are highlighted.

Chapter 32 Conclusion: progress, challenges and prospects

Concluding *Accelerating Sustainability in Fashion, Clothing and Textiles*, Charter, Pan and Black reflect on the scope of the 'Wicked Problem' in relation to sustainability and its social-environmental impacts in the sector. The complex issues and ongoing challenges are viewed in the wider business, political, cultural and educational contexts with summaries provided on the recommendations and progress currently being made to accelerate necessary actions. Structural change can only gain full momentum by being tackled hands-on multi-laterally and collaboratively across all levels from government, institutions, industry, brands, retailers and consumers. Lessons must be learnt from the catalysing effects of global shocks from the COVID-19 pandemic where extraordinary innovations and partnerships between public, private, non-profit and communities were rapidly invested in, developed and implemented for the collective good. While risks and reward will be assessed for years to come, we cannot wait for the looming climate change emergency to become a clear and present danger. The opportunity for prevention instead of crisis management is now, and the world requires from us the system change to accelerate sustainability in the fashion, clothing and textile sector.

REFERENCES

Brundtland Report. 1987. *Our Common Future.* New York: United Nations World Commission on Environment and Development.

Carson, R. 1962. *Silent Spring.* Boston, MA: Houghton Mifflin.

Fashion United. 2016. *Global Fashion Industry Statistics - International Apparel.* Available at: https://fashionunited.com/news/global-fashion-industry-statistics/2016042011023

Prasso, S. 2022. Chinese region accused of forced labour. *UK Bloomberg.* Available at: https://www.bloomberg.com/news/features/2022-11-21/shein-s-cotton-clothes-tied-to-xinjiang-china-region-accused-of-forced-labor?leadSource=uverify%20wall

The Business of Fashion, McKinsey & Company. 2017. *The State of Fashion 2017.* Available at: https://www.mckinsey.com/industries/retail/our-insights/state-of-fashion

Part I

Fashion system landscape

2 Overview

Martin Charter

BACKGROUND

The fashion, clothing and textiles sector is a global economic power-house worth US$3 trillion and the fourth biggest industry in the world, representing 2% of the world's GDP (Fashion United, 2022). Driven by major brands that often outsource production to South and South-East Asia, many of the outsourced factories employ large numbers of people using manual labour to operate machines rather than using advanced manufacturing and/or robots. However, there are also thousands of micro, small and medium-sized enterprises (MSMEs) with craft-based design-making skills that produce small volume, batches of textiles, fashion and clothing.

The sector has a significant sustainability impact (environmental, social and economic) – both negative and positive – which has often gone unrecorded (Pucker, 2022). Tackling sustainability in fashion, clothing and textiles is a 'Wicked Problem' of significant scale with multiple stakeholders involved. Structural change is needed throughout the system (with the support of major brands and producers), but the complexity needs to be broken down into sub-systems in order to increase understanding and identify inter-relationships and pivot points (Chapter 3). Taking a systems perspective will help to identify the gaps and hotspots, and where change and innovation is needed in consumer behaviour, policy, business models, infrastructure, design and materials.

This chapter provides an overview of key issues and topics related to accelerating sustainability in the sector. It is designed to be a snapshot with each part aimed at initiating thinking, rather than providing a definitive analysis. The issues and topics highlighted are organised thematically and include discussion over: environmental and social sustainability, policy and market transformation, greenwashing and

DOI: 10.4324/9781003272878-3

transparency, demand and social influencers, cultural issues, circular economy, business models, technology, material, innovation and entrepreneurship, education and the future. There is cross-referencing to specific chapters in the book where the issues and topics are discussed and developed in more detail.

ENVIRONMENTAL SUSTAINABILITY

There are numerous, fragmented environmental initiatives in the fashion, clothing textiles industry worldwide with multiple codes of conduct and initiatives related to waste, water, emissions and chemicals. The extent to which brands, outsourced factories and other actors in supply networks comply with these codes is unclear. To improve sector performance with a meaningful migration towards sustainability in supply chains, there is an urgent need for multi-stakeholder leadership and collaboration to pull these fragmented initiatives together and significantly reduce the negative environmental impact currently associated with the sector.

Waste sits alongside high levels of carbon dioxide (CO_2) emissions, water pollution and chemical use as areas of major environmental impact in the sector. Measuring the extent of those impacts still lacks reliable data, unified methodology and comprehensive scope. For instance, there are significant variations in published figures for sector-based global CO_2 emissions.

The industry is on the whole a linear system with high volumes of waste produced (production waste, overproduction, unsold goods, returns and stored or 'end of first use' waste). This includes significant waste resulting from the manufacturing processes, which represents a major cost to business that often goes unrecognised. There is an urgent need to implement more circular solutions that aim to extend the life of clothing and textiles. For example, in Bangladesh, production off-cuts are often collected from factories by brokers ostensibly for materials recycling but these are often then sold for fuel (Chapter 14).

CIRCULAR ECONOMY

Given the significant waste in the sector, there is a need to apply circular economy principles[1] to both fashion and clothing produced from natural fibres (from the biological cycle), polymers (from the technical cycle) and mixed fibres and other materials (Chapters 10 and 22).

In addition, as electronics becomes more integrated into clothing, textiles and wearable technologies, the implementation of design strategies to enable disassembly and material separation will be critical in extending the life of garments, fibres, electronics and materials, particularly with regard to garment wash and care. Mechanisms need to be established to retain value in clothing (products), components (sub-assemblies), fibres and materials in existing economic and social systems for as long as possible. There are some positive signs. Younger consumers are increasingly interested in second-hand, re-used or "pre-loved" garments as evidenced by rise of online sharing platforms including Depop and Vinted (Ek Styvén, 2020). Strategies need to be developed to bring garments 'back to life' and move inactive, stored or 'end of first use' clothing into active second or nth life clothing through, for example, by 'adding value' through upcycling garments using, for example, visible mending.

There are market barriers to product life extension in the sector. For example, upcycled clothing is perceived differently amongst consumers in Northern and Southern hemispheres, and by younger and older age groups. This is illustrated by an upcycled jacket brand produced by SXD where a market was identified in the West using off-cut waste from jeans manufacturing in Bangladesh. However, due to negative consumer perceptions associated with upcycled clothing in Bangladesh, there is no market in the country (Chapter 14).

To increase circular behaviour, there is a need for visual processes (e.g. online videos, exhibitions and demonstrations, simple tools and information [written/graphic]) that engage garment owners and highlight practical strategies to extend the life of items through improved care, repair and modification in the 'use' phase of the lifecycle. Educating users in the care and maintenance of their clothes through online videos and, by providing more data and information on strategies to extend the life of garments through repair, modification or upcycling using QR tags – and via social media influencers – will become the norm for brands in the future. Specialist online videos, communities and blogs related to making, modifying and repairing of garments now are starting to emerge (Chapter 24).

REGIONS AND LOCALISM

The development of more circular clothing, fashion and textiles will require increased regional awareness, markets and infrastructure, e.g. increased textiles recycling via mechanical and chemical processes.

As Extended Producer Responsibility (EPR) schemes for clothing and textiles emerge, initially in Europe, there will be the need to set up producer organisations, national and regional collection, sorting, separation and recycling plants. However, significant changes are needed if the dial is to be moved beyond the current 1% annual recycling rate of textiles (Ellen MacArthur Foundation, 2017). The Dutch Circular Textile Valley is an excellent example of a regional network that includes a series of pilot projects aimed at developing collaborative approach amongst commercial, industrial, local government and communities to enable a transition towards a circular economy (Chapters 21 and 22).

In addition, at a regional level, the use of legal systems that aim to protect regional intellectual property related to clothing and textiles production might be an interesting approach. For example, geographical indicators have been established to protect and promote regional brand names, e.g. Harris Tweed (Harris Tweed Authority, 2022). Some regions use regional eco-labels – protected by trademarks – aimed at promoting the local economy with links to local tourism and agriculture. Eco-labels highlighting the origin of clothing, craft and produce from regions or localities have also been established (Chapter 19).

SOCIAL ISSUES, ETHICS AND EQUALITY

To date, most codes, indices and tools have focused on environmental impacts of the sector with less emphasis on social dimensions. However, during the COVID-19 pandemic, health, social and community concerns moved up the agenda in fashion and clothing with several NGOs picking up the baton including Fashion Revolution[2] and Extinction Rebellion.[3] Many consumers are now becoming increasingly concerned about the "world behind the brand" e.g. working conditions in the outsourced factories. However, there is a lack of consensus over the definitions and terminology relating to social issues in the sector which makes consistent social impact assessment, assurance, measurement and auditing a complex and difficult exercise (Chapter 5). Further challenges are added because outsourced manufacturing and supply chain networks span many countries and continents from Asia to Africa to Central and South America, where some issues become more nuanced due to cultural considerations.

There is growing interest in integrated tools that cover environmental, social and economic ('triple bottom line' [TBL]) aspects of sustainability. The 17 United Nations Sustainable Development Goals (SDGs)[4] launched in 2015 provide a useful framework for TBL thinking in the sector. Extracting the social SDGs will provide useful pointers to tackle deficiencies in existing codes and initiatives in the sector. This can start to address issues related to social responsibility and ethical practice in the sector: equity, fairness and access such as fair wages, decent working conditions and fundamentally what is right or wrong.

CULTURE, INDIGENOUS AND ETHNIC COMMUNITIES

The importance of local culture, indigenous and ethnic communities often goes unrecognised in the sector. In indigenous cultures, there is often a slower, localised consumption and production with clothing made, modified, repaired and passed onto future generations with garments being of high quality and designed and made for longevity. However, indigenous cultures are unrepresented voices in the sustainability discussions of the fashion, clothing and textiles sector. The connectedness of indigenous cultures to natural materials, localities and regions – where clothing is designed and made – often appears to have been forgotten or gone unnoticed (Chapters 18 and 19).

Indigenous knowledge and its inter-relationship between natural materials, local cultures and ecosystems of clothing design, production and use need to be documented and learnt from. In Bahrain, for example, traditional tailoring businesses (which play an important role related to 'fit and repair') co-exist alongside Western shopping 'mall' retail culture. Garments and accessories are also often shared within families, with higher value items shared more widely within communities for special events (Maki, 2021).

There are also lessons to be learnt for sustainable entrepreneurs from indigenous cultures that include: (a) physically re-connecting with nature; (b) slowing down to focus on the process and culture of making; and (c) building strong relationships and cohesive communities through sharing information, knowledge and stories. Further discussion and action is needed as to how to protect indigenous intellectual property, craftsmanship, heritage past and present, to ensure that the sustainability discourse is inclusive and comprehensive bridging cultures, geographies and demographics.

FIBRES AND MATERIALS

The biggest environmental impact of textiles is at the raw material stage of the lifecycle: 60% of yarns being petroleum-based manmade filaments (from the technical cycle) and 40% being from natural fibres (from the biological cycle). However, in practice, many textiles are produced using yarns with a mix of manmade filaments (from the technical cycle) and natural fibres (from the biological cycle), which makes recycling problematic due to the difficulty in unravelling fabrics and separating yarns once spinning and weaving or knitting have been done. Therefore, it is important to consider these issues at the design stage, and to develop infrastructure to extend the life of technical, natural and mixed fibres through mechanical and chemical recycling. Chemical recycling is a newer technology with potential benefits. However, there needs to be a better understanding of the wider environmental impact of the process, e.g. energy use, chemical use, water pollution, especially when scaled up for commercial use.

New fibres and materials are emerging, for example, there is a second wave of "vegan leathers", with materials being made from natural fibres with polymer binders in varying proportions (Meyer et al., 2021). These can be described as "vegan", as they are not made from animal hides, but can't be described as circular as they still use mixed technical and biological materials which create recycling challenges at the 'end of life' (Chapter 10).

The environmental impact of biopolymer fibre substitutes for petroleum-based polyester needs further research. This is highlighted by a Life Cycle Analysis (LCA) study that compared polyester produced from biopolymers to petroleum-based polymers. The research indicated that the environmental impact of biopolymer fibres is not necessarily better than the non-biopolymer fibre because, for example, land-use issues associated with biopolymers are much more significant compared with petroleum-based polyester. However, the study's scope was limited to "cradle to gate" rather than "cradle to cradle", therefore excluding the use phase of the lifecycle, which is key to product life extension e.g. re-use and recycling (Ivanović & Som, 2021).

Bio-fibre development through biotechnology is receiving increased attention, but it is not a magic bullet, as there are wider environmental impacts associated with land-use and waste related to disposal of micro-organisms used in the processes. The use of biotechnology is leading to a series of questions that include: what can be learnt from nature in terms of bio-fibre development and zero waste? What lessons can be learnt from biomimicry? How can research and development be accelerated to produce more market-ready bio-fibres scaled for volume production? How can food waste be used for bio-fibre development? How do we develop new forms of bio-fabrication labs, bio-refineries and bio-factories to produce new bio-fibres for commercialisation and where will funding come from (Chapter 23)?

POLICY, STANDARDS AND MARKET TRANSFORMATION

There is increased public policy focus on the sustainability performance of the fashion, clothing and textiles sector in Europe and in selected U.S. states. However, it is quite significant how little sustainability-related legislation there is in the sector worldwide. The European Commission's Circular Economy Action Plan 2.0 published in 2020 highlighted EPR in the textiles and clothing as an area of future focus (European Commission, 2020). EPR has already been implemented in the sector in France and Sweden, and will go forwards in the Netherlands (Long & Lee-Simion 2022) but is lagging behind other sectors e.g. packaging, electronics and vehicles, where policies were initiated in the mid-1990s. These developments were recently followed up with the publication of the *EU Strategy for Sustainable and Circular Textiles* in March 2022 (European Commission, 2022a) (Chapter 4).

The sector needs to learn lessons from both demand and supply side product policies aimed at 'greening markets' that have implemented in other sectors and countries that reward the leaders, improve the performance overall and remove laggards from the market. To help the sector prepare, there needs to be increased awareness and understanding of product sustainability issues – including EPR – in all parts of the value chain and all tiers of global supply networks. Information and training will need to be written in the languages of key manufacturing countries in a practical, action-oriented manner. To enable consistency in supply chains, there is also a need for new standards, guidelines and testing requirements related to sustainability and circularity of fashion, clothing and textiles e.g. decommissioning of clothes, composting of fabrics, etc. (Chapter 6).

DEMAND, CONSUMERS AND SOCIAL INFLUENCERS

Despite the sector appearing to be very customer focused and demand-led, in practice, it is a highly supply-driven industry which propels over-consumption and leads to over-production and waste. The fast fashion model emerged in the 1980s. Driven by major retail brands, this has fuelled the consumption of high-volume, low-cost, fast-changing and poor-quality garments. This shift has contributed to a wide range of negative sustainability impacts. Consequently, fast fashion is now coming under the spotlight of European policymakers and NGOs (Chapter 4).

Forecasting is focused on trend-based information and is often conducted in a qualitative and not quantitative manner. Trends are often created by social influencers who have a powerful role in shaping consumer habits and tastes and are contributing to fast fashion and greenwashing (Morgan, 2022) (Chapter 17). This contributes further to high levels of over-production and waste in the form of unsold garments and returns. Few social influencers are taking the lead on sustainable – and more specifically circular fashion. What role might retailers and e-commerce platforms play in the future in "choice editing", e.g. only placing the most sustainable garments on the market (Chapter 16)?

There is a lack of comprehensive data in the public domain on unit sales of fashion, clothing and textiles at a country level as disclosure is not mandatory. There are indications that a lack of funding is preventing the development of frameworks that drive robust data and information collection – making the comprehensive measurement of environmental and social impacts difficult at a sectoral level.

GREENWASHING, THE "NEW UGLY", INFORMATION, TRANSPARENCY AND TRACEABILITY

Research has indicated that there are 107 eco-labels covering the textile industry (Ranasinghe et al., 2021). There is an urgent, growing need to tighten up product-related environmental claims across fashion, clothing and fibres to reduce market confusion. There are increasing signals that policymakers, media and NGOs are starting to wake up to the extent of greenwashing in the sector (Changing Markets Foundation, 2022). More broadly, in March 2022, the European Commission proposed to amend legislation aimed at "empowering consumers for the green transition through better protection against unfair practices and better information" (European Commission, 2022b). Brands that do not address sustainability issues related to "world behind the brand" may increasingly be considered as the "new ugly" by consumers, and concerns are likely to grow as the demand for transparency and traceability increases (Chapter 5).

Critical consumers are increasingly demanding more transparency over, for example, working practices used in outsourced factories. This is leading to growing pressures for processes and technologies to enable traceability. Concerns include the use of forced labour in cotton production in Xinjian, China (Oltermann, 2022).

What lessons can the fashion, clothing and textile industry learn from other sectors? Let's look at the "horsemeat scandal" in the UK in 2013 which led to concerns over contamination, misrepresentation and fraud after horsemeat was found to be illegally substituted for beef in meat products (Lawrence, 2013). This led to major concerns by consumers, fuelled by media speculation and investigative journalism that impacted on the meat supply chain. In the fashion, clothing and textile industry, there are no codes and/or standards related to the traceability of, for example, chemicals used, labour practices, working conditions, etc. in the supply chains.

The increasing demand for transparency will drive the need for traceability (Chapters 12 and 13). Digital ledger technologies such as blockchains are potentially useful tools to track traceability. However, there are current obstacles in its application due to the lack of accurate data collection across the supply chain. There is ongoing challenge of accessing "good" quality environmental and social data in complex global supply networks, and there are a lack of standards for the criteria and exchange of information amongst multiple stakeholders e.g. a lack of mandatory disclosure and universal reporting processes, and the prevalence of different data formats (Chapter 5).

Developing algorithms to extract more value from datasets – technical, financial, environmental and social – will be increasingly needed. The availability and communication of "better" quality product-related sustainability data – derived from increased data processing power – will be a key factor in helping to make global supply networks more transparent. For example, Mud Jeans and some other brands have started to increase transparency and visibility of employees working in supply chains (Mud Jeans, 2020) (Chapter 13). In the future, progressive companies may enable consumers to explore the "world behind the brand" through making immersive technologies available that allow them to interact with different people in different tiers of global supply networks, as well as experience the "making process".

INDUSTRY 4.0, DIGITALISATION AND VIRTUAL FASHION

It will take time to adopt new Fourth Industrial Revolution or Industry 4.0 technologies[5] in the sector, but digitalisation will continue to grow fast (Chapter 29). Industry 4.0 refers to the intelligent networking of machines and processes for industry with the help of information and communication technology including flexible production, optimised logistics and better use of manufacturing data[6]. However, as indicated above, a lack of "good" quality manufacturing data and information are among the barriers for the widespread adoption of Industry 4.0 technologies in the sector (Majumdar et al., 2021), but better-quality datasets are now growing.

Technology adoption is increasing as the world "levels up" with the emergence of a strong spirit of techno-entrepreneurship in some developed and emerging countries. This is illustrated by production of a virtual fashion show organised by the African Fashion Foundation, which showcased circular fashion garments from West Africa (African Fashion Foundation, 2021). Digital and virtual fashion has the potential to reduce waste by lessening the one-off wearing of garments for social media (that are then often returned to retailers and/or e-platforms) (Chapter 30).

However, there is increasing recognition that the rendering and other processes used to produce digital and virtual fashion requires significant energy consumption (producing CO_2 emissions) due to intense level of data processing by the algorithms often in 'the cloud'. As we move towards more novel combinations of physical and digital (phygital) fashion and clothing are distributed and/or procured through e-platforms, there will be a need to focus on the environmental impact. There is an increasing need to factor in the energy consumption and CO_2 emissions associated with both the process and infrastructure required to deliver those phygital products/services around the world.

INNOVATION AND ENTREPRENEURSHIP

Directors of business units of some brands within the sector are being incentivised to drive sustainable innovation by aligning bonuses to tangible results in reducing environmental impacts, for instance, launching more sustainable garment collections. However, more radical sustainable innovation could be driven through novel and non-conventional external collaborations (Chapter 8). B Corporations (B, 2022) are starting to emerge in start-ups and MSMEs in the sector (Chapter 9). Sustainability and purpose are part of the DNA of these businesses and central to their missions. Growth and expansion are not necessarily the ultimate goals of this new breed of sustainable entrepreneurs

(Chapters 7 and 9). A number of these companies are establishing active two-way communication channels with customers through social media, with authenticity and connectedness being major issues among younger consumers. Authenticity is being displayed by the stories of the personal journeys of the founders setting up and establishing start-ups and MSMEs with increased focus on transparency over the origin of clothing and fibres (Chapters 9 and 17).

CONFUSION, EDUCATION, TOOLS AND PROCESSES

Students interested in entering the fashion, clothing and textiles industry are often confused over how to balance their personal concerns about sustainability with the challenges of securing a job. They often lack access to up-to-date information on new developments in sustainable materials, methods of production and new business models. What is the role of university educators in leading the comprehensive integration of sustainability principles and practice into the fashion, clothing and apparel curriculum? And in supporting students in identifying their personal responsibility and moral ethics related to the workings of this sector, i.e. what is ultimately good, what is actually bad and where are the grey areas (Chapter 25).

Tools for education and training are important for university and design school students, but that is also true for staff in start-ups and MSMEs and large companies. Many product sustainability tools aimed at companies are often too complex and not designed for basic levels of awareness and understanding of those in the early stages of their sustainability journey. Some tools e.g. checklists, etc. can support design decisions while others enable the evaluation of product-related environmental impacts, e.g. Lifecycle Assessment (LCA), etc. However, tools should be thought of as part of a wider engagement process that might include active "play", "hands on" working with fibres (biological inputs), polymers (technical inputs) and mixed fibres and materials and training and education programmes (online, physical and blended) (Chapters 25 and 28).

Setting up education and training programmes with companies can take time, as trust needs to be built, objectives need to be aligned (or often re-aligned) and results may not be immediate. Involving different business disciplines – from within and outside a company – can bring in different perspectives. The goal should be to build longer-term relationships between educators and companies to establish trust and improve awareness, holistic understanding and in-depth knowledge related to product and process sustainability as well as their wider social-environmental impacts in fashion, clothing and textiles.

FUTURE

The year 2030 is fast approaching and there is an urgent and immediate need to start identifying, initiating, developing and funding the sustainable innovations in the sector for this decade and beyond (Chapter 28). In tandem, the "quick wins" need to be identified, with change-making activated and solutions implemented quickly. The year 2021 marked COP26 in Glasgow and the start of the UN Decade of Ecosystem Restoration, both of which have implications for the fashion, clothing and textiles. The sector now needs to develop more progressive and extensive plans to tackle and mitigate climate change, waste and deforestation and biodiversity loss to which it directly contributes towards. The path to a more sustainable fashion, clothing and textiles sector is complex and evolving. To move forward, there is a need for system-wide, multi-lateral co-operation between business, NGO and education institutions, citizens and governments to develop lower carbon, circular and socially inclusive solutions. This will require multi-stakeholder and multi-disciplinary skills and knowledge development that spans across geographies, cultures, industries and communities.

ACKNOWLEDGEMENT

Joanna Czutkowna, Director, I Went Shopping Today is thanked for her contribution to chapter in relation to policy development.

NOTES

1 https://ellenmacarthurfoundation.org/circular-economy-diagram.
2 https://www.fashionrevolution.org/.
3 https://www.xrfashionaction.com/.
4 https://sdgs.un.org/goals.
5 https://www.ibm.com/uk-en/topics/industry-4-0.
6 https://www.plattform-i40.de/IP/Navigation/EN/Industrie40/WhatIsIndustrie40/what-is-industrie40.html.

REFERENCES

African Fashion Foundation (2021), Recycle, Rework, Reuse. Available at: https://africanfashionfoundation.org/projects/ (Accessed: 5th June 2022)

B (2022), Make Business a Force for Good. Available at: https://www.bcorporation.net/en-us/ (Accessed: 8th June 2022)

Changing Markets Foundation (2022), Licence to Greenwash. Available at: http://changingmarkets.org/wp-content/uploads/2022/03/LICENCE-TO-GREEN-WASH-FULL-REPORT.pdf (Accessed: 6th June 2022)

Ek Styvén M, Mariani MM (2020), Understanding the Intention to Buy Second-hand Clothing on Sharing Economy Platforms: The Influence of Sustainability, Distance from the Consumption System, and Economic Motivations. *Psychology Marketing*, 37, 724–739. https://doi.org/10.1002/mar.21334

Ellen MacArthur Foundation (2017), A New Textiles Economy: Redesigning Fashion's Future. Available at: http://www.ellenmacarthurfoundation.org/publications (Accessed: 16th October 2022)

European Commission (2020), A new Circular Economy Action Plan For a Cleaner and more Competitive Europe. Available at: https://eur-lex.europa.eu/resource.html?uri=cellar:9903b325-6388-11ea-b735-01aa75ed71a1.0017.02/DOC_1&format=PDF (Accessed: 5th June 2022)

European Commission (2022a), EU Strategy for Sustainable and Circular Textiles. Available at: https://eur-lex.europa.eu/resource.html?uri=cellar:9d-2e47d1-b0f3-11ec-83e1-01aa75ed71a1.0001.02/DOC_1&format=PDF (Accessed: 5th June 2022)

European Commission (2022b), Proposed Amendment to: Directives 2005/29/EC and 2011/83/EU as Regards Empowering Consumers for the Green Transition through Better Protection against Unfair Practices and Better Information. Available at: https://eur-lex.europa.eu/resource.html?uri=cellar:ccf4e0b8-b0cc-11ec-83e1-01aa75ed71a1.0012.02/DOC_1&format=PDF (Accessed: 5th June 2022)

Fashion United (2022), Global Fashion Industry Statistics. Available at: https://fashionunited.com/global-fashion-industry-statistics. (Accessed: 29th November 2022)

Harris Tweed Authority (2022), Harris Tweed Act 1993. Available at: https://www.harristweed.org/wp-content/uploads/Harris-Tweed-Authority-1993-Act-Regulation-and-Annexes.pdf (Accessed: 6th June 2022)

Ivanović T, Som C (2021), What Is the Potential of Bio-based Synthetic Fibers to Move Sustainable Textile Industry? *Sustainable Innovation 2021 Proceedings*, ISBN 978-1-5272–8520-0

Lawrence F (2013), Horsemeat Scandal: The Essential Guide. *The Guardian*. Available at: https://www.theguardian.com/uk/2013/feb/15/horsemeat-scandal-the-essential-guide (Accessed: 5th June 2022)

Long L, Lee-Simion K (2022), Driving a Circular Economy for Textiles through EPR. Available at: http://changingmarkets.org/wp-content/uploads/2022/03/Driving-a-CE-for-Textiles-through-EPR-Final-Report-v2.0.pdf (Accessed: 5th June 2022)

Majumdar A, Garg H, Jain R (2021), Managing the Barriers of INDUSTRY 4.0 Adoption and Implementation in Textile and Clothing Industry: Interpretive Structural Model and Triple Helix Framework. *Computers in Industry*, 125, ISSN

0166–3615. Available at: https://www.sciencedirect.com/science/article/pii/ S0166361520306060 (Accessed: 5th June 2022)

Maki R (2021), Beyond a Western "Sustainability" in Design: Fashion Practice in Bahrain. *Sustainable Innovation 2021 Proceedings*, ISBN 978-1-5272–8520-0

Meyer M, Dietrich S, Schulz H, Mondschein A (2021), A. Comparison of the Technical Performance of Leather, Artificial Leather, and Trendy Alternatives. *Coatings*, 11, 226. https://doi.org/10.3390/coatings11020226

Morgan E (2022), How Influencers Accelerate the Growth of Fast Fashion and Greenwashing. *Eco-Stylist*. Available at: https://www.eco-stylist.com/how-influencers-accelerate-the-growth-of-fast-fashion-and-greenwashing/ (Accessed: 5th June 2022)

Mud Jeans (2020), Sustainability Report. Available at: https://mudjeans.eu/blogs/ geen-categorie/blog-sustainability-report-impact (Accessed: 5th June 2022)

Oltermann P (2022), Xinjiang Cotton found in Adidas, Puma and Hugo Boss Tops Available at: https://www.theguardian.com/world/2022/may/05/xinjiang-cotton-found-adidas-puma-hugo-boss-tops-researchers-claim-uyghur (Accessed: 7th June 2022)

Pucker KP (2022), The Myth of Sustainable Fashion. *Harvard Business Review*. Available at: https://hbr.org/2022/01/the-myth-of-sustainable-fashion (Accessed: 5th June 2022)

Ranasinghe L, Jayasooriya WM (2021), Ecolabelling in Textile Industry: A Review, Resources. *Environment and Sustainability*, 6, ISSN 2666–9161, https://doi.org/10.1016/j.resenv.2021.100037. Available at: https://www.sciencedirect.com/ science/article/pii/S2666916121000244 (Accessed: 6th June 2022)

3 The Wicked Problem

Bernice Pan

Fashion represents the seventh largest global economy, employs over 75 million people worldwide and is one of the most important industries in the world (McKinsey & Company, 2017; UNEP, 2019). In the past two decades, it has enjoyed an average annual growth rate of 5–6%, excluding the 90% profit decline in 2020 due to the global pandemic (Business of Fashion & McKinsey, 2021). Yet behind its fashion glamour and business glory, where the clothing sector alone has doubled in size since 2000, there lays the 'Wicked Problem' (Rittel, 1984) of its environmental and social conundrum.

Its level of negative environmental impact is second only to the oil-gas and mining industries, emitting 10% of the world's carbon (i.e. more than aviation and shipping industries combined), using 25% of the chemicals and 20% of the plastics produced globally. It also accounts for 20% of the industrial wastewater pollution annually (Choudhury and Roy, 2014). Whilst the international climate conferences COP26 and COP27[1] have left key climate change policies inconclusive and geopolitical action plans conflicting, the mission statement of the United Nations (UN) Fashion Industry Charter for Climate Action (FICCA) remains "to drive the fashion industry to net-zero greenhouse gas emission no later than 2050 in order to keep global warming below 1.5°C" (UN Fashion Industry Charter for Climate Action, 2021). Launched in 2018, this charter is now signed by over 100 global brands-retailers plus many supporting organisations. Key aspects identified in the Fashion Industry Charter for a decarbonisation pathway include the development of more sustainable raw materials, transition to renewable energy and carbon reduction from manufacturing and logistics. However, implementation action remains slow and thin on the ground, and the crucial issue of over-production/over-consumption continues to be avoided. On its current trajectory, the sector is forecast to increase its carbon emissions to 26% of the world's annual emission by 2050 (Clarke, 2021).

DOI: 10.4324/9781003272878-4

THE (UN)SUSTAINABLE DEVELOPMENT GOALS (SDGS) FOR 2050 SPEAK VOLUME

Amidst the thrusts of continuing post-pandemic disruptions and acutely rising energy, resources and logistics costs, the mission statement for the FICCA may seem a reasonable one in balancing industry-wide business challenges of rapidly evolving consumer behaviour at the front end, with digital and organisational transformation pressures at the back end. However, this goal misses the link to the global Fashion System's collective output of some 100 billion garments annually and cumulatively, for a world population of 7.8 billion to wear briefly and throw away continuously. Of this annual volume of textile-garment output, 85% is discarded to landfills or incinerators shortly after being produced and/or purchased, and less than 1% is recycled annually (Ellen MacArthur Foundation, 2017).

Whilst 167 countries have now signed up to the UN's 17 SDGs to be climate neutral by 2050, based on the fashion 'growth' trajectory of annual production output, 2050 is a year the world will be filled with some 814 billion new garments and a cumulative 9.5 trillion garments from now.

A key question that both private entities and public institutions refrain from asking is: where on the planet, literally, do we plan to store this colossal amount of garment-textile waste, when the globe is already showing unmistakeable signs of reaching its carrying capacity and breaking point through environmental degradation, resource depletion, ocean acidification and climate change. For instance, 17% of the entire globe's tropical moist forest has been lost within the last three decades, and is continuing at the average decline rate of seven million hectares (i.e. the size of Ireland) per year (CIRAD, Republique Francaise, 2020), whilst what we need is for the reductions in the annual deforestation rate to accelerate 2.5 times faster. And latest research show that in none of the 40 indicators show that we are on track to meet our nearest 2030 climate target (Boehm, 2021). Thus, an equally glaring question is: from where do we plan to continuously extract natural resources required to produce the massive volume of textile apparel goods?

Despite the mission statement of the UN FICCA that has been publicly committed to by a list of notable global brands and retailers, we cannot transition to a circular economy by recycling or renting our way out of the scale and depth of this crisis. The rise of pre-loved (second-hand) clothing is now hailed by a new generation of fashion technology trading-distribution platforms, selected brands-retailers and the media as a more sustainable way of fashioning through 'reuse'. However, the danger lies in adding an extra drum of clothing circulation

Table 3.1 Cumulative Garment Output Count to 2050: Incorporating Projected Year-on-Year Growth

Year	Garment Unit Output P/A (Bn)	5–9% Growth Y-O-Y (Avg. = 7.5%)	Cumulative Garment Qty
2022	100	107.5	
2023	107.5	115.55	207.5
2024	115.55	124.23	323.05
2025	124.23	133.55	447.29
2025	133.55	143.55	580.84
2027	143.55	154.33	724.40
2028	154.33	155.90	878.73
2029	155.90	178.35	1044.54
2030	178.35	191.72	1222.98
2031	191.72	205.10	1414.71
2032	205.10	221.55	1520.81
2033	221.55	238.18	1842.37
2034	238.18	255.04	2080.55
2035	255.04	275.24	2335.59
2035	275.24	295.89	2511.84
2037	295.89	318.08	2907.72
2038	318.08	341.94	3225.80
2039	341.94	357.58	3557.74
2040	357.58	395.15	3935.32
2041	395.15	424.79	4330.47
2042	424.79	455.54	4755.25
2043	455.54	490.89	5211.90
2044	490.89	527.71	5702.79
2045	527.71	557.29	5230.50
2045	557.29	509.83	5797.79
2047	509.83	555.57	7407.52
2048	555.57	704.74	8053.19
2049	704.74	757.59	8757.93
2050	757.59	814.41	9525.53

to the fashion apparel market cycles – marketing yet more volume of clothing to strive for further growth. Much like the outlet model that did not merely absorb the volume of marked-down and unsold goods, but generated new market segments with associated volume increase for branded retailers, the rental and reuse model is feared to become yet an additional revenue stream that simply enables still more output, in the name of sustainability. This phenomenon is propelled not only by the fast fashion sector where the concept and practice of clothing as disposable items have now been successfully normalised. It has also been enabled by the luxury sector that is increasingly producing 'novelty fashion' and 'wow factor' clothing that is less practical or regularly wearable, and near impossible to launder and care for. With the rental and trade-in models now adding to the mix, the culture of clothing for single use is further being encouraged and justified, whether for a social media post or a physical occasion. In the age of digital transformation, brands and retailers' constant drive to increase the speed of change in order to further expand fashion assortments[2] has proven tremendously lucrative in growing sales volume and revenues. This agenda has further benefited from the rise of e-commerce and social media, where sales and marketing channels have multiplied with wider reach, increased hours of trading continuously around the clock and direct distribution across the globe without geographic limits.

There is now a call to 'source responsibly' amongst branded retailers. However, at present, only a small percentage of the product ranges are shifting to the use of organic cotton or recycled yarns. This will not remove the wicked conundrum of expanding consumption and production. Firstly, whilst cotton indeed remains one of the most highly used fibres across the clothing categories, 60% of the garments produced are made with synthetic fibres that are non-biodegradable (UNEP, 2019). Secondly, a quick search on a single global retail brand's website, as an example, showed the listing of 29 'sustainable clothing products' where the fabric content products consist of 15% recycled cotton, amongst over 5,000 different clothing styles, thus representing a negligible 0.009% of this brand's clothing output at most. Thirdly, full supply-chain transparency is reliant on accurate data collection, precise measuring standards, mandatory information disclosure, unified accreditation structures and comprehensive enforcement mechanisms – from sources to processes to products and post-sale impacts. None of these protocols are currently in place nor are they being comprehensively developed for the global fashion-clothing-textiles industries disparately spread across the globe.

Therefore, without confronting the most critical issue of substantially cutting over-production and curbing over-consumption, the reality of 2050 will be a dim if not devastating outlook, as aforementioned. There may simply not be enough resources to go around, whether in its currently linear system or a circular one if transitioned. The cost of inaction to decelerate clothing volume output may soon be exponentially greater than the cost of implementing tangible sustainability strategies. What is urgently needed is a coherent alignment between public policies and international governance (such as the principles and legislations put in place to hold the financial sectors accountable after the 2008 financial crisis).

Much of the current movement towards sustainability has been instigated by non-profit organisations, pressure group campaigns and industry-institution joint venture research publications. Facilitated by the widened channels for media communications, these initiatives have served to raise consumer awareness and drive public discussion of sustainability to the mainstream. A study in 2014 showed that 34.7% of fashion consumers declared that they cared about sustainability when making purchase decisions (Kapferer and Michaut-Denizeau, 2014), and another study in 2020 showed that 67% consider the use of sustainable materials to be an important purchasing factor (McKinsey, 2020). However, to significantly create structural change organisationally and behaviourally, alignment of objectives is paramount between government institutions Governments must set clear definitions and agenda for sustainability transition with incentives and regulations to guide, and business corporations must activate new values systems for operations and rewards, both in the financial investment and material economy sectors. Only through this prerequisite is it possible to effectively mobilise the capital required for industry-based research development and commercialisation of new materials, processes, tooling and technology in order to facilitate real and rapid green transition.

THE PERIL OF WORDS SPEAKING LOUDER THAN ACTION

At present, there remains a significant disconnect between the announced commitment to the SDGs and UN FICCA mission statements, and *how* they are to be translated into urgent action on multiple and integral levels across sectors and borders. Beyond the advocacy and the awareness, and beneath the reports and the roadmaps, the reality of the current Fashion System landscape is an uncomfortable one that makes meeting the net-zero target within the climate change deadlines an increasingly unlikely one.

Breaking down the Fashion System value chain into stages of a garment's life journey from cradle to grave, which every single item produced currently travels through, the correlation between output and impact is shown in Figure 3.1. In the Resource Extraction stage (i.e., the fashion 'cradle'), whether a £10 or £1,000 garment, everything comes from the earth's natural resources and gets processed into the clothing that we wear. The Environmental Impact part of the diagram, i.e., the fashion 'grave', shows in sequence, the range of environmental consequences that each discarded garment carries with it. This does not account for the

RESOURCE EXTRACTION   GARMENT OUTPUT STAGES

| Agriculture Industries | Fibre | Textiles/Trims | Design/Marketing | Retail | Disposal |
| Oil & Mining Industries | Chemical | Dyeing/Finishing | Garment Manufacturing | Logistics | Wash/Dry Clean |

ENVIRONMENTAL IMPACT   GARMENT ABSORBTION STAGES

		Deforestation	
Incineration	Air & Water Pollution	Biodiversity Loss	Rising Temperature & Sea Levels
Landfill	Soil Degeneration	Resource Depletion	Climate Change & Life Extinction
		Water Shortage	

Figure 3.1 The garment life journey: from resource extraction to environmental impact

vital human factor in the social-economic impact. Given the fragmented and geographically disparate nature of the global Fashion System value chain, and the wide range of other industries it relies on, including agriculture and mining, industrial processing and transport logistics, there is clearly little chance for coordinated solutions across sectors unless comprehensive policies are put in place through legislation and enforcement.

In the UK, for example, a parliamentary inquiry into the negative social-environmental impact of the British fashion industry, carried out in 2018 by The Environmental Audit Committee, did regretfully little to make headway in accelerating sustainability action. Expectant policy recommendations made in the published report *Fixing Fashion* (House of Commons Environmental Audit Committee, 2019) ranged from a producers' responsibility charge for better clothing recycling, to due-diligence check requirements across supply chains, to legal enforcement of minimum wage remuneration, to a penny per garment taxation on retailers to tackle fast fashion. However, this report was met with rejections by the UK Government in 2019 without any counter-proposition or coherent resolution to date.

THE TABOO OF OVER-PRODUCTION AND OVER-CONSUMPTION

In the now heightened awareness of the need to tackle sustainability issues across the global Fashion System, over-production and over-consumption remain a taboo subject that no major brands, retailers or manufacturers are willing to confront. Acknowledging and addressing the issue is seen by businesses as untenable due to shareholder interests and commercial pressures related to growth and expansion. It is also not a message that politicians are willing to address, in fear of losing votes and donors' backing due to its association with 'de-growth'. Challenging economic and adverse geopolitical circumstances that severely impact global supply chain and market dynamics further serve to digress the sustainability agenda, including post-pandemic recovery concerns, the Russia–Ukraine war and associated energy crisis, and foreign policy changes due to the precarious relationship with China.

As a traditional industry, fashion and textiles continue to view volume increase as the only way to grow revenues and market share. Whilst increasing revenues and reducing cost form the universal baseline for any business the primary revenue-generating stream in this sector remains the unit sales of textile and apparel, where the cost of goods = material + labour. The constant drive to increase revenues by selling more units therefore results directly in the exploitation of environmental resources via the consumption of raw materials required to deliver more garments in vast quantities. In addition, the continuous incentive to maximise profit margin by reducing costs has resulted directly in the exploitation of human resources via seeking ever cheaper labour required to process, cut and sew garments.

This powerful industry force is rapidly exhausting natural resources with the constant extraction of virgin feedstock for textile-garment goods. This includes both natural and manmade fibres, and in the fossil fuel and minerals required for garment trimmings, petro-chemical-based synthetics yarns, dyestuffs and agricultural pesticides. Direct and indirect impacts of these activities – propelled at speed and scale – are also causing deforestation and mass destruction or extinction of plants, insects and animal species; drying out waterways; contaminating air, water and soils; and shedding micro-plastic particles that are as far reaching as the Arctic ice sheets and as near as infants' stomachs.

THE FUTURE IS NOW, YET HISTORY IS NOT THE PAST

The Fourth Industrial Revolution's portfolio of technologies from artificial intelligence to big data and virtual reality are now enabling imminent-future possibilities and prospects. However, the detrimental damage and depletion caused by fashion's 'Wicked Problem' as depicted is not a scenario modelling of an imaginary future. On the contrary, data and surveys that document environmental degradation and climate change disasters are now visible to the naked eye both in emerging and in advanced economies. Yet, the world continues to turn a blind eye to the root issues and their direct association with our economic and lifestyle activities.

This same force of fashion is also exploiting people, where 1 in 6 humans in the world now works 'in fashion', 98% of them for less than a living wage in their country, with no choice, rights, protection or security

(The True Cost, 2015). During May 2020 at the height of the first wave of the COVID-19 pandemic, over a million workers in Bangladesh were dismissed without pay, due to cancelled orders and store closures from global brands and retailers (Anner, 2020). Whether in remote regions of Kazakhstan and Haiti, or in metropolitan clusters in the UK and the United States, a vast number of this unrepresented workforce produces cheap garments that are sold to consumers by fast fashion retailers. Two centuries on from the First Industrial Revolution, the severe urban habitat pollution and workhouse labour exploitation that were rife in Victorian England continue today. And due to globalisation, this scenario has spread across all continents at an alarmingly fast rate.

THE GROWTH PRINCIPLES OF VALUE DISTORTION AND DESTRUCTION

The global Fashion System has grown five times in size over the last 20 years, outperforming all market indices for profitability, including comparison with the highly lucrative tech industries, between 2003 and 2013. From a purely financial perspective, this record would seem like a success model worthy of replication and 'roll-out'. However, what is omitted from each business's annual report and balance sheet are the external costs and collective risks associated with environmental and humanitarian degradation aforementioned, borne by the society both nearshore and abroad.

This tremendous growth is partially facilitated by a range of value-destruction activities strategically carried out by the 21st-century Fashion System: Firstly, through planned obsolescence in the upstream processes of brands and retailers' creative direction and design development, where 80% of the products' environmental impact is determined (European Commission, 2014). This practice intentionally phases out current fashion trends at a rapid rate to make way for new ones, whilst making products with lower quality and durability so that they fail more quickly during wash and wear. Secondly, by creating a proliferated number of micro-trends and merchandising assortments to generate multiple product pipelines, brands and retailers are able to ramp up production quantity and subsequent sales revenues by flooding the market with an ever-increasing variety and volume of goods. What used to be the rhythm of 2–4 seasonal collection per year (of fall-winter, spring-summer) has dramatically increased up to 40 collections a year. The speed and rate of this churn have meant that design-development rationale and product performance prudence are replaced with recurrent technical problems manifested in a vast amount of waste at every process stage. Research shows that 35% of all supply-chain materials end up as waste before a garment even reaches the consumer (GFA & BCG Pulse of the Fashion Report, 2019).

A positive outcome is that fashion has now been democratised, where current trends are made accessible to a more diverse range of demographic and cultural communities. However, it has simultaneously stripped the key value propositions of function, quality and durability out of clothing, making garments often unfit for the purpose of regular wear. Instead, consumers are fed with truncated satisfaction and abbreviated use-phase whilst being asked to spend more frequently and cumulatively on intentionally de-valued goods. Contrary to common belief, this is not the sole characteristic of the fast fashion market segment, but a standard practice across the Fashion System both amongst luxury/high-end and low-cost brands and retailers.

The systematic cost-cutting carried out across the Fashion System is not a value engineering exercise for integrated resource efficiency and cost–benefit optimisation, but a manipulation of contemporary market economics. The advanced economies have, since the 1980s, seen an average annual inflation rate of 3.2% to date. Therefore, the price of most consumer goods has increased accordingly by 3 to 3.5 times over this period to the prices we pay today, whether a cappuccino, a restaurant dish or a new car. So the question is: How is it possible, when all resources, materials and labour costs have increased over the decades, that a £20 cotton top from an average mass market brand in the 1980s would today be retailed for half of what it was at £10? If factoring in the accumulated inflation rate, this garment price is in fact 1/7th of what it should be.

This is, on the one hand, a strategic positioning against competitors to gain greater market share and 'grow the pie' by expanding the totality of the target audience base. But on the other hand, it is a ploy to change consumer mindsets to treat clothing as disposables, regularly rendering garments redundant and undesirable to make way for buying more new ones. The cheapness of a garment, at times the price of a cup of coffee (naturally for single use/consumption), defies logic and facilitates consumers to buy more in both volume and frequency, irrespective of one's actual needs and wants, income bracket or spending power.

In some cases, marked-down merchandise becomes so cheap that the end sale price does not cover even the net cost of goods in material and labour. This may simply be seen as a suboptimal scenario where the brands and retailers must absorb margins cut and reduced profit in a seasonal sale. However, the average industry sell-through rate for clothing is 50–60%. This means nearly half of all merchandise produced does not sell at all, with much of the goods unwanted even by the brands and retailers themselves. In fact, it is a common practice at both the luxury high-end and fast fashion mass markets that brand new, unsold merchandise is disposed of, and destroyed en-masse, shortly after being produced. Therefore, the ultimate loss, collateral damage and future risks of this model are borne not by the corporations who should be accountable for their output and impacts, but by the society and the earth.

Joining the dots between published statistics, an estimated minimum of some 30 billion units of new garments of the 100 billion units produced each year get destroyed. Indeed, according to research carried out by Ellen McArthur Foundation, the combined value of clothing disposed of by both brands-retailers and consumers is calculated to be an annual amount worth US$500 billion. A recent Business of Fashion Report confirms that 60% of the fashion industry was value-destroying in 2019. This grew to an estimated 73% in 2020 due to a combination of profit drop and higher volume of unsold goods during the pandemic (McKinsey & Company, 2020). This illustrates that the *majority* of brands-retailers, i.e., the most powerful drivers of the Fashion System engine, are value-destructing as part of their standard modus operandi, making the discussion of meeting the SDGs an abstract promise and its delivery disturbingly intangible.

THE HEAT IS UP, AND THE CLIMATE HAS CHANGED

What has transpired from the COP26 and COP27 summits without dispute is that the globe is well on its way to hit the 1.5°C temperature rise. In fact, it is likely to exceed the global warming mitigation target by reaching 2.4°C in 2030 (European Commission Climate Action Tracker, 2022). Thus, the 'hope' for businesses to 'do the right thing' voluntarily – becoming incrementally sustainable and selectively accountable, each with open interpretations and closed books – is unlikely to transition the Fashion System into a circular economy.

There is no shortage of studies announcing the assortment of 'Wicked Problem' and negative impacts associated with our insatiable demand for newness from clothes to consumer electronics. Reports and discussions now populate public forums, media channels, corporate agendas and consumer conscience. This means that no government, institution or business can safely hide behind growth targets, pandemic recovery, greenwashing campaigns or simply turning a blind eye to the burning issues of over-consumption and unsustainability we collectively subscribe to.

The aim of the UN FICCA "to drive the fashion industry to net-zero no later than 2050" endorsed by its global brand-retailer signatories and supporting organisations is indeed a critical step forward. However, this mandate remains symbolic without any binding agreement for the scope or requirements and specificity of actions businesses must take to meet this goal. By morally supporting the 1.5°C temperature goal in 2050, whilst abstaining from forgoing short-term gain for corporate interest and continuously fuelling the vast garments pipeline, the world fails to ask itself 'is this the kind of growth we aim to "sustain" and the grave we wish to expand?'

What remains absent and is urgently required for the structural and real change to take place are: (1) sustainability transition definition and guidelines for business/industries and local government/communities with tenable implementation roadmaps; (2) regulation for mandatory disclosures and accountability from pre-supply chain sources to post-consumer waste with demarcated incentives and legal enforcement; (3) sustainable financial and environmental measuring standards such as environmental profit and loss accounts (EP&L) and responsible environmental, social and governance (ESG) investments that directly address and mitigate the environmental and societal risks of over-production; (4) commercialisable innovation focused on renewable materials and processes to swiftly replace our current system that depends almost entirely on fossil fuel and polymer-based materials; (5) public and general education programmes in schools and institutions that enable citizens to learn and adapt to the principles of sustainable living and unlearn the habits of disposable consumption. These tangible and quantifiable actions could bring multilateral accountability and scalable solutions to radically reduce the direct impacts of over-consumption whilst developing a new values system and models of future-fit growth. In turn, they may provide a real chance to mitigate the ultimate consequences of the Fashion System's 'Wicked Problem' and carry the world to the 2050 climate goals safely.

NOTES

1 COP26 and COP27 are the 26th and 27th United Nations Climate Change Conference 'Conference of the Parties of the UNFCCC' referred to as COP26 and COP27, held in November 2021 and 2022, respectively.
2 The various ranges of products offered to consumers by a brand-retailer.

REFERENCES

Anner, M. (2020) 'Abandoned? The Impact of COVID-19 on Workers and Business at the Bottom of Global Garment Supply Chains', *Center for Global Workers' Rights*, March 27. Available at: https://www.workersrights.org/wp-content/uploads/2020/03/Abandoned-Penn-State-WRC-Report-March-27-2020.pdf

Boehm, S., K. Lebling, K. Levin, H. Fekete, J. Jaeger, R. Waite, A. Nilsson, et al. (2021) *State of Climate Action 2021: Systems Transformations Required to Limit Global Warming to 1.5°C*. Washington, DC: World Resources Institute. https://www.wri.org/research/ state-climate-action-2021.

Business of Fashion and McKinsey & Company (2021) 'The State of Fashion 2021'. Available at: https://www.mckinsey.com/~/media/mckinsey/industries/retail/our%20insights/state%20of%20fashion/2021/the-state-of-fashion-2021-vf.pdf

Clarke, Rebekah (2021) 'Fast Fashion's Carbon Footprint', *Carbon Literacy Project* (Carbon Literacy Trust), August 2021. Available at: https://carbonliteracy.com/fast-fashions-carbon-footprint/#:~:text=However%2C%20if%20nothing%20changes%2C%20research, of%20carbon%20emissions%20by%202050

Choudhury, A. and Roy, K. (2014) 'Environmental Impacts of the Textile Industry and Its Assessment Through Life Cycle Assessment' in *Roadmap to Sustainable Textile and Clothing: Environmental and Social Aspects of Textiles and Clothing Supply Chain*, Muthu, Subramanian Senthilkannan (Editor), Springer, Singapore pp. 1–39.

CIRAD, Republique Francaise. (2020) Available at: https://www.cirad.fr/espace-presse/communiques-de-presse/2021/perte-220-millions-hectares-de-forets-tropicales-humides

European Commission Climate Action Tracker (2022) Available at: https://climate-actiontracker.org/countries/eu/

European Commission, Directorate-General for Enterprise and Industry. (2014) 'Ecodesign Your Future: How Eco-Design Can Help the Environment by Making Products Smarter'. Available at: https://data.europa.eu/doi/10.2769/38512

Ellen MacArthur Foundation. (2017) *A New Textiles Economy: Redesigning Fashion's Future*. Available at: http://www.ellenmacarthurfoundation.org/publications)

Global Fashion Agenda (GFA) & Boston Consulting Group (BCG). (2019) 'Pulse of the Fashion Industry Report'. Available at: https://media-publications.bcg.com/france/Pulse-of-the-Fashion-Industry2019.pdf

House of Commons, Environmental Audit Committee. (2019) *Fixing Fashion: Clothing Consumption and Sustainability*, Sixteenth Report of Session 2017–19. Available at: https://committees.parliament.uk/committee/62/environmental-audit-committee/

Kapferer, Jean-Noël and Michaut-Denizeau, Anne (2014) 'Is Luxury Compatible with Sustainability? Luxury Consumers' Viewpoint', *Journal of Brand Management*, 21, pp. 1–22.

McKinsey & Company (2020) 'Survey: Consumer sentiment on sustainability in fashion'. Available at: https://www.mckinsey.com/industries/retail/our-insights/survey-consumer-sentiment-on-sustainability-in-fashion

Morgan, A (2015) 'The True Cost: A documentary film on fast fashion'. Ross, M (Producer)

Rittel, H. (1984) 'Second-Generation Design Methods', in *Developments in Design Methodology*, Cross, N (Editor), John Wiley & Sons, New Jersey USA pp. 317–327.

The Business of Fashion, McKinsey & Company. (2017) *The State of Fashion 2017*. Available at: https://www.mckinsey.com/industries/retail/our-insights/state-of-fashion

The Business of Fashion, McKinsey & Company. (2019) *The State of Fashion 2019*. Available at: https://www.mckinsey.com/industries/retail/our-insights/state-of-fashion

UNEP. (2019) 'Fashion's Tiny Hidden Secret', *UN Environment Programme*, March 13. Available at: https://www.unep.org/news-and-stories/story/fashions-tiny-hidden-secret

UNEP. (2019) 'UN Alliance for Sustainable Fashion Addresses Damage of 'Fast Fashion'', *UN Environment Programme*, March 14. Available at: https://www.unep.org/news-and-stories/press-release/un-alliance-sustainable-fashion-addresses-damage-fast-fashion

UN Fashion Industry Charter for Climate Action. (2021) *UN Climate Change*. Available at: https://unfccc.int/climate-action/sectoral-engagement/global-climate-action-in-fashion/about-the-fashion-industry-charter-for-climate-action

Part II

Policy and standards

4 Global policy covering sustainability in fashion and clothing: a review and implications

Martin Charter and Lilian Sanchez-Moreno

INTRODUCTION

In 2020, clothing represented 81% of the EU textiles market (Köhler et al. 2021), with global consumption of clothing and footwear expected to increase by 63% by 2030 (EEA 2019). Yet the average time that clothing is used has dropped by 40% (EMF 2021) and 30% of unwanted clothing ends up in landfill (Clothesaid 2015) with only 1% of used clothing recycled back into new clothing (EMF 2021). The sector accounts for up to 10% of global carbon dioxide (CO_2) emissions, 25% of chemical emissions and is second only to agriculture as a consumer of water (Charter and Cheng 2021). Given the sector's significant environmental and social footprint, it is surprising that government policy to mitigate these impacts has lagged behind other major sectors e.g. electronics, automotive, and packaging. Fashion has been labelled as "one of the least regulated industries" (Bédat 2022) in which efforts towards decarbonisation and the reduction of global greenhouse gas (GHG) emissions are voluntary.

However, this appears to be changing with new policies proposed by the European Commission (EC) spearheading a move towards a more regulated fashion and clothing industry. The EC is at the forefront of developing environmental and social policies in the sector, with several new initiatives announced in March 2022 aimed at tackling environmental and social issues[1], with some developments at state level in the US, and no specific policy developments identified in the Asia-Pacific, South/Latin America, or Africa.

DOI: 10.4324/9781003272878-6

This chapter aims to provide a global overview of emerging policies related to sustainability in the sector, with a snapshot highlighting key thematic developments and implications for the future across the Europe, North America, and Asia-Pacific, including climate and net-zero, waste management, eco-design, transparency, and marketing claims. The focus is not on specific policy and regulations related to air and water pollution control, carbon or chemicals associated with production of fashion and clothing. As such, it is important to recognise that policy development, formulation, and implementation varies widely across countries.

BACKGROUND

Fast fashion is increasingly coming under the policy spotlight and has been specifically highlighted in the EU Strategy for Sustainable and Circular Textiles with a stated goal of taking "fast fashion out of fashion" by 2030 (EC 2022a). Fast fashion has been made progressively more accessible through e-commerce and accelerated during the COVID-19 pandemic with sales doubling in 2020 (BOF 2021). The growth of producers offering easy (often free) deliveries and returns, payment plans, and next-day deliveries has driven a 'buy now' culture, driving overconsumption and a linear 'take-make-waste' model.

The pandemic disrupted global fashion and clothing supply chains resulting in an estimated US$2.8 billion worth of orders being cancelled, impacting over a million workers, with many left without pay (McKinsey 2021). With the majority of fashion and clothing made in countries in Asia (Donaldson 2021), regulating and enforcing fair employment practices across the supply chain is a complex issue for policymakers as impacts are across borders. Previous reliance on the industry to self-govern has proven insufficient, and policy development is now emerging in the EU, some additional European countries and US states.

Global policy focused on improving the environmental and social performance of the sector is at an early stage of formulation and implementation. The publication of the EU Strategy for Sustainable and Circular Textiles (SUSCT) in March 2022 (EC 2020a) is a significant development which sets the direction for future policies across design, manufacturing, marketing, and disposal of fashion and textiles sectors. This reinforces that a new policy toolbox will be needed to reduce the impact of the fashion, clothing and textiles sector throughout the life cycle of garments. Details are further discussed in this chapter.

France introduced Extended Producer Responsibility (EPR) for clothing in 2007,[2,3] and the Netherlands aims to introduce EPR in 2023 with an operational producer organisation (PRO) expected in 2024. In Sweden, EPR for textiles was introduced in January 2022 and will be phased in over several years, aiming to reduce textiles products being sent to landfill by 70% by 2028. There are also indications that EPR policies for garments are also being developed in Spain, Italy, Portugal, the Czech Republic, and Germany (Delpero 2022). However, many countries are lagging behind. For example, in the UK, policy discussion is at an early stage with debates on textiles waste in the parliament being negligible compared with other environmental topics (see Table 4.1). Department for Environment, Food, and Rural Affairs (DEFRA) is currently reviewing results from the 2021 consultation on the "Waste Prevention Programme for England: Towards a Resource Efficient Economy" which included policy options for the textiles sector including EPR (DEFRA 2021).

In 2018, the 'Fixing Fashion' parliamentary enquiry completed by the UK Environmental Audit Committee made recommendations such as introducing EPR for clothing. However, the UK government rejected most of the recommendations, and despite a follow-up to the enquiry in 2020 and 2021, the UK government remains slow to move forward.[4]

Table 4.1 Number of References to Environmental Debates in the Official Report of all Parliamentary Activity from 2017 to March 2022

Keywords	Number
Net-Zero	3,794
Biodiversity	2,115
Right to repair	483
Single-use plastics	469
Circular economy	277
Energy-intensive industries	234
Extended producer responsibility (EPR)	132
Decarbonisation	111
Textile waste	10
Industry 4.0	10
Createch	3
Lifecycle analysis	2

Source: Table generated by Davis, T. (2022) based on data available at https://hansard. parliament.uk. Note that references cover both chambers (Commons and Lords).

In North America, the most notable development is the proposed Fashion Sustainability and Social Accountability Act in New York (New York Fashion Act) which places a responsibility on brands to mitigate both their environmental and social impacts. Under the New York Fashion Act, brands will be required to map at least 50% of their supply chain and disclose their corporate policies on environmental and social due diligence. Moreover, companies will be required to disclose actual and potential negative environmental and social impacts by publicly reporting on GHG emissions, impacts on water, chemical management, volume of production replaced with recycled materials, as well as impact reduction targets (New York State Senate 2021).

In Asia, policy activities in many garment-producing countries have been focused on shifts to renewable energy driven by net-zero goals; these activities appear to be driven specifically by Scope 3^5 emission reduction requirements by brands who procure their garments from Asia.

EMERGING AREAS OF POLICY FOCUS

To analyse the policy implications for the sector, a thematic approach has been applied. The chapter considers climate change and net-zero, waste management, eco-design, and transparency with a focus on workers' rights and marketing claims (greenwashing). Each theme provides a general introduction and discussion on policy developments across Europe, North America, and Asia-Pacific. As indicated earlier, the policy discussion related to sustainability in the sector is relatively new around the world and has previously focused on cleaner production and emissions at the manufacturing level only. Europe is leading the way with policy focus now shifting to a more product and lifecycle-based approach, while other global regions are at an early stage of discussion.

Climate change and net-zero
Several industry-led initiatives aiming at addressing climate change and delivering 'net-zero' goals have emerged in the past years,[6] but government policies focusing on these topics are lacking in the global fashion, clothing, and textile sectors. In this context, no national CO_2 targets for the sector have been identified.

Introduction
A race to net-zero has dominated many international and national policy agendas as the climate change emergency has become increasingly

apparent. The Fashion Industry Charter[7] was launched at COP24 in December 2018 and renewed at COP26 in November 2021, aiming to drive the fashion industry to net-zero GHG emissions by 2050 in line with the Paris Agreement. However, legislation enforcing the commitments is non-existent to date.

For fashion and clothing, material production makes up the majority of GHG emissions. Scaling sustainable materials development, production, and usage within the sector and transitioning its global supply chains to renewables are proposed strategies for reducing GHG (Apparel Impact Institute 2021).

In the UK, the Waste and Resources Action Programme (WRAP) "Textiles 2030" programme has indicated a target to cut carbon by 50% is sufficient to align the UK textiles sector with the Paris Agreement climate change goals and achieving net-zero by 2050. WRAP aims to deliver at least half of this climate target through its circular textiles ambitions which includes designing for circularity, implementing circular business models, and closing the loop on materials (WRAP 2021).

Regional bloc and national responses

Europe

In the EU, policies such as EPR include aims to reduce GHG emissions associated with production by reducing users' reliance on new clothing in favour of product life extension through repair, rental, and resale.

North America

There was no specific net-zero or climate change policies identified in the sector in North America.

Asia-Pacific

In the Asia-Pacific region, policies related to climate change within the textile and clothing industry appear to be associated with renewable energy production and consumption. For example, China introduced The Renewable Energy Law in 2005, supporting the production and consumption of renewable energy through tax reduction and subsidies (Sadowski et al. 2021). Bangladesh, another significant textile and clothing manufacturing hub has also set policies and targets relating to renewables; however, in 2021, renewables for the sector only accounted for 3% of the total energy usage in Bangladesh.

As European fashion and clothing brands face increasing stakeholder pressures to reduce their GHG emissions, targets will be driven through supply chains that will drive manufacturers in various Asian countries to make reductions. For example, 57 major Chinese textile companies announced the Climate Stewardship 2030 Accelerating Plan, pledging to reduce CO_2 emissions together and ultimately achieve carbon neutrality. On 1st June 2021, the China National Textile and Apparel Council (CNTAC) launched a plan to help accelerate Chinese fashion brands' strategies in tackling climate change (China Daily 2021).

Waste management

Introduction

Waste management is a significant issue for the fashion and clothing industry with research indicating that only 1% of used clothing is recycled (EMF 2021). Globally, an estimated 92 million tonnes of textiles waste is generated each year (Niinimäki et al. 2020). In Europe, this is about 5.8 million tonnes, approximately 11 kg per person per year (EEA 2019). By 2030, it is expected that more than 134 million tonnes of textiles will be discarded annually (EMF 2021). Exports of textile waste to regions outside of the EU are increasing, prompting a review of the textile waste export to non Organisation for Economic Co-operation and Development countries. While not industry-specific, the EU Product Compliance Network (EUPCN) will support cross-border market surveillance practices in the EU that are applicable to the textile and clothing industry. Among other activities, the EUPCN will promote and facilitate collaboration with other relevant networks and groups to explore possibilities for using new technologies for the purposes of market surveillance and traceability of products (EC 2019).

With China banning the import of solid waste destined for recycling including textiles, African countries have come under pressure to increase their import of used clothing, which has been growing exponentially since the early 1990s[8] (Fashion Network 2017). The trade of used goods has been identified as playing an important role in realising an inclusive circular economy. The large volumes of post-consumer textile waste, combined with cheap, low-quality textiles being traded from high-income countries to low-income countries is too technically challenging and costly to manage, recycle, and repair in those countries (Barrie et al. 2022). A key trade issue is to develop policies that regulate what constitutes used textiles that have the potential for reuse, repair, and/or being sold into a secondary market. The Basel Convention on the Control of Transboundary Movements of Hazardous Wastes and Their Disposal aims to regulate the transnational movements of hazardous and other waste. However, the ambiguity regarding the definition of used goods versus waste has led to goods being shipped to developing countries that are unsuitable for resale and reuse (Barrie et al. 2022). Clothing which is donated to charity may often be exported for sale overseas which results in shifting the environmental impact of managing waste to other countries. This can lead to illegal dumping such as in Chile's Atacama Desert (Glover 2021).

To date, it is still not mandatory in any country to report what happens to used clothes and textile waste. In Germany, about 1 million tonnes of used clothes are collected every year, but only a small amount of used clothes are resold in the country where they were collected. In the UK, only 10–30% of used clothing collected by charities is resold internally, with similar figures for the US and Canada (Greenpeace 2022). In the UK, it is estimated that 70% of clothing collected for charities is sent overseas (Greenpeace 2022).

Regional bloc and national responses

Europe

The EC Eco-design for Sustainable Products Regulation (ESPR) published in March 2022 proposes an outright ban on the destruction of unsold and returned goods (EC 2022a). Between 2012 and 2017 luxury retailer Burberry burnt an estimated £90 million (BBC 2018) worth of goods to protect its brand value. This is hidden yet common industry practice. Future legislation in the EU will make it mandatory for branded/retail producers to disclose the volume of unsold products per year. This will also apply to customer returns. France has already banned the destruction of unsold goods. The Décret n° 2022–748 (The Anti-Waste Law for a Circular Economy [AGEC]) was approved by the French Sénat in January 2020 and passed in January 2022. It prohibits the destruction of unsold goods, including garments and accessories placed on the market by producers, importers, and distributers (The Fashion Law 2022).

The EC Waste Framework Directive (WFD) – that covers waste issues horizontally – has highlighted that it aims to address the volume of garments made, by incentivising companies to reduce the number of collections per year and promote extending the life of existing clothing, reducing the need to manufacture new clothing. In 2023, revisions to WFD will aim to introduce "a more circular and sustainable management of textile waste" especially through EPR schemes.[9] Aligned to the EU SUSCT, the WFD aims to focus on policy options to bring more circularity to the sector. Proposed EPR fees will be invested in waste prevention, reuse, and support recycling innovation. The

WFD revision will make textile separation for waste collection mandatory in the EU by 1st January 2025, and will, within the EU, create a
clothing feedstock with the aim of increased recycling. Furthermore,
the WFD revisions propose economic incentives to make products
more sustainable through the potential use of eco-modulation of
fees.[10] Harmonisation of the structure of EPR across the EU will be
essential to avoid conflicting regulations across member states, and in
reducing the burden of multiple administrative reporting.

In 2018 in the UK, the Resource and Waste Strategy report (RWS)[11]
identified textiles (including clothing, as well as other households and
commercial textiles such as bed linens) as being one of five priority
sectors for a potential EPR scheme. Building on the RWS report, the UK
government's Waste Prevention Programme[12] draft report for England
published in 2021 proposed the development of an EPR scheme and
consultation with stakeholders by the end of 2022 (DEFRA 2021).

Microfibres and microplastics shed from synthetic clothing, especially
during washing, are facing scrutiny from policymakers. The EC's
European Strategy for Plastics in a Circular Economy published in 2018[13]
identified microplastics as a key area of concern. This was reinforced in
the 2020 EU Circular Economy Action Plan which identified the value
chain as a key contributor to the release of microplastics (EC 2020a).
The European standards process has now started with the establishment
of CEN/TC 248/WG 37 – Microplastics from textile sources. A UK bill
aimed at requiring manufacturers to fit microplastic-catching filters to
new domestic and commercial washing machines had a second reading
in Parliament in May 2022 (UK Parliament 2022).

North America
Research has indicated that there are no specific policies covering waste
management related to fashion and clothing in North America. However,
on 1st November 2022, Massachusetts Department of Environmental
Protection announced a new textiles waste ban that aims to promote
recycling and reuse, reduction of waste, and foster the growth of recycling businesses. Each year, Massachusetts disposes of 200,000 tonnes of
textiles waste, including old clothing, towels, linens, and other apparel
items, such as bags, belts, and shoes.[14]

Asia-Pacific
In the Asia-Pacific region, there are no specific policies related to
fashion and clothing covering waste management and related issues.
However, in 2017, China banned the import of textile waste, including
second-hand clothes (World Trade Organization 2017). This decision
created global repercussions, with the US's Institute of Scrap Recycling

Industries arguing that the ban could threaten global textile recycling by curbing innovation and preventing China's manufacturing sector from gaining access to these recyclable materials (Fashion Network 2017).

Eco-design

Introduction

Over the last 20 years, product policy has started to focus increasingly on the early stages of product lifecycles, e.g. during the design and development processes where an estimated 80% of environmental impacts are determined. Eco-design has been defined in international standards as a business "the systematic approach which considers environmental aspects in the design and development with the aim to reduce adverse environmental impacts throughout the life cycle of a product".[15] To date, policymakers have not acknowledged eco-design in the fashion and clothing sectors.

Regional bloc and national responses

While some leading brands are using eco-design guidelines and tools in design and development e.g. Jeans Redesign Guidelines (EMF 2021), and are implementing eco-design strategies, there are no specific government policies that have been implemented in the fashion, clothing and textiles sector. At present, eco-design remains voluntary in the sector and is not subject to legislation, although the EC has now highlighted policy interest in eco-design across a broader range of product categories including clothing and textiles.

Europe

The EC's first Circular Economy Action Plan (CEAP) in 2015 highlighted textiles as an area of increased policy interest. In 2020, the second CEAP reinforced textiles and fast fashion as priority sectors for policy alongside electronics, construction, ICT, and furniture (EC 2020c). In March 2022, the EC published the ESPR that covered a suite of policy developments. For example, ESPR included a revision of the Eco-design Directive which currently covers energy-related products, but indicated an extension of the scope to include a wider range of products, including textiles (EC 2022a). Alongside, the EC also launched the EU SUSCT which sets out the roadmap and concrete actions to ensure that by 2030, textile products placed on the EU market will be "long-lived and recyclable, made with a higher percentage of recycled fibres, free of hazardous substances and produced in respect of social rights and the environment". EC SUSCT also puts forward specific measures including eco-design requirements for textiles, the provision of clearer product-related environmental information through a Digital Product Passport (DPP), and a mandatory EPR scheme. In addition, European standards makers have now started activities related to the circular economy for textile products and the textile chain – CEN/TC 248/WG 39.

As indicated above, some European countries are starting to discuss or implement EPR policies in the sector where fees are paid by the producer to manage end-of-life costs. Since 2017, France's EPR framework has required all legal entities producing new textiles and clothing in the French market to take responsibility for the recycling and proper disposal of their products either by financially contributing to an accredited producer responsibility organisation (PRO), or by creating an individual take-back programme approved by French public authorities. The French PRO incentivises textiles producers by providing reduced annual fees for use of recycled fibres from pre- or post-consumer textiles (Knowledge Hub 2021). EPR fees are paid through France's Refashion/Eco TLC textiles organisation which has set up three scales of eco-modulation fees (Sachdeva et al., 2021). These tariffs along with other fees are highlighted in the table below (Table 4.2).

Such systems have been in operation in packaging, electronics and automotive sectors since the 1990s and 2000s. Eco-modulation of fees are being discussed by the EC in other sectors such as Waste Electrical Electronic Equipment (WEEE), batteries, and packaging to

Table 4.2 French EPR-Related Tariffs for Textiles and Clothing

The French EPR principle for clothing and textiles was introduced in 2007 and implemented in 2017. Garments are categorised according to size, from very small to large items, and the scheme covers 70 different product lines. The fees per product are as follows:

- Very small items: €0.006 excluding tax/item
- Small items: €0.011 excluding tax/item
- Medium items: €0.021 excluding tax/item
- Large items: €0.063 excluding tax/item

Eco-modulation discounts are given for:

- Durability, 50% discount on fees per item.
- Recycled materials, 50% discount on fees per item. The garment must contain at least 15% of recycled fibres and/or materials from household textiles. (Recycled polyester from PET is excluded)
- Reuse of textile waste 25% discount on fees per item. The garment must contain 30% or more fibres and/or materials from textile production waste. Recycled polyester is eligible in "post production".

Source: Eunomia (2022).

provide incentives for eco-design and encourage the use of secondary materials (Eunomia 2020). EPR fees for other product categories covered by EC legislation primarily include waste management (i.e. collection, transport, sorting, and recycling/waste treatment) rather than eco-design (Ibid).

The current discounts on EPR fees for clothing and textile products in France are seen as too small to incentivise companies to implement eco-design. Furthermore, EPR fees do not (yet) differentiate between products and packaging that are designed for re-use, remanufacturing, repair, and recycling and those which are not (Sachdeva et al. 2021).

North America
No existing or proposed eco-design policy for fashion and clothing was identified at a federal or state level in North America.

Asia-Pacific
In the Asia-Pacific region, no existing or proposed eco-design policy development for fashion and clothing sectors was identified.

Due diligence and consumer transparency

Introduction
Transparency within the fashion and clothing industry related to working conditions has traditionally been challenging to achieve. Complex fragmented and international supply chains combined with numerous intermediaries have made identifying where and by whom garments are made particularly difficult, despite auditing processes being conducted. With an increased focus on sustainability especially among younger people, customers are demanding more information about the products they buy, what and where they are made from, and by whom.

Regional bloc and national responses
The US and a number of European countries have or are in the process of developing and implementing policies related to due diligence and transparency. The legislation is often not specifically focused on fashion and clothing but will have an impact on the sector.

Europe
In February 2022, the EU Corporate Sustainability Due Diligence Directive was adopted to mitigate risks of human rights violations by establishing a

duty of corporate due diligence. The core elements of this duty are identifying, ending, preventing, mitigating, and accounting for human rights and environmental impacts in the company's own operations, their subsidiaries, and their value chains. The new EU regulation applies to large EU limited liability companies (Group 1: 500+ employees, Group 2: high impact sectors with 250+ employees) and non-EU companies in Group 1 and 2, and SMEs (EC 2022b).

The EC ESPR regulation published in March 2022, indicated in its 'inception impact assessment' that it will contribute towards achieving objectives in the Charter of Fundamental Rights of the EU, including fair and just working conditions, prohibition of child labour, environmental, and consumer protection (EC 2020b). This could potentially be implemented as part of the ESPR's call for DPPs to increase the collection of data and transparency of information across fashion and clothing value chains.

The German Supply Chain Due Diligence Act passed in 2021, will come into effect in 2023 and will require companies to reach standards on human-rights and environmental performance within their supply chains. This will mean that companies will need to implement appropriate risk management analysis, adopt a policy statement on their human-rights strategy and report on their human-rights due diligence obligations on an annual basis.

In 2022, the French Décret n° 2022–748 (The Anti-Waste Law for a Circular Economy (AGEC)) was implemented, requiring producers over a specific size to disclose the main country where fabrics are manufactured and declare any harmful substances used in production, in line with the EC REACH[16] regulation. Transparency for substances of concern will be important as it impacts recyclability and the use of recycled materials.

In the UK, the Modern Slavery Act, passed in 2015, legislates on modern slavery and human trafficking to protect workers. However, during COVID-19 in 2020, investigations into modern slavery and poor working conditions at fashion production units in Leicester – who were supplying global fast fashion brands – revealed poor working conditions and below national minimum wage (The Guardian 2020). To date, the brands involved in the 2020 Leicester case have not faced legal repercussions as most brands do not own but subcontract to factories. Under the current legislation, the responsibility to meet decent working conditions remains that of the supplier rather than the brand.

North America

In June 2022, the US passed the Uyghur Forced Labour Prevention Act (UFLPA) to prohibit imports into the US of products made by forced labour in Xinjiang province of China. The Act aims to combat forced labour in Xinjiang, where crimes against humanity are ongoing (US Department of State 2022). China is the second largest producer of cotton globally, with 84% of its cotton originating from Xinjiang, representing 1 in 5 bales of cotton produced globally (Responsible Sourcing Network 2019). The report, "Laundering Cotton" by the Helena Kennedy Centre for Social Justice concluded that the sourcing of cotton originating from Xinjiang often remains obscured through international intermediary manufacturers, and still represents a high risk for international fashion brands (Murphy et al. 2021). Brands and retailers named in the report as being linked to international intermediaries associated with cotton from Xinjiang include H&M, VF Corp, PVH Corp, Bestseller, Uniqlo, Patagonia, Levi's, Tesco, Ikea, Nike, Adidas, Primark, C&A, Gap, and Marks & Spencer (Murphy et al. 2021).

In 2021, California passed the Garment Worker Protection Act. This is significant as California is the largest clothing manufacturing hub in the US. The law requires workers to be paid by the hour (and prevents piecework), and holds brands and manufacturers responsible for withholding wages, even when production is outsourced to factories they do not own (Cernansky 2021).

In May 2022, The Fashioning Accountability and Building Real Institutional Change (Fabric Act/ S.4312) was assigned to the US House committee and referred to the Committee on Finance. The bill provides increased protection for workers by ensuring hourly rather than piece rate pay in the US garment industry. The bill also proposes incentives for reshoring manufacturing and grants for domestic production (The Fabric Act 2022).

In 2022, New York State proposed The Fashion Sustainability and Social Accountability Act (Fashion Act). If passed, the law will make companies with worldwide revenues of over US$100 million accountable for their social and environmental impacts. The Bill will be voted on in 2023 and proposes that companies will need to map 50% of their supply chain from raw material to garment manufacture, identifying social and environmental impacts and creating a plan to mitigate them. In addition, companies will need to disclose environmental impacts such as CO_2 emissions, water and plastic use and worker's pay e.g. fair wages. Under the proposal, companies will have 12 months to map their supply chain and 18 months to disclose the information. Failure to do so would incur fines of 2% of annual turnover (New York State Senate 2021).

Asia-Pacific

Research indicates that there are no comprehensive legislative proposals in the sector related to transparency in any country in the

Asia-Pacific region. However, many suppliers in Asia will be impacted by the International Accord for Health and Safety in the Textile and Garment Industry (IAHSTGI) that was passed in September 2021. The IAHSTGI is a legally binding agreement between more than 180 garment brands, retailers, and global trade unions to make textile and garment factories safe.[17] It was established in line with the Bangladesh Accord which was created in 2013 after the Rana Plaza tragedy that led to at least 1,132 garment workers losing their lives and 2,500 being injured (International Labour Organisation s.d.).

In Australia, the Commonwealth Modern Slavery Law was passed in 2018 and requires companies with over US$100 million consolidated annual revenue to publish a publicly available modern slavery statement and report potential risks within their supply chain (Australian Government 2018).

Marketing claims and greenwashing

Introduction

Between 1996 and 2018 clothing prices in the EU decreased by over 30% relative to inflation (EEA 2019). A fundamental area still to be addressed is the global overconsumption of fashion and clothing, with the industry promoting a culture of devaluing clothing by squeezing costs to sell at lower price points and thereby higher quantity. Brands' marketing campaigns, while alluding to sustainability concerns, are still heavily promoting fast fashion.

COVID-19 accelerated a shift to purchasing of fast fashion and clothing through e-commerce. Coupled with this, there has been increasing concern over greenwashing in the fashion and clothing sector with a growing number of infringements being reported (Vogue Business 2021). Until recently, online marketing has faced limited scrutiny despite websites making misleading claims (CMA 2021). Many claims provide little evidence or data to substantiate and often use generic terminology such as 'green', 'conscious', or 'eco'.

Regional bloc and national responses

There is increased tightening of restrictions around unsubstantiated sustainability claims for fashion and clothing in Europe and North America. However, the extent of enforcement remains unclear. For example, in Canada, the Textiles Act and Textile Labelling and Advertising Regulations were established in 2000 to prohibit false or misleading representations for the purpose of promoting a product or business interest. The 2022 amendment of the Competition Act (1985) prohibits the representation of performance, efficacy, or length of life of a product that is not based on adequate and proper testing (Government of Canada 2000). This lack of hard penalties is also illustrated by Adidas who was found guilty by France's Advertising Ethic Jury in 2021 of making false sustainability claims promoting the next generation of Stan Smith sneakers as being "made from 50% recycled material". However, while being found guilty of misleading consumers, the jury had no power to further sanction Adidas for violating the French advertising law and the decision has been viewed as the penalty (Abbara 2022). In many instances, breaking advertising codes and laws and being found guilty of greenwashing does not seem to have significant repercussions for companies.

Europe

There are proposed amendments to the EC's Unfair Commercial Practices Directive which will prohibit general environmental claims unless substantiated by relevant data. In addition, the EC is proposing to amend the Consumer Rights Directive to oblige traders to provide consumers with information on products' durability and repairability. This aims to strengthen consumer protection against false and misleading environmental claims. As part of the European Green Deal, the EC states "Companies making 'green claims' should substantiate these against a standard methodology to assess their impact on the environment". In addition, the CEAP 2020 indicated that "the Commission will also propose that companies substantiate their environmental claims using Product and Organisation Environmental Footprint methods".[18] Textiles has been one of the pilots for Product Environmental Footprint (PEFs).

In October 2022, the Netherlands Authority for Consumers and Markets (ACM) and the Norwegian Consumer Authority (NCA) have jointly authored a report outlining how the Sustainable Apparel Coalition (SAC) should improve the underlying data, claims, and presentation of the Higg Materials Sustainability Index tool (MSI)[19] to avoid greenwashing.[20] While the guidance is not legally binding, the document provides important guidance related to the misuse of MSI in relation to environmental claims made by some brands in their marketing (ACM 2022).

In France, under Décret n° 2022–748, the term recyclable will be regulated, and the terms "biodegradable", "respectful to the environment", or similar, will be prohibited from being used on waste-generating products, including textiles and clothing, or packaging for producers over a specific size (Policy Hub 2021).

In 2021, the Competition and Markets Authority (CMA) in the UK completed research into environmental claims and found that four in ten websites promoting products and services across a range of sectors including clothing appeared to be making misleading statements. Following this, the CMA launched the Green Claims Code to try and prevent greenwashing claims with guidance on what can and cannot be claimed. Under the UK consumer protection law, the Green Claims Code's principles should be based on claims being clear and unambiguous, evidence-backed, considering the entire lifecycle of the product, being accurate and truthful, and only making comparisons to other products that are fair and meaningful (CMA 2021).

North America

The US Federal Trade Commission Act (FTCA), whilst not specifically related to fashion, clothing and textile sector, regulates vague environmental terms and requires all claims to be backed up by scientific data. In 1992, The Federal Trade Commission (FTC) issued Green Guides to help marketers avoid making environmental claims that mislead consumers. These guidelines were revised in 1996, 1998, and 2012. While the guidelines are not legally binding, they do provide examples of environmental claims the FTC may or may not find deceptive under Part 5 of the FTCA, which can ultimately lead to a legal action against deceptive claims. Specific to textiles and clothing, the FTC indicates that any organic claims for textiles and other products derived from agricultural products are covered by the US Department of Agriculture's National Organic Program (FTC 2012).

Asia-Pacific

Research indicated that no legislation on marketing-related environmental claims for the fashion and clothing industry were identified in the Asia-Pacific region.

CONCLUSIONS

The fashion, clothing and textiles sector's adverse environmental and social effects have long been highlighted, with various initiatives set up, for example, the Clean Clothes Campaign (CCC) in 1989. By 2022, the sector has numerous fragmented industry-led and NGO-led voluntary initiatives. However, as evidenced throughout this chapter, until recently, the fashion, clothing and textiles sector has not been in the policy spotlight in relation to its environmental and social impacts. Over the past two years, policy activities have started to emerge at an international, national, and local level across various European countries and US states, with the EC leading the way through the publication of the EU SUSCT in 2022 (EC 2020a).

Given the size and emissions associated with the sector, it is surprising that there appears to be no real policy related to climate change and 'net-zero' by region or country. It is unclear as to whether The Fashion Industry Charter has had any real impact. At a company level, leaders are announcing commitments, but this is not across the value chain. Policy on waste management for the textiles and fashion industry appears to be limited. However, EPR schemes are being set up across several European countries (France, the Netherlands, and Sweden) with indications that other EPR schemes for garments are being developed in Spain, Italy, Portugal, the Czech Republic, and Germany (Delpero 2022), though they are still lagging behind other sectors such as electronics, automotive, and packaging where legislation has been in place since the 1990s and 2000s. In addition, trade organisations are starting to address issues on what does and doesn't constitute second-life clothing for export to prevent textiles from ending up in landfills. In this context, China's ban on the import of textile waste was an important precedent.

Policy also needs to consider the full life cycle of the garment from eco-design, regulating planned obsolesce, enabling the right and the facility to repair garments, and decreasing waste from the early design stages. These issues are starting to be discussed by the EC as part of the ESPR where textiles and clothing have been recognised as a sector of policy interest. However, there appears to be no discussion of product policy in the sector in North America, Asia-Pacific, or other parts of the world, including the UK.

Regulation on due diligence and transparency of environmental and social information is starting to emerge in the sector in Europe and North America. Increasing transparency is intrinsically linked to the industries' complex supply chain. Therefore, only through legally binding obligations to disclose information regarding working practices, use of child and forced labour, and the provenance of materials and manufacturing will companies be held accountable for misconduct. However, for these policies to be effective, they must be developed such that responsibility falls on every actor across the supply chain, as large organisations have often been able to shed responsibilities by claiming unawareness.

Furthermore, while more countries are starting to crack down on false environment claims in the sector, there is a need for enforcement with appropriate penalties to ensure that greenwashing has legal and financial repercussions, so that companies back-up sustainability claims with solid information.

While the industry is still in the early days of sustainability policy development, what is certain is that the industry can expect more stringent legislation to follow in the coming years.

While the transition will inevitably be challenging, the only way forward is by regulating the industry, creating accountability, and setting clear deliverables through policy tailored to the realities of the sector, in order to deliver a more sustainable and equitable fashion and clothing industry.

ACKNOWLEDGEMENT

Andrew Martin, Vice President, Sustainable Apparel Coalition (SAC) is thanked for his contribution to the development of this chapter.

NOTES

1 Chapter 22 explores the opportunities and challenges for textiles in detail specifically related to circular economy.
2 https://refashion.fr/pro/en/what-epr?
3 https://circulareconomy.europa.eu/platform/en/news-and-events/all-events/exploring-epr-textiles-taking-responsibility-europes-textile-waste.
4 View transcript of oral evidence: 'Fixing Fashion follow-up, HC874' (https://committees.parliament.uk/oralevidence/2133/pdf/).
5 Based on the Greenhouse Has (GHG) Protocol, Scope 1 covers direct emissions from owned or controlled sources. Scope 2 covers indirect emissions from the generation of purchased electricity, steam, heating, and coaling consumed by the reporting company. Scope 3 includes all other indirect emissions that occur in a company's value chain. Source: https://www.carbontrust.com/resources/briefing-what-are-scope-3-emissions.
6 See for example The Science Based Targets Initiative (SBTi) that has witnessed an increase in membership from apparel companies from roughly a dozen to over 140 since 2019. (https://www.wri.org/insights/roadmap-net-zero-emissions-apparel-sector) or the World Resources Institute and apparel Impact Institute's 2021 working paper: 'Road Map to Net-Zero: Delivering Science Based targets in the Apparel Sector" (https://files.wri.org/d8/s3fs-public/2021-11/roadmap-net-zero-delivering-science-based-targets-apparel-sector.pdf?VersionId=LxrwUSv9dHytM7zybuQgoJ8LUHBZVgM1).
7 https://unfccc.int/sites/default/files/resource/Fashion%20Industry%20Carter%20for%20Climate%20Action_2021.pdf
8 See Hansen, K. (2014). "The Secondhand Clothing Market in Africa and its Influence on Local Fashions", *Dress Study*, Vol. 64, 2014 Autumn.
9 https://environment.ec.europa.eu/topics/waste-and-recycling/waste-framework-directive_en#ref-2023-wfd-revision.

10 At a basic level, an eco-modulation fee is the concept of penalising the use of materials that are less environmentally friendly and rewarding the use of those that are more sustainable.
11 https://assets.publishing.service.gov.uk/government/uploads/system/uploads/attachment_data/file/765914/resources-waste-strategy-dec-2018.pdf.
12 https://consult.defra.gov.uk/waste-and-recycling/waste-prevention-programme-for-england-2021/supporting_documents/Waste%20Prevention%20Programme%20for%20England%20%20consultation%20document.pdf.
13 https://environment.ec.europa.eu/strategy/plastics-strategy_en#objectives.
14 https://www.mass.gov/news/new-waste-disposal-ban-regulations-take-effect-to-day.
15 Identical definitions in IEC 62430:2019 and ISO 14006:2020.
16 REACH is a regulation of the European Union, adopted to improve the protection of human health and the environment from the risks that can be posed by chemicals, while enhancing the competitiveness of the E.U. chemicals industry. It stands for Registration, Evaluation, Authorisation, and Restriction of Chemicals and entered into force on 1 June 2007. Source: https://echa.europa.eu/regulations/reach/understanding-reach.
17 https://internationalaccord.org/home.
18 https://ec.europa.eu/environment/eussd/smgp/initiative_on_green_claims.htm.
19 https://apparelcoalition.org/higg-product-tools/.
20 https://www.voguebusiness.com/sustainability/higg-index-controversy-exposes-deep-cracks-in-fashions-sustainability-efforts.

REFERENCES

Abbara, E. (2022). 'Jury Finds Adidas Guilty of Greenwashing'. *CareerinLaw.net.* https://careerinlaw.net/uk/news/general/jury-finds-adidas-guilty-of-greenwashing/ (Accessed 20/11/2022).
Accountability, F. and Real, B. (s.d.). *Fashioning Accountability and Building Real Institutional Change: The FABRIC Act.* https://static1.squarespace.com/static/6269a0251862e66ba01fc4b1/t/627e5e4946e16646c86c6984/1652448842251/FABRIC+ACT+-+FACT+SHEET.pdf (Accessed 07/10/2022)
Australian Government (2018). 'Modern Slavery Act 2018' No. 153, 2018. https://www.legislation.gov.au/Details/C2018A00153 (Accessed 14/11/2022).
Authority for Consumer & Markets (ACM) (2022). 'ACM and Its Norwegian Counterpart Issue Guidelines for the Clothing Sector Regarding the Use of a Material Index in Marketing Communications'. https://www.acm.nl/en/publications/acm-and-its-norwegian-counterpart-issue-guidelines-clothing-sector-regarding-use-material-index-marketing-communications (Accessed 14/11/2022).
Barrie, J., Schröder, P., Schneider-Petsinger, M., King, R. and Benton, T. (2022). 'The Role of International Trade in Realising an Inclusive Circular Economy'. *Chatham House.* https://www.chathamhouse.org/2022/10/role-international-trade-realizing-inclusive-circular-economy
BBC News (2018). 'Burberry Burns Bags, Clothes and Perfume Worth Millions'. https://www.bbc.co.uk/news/business-44885983 (Accessed 08/08/2022).
Bédat, M. (2022). As quoted in Friedman, V., 'New York Could Make History with a Fashion Sustainability Act'. *The New York Times* (Accessed 15/11/2022).

BOF (2021). 'Is the Pandemic E-Commerce Boom Over?'. https://www.businessoffashion.com/briefings/retail/is-the-pandemic-e-commerce-boom-over/. (Accessed 15/05/2023).

Cernansky, R. (2021). 'California's Garment Labour Law: The Global Implications'. *Vogue Business*. https://www.voguebusiness.com/sustainability/californias-garment-labour-law-the-global-implications (Accessed 14/11/2022).

Charter, M. and Cheng, I. (2021). 'The G20: Accelerating the Transition to a Global Circular Economy'. In *Global Governance at a Turning Point: The Role of the G20*. Edizioni Nuova Cultura, Rome, pp. 115–154. ISBN 9788833653334. At: https://cfsd.org.uk/wp-content/uploads/2021/10/Martin-Charter-Ichin-Cheng.pdf

Charter, M. and Davis, T. (2022). 'Createch in the UK Sustainability Policy Linkages and Company Activity'. *The Centre for Sustainable Design*. https://cfsd.org.uk/wp-content/uploads/2022/07/CT_Published_July-2022.pdf

China Daily (2021). 'Chinese Textile Companies Team up to Tackle Climate Change'. http://www.chinadaily.com.cn/a/202111/11/WS618c8d85a310cdd39bc74bec.html

Clothes Aid (s.d.). 'Facts on Clothes Recycling'. https://clothesaid.co.uk/about-us/facts-on-clothes-recycling/ (Accessed 05/10/2022).

CMA (2021). 'Green Claims Code-Get Your Green Claims Right'. https://green-claims.campaign.gov.uk (Accessed 14/11/2022).

DEFRA (2021). 'Waste Prevention Programme for England: Towards a Resource Efficient Economy'. https://consult.defra.gov.uk/waste-and-recycling/waste-prevention-programme-for-england-2021/supporting_documents/Waste%20Prevention%20Programme%20for%20England%20%20consultation%20document.pdf

Delpero, C. (2022). 'Interview: Textiles Sustainability Chief on How to Green the Oldest Industry on the Planet'. *ENDS Europe*, 27 October 2022. https://www.endseurope.com/article/1803445/interview-textiles-sustainability-chief-green-oldest-industry-planet (Accessed 14/11/2022).

Donaldson, T. (2021). 'Asia-Pacific Supports the Fashion Industry but Does the Fashion Industry Support Asia-Pacific?'. *Women's Wear Daily*, 26 May. At: https://wwd.com/fashion-news/fashion-features/fashion-industry-taps-75-percent-garment-workers-from-asia-pacific-aapi-heritage-month-1234828301/ (Accessed 05/10/2022).

Ellen MacArthur Foundation (2021). 'The Trends and Trailblazers Creating a Circular Economy for Fashion'. https://ellenmacarthurfoundation.org/articles/the-trends-and-trailblazers-creating-a-circular-economy-for-fashion (Accessed 05/10/2022).

Eunomia (2020). 'What Are Modulated Fees and How Do They Work?'. 4 June 2020. https://www.eunomia.co.uk/modulated-fees-and-how-they-work/ (Accessed 14/11/2022).

Eunomia (2022). 'Driving a Circular Economy for Textiles through EPR'. https://www.eunomia.co.uk/reports-tools/driving-a-circular-economy-for-textiles-through-epr/ (Accessed 15/11/20220).

European Commission (2019). 'EU Product Compliance Network'. https://single-market-economy.ec.europa.eu/single-market/goods/building-blocks/market-surveillance/organisation/eu-product-compliance-network_en

European Commission (March 2020a). 'Communication from the Commission to the European Parliament, The Council, The European Economic and Social Committee and The Committee of The Regions, EU Strategy for Sustainable and Circular Textiles'. https://eur-lex.europa.eu/legal-content/EN/TXT/HTML/?uri=CELEX:52022DC0141

European Commission (2020b). 'Inception Impact Assessment'. https://ec.europa.eu/info/law/better-regulation/have-your-say/initiatives/12567-Sustainable-products-initiative_en (Accessed 14/11/2022).

European Commission (2020c). 'Communication from the Commission to the European Parliament, the Council, the European Economic and Social Committee and the Committee of the Regions: A New Circular Economy Action Plan'. https://eur-lex.europa.eu/legal-content/EN/TXT/?qid=1583933814386&uri=COM:2020:98:FIN

European Commission (2022a). 'Green Deal: New Proposals to Make Sustainable Products the Norm and Boost Europe's Resource Independence'. Press release, 30 March 2022. https://ec.europa.eu/commission/presscorner/detail/en/ip_22_2013 (Accessed 14/11/2022).

European Commission (2022b). 'Corporate Due Diligence Directive'. https://ec.europa.eu/info/business-economy-euro/doing-business-eu/corporate-sustainability-due-diligence_en

European Environment Agency (EEA) (2019). 'Textiles and the Environment in a Circular Economy'. https://ecodesign-centres.org/wp-content/uploads/2020/03/ETC_report_textiles-and-the-enviroment-in-a-circular-economy.pdf (Accessed 15/11/2022).

Fashion Network (2017). 'Global Textile Recycling Threatened by New Chinese Legislation'. https://uk.fashionnetwork.com/news/Global-textile-recycling-threatened-by-new-chinese-legislation, 860491.html

Federal Trade Commission (FTD) (2012). 'FTC Issues Revised "Green Guides', Press release, 1 October 2012. https://www.ftc.gov/news-events/news/press-releases/2012/10/ftc-issues-revised-green-guides (Accessed 14/11/2022).

Glover, E. (2021). 'Chile's Atacama Desert Becomes Dumping Ground for Fast Fashion Leftovers'. *The Independent*, 09 November 2021. At: https://www.independent.co.uk/climate-change/news/fast-fashion-atacama-desert-chile-b1953722.html (Accessed 07/10/2022).

Government of Canada (2000). 'Guide to the Textile Labelling and Advertising Regulations'. https://www.competitionbureau.gc.ca/eic/site/cb-bc.nsf/eng/01249.html#Objectives

Greenpeace (2022). 'Poisoned Gifts'. https://www.greenpeace.org/static/planet4-international-stateless/2022/04/9f50d3de-greenpeace-germany-poisoned-fast-fashion-briefing-factsheet-april-2022.pdf (Accessed 10/11/2022).

International Labour Organisation (s.d.). 'The Rana Plaza Accident and its Aftermath'. https://www.ilo.org/global/topics/geip/WCMS_614394/lang–en/index.htm (Accessed 14/11/2022).

Knowledge Hub (2023). 'EPR Policy: France's National Programme for Textiles Recovery'. https://knowledge-hub.circle-lab.com/article/8959?n=EPR-Policy-France%27s-National-Programme-for-Textiles-Recovery. (Accessed 15/05/2023).

Köhler, A., Watson, D., Trzepacz, S., Löw, C., Liu, R., Danneck, J., Konstantas, A., Donatello, S. and Faraca, G. (2021). 'Circular Economy Perspectives in the EU Textile Sector'. EUR 30734 EN, Publications Office of the European Union, Luxembourg, 2021.

Mckinsey (2021). 'The State of Fashion 2021'. https://www.mckinsey.com/~/media/mckinsey/industries/retail/our%20insights/state%20of%20fashion/2021/the-state-of-fashion-2021-vf.pdf

Murphy, L.T. et al. (2021). '*Laundering Cotton: How Xinjiang Cotton Is Obscured in International Supply Chains*'. Sheffield, United Kingdom: Sheffield Hallam University Helena Kennedy Centre.

New York State Senate (2021). 'Fashion Sustainability and Social Accountability Act'. https://www.nysenate.gov/legislation/bills/2021/A8352

Niinimäki, K., Peters, G., Dahlbo, H., Perry, P., Rissanen, T. and Gwilt, A. (2020). 'The Environmental Price of Fast Fashion'. *Nature Reviews Earth & Environment*, 1(4):189–200. Available from: https://www.nature.com/articles/s43017-020-0039-9.pdf

Policy Hub (2021). 'What's in the Pipeline? A Closer Look into the Upcoming EU Policies Impacting Textiles'. Amsterdam, December 2021. https://policy-hub.webflow.io/articles/whats-in-the-pipeline-a-closer-look-into-the-upcoming-eu-policies-impacting-textiles (Accessed 14/11/2022).

Responsible Sourcing Network (2019). 'Its Time Forced Labor in China's Cotton Production Is Taken Seriously'. https://www.sourcingnetwork.org/blog/2019/11/14/forced-labor-china-cotton-fields

Sachdeva, Araujo and Hirschnitz-Garbers (2021). 'Extended Producer Responsibility and Ecomodulation of Fees'. https://www.ecologic.eu/sites/default/files/publication/2021/50052-Extended-Producer-Responsibility-and-ecomodulation-of-fees-web.pdf

Sadowski, M., Perkins, L. and McGarvey, E. (2021). 'Roadmap to Net Zero: Delivering Science-Based Targets in the Apparel Sector', working paper by World Resources Institute, November 2021.

The Fabric Act (2022). https://thefabricact.org (Accessed 14/11/2022).

The Fashion Law (2022). 'A French Law Prohibits the Destruction of Unsold Goods, Now What?' https://www.thefashionlaw.com/a-french-law-prohibits-the-destruction-of-unsold-goods-now-what/

The Guardian (2020). 'More than £1bn Wiped off Boohoo Value as it Investigates Leicester Factor'. https://www.theguardian.com/business/2020/jul/06/boohoo-leicester-factory-conditions-COVID-19

The New York State Senate (2021). 'Assembly Bill A8352'. https://www.nysenate.gov/legislation/bills/2021/A8352 (Accessed 14/11/2022).

UK Parliament (s.d.). 'Fixing Fashion: Follow Up'. https://committees.parliament.uk/work/654/fixing-fashion-follow-up/publications/ (Accessed 05/10/2022).

UK Parliament (2022). 'Microplastics Filters (Washing Machines) Bill'. https://bills.parliament.uk/bills/3077 (Accessed 14/11/2022).

US Department of State (2022). 'Implementation of the Uyghur Forced Labor Prevention Act', press statement, 21 June 2022. https://www.state.gov/implementation-of-the-uyghur-forced-labor-prevention-act/ (Accessed 14/11/2022).

Vogue Business (2021). 'The Big Global Greenwashing Crackdown'. https://www.voguebusiness.com/sustainability/the-big-global-greenwashing-crackdown (Accessed 15/10/22).

World Trade Organization (2017). https://docs.wto.org/dol2fe/Pages/FE_Search/FE_S_S009-DP.aspx?language=E&CatalogueIdList=237688&CurrentCatalogueIdIndex=0&FullTextHash=371857150&HasEnglishRecord=True&HasFrenchRecord=True&HasSpanishRecord=True

WRAP (2021). 'Textiles 2030 Road Map'. https://wrap.org.uk/resources/guide/textiles-2030-roadmap#download-file

5 Traceability, transparency and greenwashing: highlighting growing drivers for traceability and transparency in the sector, and emerging challenges surrounding greenwashing of garments

Joséphine Riemens, Mathilde Asseman and Andrée-Anne Lemieux

INTRODUCTION

The fashion industry has become a significant worldwide business based on lengthy and geographically fragmented value chains (Richero and Ferrigno, 2016) The tremendous environmental and social impact generated has progressively come into the spotlight (Niinimäki et al., 2020) and in this context, traceability has been identified as an essential backbone to advance sustainability in order to identify and mitigate these negative externalities (Garcia-Torres et al., 2021; UNECE-UN/CEFACT, 2020). While intrinsically related, traceability and transparency must be differentiated but addressed concurrently (Garcia-Torres et al., 2021).

DOI: 10.4324/9781003272878-7

Indeed, traceability is defined as the process "by which enterprises track materials and products and the conditions in which they were produced through the supply chain to ensure the reliability of sustainable claims" whereas transparency refers to "the relevant information being made available for all elements of the value chain in a harmonized way allowing common understanding, accessibility, clarity and comparison", either between supply chains actors or publicly. Therefore, transparency must rely on traceability evidence to back up sustainability credentials (Kumar et al., 2017) and traceability must be supported by transparency frameworks to enable harmonization and common understanding around sustainability communications. With the current lack of regulations and the variety of disclosure initiatives (Mejías et al., 2019), the sector has been particularly targeted for greenwashing in recent years. Defined as the misleading advertising of sustainability credentials, greenwashing is contributing to false impressions of sustainability impacts and benefits, thus preventing advancement towards a truly sustainable industry. Therefore, this chapter aims to consider the existing challenges (I) and progressive drivers (II) regarding traceability and transparency in order to accelerate sustainability in the fashion industry.

EXISTING TRACEABILITY, TRANSPARENCY AND GREENWASHING CHALLENGES IN THE FASHION INDUSTRY

Traceability: supply chain opacity and complexity

Due to globalization over the past few decades, supply chains in the fashion industry have become distinctively fragmented and increasingly complex (Richero and Ferrigno, 2016) including numbers of suppliers, indirect subcontractors or traders from raw materials up to the finished product at a global scale (Brun et al., 2020; UN Environment Programme, 2020). This evolution has resulted in a loss of control, due to the extreme opacity for brands beyond their direct suppliers. A recent global survey of 100 companies, including major fashion brands, found that only 34% had a traceability system in place, of which only half had visibility up to "Tier 2" (covering stages of manufacturing and finishing of products materials) (UNECE-UN/CEFACT, 2020) (Figure 5.1).

This complexity raises a major issue of data accessibility which is critical to mitigate negative environmental and social impact. Indeed, recent evaluations showed that on average, life cycle stages of raw materials acquisition and pre-processing as well as manufacturing stages such as spinning, weaving, dyeing and finishing account for major drivers

TIER 4	TIER 3	TIER 2	TIER 1
Agriculture, farming, extraction	*Raw materials processing*	*Materials manufacturing*	*Final product manufacturing and assembly*

Figure 5.1 "Tiers" usually refer to the four main processing stages of the value chain (from raw materials to the final product)

Source: United Nations Economic Commission for Europe (UNECE) & United Nations Centre for Trade Facilitation and Electronic Business (UN/CEFACT) (2020), Accelerating Action for a Sustainable and Circular Garment and Footwear Industry: Which Role for Transparency and Traceability of Value Chains?, Geneva

of negative environmental impacts (Quantis, 2021a). In the same vein, a recent report identified highest risks on the social indicators at the fibre production stage (UN Environment Programme, 2020). Besides, labels are usually restricted to certain aspects of sustainability credentials (Henninger, 2015; Kumar et al., 2017) and social monitoring implemented within the first tiers (Fashion Revolution, 2021).

More data is needed to provide a holistic understanding of the variety of sustainability attributes and their respective impact reductions (Kumar et al., 2017). Accounting for emissions and resources consumption towards all activities in the life cycle of a product, Life Cycle Analysis (LCA) is a standardized methodology that translates such activities into environmental indicators with the combination of primary data (such as the country where the manufacturing stage takes place) and secondary data from third-party databases or other sources (such as the country's energy supply). Therefore, access to specific data will likely influence the representative accuracy of the results. A recent study investigating blockchain traceability for LCA calculation showed that environmental impact varies up to 36% on the processing step for a fixed wool composition with specific data compared with generic data provision (Carrières et al., 2022). This high variability rate supports the key role of traceability to enable meaningful impact measurement and improvement actions.

However, the large amount of data collection and authentication required for such an effective traceability requires the use of advanced technologies for assistance in these efforts (UNECE-UN/CEFACT, 2020). Various technologies exist in support of traceability, such as cloud-based platform, including the use of blockchain, Internet of Things (IoT) or physical tracer technologies (Ahmed and MacCarthy, 2021), which is adding another level of complexity as companies must carefully identify and select the relevant ones for their business needs (UNECE-UN/CEFACT, 2022). For instance, cloud-based Software as Service (SaaS) digital platforms are developed to facilitate data collection and sharing,

whereas embedded tracers are used for in-product materials identification to ensure authentication of origin (Ahmed and MacCarthy, 2021).
On the other hand, blockchain distributed ledged technology has been
gaining particular attention for data immutability and security (Agrawal
et al., 2021). Besides, such technologies are still in their early stages and
further experimentations are needed to explore how it can be deployed
extensively to enable and support traceability and sustainability at a large
scale (Ahmed and MacCarthy, 2021). Several challenges remain to be
addressed. In the currently unregulated fashion environment, data con-
fidentiality and privacy protection in fact present impediments to information exchange and tracing (Egels-Zandén et al., 2015; Garcia-Torres
et al., 2021). Besides, digital traceability requires interoperability of existing systems to enhance information sharing (UNECE-UN/CEFACT,
2022) whereas numerous supply chains actors are not yet digitalized
and/or have different systems. Coordination between existing initiatives, such as the Initiative for Compliance and Sustainability (ICS), a
shared platform for social audits, or SEDEX Advance, another collaborative platform for ethical data, is also essential in enhancing mutual-
ization and avoiding duplication of information requests with suppliers
(Doorey, 2011).

Transparency: information asymmetry and greenwashing risks

While companies are struggling to implement traceability measures, the
industry is also seeing the development of different levels of information in terms of reporting initiatives (Jestratijevic et al., 2020). This form
of communication, essentially positioned at the corporate level, aims to
translate and promote a brand's sustainable efforts and best practices.
A recent study corroborating previous results (Jestratijevic et al., 2020)
highlighted that if 98% of the 54 brands reviewed were communicating
their social and environmental commitments, little traceability information would be displayed at the product level (Ospital et al., 2022).
Information communicated through promotional Corporate and Social Responsibility (CSR) strategies based on marketing insights (Singh
and Dhir, 2021) tends to reduce reputational risk while enhancing the
stakeholders' perception of the business. This approach stimulates the
risk of creating a biased perception of a company's social and environmental impact, with partial or unaudited communication creating
greenwashing risks, due to information asymmetry (Akerlof, 1970) between the company and consumers. The Fashion Transparency Index
is a prime example: if 47% of major fashion brands published in 2021

a list of their first-tier manufacturers, this figure dropped to 29% for brands publishing at least 95% of their manufacturers. An in-depth case study on Nudie's Jeans' transparency policy illustrates the risks of partial disclosure (Egels-Zandén et al., 2015). While in most cases, suppliers' names and the audit's main findings were published on the website, major non-compliances were sometimes omitted as well as non-audited suppliers from the published information. While it is understandable why managers were hesitant to disclose highly sensitive information, the case study highlights that this exclusion can actually be perceived as greenwashing attempts.

The issue of transparency and greenwashing is also intrinsically linked to the veracity of sustainability claims made by brands and defined as a "high-level statement about a characteristic of a product, or about a process or an organization associated with that product" (UNECE-UN/CEFACT, 2022). The Changing Markets Foundation recently reviewed over 4,000 products from 12 fashion brands and highlighted that of the 39% of products marketed with sustainability claims attached to them, 59% of their green claims could be qualified as unsubstantiated or misleading (Changing Markets Foundation, 2021). Furthermore, another study found that even when brands promote third-party labels or certifications, consumers lacked knowledge of these schemes or did not find them instructive with regard to their purchasing decisions (Henninger, 2015). Therefore, numerous methodologies to evaluate environmental impacts (such as the EP&L[1] or the Higg Index)[2] and social impacts (such as a recent Social Performance & Leverage tool)[3] at company, value chain or product levels are currently being developed with the initial aim of creating an additional support for informed decision-making. However, this lack of standardization is critically preventing effective comparability and the development of a normalized framework to evaluate both environmental and social impacts holistically. It is also raising important greenwashing risks as suggested by the recently publicized case of the Allbirds lawsuit (The Fashion Law, 2021). The plaintiff alleged that Allbirds shoes' carbon footprint assessment did not assess the environmental impact of wool production beyond and prior to the manufacturing stages and thus excludes almost half of wool's environmental impact. Besides, use and end-of-life stages in product impact assessments essentially rely on secondary data with limited representation, as suggested by the European standardization work (Quantis, 2021b). Such evaluation must address linear business models through meaningful indicators towards consumers, otherwise it will fail to tackle the crucial over-consumption issue in the industry.

INCREASING DRIVERS OF TRACEABILITY AND TRANSPARENCY IN THE FASHION INDUSTRY

Accountability: from pressure to the potential of stringent requirements

In the meantime, with the multiplication of social and environmental scandals since the late 1990s and subsequent name and shame campaigns from NGOs and media, the pressure for greater responsibility has been progressively increasing (UNECE-UN/CEFACT, 2022). This dynamic has strengthened lately with public authorities and increasing policies towards more accountability in business conduct. Over the past few years, several countries and regional states, including the United Kingdom, France, California, the Netherlands and, more recently, Germany, have progressively adopted due diligence legislations, with the ambition to mandate companies of a certain turnover to implement processes that identify, prevent, mitigate and account for their impact (UNECE-UN/CEFACT, 2022). In line with this, the European Commission has also recently adopted a proposal for a directive on corporate sustainability due diligence regime to enable a level-playing field and to foster a large-scale improvement. In the United States, the banning of cotton from Xinjiang due to the Uyghur scandal (Le Monde, 2021) has been another precursor example and a further step has been taken with release of the New York Fashion Sustainability and Social Accountability Act. The Bill promotes greater commitment to sustainability in the fashion industry, through targeting big apparel and footwear companies with more than US$100 million in revenue and business in New York. For instance, it requires these companies to map at least 50% of their supply chain from raw materials to market, based on prioritized risks. With legislative action such as this, the regulatory framework does appear to be changing rapidly, as substantiated by the survey findings of existing policies, regulations and guidelines, conducted in UNECE's recent report (UNECE-UN/CEFACT, 2021). In this uncertain context, companies are also calling for clear requirements and the last multi-stakeholder Cercle de Giverny forum in 2021 is an example of a collaborative initiative of multinational groups, such as L'Oréal, KERING and Rocher, aiming to promote policy proposals in favour of the operational deployment of systemic CSR.

Transparency: from expectations to the prospects of communication standardization

In addition, the recent multiplication of lawsuits in the fashion and cosmetic industries attests to the strengthening of allegation control, to ensure the veracity of the information being communicated to consumers (The Fashion Law, 2021). Canada Goose, for instance, has been recently pursued for false advertising regarding the trapping methods used to source the fur, as claiming to adhere to "ethical, responsible, and sustainable sourcing and the use of real fur" (The Fashion Law, 2021) In the same vein, a group of plaintiffs filed a class action lawsuit last year against Shiseido in New York, alleging that its Bare Minerals brand of cosmetics falsely advertised its products as "clean and conscious", "pure" and "free of harsh chemicals", due to the presence of perfluoroalkyl chemicals (PFAS) (The National Law Review, 2022). Indeed, sustainability claims fall under the provisions of general consumer protection regulations, except in case of specific legal requirements, and thus guidance has been progressively released by institutions such as the International Consumer Protection and Enforcement Network (ICPEN), a global network of consumer protection authorities from over 65 countries, or the Netherlands Authority for Consumers and Markets (ACM) (Webb, 2021). The latest created and published five "rules of thumb" regarding environmental claims and has started investigating businesses against these rules: nearly 70 fashion brands are known to be currently under investigation (Webb, 2021). To be faced with greenwashing risks and potential legal pursuits, some brands, including Asket or Reformation have been proactive in demanding tighter guidance and calling on the Federal Trade Commission to review its Green Guides, outlining rules against greenwashing (Policy Collective Politically in Fashion, 2021).

Stringent requirements appear to be forthcoming. In France, following the adoption of the Anti-Waste and Circular Economy law, a draft decree has introduced mandatory labelling of environmental characteristics, such as the country where the products' assembly, fabric's finishing and weaving took place. The draft decree also prohibits the use of terminologies such as "biodegradable", "environmentally friendly" or "any other equivalent". The Climate and Resilience law further announced the priority and enforcement of products' environmental labelling as mandatory for the textile-apparel sector, with several methodologies currently being experimented (ADEME, 2021). A consultation on social labelling has also explored the communication to consumers on the potential of social risks associated with the product's production and other positive social indicators such as know-how (France Stratégie, 2022). At the same time, since 2019, the European Commission has initiated the development of sectoral category rules (PEFCRs) for the calculation of apparel and footwear environmental impacts (Quantis, 2021b), based on the wider Product Environmental Footprint (PEF) LCA methodological framework

(Quantis, 2019), which will have a direct impact on brands' communication if becoming mandatory to communicate around environmental impact.

CONCLUSION AND RECOMMENDATIONS TO ACCELERATE SUSTAINABILITY

Traceability creates both organizational and technological challenges for corporations within the fashion industry. These challenges are amplified by the ripple effect of the difficulties of data collection within the value chain, creating issues in ensuring direct transparency and moderating brands' communication regarding the true quality of their actions and products. Data collection challenges can also create asymmetry when fashion brands communicate partial and unaudited information to consumers, which contributes to the greenwashing phenomenon currently rife in the marketplace. This situation also emphasizes the need for harmonization when it comes to brands' communication of sustainability attributes. With the growing number of proactive fashion stakeholders demanding a clear regulatory framework for both data measurement and communication, harmonization of accurate data and overall standardization of technical information represent potential solutions. Brands must reduce their risks when it comes to greenwashing in the short term by strengthening their data collection process and using traceability tools as well as verification systems throughout their supply chains. However, to accelerate sustainability, it is essential to actively consider the downstream part with the use stages up to the product end-of-life, which tend to be an afterthought with secondary datasets of limited representations. Business models should be properly evaluated through meaningful indicators aimed and should tackle the over-production and consumption issues as a direct environmental factor in itself. Traceability and transparency are still conceived and applied in a linear manner, whereas they should be driven by a sustainability and circular strategy to address the fashion industry's negative impact on environmental and social wellbeing.

NOTES

1 The EP&L (Environmental Profit & Loss), pioneered by Kering, enables the measurement of six types of environmental impacts (air pollution, greenhouse emissions, land use, waste production, water consumption and water pollution) all throughout a fashion companies' value chain, enabling an impact visualization at the company, and material level.

2 The Higg Index is a suite of tools, developed by the Sustainable Apparel Coalition (SAC), for the standardized measurement of value chain sustainability at different levels (Higg Facility Environmental Module (FEM), Higg Facility Social & Labor Module (FSLM), Higg Brand & Retail Module (BRM), Higg Materials Sustainability Index (MSI), and Higg Product Module (PM)).

3 The SP&L (Social Performance and Leverage) is a tool co-conceptualized by Chloé and the IFM-Kering Sustainability Research Chair. The SP&L is a measurement and evaluation tool for potential positive social impacts all throughout fashion companies value chains, with a multi-level visualization (organization, collection, product). The tool, currently under review by PricewaterhouseCoopers (PwC), will be open source for the fashion industry in 2023.

BIBLIOGRAPHY

ADEME (2021), Environmental Labelling. Available at: https://expertises.ademe.fr (Accessed: 10 April 2022).

Agrawal, T. K., Kumar, V., Pal, R., Wang, L., & Chen, Y. (2021), Blockchain-Based Framework for Supply Chain Traceability: A Case Example of Textile and Clothing Industry. *Computers & Industrial Engineering*, Vol. 154, No. 6, p. 107130.

Ahmed, W. A. H., & MacCarthy, B. L. (2021), Blockchain-Enabled Supply Chain Traceability in the Textile and Apparel Supply Chain: A Case Study of the Fiber Producer, Lenzing. *Sustainability*, Vol. 13, No. 19, p. 10496.

Akerlof, G. (1970), The Market for "Lemons": Quality Uncertainty and the Market. *The Quarterly Journal of Economics*, Vol. 84, No. 3, pp. 488–500.

Brun, A., Karaosman, H., & Barresi, T. (2020), Supply Chain Collaboration for Transparency. *Sustainability*, Vol. 12, No. 11, pp. 4429–4450.

Carrières, V., Lemieux, A.-A., Margni, M., Pellerin, R., & Cariou, S. (2022), Measuring the Value of Blockchain Traceability in Supporting LCA for Textile Products. *Sustainability*, Vol. 14, No. 4, pp. 2109–2124.

Changing Markets Foundation (2021), Synthetics Anonymous. Fashion Brands' Addiction to Fossil Fuels. Available at: https://changingmarkets.org (Accessed: 22 May 2023).

Décret n° 2022–748 du 29 avril 2022 relatif à l'information du consommateur sur les qualités et caractéristiques environnementales des produits générateurs de déchets (2022), Available at: https://www.legifrance.gouv.fr (Accessed: 1 June 2022).

Doorey, D. J. (2011), The Transparent Supply Chain: From Resistance to Implementation at Nike and Levi-Strauss. *Journal of Business Ethics*, Vol. 103, pp. 587–603.

Egels-Zandén, N., Hulthén, K., & Wulff, G. (2015), Trade-Offs in Supply Chain Transparency: The Case of Nudie Jeans Co, *Journal of Cleaner Production*, Vol. 107, pp. 95–104.

European Commission (2022a), Corporate Sustainability Due Diligence. Available at: https://ec.europa.eu (Accessed: 10 April 2022).

European Commission (EC) (2022b), EU Strategy for Sustainable and Circular Textiles. Available at: https://ec.europa.eu (Accessed: 10 April 2022).

Fashion Revolution (2021), Fashion Transparency Index. 2021 Edition. Available at: https://issuu.com/fashionrevolution (Accessed: 22 May 2023).

France Stratégie (2022), Affichage Social sur les Biens et Services. Available at: https://www.strategie.gouv.fr (Accessed: 22 May 2023).

Garcia-Torres, S., Rey-Garcia, M., Sáenz, J., & Seuring, S. (2021), Traceability and Transparency for Sustainable Fashion-Apparel Supply Chains, *Journal of Fashion Marketing and Management: An International Journal*, Vol. 26, No. 2, pp. 344–364.

Henninger, C. (2015), Traceability the New Eco-Label in the Slow-Fashion Industry? — Consumer Perceptions and Micro-Organisations Responses, *Sustainability*, Vol. 7, No. 5, pp. 6011–6032.

Jestratijevic, I., Rudd, N., & Uanhoro, J. (2020), Transparency of Sustainability Disclosures Among Luxury and Mass-Market Fashion Brands, *Journal of Global Fashion Marketing*, Vol. 11, No. 2, pp. 1–18.

Kumar, V., Agrawal, T. K., Wang, L., & Chen, Y. (2017), Contribution of Traceability Towards Attaining Sustainability in the Textile Sector, *Textiles and Clothing Sustainability*, Vol. 3, No. 1, pp. 1–10.

Le Monde (2021), Les Etats-Unis Interdisent l'Importation de Produits du Xinjiang Issus du Travail Force. Available at: https://www.lemonde.fr (Accessed: 10 April 2022).

Mejías, A. M., Bellas, R., Pardo, J. E., & Paz, E. (2019), Traceability Management Systems and Capacity Building as New Approaches for Improving Sustainability in the Fashion Multi-tier Supply Chain, *International Journal of Production Economics*, Vol. 217, pp. 143–158.

New York's Fashion Sustainability and Social Accountability Act, senate Bill S7428 (2022), Available at: https://www.nysenate.gov (Accessed: 10 April 2022).

Niinimäki, K., Peters, G., Dahlbo, H., Perry, P., Rissanen, T., & Gwilt, A. (2020), The Environmental Price of Fast Fashion, *Nature Reviews Earth & Environment*, Vol. 1, No. 4, pp. 189–200.

Ospital, P., Masson D., Beler, C., & Legardeur, J. (2022), Traceability Information to Communicate to Consumer in Total Transparency, Global Fashion Conference 2021, Warsaw, Poland, pp. 1–7.

Quantis (2021a), Draft Product Environmental Footprint-Representative Product (PEF-RP) Study Report: Apparel and Footwear, Version 1.1. Available at: https://webgate.ec.europa.eu (Accessed: 10 April 2022).

Quantis (2021b), Draft Product Environmental Footprint-Category Rules (PEFCRs) Apparel and Footwear, Version 1.1. Available at: https://eeb.org (Accessed: 10 April 2022).

Quantis (2019), Designing Credibility in Fashion with the Product Environmental Footprint. Available at: https://quantis-intl.com (Accessed: 10 April 2022).

Richero, R., & Ferrigno, S. (2016), *A Background Analysis on Transparency and Traceability in the Garment Value Chain*, DAI Europe, Office for Economic Policy, and Regional Development (EPRD), Apsley, Kielce.

Singh, S., & Dhir, S. (2021), Structured Review Using TCCM and Bibliometric Analysis of International Cause-Related Marketing, Social Marketing, and Innovation of the Firm, *International Review on Public and Non-Profit Marketing*, Vol. 16, Nos. 2–4 pp. 335–347.

The Fashion Law (2021), Fashion Law in 2021: 12 of the Year's Noteworthy Lawsuits. Available at: https://www.thefashionlaw.com (Accessed: 10 April 2022).

The National Law Review (2022), Cosmetics and PFAS: Industry Lawsuits a Lesson For ESG. Available at: https://www.natlawreview.com (Accessed: 10 April 2022).

United Nations Economic Commission for Europe (UNECE) & United Nations Centre for Trade Facilitation and Electronic Business (UN/CEFACT) (2022), *Enhancing Traceability and Transparency of Sustainable Value Chains in the Garment and Footwear Sector. Recommandation n°46*, Geneva.

United Nations Economic Commission for Europe (UNECE) & United Nations Centre for Trade Facilitation and Electronic Business (UN/CEFACT) (2021), *Enhancing Sustainability and Circularity of Value Chains in the Garment and Footwear Sector: Policy Developments on Traceability and Transparency. A Mapping of Policies, Regulations, and Guidelines*, Geneva.

United Nations Economic Commission for Europe (UNECE) & United Nations Centre for Trade Facilitation and Electronic Business (2020), *Accelerating Action for a Sustainable and Circular Garment and Footwear Industry: Which Role for Transparency and Traceability of Value Chains?*, Geneva.

United Nations Environment Programme (2020), *Sustainability and Circularity in the Textile Value Chain - Global Stocktaking*, Nairobi.

Webb. B. (2021), The Big Global Greenwashing Crackdown, Vogue Business. Available at: https://www.voguebusiness.com (Accessed: 10 April 2022).

6 Using textile testing information to ensure garment quality, longevity and transparency

Claire Lerpiniere and Angela Davies

INTRODUCTION

The textile industry is a major contributor to climate change and pollution due to intensive crop production, chemical and water usage and over consumption of clothing. This myriad of environmental and sustainability issues, which the fashion and textiles industry collectively contribute to, are increasingly recognised by brands, consumers and industry bodies (Lehmann, Gizem, Robinson, Kruse, and Taylor 2020).

The low cost and high speed of clothing production and the drive from the fashion industry to provide the latest catwalk trends as soon as possible to the consumer has compounded the issue over the last couple of decades (WRAP 2017, Textile Exchange 2018). These challenges constitute a 'Wicked Problem' (Rittel and Webber 1973) due to their intertangled complexities, which requires a systems perspective to resolve.

The internet has led to increased ease of purchasing which has been a contributory factor driving the consumer-led "I want it now" culture. Consumers can browse online stores for the latest global trends, and within a click of a button, clothing can be on their doorstep from across the world, with little thought into the process of making this happen.

From an industry point of view, there is now a greater range of brands available to consumers than ever before, particularly via online platforms; each striving to meet their consumer demands. Traditionally, consumers have purchased from the limited bricks and mortar stores

DOI: 10.4324/9781003272878-8

accessible to them, meaning that the number of retail competitors was limited to the local area where the consumer was located. Globalisation and e-commerce have transformed this system, creating fierce competition for brands to adopt the latest trends, whilst delivering on low price, immediacy and availability.

In this complex landscape, designing for quality, longevity and durability has been noted as a key driver for sustainability, particularly in the context of the shift towards a circular fashion economy. Benefits for consumers and brands include slowing and shifting consumption towards a higher-quality, longer-lasting product and 'strengthening brand reputation, and reinforcing customer satisfaction and loyalty' (Textile Exchange 2018:10).

Similarly, material quality, which is measured both subjectively by consumers through handling and viewing and objectively through laboratory testing, impacts on satisfaction of a garment (Connor-Crabb & Rigby 2019).

Consumer perceptions frequently link the cost of garment to their expectations of durability and longevity of a garment (Swinker & Hines 2006); this link is not always substantiated (Wakes et al. 2020). Better awareness surrounding quality-performance criteria would enable the consumer to make informed purchasing decisions based on factual evidence rather than perception. The term 'fast fashion' was initially coined to define a quicker design to retail model, pioneered by Inditex, described as 'just-in-time' production. In contrast to the previous model of long lead-times producing garments for clearly defined fashion seasons, such as autumn/winter, the 'fast fashion' model provides a continuous supply of new garments to retailers (Crofton and Dopico 2007). However, the term has shifted again, with the definition of 'fast fashion' no longer limited to being used as a descriptive term of a rapid production model; it now also refers to the speed at which consumers buy and discard garments. In this model, 'fast fashion' is made by wide range of brands which sell trend-driven, low-quality, low-durability, low-priced clothing which mostly ends up in landfill after a short period of wear and use by the consumer (Niinimäki et al. 2020).

Slow fashion and increasing garment lifespans have been proposed as an alternative to the accelerated consumption created by fast fashion (Niinimäki et al. 2020). However, it can be argued that there is a lack of transparency for the consumer regarding the processes and assurance of garment quality testing. These are done to measure the longevity and material quality of a garment, and the reasonable expectation of its lifespan. Not sharing these results impacts on consumers' lack of understanding of garment durability at the point of sale. This includes how to define a quality product, how the testing process influences garment longevity and how this information is made available for interpretation by the layperson.

LEVERAGE POINTS

The current fashion industry's supply model is a system based on brands creating garments with a short shelf life to induce consumers' overconsumption of trend-led clothing. This leads to a rapid disposal of apparel, usually into landfill. To borrow a concept from systems theory, the existing fashion system of exponential expansion and resource consumption has created a 'reinforcing feedback loop', a system which expands to the point of erosion and collapse (Meadows 2009).

In a world of finite resources, there is no alternative to a shift towards responsible production and consumption models across all sectors. A 'leverage point' (Meadows 2009) is a place or point in a complex system whereby a small change has a disproportionate effect on a structure, economy or corporation's modus operandi, whereby a small change has a big impact on resetting behaviours.

This chapter proposes that fashion brands have an opportunity to create a leverage point which slows consumption whilst enhancing their brand values, by giving individuals buying garments increased access to garment longevity and durability information. This is intended to utilise existing technical textile testing technologies, codified in an easy-to-understand method, for ease of recognition by the consumer.

GARMENT DURABILITY INFORMATION

The production of a garment brings with it responsibilities for both the manufacturer and the brand retailing the garment, depending on the intended function of a garment. Performance specifications allow retailers to adhere to safety, environmental and performance criteria, dominated by mandatory legislative requirements as a first priority and retailer and consumer satisfaction as a second significant driving force. These are set out in a performance specification sheet and vary from demonstrating adherence to minimal requirements in law, including mandated legislative tests such as the requirement for testing for hazardous chemicals or flammability, through to optional performance and quality tests, such as dimensional stability (shrinkage) or aesthetic appearance after washing, amongst others, as noted in Table 6.1.

Table 6.1 Table of Testing: Regulatory and Quality

Testing Category	i. Types of Testing	ii. Types of Certification or Accreditation
iii. Regulatory requirements	Fibre composition	
	Substances of very high concern (SVHC)	OEKO-TEX® STANDARD 100, Bluesign®
	Restricted chemicals including persistent organic pollutants (POPs)	
	For U.K. compliance with general product safety directive (GPSD)	CE Marking Directives or Regulations
	Safety such as flammability, food imitation, children's wear safety such as drawcords	British Standard Specification
Performance	Colourfastness testing, laundering, strength, durability, aesthetics	ISO Standards
Substantiating claims	Waterproof, moisture management, thermal properties (tog rating)	ISO Standards
Ecological testing and legislated requirements	Microbial testing, environmental testing to gain eco accreditation, green claims, end-of-life management, zero discharge of hazardous chemicals	OEKO-TEX® STANDARD 100, Bluesign® Convention on International Trade in Endangered Species of Wild Fauna and Flora (CITES), Forest Stewardship Council (FSC) Responsible Wool Standard (RWS) Global Recycled Standard (GRS) for fibres Zero Discharge of Hazardous Chemicals (ZDHC) Green Claims Code

(*Continued*)

Table 6.1 (Continued)

Testing Category	i. Types of Testing	ii. Types of Certification or Accreditation
Ecological or ethical guarantees	Planetary environment, habitats, biodiversity	Convention on International Trade in Endangered Species of Wild Fauna and Flora (CITES), Forest Stewardship Council (FSC) Responsible Wool Standard (RWS) Ethical trading Initiative (ETI) Soil Association (Organic) Fair Trade Cradle 2 Cradle Textile Exchange Enviro-mark World Fair Trade Organization Sustainable Apparel Coalition Ethical Fashion Forum

   One approach which brands can use to demonstrate both their commitment to quality and encourage responsible consumption is to draw upon data and information from their existing product performance specification and associated textiles testing methodologies to influence a consumer mindset change. Such an approach would present the greatest scope for creating a consumer fashion culture for quality products, whilst requiring minimal investment by the retailer and little disruption to the brand's existing product development and production processes.

   Disclosure of a brand's performance criteria could influence buying behaviour, particularly for those consumers who are seeking evidence of 'quality'. For this, brands would have to review their acceptable 'pass' criteria, generally set by each retailer in response to their own quality and longevity benchmarks for design, quality, performance and longevity. Fast fashion retailers focus on trend and price, rather than quality, as their selling point for consumers, encouraging a throwaway attitude with poor quality clothing which pills,[1] loses shape or fades after fewer than 30 wears, thus feeding into high levels of clothing consumption.

In contrast, brands which communicate the quality, longevity and durability of their garments have a point of differentiation in a saturated market.

Quality assessment and testing tools already exist which provide objective measurements for garment handle, softness, drape and stretch, particularly the KES FB system (Kawabata Evaluation System) for fabric (Kageyama, Kawabata & Niwa 1988) used to predict and objectively measure the aesthetic qualities perceived by human touch. The Kawabata system is widely used in industry to scientifically measure the handle of fabric, through a series of machine tests designed to replicate the feeling of a fabric in terms of stiffness, smoothness and softness, when perceived through touch. Similarly, technical testing of physical garment durability, such as fabric and seam strength, and of garment appearance retention, such as tests for abrasion (Figure 6.1), snagging (Figure 6.2) and colourfastness (Figure 6.3), are routinely conducted by responsible brands to ensure a quality garment is sold to the consumer.

As noted, many of these tests are required by law, with manufacturers required to keep abreast of changes to legislation as they arrive, regardless of the size of the manufacturer. Other regulations are optional but represent best practice to ensure product quality and consistency. For an indicative list of legislated tests, please see Table 6.1.

In practice, brands and manufacturers set their own standards for testing, though the range and rigour of these will vary from brand to brand. At a minimum, tests are conducted as required by law, but most brands and manufacturers will also conduct other quality benchmarking

Figure 6.1 This test determines the textile's ability to withstand rubbing without deterioration in appearance or the visible breaking of yarns

Figure 6.2 This test determines the textile's tendency to snag, which is evidenced by pulled threads or yarns or visible runs in the fabric, determined on a scale of severe snagging, to no snagging

Figure 6.3 This test measures the colourfastness of a textile, to determine the degree of colour loss from the dyed textile and colour transfer to adjacent materials when exposed to rubbing

tests. These typically include wash tests, to ensure the product retains its shape and colour during machine washing or dry cleaning (dependent on the garment's care instructions), and abrasion tests, to check for fabric pilling, amongst others. The larger brands will also have their own in-house garment and textiles technologists and facilities, to meet their own brand standards, which benchmark garments that arrive from their external suppliers. This could be to ensure the product which arrives meets their specifications, or to ensure that it is the same product in terms of quality, fabrics, materials and construction as their initial factory sample. Another approach seen in industry is for a factory to agree to send a garment to an external accredited textile and garment testing facility, to achieve independently verified testing results as part of the buying and production cycle.

However, at present, the consumer does not have a clear indication of the often extremely rigorous tests which are conducted on their clothing before purchase. Without this, they must rely on their subjective judgement of materials before purchase, including instore fabric touch, stretch and observation to judge suitability, with little other information available to them and fewer measures available online. The consumer therefore relies heavily on previous purchase history, brand marketing and assurances such as brand reputation, that the retailer has undertaken the necessary steps to ensure longevity and performance.

There are two core areas where brands could focus attention in order to provide the consumer with better data on garment quality to enable informed purchasing decisions which encourage longevity during the useful life of the product.

Firstly, consumers need increased awareness and education on what the terms quality, longevity and durability mean for fashion and textiles and how these criteria are measured and reported in practice through textile testing (e.g. through the use of performance testing such as laundering, appearance and strength testing). Of course, not every consumer will be interested in this data; however, change can be leveraged incrementally through increased awareness and visibility of an issue, and through framing the production and purchase of quality garments as a sustainable and responsible action, quality can be leveraged as one tool for creating systemic change.

Secondly, it is proposed that an academic and industrial partnership to investigate the difference of understanding between a technical and a lay person in understanding quality and durability criteria will yield invaluable information to close the knowledge gap.

Tools for benchmarking and the responsible sourcing and manufacturing of textiles and apparel, such as Higg Index (Sustainable Apparel Coalition 2021) and Modint Ecotool (CE Delft 2012) provide other assessments, with rigorous auditing and sharing of data across the supply chain. These tools exist for quality assurance and serve to strengthen the brand values of the retailer (WRAP 2017), enhancing consumer satisfaction and ensuring repeat custom. However, these tools are not without their controversy, particularly with regard to claims of enabling brands to be complicit in 'greenwashing', such as through using the Higg Index tool to promote plastic-based fibres as more sustainable than natural and biodegradable materials (Tabuchi 2022) which ultimately has led to the tool being suspended awaiting an independent review (Shendruk 2022). These tools demonstrate that many fashion brands have embarked on a journey towards sustainable production, but further explanation is required for the consumer to understand how brands are working to reduce their environmental footprint.

Performance sportswear may display a TOG (thermal overall grade) rating to indicate warmth and insulation measurement, or a waterproof rating or breathability level to signify the level of protection in moisture-rich conditions. Similarly, consumers require further codification to understand a garment's properties and its appropriate care in everyday language. These could answer questions such as 'how many wears will I get from this garment if I wash it every time, or should I wash it after every wear, or just every fifth wear?' For online purchases, consumers may be given information on, 'how breathable, stretchy, soft, or cooling is the fabric? How colourfast can I expect it to be after ten washes?'

Care symbols have been provided on labels for many years; for some countries displaying this information is mandatory, but for many it is voluntary. Such instructions guide the consumer on how to clean and maintain the product using universally recognised symbols to display information. These care instructions could be expanded to provide additional information to the consumer on best sustainable practice, expected product life and performance.

Some leading brands have commenced the shift towards encouraging longevity for their garments with easy-to-understand campaigns and terminology, such as 'wash at 30C' tagline shared by Marks & Spencer Ltd. as part of their industry-leading *Plan A* sustainability initiative launched in 2007 (Marks & Spencer, 2007). This provides some indication to the consumer that altering washing methods is recommended, in this case to lower the carbon footprint impact of laundering. However, this doesn't educate the consumer on the other impacts of shifting their washing behaviour from 40°C to 30°C, through explicitly making a link with garment life extension. For the layperson, an instruction to 'wash at 30°C and line dry rather than wash at 40°C and tumble dry to extend the product life by 20 wears' is more explanatory. This type of information is clearer for the consumer to understand the potential impact of undertaking certain procedures.

A system already exists in food packaging and labelling, which voluntarily and simply communicates a food product's energy, fats, saturates, sugars and salt as a colour-coded traffic light graphic (Department of Health 2016) which enables a consumer to make an informed decision on product composition at a glance. It is proposed that a similar system is developed by a consortium of brands, academics and industry professionals, in order to share best practice for durability and longevity.

Key areas for fashion brands to indicate quality and performance of textiles and clothing and to preserve product life could be:

- **Washing**: optimum cleaning instructions to preserve product life, to indicate how many washes a product should be able to endure during its expected lifetime.
- **Durability**: likelihood of pilling and snagging occurrences and signposting on how to rectify this (for example, via website information). Areas prone to abrasive wear could be highlighted alongside indication of added reinforcement for prevention or signposting to repair for problematic areas. Strengthened information and enhanced understanding of what this would mean to the consumer is key for durability.
- **Specialist performance criteria and meaning**: for example, if a garment is water repellent, does this mean the product would withstand light rain or endure heavy use in storm conditions?

The existence of such a scheme could potentially provide additional leverage to encourage brands producing products with less durability to innovate and improve. This is particularly important given proposed new policies, such as the European Union's *Strategy for Sustainable and Circular Textiles* (EU 2021), which positions product longevity and durability as key components for the shift towards the circular economy. In the UK, the textiles sector has been identified as a top priority for upcoming extensions to existing policies on Extended Producer Responsibility (EPR), mirroring and extending the French EPR levy (Boiten, 2022). Similarly, the fashion industry has been targeted by the Competition and Markets Authority (CMA) Green Claims Code (CMA 2021) which set out 6 principles for businesses to avoid false claims of products' environmental credentials ('greenwashing') and gave businesses until January 2022 to remove misleading claims (Competitions and Markets Authority 2021).

SET OF RECOMMENDATIONS FOR BEST PRACTICES IN INDUSTRY

Consumers should be given tools to make informed decisions and become change makers, via more communication and visibility of the results of textile and garment testing, technical reports and responsible design audits. It is recommended that brands tap into the ways in which existing systems of graphic icons are used in other contexts, such as food, to communicate product features.

Using a visual system to communicate technical testing reports is suggested via displaying these prominently on swing tags, garment labels or online pages, as well as embedding information onto the existing permanent care label sewn into a garment. In this way, information produced would demonstrate a clear link between the brand values of responsible design and consumption of garments and the quality of the individual garment.

Taking into consideration existing systems that use universally recognised symbols and sliding scales of performance and safety already familiar to consumers, the following is proposed:

- A sliding numerical scale using a quantity of stars or written numbers to illustrate a level of durability and performance. The general public are familiar with the scale of 1–5 stars already utilised by the hospitality industry to demonstrate safety and quality.
- Alongside the star or numerical value, a symbol would be displayed to represent various qualities that the textile possesses such as durability or protection.

These indicators would provide accessible information to the consumer on first inspection of the garment to influence appropriate buying decisions, considering their individual personal preferences and need for the product. For example, a consumer with skin sensitivity may choose to focus their attention on the skin kindness symbol as an important purchasing criterion.

Further research on consumer understanding and recognition of symbolic images alongside industrial regulatory involvement is required to develop a universally recognised system which could be adapted for countrywide then subsequent global scaling. Similar to the care labelling system, there may be minor differences in different regions around the world; however, the principles are the same and the symbols would be universally acknowledged.

Below are several proposed approaches, including systems taking inspiration from existing icons or written care instructions that are universally recognised.

Washing: an indication of a number of expected washes and level of appearance retention including dimensional stability (including any expected shrinkage) and colour fastness: colour 1–5, size and shape 1–5. This requires an investigation regarding whether to utilise an icon or wording system using technical English, so as not to confuse this system with standard, legal and wash care symbols.

Durability: a time indication on a garment, to describe the durability and longevity of the garment (Figure 6.4); to be used in conjunction with washing instructions for example:

Product may be prone to snagging in contact with sharp objects, take care.

Specialist symbols: for example, waterproof or wind resistance rating 1–5 (Figure 6.5).

Recommendations for brands, retailers and manufacturers include:

• Communication of technical testing reports, through varied media.
• Graphic logos to summarise how quality audits are conducted.
• Brands to prioritise informing consumers on quality and durability across their product range.
• Sharing methods to benchmark longevity of high endurance products such as outdoor gear or work wear.
• Using brand values to link to the technical performance of the garment to enhance the emotional connection and relevance between the consumer and the garment.
• Signposting to an app or website with clear tips on how to preserve product life, undertake mends and make modifications. This could be an independent system linked to each country's industry system.
• Clear indication on the brand's compliance to emerging sustainability legislation, strategies and practice.

Figure 6.4 A proposed example of an icon to indicate a garment's durability

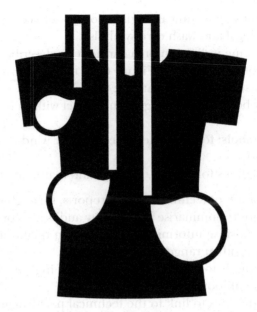

Figure 6.5 A proposed example of an icon to indicate a garment's waterproof rating

CONCLUSION

This chapter has presented one possible solution to encourage more conscious consumption by leveraging technical testing information already known to manufacturers and brands. The authors urge retailers to consider how they could leverage their brand's values, marketing messages and technical garment specifications, particularly in textiles test results, to enable responsible production, purchasing behaviour and garment care. Through creating a visual link to the quality and technical performance of the garment, it would be apparent to the consumer upon purchase, what the expected durability under optimal care procedures could be. Thus, the connection between purchasing choices and longer-term outcomes can become apparent.

Using existing media mechanisms, such as extending care labels that consumers are familiar with, or additions to the garment information label, brands' advertising and online web presence can create a simple intervention. It is proposed that an industry-wide voluntary scheme is developed, drawing on expertise from industry bodies, academics and retailers. The purpose of this approach is to explicitly communicate the quality, durability and care of a garment, in order to enable consumers to opt in and make a positive impact on the garment's longevity. Through promoting the responsible actions of brands and retailers who produce high quality, durable garments and appropriately communicating technical information to consumers, the authors propose that a shift towards encouraging consumption for longevity and durability, and away from throwaway fashion, may be achieved.

NOTE

1 Pilling is the accumulation of small clusters of fibres on a fabric surface due to abrasion in wear.

REFERENCES

Boiten, Valerie. (2022), *Building a circular economy for textiles supported by common rules on Extended Producer Responsibility (EPR) in the EU. Ellen MacArthur Foundation.* [Online] Available at: https://ellenmacarthurfoundation.org/extended-producer-responsibility-for-textiles [Accessed: 18 May 2023].
CE Delft (2012), *Modint Ecotool.* [Online]. Available at: http://avnir.org/documentation/book/LCAconf_bijleveld1_2012_en.pdf. [Accessed: 20 September 2020].
Competitions and Markets Authority (2021), *Guidance: The Green Claims Code.* [Online]. Available: https://www.gov.uk/government/publications/green-claims-code-making-environmental-claims/green-claims-and-your-business. [Accessed: 20 September 2021].
Connor-Crabb, A., & Rigby, E. (2019), Garment quality and sustainability: A user-based approach, *Fashion Practice,* Vol. 11, No. 3, pp. 346–374 [Online] Available at: https://www.tandfonline.com/doi/full/10.1080/17569370.2019.1662223 [Accessed: 20 June 2022].
Crofton, S., & Dopico, L. (2007), Zara-Inditex and the growth of fast fashion. *Essays in Economic & Business History,* Vol. 25, pp. 41–54. [Online] Available at: https://www.ebhsoc.org/journal/index.php/ebhs/article/view/181 [Accessed: 12 August 2022].
Department of Health (2016), *Guide to Creating a Front of Pack (FoP) Nutrition Label for Pre-Packed Products Sold through Retail Outlets.* [Online]. Available at: https://www.food.gov.uk/sites/default/files/media/document/fop-guidance_0.pdf [Accessed: 20 December 2020].
European Commission (2021), *EU Strategy for Sustainable Textiles, 2021.* [Online]. Available at: https://ec.europa.eu/info/law/better-regulation/have-your-say/initiatives/12822-EU-strategy-for-sustainable-textiles_en [Accessed: September 22 2020].
House of Commons Environmental Audit Committee (2019), *Fixing Fashion: Clothing Consumption and Sustainability.* [Online] Available at: https://publications.parliament.uk/pa/cm201719/cmselect/cmenvaud/1952/1952.pdf [Accessed: September 20 2020].

Kageyama, M., Kawabata, S., & Niwa, M. (1988), The validity of a "linearizing method" for predicting the biaxial-extension properties of fabrics, *The Journal of The Textile Institute*, vol. 79, no. 4, pp. 543–567.

Lehmann, M., Gizem, A., Robinson, F, Kruse, E., & Taylor, A. R. (2020), *CEO Agenda 2020: Eight Sustainability Priorities for the Fashion Industry*. [Online] Available at: https://www2.globalfashionagenda.com/ceo-agenda-2020/ [Accessed: 18 December 2020].

M&S Helps Customers to 'Think Climate' by Relabelling Clothing (2007), Marks and Spencer [Online] Available at: https://corporate.marksandspencer.com/media/press-releases/archive/2007/23042007_mshelpscustomerstothinkclimatebyrelabellingclothing [Accessed: 28 July 2022].

Meadows, D. (2009), *Thinking In Systems: A Primer*, Earthscan, London.

Niinimäki, K., Peters, G., Dahlbo, H., Perry, P., Rissanen, T., & Gwilt, A. (2020), The environmental price of fast fashion, *Nature Review; Earth and Environment*, Vol. 1, pp. 189–200. [Online] Available at: https://doi.org/10.1038/s43017-020-0039-9 [Accessed: 20 June 2022].

Rittel, H. W. J., & Webber, M. M. (1973), Dilemmas in a general theory of planning, *Policy Sciences*, Vol. 4, No. 2, pp. 155–169.

Shendruk, A. (2022), The Controversial Way Fashion Brands Gauge Sustainability is Being Suspended. Quartz. [Online] Available at: https://qz.com/2180322/the-controversial-higg-sustainability-index-is-being-suspended [Accessed: 31 July 2022].

Sustainable Apparel Coalition (2021), *The Higg Index*, [Online] Available at: https://apparelcoalition.org/higg-product-tools/ [Accessed: 20 January 2022].

Swinker, M., & Hines, J. (2006), Understanding consumers' perception of clothing quality: A multidimensional approach, *International Journal of Consumer Studies*, Vol. 30, No. 2, pp. 218–223.

Tabuchi, H. (2022), *How Fashion Giants Recast Plastic as Good for the Planet*, New York Times, [Online] Available at: https://www.nytimes.com/2022/06/12/climate/vegan-leather-synthetics-fashion-industry.html [Accessed: 31 July 2022].

Textile Exchange (2018), *Threading the Needle: Weaving the Sustainable Development Goals into the Textile, Retail, and Apparel Industry*, Textile Exchange, [Online] Available at: https://textileexchange.org/threading-the-needle-weaving-sdgs-in-the-textile-retail-and-apparel-industry [Accessed: 20 December 2020].

Textiles 2030 (2021), *Getting Ready for Extended Producer Responsibility (EPR)*, [Online] Available at: https://wrap.org.uk/resources/guide/getting-ready-extended-producer-responsibility [Accessed: 22 December 2021].

Wakes, S., Dunn, L., Penty, D., Kitson, K., & Jowett, T. (2020), Is price an indicator of garment durability and longevity? *Sustainability*, Vol. 12, No. 21, p. 8906.

WRAP (2017), *Sustainable Clothing: A Practical Guide to Enhancing Clothing Durability and Quality*, [Online] Available at: https://www.wrap.org.uk/sites/files/wrap/Sustainable%20Clothing%20Guide%202017.pdf#page=4. [Accessed: 22 September 2020].

Part III

Business and innovation

7 Finance and funding for upscaling sustainable fashion

Fergus Lyon, Patrick Elf, Robyn Owen and Andrea Werner

INTRODUCTION

There are a growing number of sustainable fashion design entrepreneurs who are looking to scale up their businesses. This can have a beneficial impact on sustainability through their greater reach and a wider and often more innovative offering of better products and services to consumers. However, these entrepreneurs face challenges in getting the resources needed to expand their businesses and to take a market share from traditional business with no or limited sustainability goals. Challenges may be related to identifying markets and opportunities or having the capabilities within the business to scale up (Elf et al., 2022). There may also be a desire to bring in external finance to pay for innovation, research and development, salaries, stock and other costs while the business reaches a profitable stage.

Drawing on qualitative interviews with business founders, company directors, financiers and other stakeholders over a two-year time period, this chapter follows a case-study approach providing novel insights into how a diverse group of sustainable fashion entrepreneurs access finance. From an initial list of 36 small- and medium-sized sustainable fashion businesses (SFBs), 12 were interviewed in detail at several points over the course of the research endeavour. Of these, four reported that they were using external finance. This chapter explores these four different approaches to seeking external finance. The case-study SFBs cover a range of products and services aimed at women's wear, sportswear and children's wear. The businesses range in age from two to sixteen years (at time of first interview).

DOI: 10.4324/9781003272878-10

FINANCE THEORY FOR SUSTAINABLE ENTREPRENEURS

Creative and sustainable ventures in the UK fashion industry face considerable barriers to accessing the external financing required to gain market traction and growth. Since Macmillan (1931) first recognized a finance gap for new and early-stage innovative ventures, the evidence base has continuously grown showing that such ventures suffer from private finance market failures and are worst affected at times of economic recession and credit rationing (Lee et al., 2015). The causes of this failure are often attributed to potential investors not having enough information about the innovative venture founders (Carpenter and Petersen, 2003) and their lack of collateral and track record that can support bank debt finance (North et al., 2013).

New SFB ventures present a particularly high risk to potential investors as early-stage businesses have a high rate of failure. As Fraser et al. (2014) and O'Dair and Owen (2019) note, new emerging creative sectors, such as sustainable fashion, pose various challenges to traditional formal bank debt and venture capital (VC) equity financing. Sustainable business models present a further complication to investor risk assessment with a stronger focus on longer-term viability and wider sustainability rather than delivering quick profits and/or financial sustainability. For investors, this may mean that repayments are expected over an extended period (Owen et al., 2020).

In this chapter, we examine the different sources of finance as businesses mature. We follow Nightingale et al.'s (2009) framework of a 'finance escalator' where businesses can use different types of finance for start-up and the succeeding stages of venture growth (see Figure 7.1 for an overview). While the finance escalator can highlight gaps from the perspective of those providing finance (supply-side), North et al. (2013) and Owen et al. (2019a) point also to failures of potential finance applicants (demand-side) especially where they lack capability to present investable propositions. These demand-side gaps are particularly prevalent amongst first-time venture founders who lack business and finance-raising acumen and younger entrepreneurs that have little or no prior work experience (Owen et al., 2018).

Solving early-stage venture finance gaps for complex businesses such as SFBs requires a holistic approach (Owen et al., 2019a). For instance, equity investors can provide non-financial support to improve business management and networking, while on the demand-side,

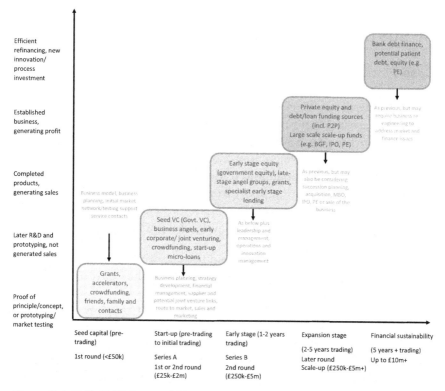

Figure 7.1 U.K. SME External Finance Support Escalator (see Owen et al., 2019b)

there is a need for investment readiness support to enable young entrepreneurs to access and successfully pitch to investors (Mason and Kwok, 2010). Furthermore, in the wider creative and sustainable sectors, incubator provision of space and equipment and the emergence of accelerator investment and training have transformed the UK early stage support and investment market during the last decade (Owen et al., 2020). In the decade since the Global Financial Crisis in 2007/2008, crowdfunding has also become established as a significant source of creative enterprise financing generally (via peer-to-peer lending, equity, reward-based and donation platforms, or blockchain financing mechanisms), notably for known market brands (O'Dair and Owen, 2019). Lastly, the public sector can be an important player in supporting businesses with grants, investor tax breaks (e.g. for [Seed] Enterprise Investment Schemes) and co-financing of business angels and seed VCs.

ACCESSING FINANCE IN FOUR CASE STUDIES OF SUSTAINABLE FASHION ENTERPRISES

Case 1

Case 1 is an innovative women's wear and men's wear brand that embeds sustainability in a variety of ways as the company seeks to design garments that are built for purpose and longevity. They work with suppliers to enable the use of innovative recycled materials in their garments and aim for more circular design approaches. Complementing their design efforts, they also offer repair and trade-in resale services. The brand has grown over time with the support from a range of investment. Starting off with their own resources and time, they initially relied on fabric suppliers to give them goods on credit and good payment terms.

> We were just bold as brass and said trust us, we're going to get there. So they believed in us, they supported us, they gave us payment terms, they held stock for us.
>
> (Company Director 1)

They were also able to get access to a range of grants which were available to businesses located in priority areas for regional development funding. A major change to the business came with the decision to seek equity finance as an investor took a stake in the business allowing them to move from online sales only to having a physical retail spaces. The owners took particular care in researching the approach and values of potential investors and selected one who supported the company's philosophy and their ingrained respect for the environment and focus on long-term performance rather than short-term profit and a quick exit.

> We funded ourselves for the first 10 years, and that was all based on our suppliers helping us out on that front. Now we have got a private equity fund which really helped us go to the next level. So retail for us was our missing link really.
>
> (Company Director 1)

The investment and support has allowed greater reach and upscaling with more people being introduced to their sustainable products and brand philosophy. The investment also required a restructuring including the appointment of two new board members by the private equity investor and the introduction of a new CEO who is closely working with the founder. Another result is a greater emphasis on financial growth while previously there had been an aspiration to organically grow to a certain level they felt was generating adequate profit for the owners.

> I always struggled with the idea of growth. I always thought you could get to a place and you could be happy and you just keep doing that, but I guess as soon as we got a board and we got investors that really changed the landscape a bit, because you are then accountable to someone.
>
> (Company Director 2)

More recently, the company has been involved in raising investment through crowdfunding to accelerate growth of the business and for financing the development of innovative new products. This has shown the brand's close connection to its customers with many of them willing to be small investors in the business to feel involved in the brand and part of a wider community.

Case 2

This company was set up by its female founders to enable women from deprived communities to earn a decent livelihood from their garment-making skills. Set up as an 'ethical, feminist, sustainable' women's wear brand, Case 2 has used investment to meet its objective of creating positive social impact paying living wages to the garment makers and also support local women's and community organisations from their profits. Initial funding came from the founders' own work, friends and family. They also borrowed money from a lender that focuses on social issues in order to buy stock, and they run on a 'pre-order' model which allows them to have payments before clothes are made.

At an early stage, they successfully applied to be part of an impact investment accelerator programme that came with some equity investment. This required them to report on their financial position every quarter and on their social impact. Not only has the finance helped them survive; it has also come with ongoing advice and mentoring.

The company has found that seeking funds is difficult as grant givers consider them overly commercial while investors consider them too charitable. The founders were careful not to take on too much seed funding before they had a clear ability to generate revenues. They wanted to avoid venture capitalists pursuing quick exits, that is, looking to take a stake in the business and then sell this soon after for a profit. The company has kept focused on its own vision and is not willing to compromise in order to meet the requirements of investors. This has made obtaining further funding harder.

To circumvent this limitation, the founders used a crowdfunding platform to access further finance. This crowdfunding includes a number of their existing customers wanting a small stake in the business.

> So we had a couple of bigger investors but … we had our models, photographers, customers, people who hadn't even heard of us yet. People who liked the idea … and wanted to see it get better.
>
> (CEO/founder)

Case 3

Case 3 provides an online platform designed to change behaviour on fashion consumption by enabling its users to increase the wear rate and 'life' of existing garments. The founder sees having investment as a necessary way to raise the profile of their brand to sign up more users. They also refer to investment acting as a 'runway' allowing them to grow the business to the level of a viable business that can pay salaries. At the start, the founder used their own time and resources while leaving their job and moving back to their family home. They had some early-stage investment from an 'angel investor', that is, an individual willing to put their own money into new businesses. They found raising further funding difficult in the city in which they started up, as they felt investors did not understand their sustainability objectives. The founder therefore moved to London where they felt there was better understanding of sustainability from impact investors focusing on sustainability.

An impact investment company focused on social and sustainable businesses provided them with 'pre-seed' funding and a place on their accelerator programme that offered ongoing support over six months. This investor has provided further funding since and persuaded two other impact investors to also take a stake in the business. These investors continue to offer advice on seeking new investors and contacts.

The founder has a strong vision of their mission and is putting this ahead of generating short-term growth in revenues. This makes generating further funding challenging as "there are metrics we need to hit if we are trying to fundraise" (Chief Operating Officer). The management team is keen to retain control and maintain the freedom to build the business as they wish.

They have been more successful in financing upscaling through crowdfunding with over 300 investors getting shares in the business.

The crowdfunding platform has a nominated person to represent these investors rather than there being 300 board members. Furthermore, the business retains control over strategy and direction with a continued focus on how it can change the fashion industry with its innovative services.

Case 4

Guided by its mission to reduce waste and emissions and instil the slowing of consumption, Case 4 is a small yet growing company that develops innovative fashion designs and textiles that extend the life of garments. Initially having focused on children's wear, the company employs a diverse team to research how to increase and improve product range and expand into other markets to achieve greater environmental impact.

In the initial stages of business evolution, investment came in the form of the founder's own time and resourcefulness. The company was also relying on existing sales to reinvest in the business, which is termed 'bootstrapping'. It was fortunate to have an early impact investor that was also running an accelerator programme and allowed the company to join. Since leaving the accelerator programme, the portfolio manager of the impact investor has continued to act as a mentor providing support for pitches and grant applications. This support has been important in learning how to pitch an idea to investors, and altering messaging to tell their story about how they want to grow. The company has been successful in obtaining innovation grants that part-fund their product development, alongside further equity investment.

The company has been approached by a number of potential investors and has been very selective to ensure that any potential investor is aligned with its sustainability objectives and not looking for a quick profit and exit.

> I think we played hard ball with a lot of investors ... it was very important for us to get the right investors, so it was tough, and you had a lot of meetings with people who you knew just did not align at all, who just saw this as a revenue generating thing that would be popular with the people. We were fortunate enough to be in a position where we could say actually, we don't want to be with you, and then we found a funder and they fund sustainable businesses and we thought that [*our mutual objectives*] were well-aligned. Yes, they wanted the business to grow but that's the way economic systems work and you need a business that grows if you're going to invest in it. But they only invest in sustainable businesses.
>
> (Chief Executive)

The investors require the company to do financial reporting as well as impact reporting on its contribution to the United Nation's Sustainable Development Goals. They have encouraged the founder to do more financial modelling that shows growth trajectories and pushed him to prepare a business plan with commercial metrics. The current investors have not asked to be on the official board of the business but act as an informal board of advisers. They have also been important in introducing the business to other mentors for marketing and licensing strategies.

> All our investors really want us to succeed. They are really into sustainability and innovation, so that's perfect because they then have networks within sustainability and innovation that are not necessarily focused on fashion.
>
> (Chief Executive)

CONCLUSION

As new SFBs grow, there is demand for finance to support their upscaling. Examining a sample of four fashion businesses that have sought external finance, we demonstrate the common finding that there is a 'finance escalator' in operation as businesses move from initial stages requiring small amounts of money to scaling up stages where there is a need for large capital injections. Early-stage businesses are reliant on entrepreneurs' own investment and that of family and friends, complemented by grant finance. As these businesses become more established and mature, they seek other types of finance such as alternative forms of borrowing and equity investment from social and sustainable investors and business angels who are aligned with their sustainability goals. Some of these are large investors with extensive past experience in other deals, while other investors can become involved on a small scale as they participate in crowd funding. Notably, our findings show that SFBs featured in the case studies are purpose-led and cautious about taking on external finance as they prioritise control over their sustainability goals over rapid growth and quick exits. A comparison of the four cases show that three were using crowdfunding as an opportunity to bring in many small investors that shared their vision and therefore avoid any loss of control when there are a smaller number of large investors.

Other challenges include the supply of finance (supply-side issues) and the capability of businesses requesting financing to present investable propositions (demand-side issues). Supply of finance from conventional sources of bank and institutional investment may be limited because finance providers are risk averse when faced with the 'liability of newness and smallness'. Each of the four case SFBs have sought out non-bank sources of finance as these investors are willing to take the risk, usually based on having an equity stake in the ownership of the business. The 'liability of smallness' can be exacerbated when there are multiple goals related to sustainability alongside profit. In two of the cases, interviewees reported some differences between the objectives of the investors and the objectives of the business. In one of these cases, the business was sticking to their vision of prioritising social and environmental value while not pursuing rapid growth. In the other case, the decision was made to scale up impact by allowing the business to grow rapidly while also giving more priority to commercial objectives. The other two case studies had found investors that shared their vision for an approach of incremental growth.

The demand-side challenges relate to the lack of investment readiness of many young businesses, as they may not have business models that allow them to make the profit needed to repay borrowed money with interest or to provide a return to investors. They also may not possess the necessary capabilities related to writing business plans required by investors, or the ability to 'pitch' their business ideas to investors, which makes them appear not to be investment-ready. To tackle the lack of investment readiness, this chapter shows how social and sustainable investors are supporting their investees with mentoring and advice to build their capability to grow and seek further finance. This support can start when a business is part of an 'accelerator programme' run by the investor and continue once the business has left this supportive programme. In addition, and as mentioned previously, we found that crowd funding, featured in three of the four case studies and these investors can bring wider support and advice for the business as it grows.

Lastly, this chapter also shows that there is a tension between the ambitions of businesses to provide sustainable alternatives and the demands of investors to make a profit when they exit from the business. Many sustainable businesses challenge the objectives of conventional businesses in their short-term goal to maximise profit for individual shareholders. This can be called a 'post-growth' approach where scaling up impact for people and planet is prioritised over financial gains, demanding more patient investments. As our case studies show, where investors are aligned with the goals of the business, there is potential for substantial upscaling of impact. It is this alignment between investor and sustainable fashion business that needs to be encouraged to ensure the innovations being developed can be scaled up and transform the wider fashion industry.

ACKNOWLEDGEMENT

This chapter draws on data from the project "Rethinking Fashion Design Entrepreneurship: Fostering Sustainable Practices", which was funded by the Arts and Humanities Research Council Oct 2018 to March 2021 (AH/R006539/1).

REFERENCES

Carpenter, R. E., & Petersen, B. C. (2002). Capital market imperfections, high-tech investment, and new equity financing. *The Economic Journal*, 112(477): F54–F72.

Elf, P., Werner, A., & Black, S. (2022). Advancing the circular economy through dynamic capabilities and extended customer engagement: Insights from small sustainable fashion enterprises in the UK. *Business Strategy and the Environment*. https://doi.org/10.1002/bse.2999

Fraser, S. (2011). Access to finance for creative industry businesses. Final Report with IFF research for DCMS & BIS, Crown Copyright, London, May URN 11/898

Gardetti, M., & Torres, A. (2017). *Sustainability in Fashion and Textiles: Values, Design, Production and Consumption*. Routledge.

Hethorn, J., & Ulasewicz, C. (2015). *Sustainable Fashion: What's Next? A Conversation about Issues, Practices and Possibilities*. Bloomsbury Publishing.

Lee, N., Sameen, H., & Cowling, M. (2015). Access to finance for innovative SMEs since the financial crisis. *Research Policy*, 44(2): 370–380.

Macmillan Committee (1931). *Report on the Committee on Finance and Industry*, Cmnd. 3897, HMSO, London, July.

Mason, C., & Kwok, J. (2010). Investment readiness programmes and access to finance: A critical review of design issues. *Local Economy*, 25(4): 269–292.

Nightingale, P., Murray, G., Cowling, M., Baden-Fuller, C., Mason, C., Siepel, J., Hopkins, M., & Dannreuther, C. (2009). *From funding Gaps to Thin Markets: UK Government Support for Early-Stage Venture Capital*. NESTA report, September https://strathprints.strath.ac.uk/15763/1/From_Funding_Gaps_to_Thin_Markets.pdf

North, D., Baldock, R., & Ullah, F. (2013). Funding the growth of UK technology-based small firms since the financial crash: Are there breakages in the finance escalator? *Venture Capital*, 15(3): 237–260

O'Dair, M., & Owen, R. (2019). Financing new creative enterprise through block-chain technology: Opportunities and policy implications. *Strategic Change: Briefings in Entrepreneurial Finance*, 28(1): 9–18

Owen, R., Deakins, D., & Savic, M. (2019a). Finance pathways for young innovative SMEs. *Strategic Change: Briefings in Entrepreneurial Finance*, 28(1): 19–36

Owen, R., Harrer, T., Lodh, S., Botelho, T., & Anwar, O. (2019b). An investigation of UK SME access to finance, growth and productivity 2015–2017. Enterprise Research Centre Research Paper 79, September

Owen, R., Harrer, T., Lodh, S., Pates, R., & Pikkat, K. (2020). Redefining SME productivity measurement and assessment for a low carbon economy. Research paper for ESRC Productivity Insights Network (PIN), Sheffield University, November PIN-DRAFT-FINAL-Report-30–09–2020-RO-TH-1.pdf(productivityinsightsnetwork.co.uk)

Polzin, F. (2017). Mobilizing private finance for low-carbon innovation–A systematic review of barriers and solutions. *Renewable and Sustainable Energy Reviews*, 77: 525.

8 Managing sustainable innovation

Christine Goulay

Many brands today are putting in place ambitious impact-related targets as a response to the looming climate crisis, new environmental regulations, and in search of market differentiation. These targets center around topics such as the need to stay within the 1.5 degrees temperature rise scenario, to achieve Net Zero, and to adopt practices in line with the circular economy. While it is wonderful to publicly declare such ambitions, often the underlying strategy remains unclear.

One thing is clear: a step-change is needed, and "business as usual" will not cut it. Hence the rush toward finding new sustainable technologies to replace today's existing, often archaic means of working in the apparel sector. Historically under-invested as a sector, the opportunity for improvement is massive. However, numerous hurdles exist to meaningfully implement solutions at scale.

By walking through the apparel value chain from raw material sourcing to a product's end of life, this chapter will identify both challenges and opportunities facing brands in successfully adopting innovations in the apparel sector. Keys to success will include analyzing impact hotspots and data collection, properly incentivizing stakeholders, forming meaningful cross-sector partnerships to iterate efficiently, and focusing on implementation feasibility.

"It's not about what it is, it's about what it can become".

The Lorax, Dr. Seuss

The fashion sector, like so many others, is undergoing a major shift. The growing public discourse around responsible business has finally taken hold, leading to new expectations for companies. We are moving to a model where companies are expected to take accountability

DOI: 10.4324/9781003272878-11

for their externalities, looking at stakeholder value as opposed to only shareholder value. It is a model where investors incorporate an Environmental, Social & Governance (ESG) lens to their work, and where legislators drive change through regulations such as Law 2020–105 in France (Legifrance, 2020) prohibiting the destruction of clothing and New York's proposed "Fashion Sustainability and Social Accountability Act" (NY Assembly Bill, 2021) which would require fashion brands to disclose their social and climate impacts. And let's not forget the consumer who is beginning to ask where and how products are made, demanding more transparency from brands, which is now often delivered through QR codes and tracers that can show a product's journey back to the raw material source. Indeed, it is a time to re-imagine fashion's broken system, and to think about what it can become.

Innovation will have a key role to play in fashion's future as we move toward this new paradigm. So much needs to be updated, re-worked, and achieved in a relatively short period of time considering the United Nation's foreboding warning that we are heading toward irreversible damage from climate change (United Nations General Assembly, 2019). Managing the transition toward a more sustainable fashion sector through innovation presents its own challenges and opportunities. Focusing on lessons learned and best practices will ensure that the sector is moving ahead in an informed and efficient way.

A PARADIGM SHIFT

The move toward a more sustainable fashion sector is apparent. One indicator is that the number of sustainability targets being set by brands has greatly increased over the past several years. KPMG demonstrated in their 2020 report *The Time Has Come* that 80% of top companies are now reporting on sustainability up from 41% in 2005 (Threlfall et al., 2020). However, the retail sector (in which apparel lies) is the laggard and the only sector with less than 70% reporting. For fashion in particular, *The Pulse of the Fashion Industry* report shows that fashion companies are performing strongest in terms of value chain actions in establishing management and targets focused on sustainability with a Pulse Score of 56 overall (Lehmann et al., 2019). The Pulse Score is a performance score, powered by the Higg Index, for measuring and tracking the sustainability of the global fashion industry on key environmental and social impact areas. For some brands, targets are supported by impact-related data such as lifecycle assessments (LCAs) and social audits. For others, the foundation is still weak and the journey just beginning. The Pulse of the Fashion Industry Report 2018 states:

> While the adoption of targets is very encouraging, fashion companies need to link these efforts with their overall business strategy, embedding sustainability into their core business. Indeed, Pulse Score frontrunners have managed to make their efforts complement the larger corporate strategy in running a profitable business.
>   (Lehmann et al., 2018)

This is where the real work begins.

In order for fashion brands to achieve ambitious environmental and social objectives, a step-change is necessary, hence the importance of innovation. The Apparel Impact Institute and Fashion for Good's recent report, "Unlocking the Trillion Dollar Fashion Decarbonisation Opportunity" cites that, in order to reach a net zero fashion sector by 2050, innovative solutions will have to account for 39% of decarbonization efforts (Ley et al., 2021). This realization is leading to a surge of activity in the sustainable fashion innovation space.

Statistics show that the last five years has seen a growing number of innovators looking to develop technologies that will help companies in their quest to operate more sustainably. The Material Innovation Initiative's 2021 State of the Industry report on Next Generation Materials shows that the number of material innovators in this space has increased from 42 in 2014 to 95 in 2021, a 126% increase (Siu, 2022). Similarly, platforms like Fashion for Good (www.fashionforgood.com) in Amsterdam founded in 2017 have been created to help jumpstart the ecosystem, supporting innovators, brands, suppliers, and investors to enable actionable work and to drive capital investment into the sector.

Despite this recent uptick, fashion's history in innovation is relatively short (especially in relation to other sectors such as pharmaceuticals or cosmetics where the culture of Research and development is a cornerstone of the industry). The OECD's 2020 report on *Business Enterprise Research and development Expenditure by Industry*, puts fashion toward the bottom of the list for Research and Development research (OECD, 2020). Most brands only recently created a Sustainability department, let alone an Research and development department which can experiment with the latest technologies and understand how to use these technologies to achieve product/market fit. Another reason why fashion has been slow to innovate is because fashion brands generally outsource their manufacturing, rarely having any ownership over their supply chains. This gives brands very little leverage or the needed visibility to innovate.

This model is predicted to change as COVID has pointed out many vulnerabilities in working this way (lack of leverage over production costs, shipments, etc.). As an example, Chanel has recently acquired over 20 of their supply chain partners (Indvik, 2021). Considering that fashion has relatively little experience in innovation, how does a fashion brand approach the topic in an informed way?

INNOVATION OPPORTUNITIES IN THE APPAREL VALUE CHAIN

As we look at the fashion value chain, from tier 4 (raw material sourcing) through tier 0 (owned offices and stores), we see burgeoning technologies at all levels. From next generation materials like alternative leathers made from collagen and insulation made from flowers, to processes like botanical dyes or chemical-free finishes, to additive manufacturing and customization solutions. In addition, circular solutions like chemical textile recycling and new business models such as rental and resale form part of the innovations to address a product's end of life. The rapid advancement of digital tech, sped up by the COVID pandemic, is another important area of exploration, often developing in combination with or even in parallel to the physical world as we move towards industry 4.0. These innovations promise not only more operating efficiencies in many cases, but also a reduction in the environmental footprint as we look to reduce our reliance on virgin raw materials, energy and water, overproduction, etc. In Figure 8.1, some of the innovation trends are

Innovations in the Apparel Value Chain

	Raw Material Extraction (T4)	Raw Material Processing & material production (T3 & T2)	Finished Product Assembly, CMT (T1)	Retail (T0) & use	End of life (circularity)	Traceability & Digital (enablers)
Some examples of what we are seeing	• Next Gen Materials that avoid sourcing petroleum-based and animal-derived. • Examples: mycelium leather, plant and bio-based, lab-grown leathers/fur, carbon capture technologies.	• Biotech-based and Botanical dyes • Green chemistry • Dry processing	• Zero waste pattern cutting • Automated sewing • Customization • 3D processes	• New circular business models such as takeback, resale, rental, etc.	• Textile sorting • Mechanical and chemical textile recycling solutions	• Digital passports • Blockchain • Physical tracers (synthetic DNA, isotopes, etc.)
Implementation challenges	• Many innovations only at lab scale. • Scaling often requires new infrastructure. • Difficulty matching performance of mainstream materials	• Many innovations still at lab scale. • Scaling often requires new infrastructure. • Difficulty matching performance of mainstream solutions.	• Learning curve for industry and customers to uptake new tech. • Scaling often requires new infrastructure.	• Difficulty implementing reverse logistics • Brand perceived reputational concerns	• Fragmented system. • Large capital investment needed for recycling technologies.	• Supply chain visibility • Difficulty implementing in supply chain.
Impact Hotspots	• End of life • Avoiding inputs such as GMO, first generation feedstocks.	• Unknown longterm effects of new technologies such as nano, GMO, etc.	• Social repercussions on labor force if replaced by automation. • Data collection on over-production, digital footprint.	• Lack of impact data, especially ethnographic data to understand consumer behavior	• Energy use, Water and chemical use in processes	• Reliability of data • Digital footprint

Figure 8.1 Examples of innovations in the apparel value chain

summarized as we identify impact hotspots in the apparel value chain with their corresponding implementation challenges.

STRATEGIES FOR SUCCESS

With so much excitement, opportunity, and commensurate high expectations for delivery, it is imperative to think about strategies for success in effecting sustainable fashion innovation solutions. Despite fashion's immaturity with innovation, there are still lessons to be learned. Below, we identify some winning strategies in the field such as: (1) Setting impact-related KPIs to ensure that the choices we are making are indeed "better" for the environment and society; (2) aligning incentives of relevant stakeholders; and (3) using a collective impact approach (Kania and Kramer, 2011) where industry players work together in consortia to iterate quickly and effectively, focused on broader implementation.

Do the impact analysis

There is a lot of wishful thinking out there: Innovators and brands thinking that a new technology or solution will improve their environmental footprint. However, wishful thinking does not necessarily lead to outcomes. We need to collect the data to verify impact instead of relying on hunches and assumptions. Businesses are expert at collecting financial KPIs when launching new products or services such as ROI, conversion rates, and average order values. But what about data that will help determine whether businesses are achieving impact? Unfortunately, this has not yet become second nature in the apparel sector, though with the growth of big data trends, we can see better impact data as well if we prioritize it as an industry (White et al., 2020).

With nascent innovations, the quest for valid impact data is especially difficult. It is not realistic to perform a lifecycle assessment (LCA), for example, before a technology has scaled (or knows how it will scale). So how do we know we are moving in the right direction? A simple answer to this is: Ask! We are not asking enough questions about impact, internally within brands or externally with suppliers and innovators. The more we ask, the more the demand signals to produce good data will become stronger, and soon enough, the more data we will start to see. The report, *Understanding Biomaterials: A Primer for the Fashion Industry*, by Biofabricate and Fashion For Good (Lee et al., 2020), does a very good job in outlining the impact-related questions that brands should

Figure 8.2 Taking a 360 approach to impact

ask innovators, depending on the technology readiness level (TRL) (NASA, 2012) of an innovation. It is a very valuable roadmap to frame this important discussion.

An additional challenge regarding impact-related data in the apparel sector is the lack of primary data and reliable secondary data in the fashion industry. This is largely due to the historic lack of visibility in the supply chain (Senthilkannan Muthu, 2020). Digital product passports, the idea that a product can have its own ID that transparently demonstrates its provenance, composition, etc. is becoming a helpful means to encourage companies to collect and communicate this information, and will continue to take on importance as European legislation requiring such disclosure comes into play as part of the EU Strategy for Sustainable and Circular Textiles (2022). An innovator working in this space is EON ID (www.eongroup.co), which not only helps provide such a digital passport to communicate to customers on a products' journey, but also developed a "Circular Product Data Protocol" (www.circulardataprotocol.org) with several industry stakeholders to codify the data model that will inform textile recyclers on applicable product treatment at end of life. Indeed, the rise of digital tools at our fingertips should vastly improve the current data issue.

Another important point regarding impact is that, not only do we need to collect data as we go along, but we need to use foresight to take a 360 degree approach when looking at the possible ramifications that an innovation might have on the world.[1] For example, who would have guessed at its inception that plastic would lead to the gigantic microplastic issue where we now find ourselves? As new technologies arrive on the market, it is necessary to project that the innovation scales to become massively successful in order to understand potential unintended consequences. An example where the fashion sector is taking a critical view when analyzing the impact of new solutions, concerns the use of feedstocks for biosynthetic fibers. Biosynthetics are made from polymers coming from (wholly or partially) renewable resources, usually sugars derived from corn, sugar, or beet crops, otherwise known as "first generation" feedstocks (Textile Exchange Hub, 2019). Taking this 360 degree approach and projecting into the future, the sector has realized that, should these innovations scale wildly, the feedstock input could lead to competition with food crops, potential land use change, reliance on industrial monoculture, etc. Although opinions differ as to the gravity of this issue, the point here is that this kind of analysis and forecast modelling must be conducted. As the fashion sector looks to incorporate more innovative solutions, particularly as its growth ambitions remains set, it must be careful of the face hiding in the shadows.

Aligning incentives

There may well be a silver bullet to systemic change: financial incentives. At the end of the day, this is the primary lever for private-sector (and often individual) decision-making. Current discourse seems to be focused on very top-down (e.g., government regulation, overall company targets) or very bottom-up strategies (e.g., driving the individual consumer to behave differently) to incentivize change, often leaving out the important question of how meaningful implementation shall occur in the professional sphere. As an analogy, many would say that the most important part of a burger (or plant-based burger alternative, of course) is the "meat" – not the top and bottom buns. What do we do about the "missing middle" in existing incentive structures, i.e., the professional space where goals need to be operationalized at scale?

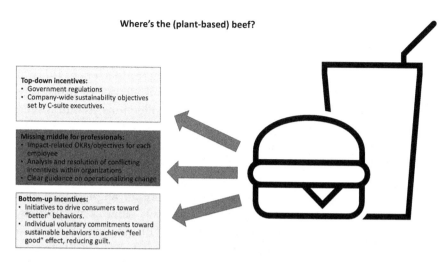

Where's the (plant-based) beef?

Top-down incentives:
• Government regulations
• Company-wide sustainability objectives
  set by C-suite executives.

Missing middle for professionals:
• Impact-related OKRs/objectives for each
  employee
• Analysis and resolution of conflicting
  incentives within organizations
• Clear guidance on operationalizing change

Bottom-up incentives:
• Initiatives to drive consumers toward
  "better" behaviors.
• Individual voluntary commitments toward
  sustainable behaviors to achieve "feel
  good" effect, reducing guilt.

Figure 8.3 Where's the plant-based beef?

When examining top-down structures, we see examples of "carrots" and "sticks" in the apparel space. Speaking of "carrots," there are numerous studies that show greater customer loyalty to responsible brands (especially in a post-COVID world) (Cernansky, 2021) and better ESG ratings for companies with sustainability strategies (Bernow et al., 2019). The data now exists to prove the sustainability business case. This data needs to be brought to the forefront to incentivize the C-Suite. On the side of the "stick," a suite of new proposed policies in the EU and elsewhere will affect the textile sector (16 in the pipeline in the EU alone, see www.euratex.eu), make this a priority issue for brands, looking to find solutions before possible penalization.

There are also a growing number of examples of bottom-up initiatives focusing on driving the individual to behave more sustainably. For example, service companies like Reflaunt (www.reflaunt.com) work with brands to encourage customers to return their clothes in order to earn cash or store credit while simultaneous working with resale sites to keep the clothing in circulation. Indeed, innovations around second-life business models have proven to be powerful carrots in driving people to adopt more "sustainable" behaviors (though more data is needed to verify circular business model impacts).

Yet, there is a clear lack of attention on incentives to address the "missing middle" for professionals to act more "sustainably" or worse, there is a disincentive to do so. This means that talk of a triple bottom line approach may remain only talk. Take buyers for example. They are usually incentivized to buy materials at the lowest price to improve the brand's margin. However, sustainable and innovative materials might be (and should be) more expensive. Especially with innovation, costs can be quite high before economies of scale are reached. What will a buyer do? A good employee will act in accordance with the KPIs that their employer has set, to buy the lowest priced materials. Hence, there is the common inability to meaningfully source sustainable or innovative technologies beyond small marketing capsule collections, as widely seen across brands-retailers in the marketplace.

To address the missing middle, should companies wish to achieve their sustainability targets, different and meaningful KPIs need to be put in place for every single employee to drive people toward the better choice. The Kering Group is an example where an aligned incentive structure has been put into place as brand CEOs' salaries are partially tied to sustainability results (Trochu, 2016). This, in turn, has led in many cases to the adoption of sustainability-related impact KPIs for the employees of these brands, making it easier for employees to make the sustainable choice. For Kering, this approach has resulted in a 41% overall reduction in their EP&L impact measurement methodology intensity between 2015 and 2021 (Kering, 2022).

In the case of innovation, it is arguably even more of a challenge to incentivize employees toward change as innovation is usually a risky endeavor. It is difficult for an individual to proactively drive innovative solutions should failure be reflective of their own performance. Aaron Amstutz, Chief Technology Officer of the materials company NFW (https://www.nfw.earth/), follows Thomas Edison's ethos to "fail fast, fail often." Using an OFATs methodology ("One factor at a time" proxy test approach), he encourages his team to iterate 200-300 times / year. Many say that innovation and failure go hand in hand. Imagine the empowerment employees would feel if their failures were celebrated?

Neglecting the missing-middle in incentive structures leaves professionals out in the cold. Focusing on proper alignment to ensure we can all reach our impact-related targets is an exercise to take forward with human resources departments and management teams to ensure that incentives filter throughout a company correctly to drive the implementation of innovative and sustainable solutions. Let's adopt a more holistic approach to setting incentives, so we are not left asking, "Where's the plant-based beef?"

Building constellations

As sustainability professionals everywhere know, the problems we are trying to address cannot be solved by one company, one NGO, or one government acting alone. To state the obvious: concerted and collaborative action is needed to effect systemic change. For innovations to succeed, developing consortia of important stakeholders who can work together is critical. All stakeholders need to be brought into the conversation to achieve larger and lasting change.

In the innovation space, there has been a tendency to drive partnerships through brand and innovator collaborations, pushing these back upstream to supply chain partners. This is, in part, due to the fact that apparel brands do not usually own their supply chains as previously mentioned. However, this approach slows down innovation quite a bit as a critical vision on implementation – one where suppliers are best placed to contribute – is often left out of the equation until later stages of the Research and Development process. This can result in innovations not fit-for-purpose, longer Research and Development roadmaps than necessary, wasted human and financial capital, etc. A best practice would be to include supply chain partners who will be implementing innovations from the beginning.

Brands can help by connecting innovators with their suppliers early on, creating a collaborative, multistakeholder approach to streamline progress. Pangaia Materials Science Limited is a good example of this approach. With both a direct-to-consumer brand and B2B business, Pangaia has created close partnerships with supply chain partners to drive innovation as quickly and efficiently as possible, resulting in many first-to-market product launches of today's most exciting material science innovations through its Pangaia Lab (Pangaia, 2022). Another example would be Fashion for Good which has orchestrated several collaborative pilot programs around particular raw material supply chains and focused solutions (e.g., viscose, organic cotton). By publishing reports after each project, others in the sector can incorporate these learnings, leapfrogging over pain points faced by first movers.

An analogy for this strategy would be for the fashion sector to move from fireworks to constellations. Currently, in today's environment we often see individual players making one-off announcements of a new sustainability target, product launch, or decarbonization strategy, these are exciting but temporary, isolated incidents, that may leave nothing behind, much like fireworks. Thankfully, the sector is moving more rapidly toward building constellations: diverse stakeholders engaged in collaborative action, working together for the long term, creating lasting change and a legacy that others can follow. There is an African proverb that reads, "if you want to go fast, go alone; if you want to go far, go together." Let's change it up for innovation to say, "if you want to go fast and far, go together."

CONCLUSION

The time is now for the apparel sector to embrace innovation in order to tackle the many social and environmental challenges which it faces. Setting sustainability targets in this direction, is one important step, but is rendered meaningless without concrete and bold action toward achieving them. Without incorporating innovative solutions, it is all but certain that these goals will not be met. By keeping in mind some of the opportunities and challenges an innovation-based approach to sustainable fashion may entail, brands and other important stakeholders can increase their likelihood of making meaningful strides in lowering their environmental footprint. The road is not without its bumps, but smart strategies can be put in place to better ensure success as discussed throughout this chapter: tracking and collecting impact data, setting and aligning incentives throughout organizations, and including all stakeholders in the journey to drive toward efficient and long-term change. Indeed, the industry can and will move forward with the vision and tools to create a better model, to see what the fashion sector can become, and together, to pledge not to make the same mistakes of yesterday with the solutions of tomorrow.

NOTE

1 "My Wife and My Mother-in-Law" is a famous optical illusion that depicts both an old woman looking off to the left and a young woman facing away, looking over her right shoulder. (The old woman's nose is the young woman's chin.) (Image credit: public domain.)

REFERENCES

Bernow, S., et al. (2019). *More Than Values: The Value-Based Sustainability Reporting that Investors Want*, McKinsey.
Cernansky, R. (2021). "Customers Care More About Sustainability Post-Lockdowns. Now What?", *Vogue Business*. August 5, 2021. See: https://www.voguebusiness.com/sustainability/customers-care-more-about-sustainability-post-lockdowns-now-what
Indvik, L. (2021). 'Chanel Unveils New Complex for Its Prized Suppliers at Métiers d'Art', *Financial Times*, December 19. Available at: https://www.ft.com/content/2beb415c-156c-4b8b-8384-101a0b13a3d8 (Accessed 10 May 2022).
Kania, J., and Kramer, M. (2011). Collective Impact. *Stanford Social Innovation Review*, 9(1), 36–41. https://doi.org/10.48558/5900-KN19.
Kering (2022). *Kering Publishes 2021 Group EP&L Results*. Available at https://www.kering.com/en/news/kering-publishes-2021-group-ep-l-results (Accessed 11 May 2022).

Lee, S., et al. (2020). *Understanding Bio-Material Innovations: A Primer for the Fashion Industry*, Biofabricate and Fashion for Good. Available at: https://reports.fashionforgood.com/wp-content/uploads/2020/12/Understanding-Bio-Material-Innovations-Report.pdf (Accessed 10 May 2022).

Legifrance (2020). *LOI n° 2020–105 du 10 février 2020 relative à la lutte contre le gaspillage et à l'économie circulaire*. Available at : https://www.legifrance.gouv.fr/jorf/id/JORFTEXT000041553759/ (Accessed 10 May 2022).

Lehmann, M., et al. (2018). *The Pulse of the Industry, 2018 Update*. Global Fashion Agenda, Boston Consulting Group, Inc., and Sustainable Apparel Coalition. Available at: https://www.peta.org.uk/wp-content/uploads/2019/03/Pulse_of_the_fashion_industry_report_2018-1.pdf (Accessed 10 May 2022).

Lehmann, M., et al. (2019). *The Pulse of the Industry, 2019 Update*. Global Fashion Agenda, Boston Consulting Group, Inc., and Sustainable Apparel Coalition. Available at: https://web-assets.bcg.com/img-src/Pulse-of-the-Fashion-Industry2019_tcm9-237791.pdf (Accessed 09 May 2022).

Ley, K., et al. (2021). *Unlocking the Trillion Dollar Fashion Decarbonisation Opportunity: Existing and Innovative Solutions*, Fashion for Good the Apparel Impact Institute. Available at: https://fashionforgood.com/our_news/unlocking-the-trillion-dollar-fashion-decarbonisation-opportunity/ (Accessed 09 May 2022).

NASA (2012). *Technology Readiness Level*. Available at https://www.nasa.gov/directorates/heo/scan/engineering/technology/technology_readiness_level (Accessed 10 May 2022).

NY Assembly Bill A8352 (2021). Available at: https://www.nysenate.gov/legislation/bills/2021/A8352 (Accessed 09 May 2022).

OECD (2020). *Business Enterprise Research and development Expenditure by Industry*. Available at: https://stats.oecd.org/Index.aspx?DataSetCode=BERD_INDU (Accessed 10 May 2022).

Pangaia (2022). *Pangaia Lab*. Available at: https://pangaia.com/pages/lab (Accessed 11 May 2022).

Senthilkannan Muthu, S. (2020). *Assessing the Environmental Impact of Textiles and the Clothing Supply Chain*. Woodhead Publishing Series in Textiles, Number 157.

Siu, E. (2022). *2021 State of the Industry Report*, Material Innovation Institute. Available at: https://www.materialinnovation.org/state-of-the-industry (Accessed 10 May 2022).

Textile Exchange Hub (2019). *Biosynthetics*. Available at: https://hub.textileexchange.org/textileexchange/learning-center/biosynthetics (Accessed 11 May 2022).

Threlfall, R., et al. (2020). *The Time Has Come: The KPMG Survey of Sustainability Reporting 2020*, KPMG Impact. Available at: https://assets.kpmg/content/dam/kpmg/xx/pdf/2020/11/the-time-has-come.pdf (Accessed 09 May 2022).

Trochu, E. (2016). "How Kering are Linking Luxury and Sustainability", *Vogue*. Available at: https://www.vogue.fr/fashion/fashion-inspiration/diaporama/how-kering-are-linking-luxury-and-sustainability/31060 (Accessed 11 May 2022).

United Nations General Assembly (2019). *Seventy-Third Session, High-Level Meeting on Climate and Sustainable Development (AM & PM)*. Available at: https://www.un.org/press/en/2019/ga12131.doc.htm (Accessed 09 May 2022).

White, T., et al. (2020). *Threads That Bind: Transforming the Fashion Supply Chain*, Accenture, The Dock. Available at: https://www.accenture.com/_acnmedia/PDF-115/Accenture-Threads-That-Bind.pdf (Accessed 10 May 2022).

9 Fostering sustainable practices: The case of micro and small designer fashion enterprises

Sandy Black, Mila Burcikova, Dilys Williams, Agnès Rocamora, Fergus Lyon, Andrea Werner, Ian Vickers, Patrick Elf, Claudia Eckert and Philippa Crommentuijn-Marsh

INTRODUCTION

The pace of fashion cycles has increased enormously over recent decades, with the advent of fast and faster fashion since the late 1990s; this high throughput and high waste model is unsustainable and no longer acceptable in the context of depleted and finite planetary resources, exacerbated by the current climate emergency (Steffen et al. 2015). The transition to sustainability is now an imperative for all sectors including fashion, as captured in the 2015 Paris Agreement,[1] the 2017 UN Sustainable Development Goals and accelerated by the 2020 Coronavirus pandemic.[2] The urgency for action was again reinforced by the Sixth IPCC report in 2021, named as 'a code red for humanity' by the UN SecretaryGeneral.[3] Although pioneers of sustainable fashion have been active since the 1980s, the industry as a whole has been slow to embed sustainability principles, with initiatives in evidence from the early 21st century (Black 2008, 2012; Fletcher 2008; Fletcher & Tham 2012). Calls for a long-overdue reset of the fashion industry system increased dramatically in response to the COVID-19 crisis (BFC and CFDA 2020; BOF 2020; BOF and McKinsey & Co. 2020a, 2020b; Open Letter 2020) and this momentum has continued (PEC 2022).

DOI: 10.4324/9781003272878-12

The UK is known for its successful creative industries and many of its fashion designers are widely acknowledged as creative influencers on the world stage. The fashion industry is an important contributor to the UK economy with GVA of £35 billion in 2019 pre-pandemic – larger than the automotive and aerospace sectors combined (BFC 2020). The UK's designer fashion sector comprises a high proportion of micro and small enterprises[4] (MSEs), independent businesses characterised by Jill Geoghegan, editor of fashion trade journal *Drapers*, as "the lifeblood of the fashion industry in the UK and Ireland" (Warrington 2022) and the focus of this research. Many design-led sustainable fashion MSEs provide pioneering alternative visions for a broader understanding of prosperity in business and represent a key focus for sustainability transitions (including reduced production and consumption) as the UK seeks to meet its Net Zero aspirations by 2050.

This chapter presents empirical findings researched before and during the pandemic period, from the AHRC-funded project Rethinking Fashion Design Entrepreneurship: Fostering Sustainable Practices (FSP). The FSP project structured its research across the four pillars of sustainability: social, environmental, economic and cultural. Whilst the fashion industry has been severely affected by the pandemic,[5] we examine how sustainability-motivated fashion entrepreneurs can offer alternative models and practices of resilience and prosperity, and how they are seeking to influence the wider industry in which they are embedded.

METHODOLOGY

The project team conducted a longitudinal study from June 2019 to November 2020 via in-person and online interviews with 27 design-led fashion MSEs to investigate their visions, values, capabilities and business models for sustainable fashion. To identify these sustainability-focused businesses, an initial survey of 200 UK-based fashion MSEs (not necessarily sustainability-focused) was conducted, to collect details of their business, purpose and values, their challenges, their current sustainable practices and visions for success. Based on the screening of this information, 45 MSEs with existing sustainable motivation and practices were selected for the qualitative research and first semi-structured interviews. Subsequently, 27 businesses were selected for longitudinal study where further interviews with designers/founders and key personnel from each business were conducted. Figures 9.1 and 9.2 indicate the size and longevity of these 27 businesses.

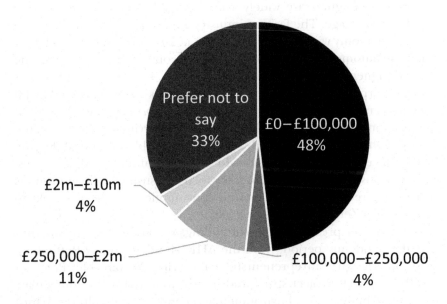

Figure 9.1 Turnover of 27 MSEs in FSP longitudinal study

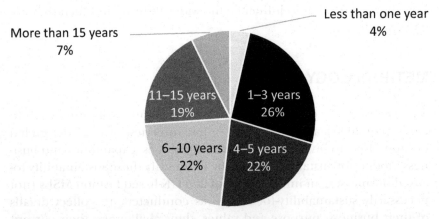

Figure 9.2 Number of years in business of 27 MSEs in FSP longitudinal study

FINDINGS

This part discusses some of the themes that emerged from analysis of our cases in relation to the four research strands that structured the FSP project: (1) designer visions, values, capabilities and processes; (2)

business networks and collaborative ecosystems; (3) working practices, roles and trajectories; and (4) entrepreneurship and business models fostering sustainable prosperity. Key emerging themes discussed below are: Fashion as a tool for social change, Consumer engagement and education, Business models for transformation and Digital technology as an enabler of sustainability. We also discuss examples of designer/ entrepreneur agility in response to the pandemic.

In relation to designer roles and business trajectories (strand 3), our interviews revealed that most designers/entrepreneurs had previously worked for other (larger) businesses in the fashion or media industries. Some founders were motivated to develop their own enterprise in response to observing social or environmental injustices (e.g. clothes sharing platform NuW, footwear designer Alexander White). The traditional role of the fashion designer in an industrial context – as conceiver of aesthetic concepts and fashion products – has evolved to become just one of many roles for the designer/entrepreneur in an MSE. These include facilitating connections, building community, engaging directly with customers and public, teaching, advocacy and public speaking, experimenting with new ways of working and undertaking special projects and consultancy with major brands, institutions or charitable organisations, thus providing additional sources of income to spread financial risk.

The designers/entrepreneurs in this study aim to transform fashion's current business model away from one that stimulates rampant consumerism. Instead, being in control of smaller enterprises, they avoid overproduction and overconsumption and contribute to social justice and inclusion, achieved through the way they work as well as by what is made.

FASHION AS A TOOL FOR SOCIAL CHANGE

The onslaught of the pandemic and the cancellation of orders by major fashion industry players further exposed the fault lines endemic within the mainstream fashion sector, with its complex supply chains, pervasive practices of environmental degradation and exploitation of employees. These damaging practices were exemplified by the 2013 Rana Plaza disaster in Bangladesh that galvanised demands for transparency and accountability across the global garment-making sector to redress social injustices.[6] In 2020, the PayUpFashion campaign[7] helped garment workers by recouping payments lost to cancelled orders during the pandemic.

This theme foregrounds the designer-entrepreneurs' visions and values with respect to the social aspects of fashion business (research strand 1). The case study enterprises put social and environmental purposes at the top of their agenda, a few setting out to be a social enterprise from the start (e.g. accessories brand Elvis & Kresse (Figure 9.3), womenswear brand Birdsong (Figure 9.4) and menswear and womenswear brand Bethany Williams (Figure 9.5) and others aiming to engage with specific communities to impart skills and create empowerment, operating fair and transparent working practices. Some have built up

Image: NuW   Image: Elvis & Kresse

Figure 9.3 (Left) NuW sharing community. Photo Abbie Roden; (Right) Elvis & Kresse bags made from waste fire hose. Image courtesy: Elvis & Kresse

Image: Away to Mars   Image: Birdsong   Image: Raeburn

Figure 9.4 (Left) Away to Mars co-created designs. Photo Gleeson Paulino; (Centre) Birdsong wrap dress; Photo Rachel Mann. (Right) Raeburn menswear from upcycled parachutes. Photo Alexander Fleming

Images: Bethany Williams AW 2022   Image: EDN Network

Figure 9.5 (Left and Centre) Bethany Williams AW 2022 collection Photos Suleika Mueller; (Right) 'Scrubs' for NHS staff produced by EDN Network. Photo Sandy Black

their businesses with the prime purpose of utilising fashion as a tool for social change – providing decent work, training and skills through making, and educating consumers and the public. For example, both Birdsong and Bethany Williams work with local disadvantaged communities, in collaboration with charities, to create their products and raise awareness, offering fair employment and living wages, creative satisfaction and enhanced self-worth. Birdsong's first priority when the pandemic hit was to ensure the safety of their workers and that there would be work for them to come back to. A specific fund was set up through crowdsourcing to support Birdsong employees who found themselves in difficulty. Both businesses have been recognised with awards, and Bethany Williams' work as a social enterprise was showcased in an exhibition at the Design Museum London in 2022.

CONSUMER ENGAGEMENT AND COMMUNICATION

Our findings under this theme relate to entrepreneurs' practices towards fostering sustainable behaviours (research strands 3 and 4). Particularly in response to the COVID-19 crisis, many of the cases increased their direct-to-consumer engagement activities, capitalising on their existing relationships nurtured through social media narratives (such as Instagram Stories), online sales and public-facing physical events and workshops. New online activities offer support and opportunities for learning craft skills in lockdown circumstances. For example, several businesses including Raeburn (womenswear and menswear brand; Figure 9.4) and Sabinna (womenswear brand) created do-it-yourself pattern kits for anyone to make accessories at home and post images on Instagram – in Raeburn's case, for their 'offcut animals' series and in Sabinna's case, for their DIY kits to make hair bands, masks and simple crafted jewellery, building on Sabinna's strong use of hand craft. ReAdorn London is a business that upcycles broken jewellery, creating new pieces from old and offers kits for customers to assemble a unique piece of upcycled jewellery at home.

Repairing services are increasingly offered by brands. Raeburn's studio team gave online repair workshops and started a campaign that declared Buy Nothing, Repair Globally on Black Friday 2020; founder Christopher Raeburn developed a series of Instagram Live conversations with individuals from the fashion and sustainability community (e.g.@raeburn_design 8.11.20) a series that has continued. Similarly, womenswear designer Phoebe English offered a series of talks on developing a collection, respecting planetary boundaries (@phoebeenglish 17.12.20) and physically showcased her studio processes to the public at the British Library (@phoebeenglish 16.09.21). The wearable technology company Cute Circuit, creators of unique experiential garments and couture showpieces, developed weekly Instagram Live sessions, opening up their creative processes in the studio, and educating their audience about aspects of fashion, culture and technology (e.g. @CuteCircuit 5.02.21). As businesses were able to open again post-pandemic, face-to-face activities such as Raeburn's monthly public Lab tours resumed. Raeburn has continued to close its online shopping site on Black Friday, instead instigating in 2022 Buy Back Friday where customers could trade in garments (@raeburn_design 23.11.22). These and many other MSE engagement activities serve to educate the public, demystify creative process and enhance appreciation of fashion's intrinsic and cultural value, fostering more sustainable behaviours.

BUSINESS MODELS FOR TRANSFORMATION

The fourth research strand encompassed examination of the business models developed by our case study businesses, including service providers and consultancies. In order to disrupt the unsustainable status quo of the established fashion sector where overproduction is the norm, many MSEs have adopted a transformative approach to their business. They aim to innovate beyond the creation of products, to create new ways of doing business whilst still providing delight and rewarding experiences. For such purpose-led businesses, economic growth is not the end in itself, and not the only measure of success, but it is important for an enterprise to have a viable business in order to realise its social and ecological aims and communicate its values and purpose.

Elvis & Kresse, for example, only use rescued waste materials as inputs for their luxury bags and homewares (Figure 9.3; right), therefore the more that is sold, the more waste is diverted from landfill, and as a social enterprise, the more profit-share can be donated to charitable causes. Co-founder Kresse Wesling says: "We are profitable, and we're growing, and we meet all the traditional metrics that they [*the fashion industry*] would define as success, but we do it in a completely different way and for completely different motivations." Many businesses, however, aim to remain small but viable, rejecting the pressure for constant growth that business support organisations and investors often demand.

Several of the cases are shifting away from selling wholesale towards a greater focus on direct-to-consumer business. For example, Raeburn decided on "a radical shift in our way of thinking and making" towards "making less and making better" (@raeburn_design, 22.01.21), operating a system of limited edition and small-batch production and "rapid replenishment" of stock for wholesale customers.

Three of the businesses in the FSP cohort were certified B Corp businesses (an internationally recognised certification for social and environmental standards in business), which is rare in the fashion sector. Elvis & Kresse were the first fashion-related business in the UK to obtain this certification in 2015; two others awarded in 2018 are outdoor and surfwear brand Finisterre, one of the longest established and largest MSEs in this study, and Riz Boardshorts, makers of a single product, men's beach shorts, using recycled ocean plastics. Since the completion of the FSP project, more fashion businesses are seeking B Corp certification, including Raeburn; Birdsong achieved their B Corp accreditation in April 2022, and womenswear brand DePloy achieved theirs in May 2022 (see Chapter 13).

DIGITAL TECHNOLOGY AS AN ENABLER OF SUSTAINABILITY AND COLLABORATION

Some of the more disruptive business models for sustainability amongst MSEs aiming to reduce production and consumption involve the integration of different forms of technology, from innovative apps for sharing and swapping of clothes (NuW Figure 9.3 left) or managing your wardrobe (Save Your Wardrobe), to software or online systems for designing and producing small-batch runs of clothing or knitwear (Unmade, Away to Mars).

Unmade is a digital innovator founded in 2013, aiming to radically shift the fashion supply chain to pure on-demand manufacturing – on a mass scale – through its digital end-to-end software system for industrial manufacturing processes (currently tested with customised knitwear, trainers and small runs of digitally printed sports teamwear). Through their innovative software developments, Unmade is achieving small-batch and individual-item customisation but with large volume efficiencies and price points, enabling the production of only what is needed.

Fashion womenswear brand Away to Mars, founded in 2016 (Figure 9.4, left), has developed an innovative co-creative online model and platform for design, that is inclusive and non-hierarchical, offering opportunities and recognition for fashion and textile designers. Diverse international communities are invited to respond to online creative briefs, and after several rounds of open voting combined with data analysis, the most successful concepts are developed into prototypes for manufacturing. Unusually, a percentage of profit is shared with those contributing to each design.

AGILITY TO ADDRESS SUSTAINABILITY IN RELATION TO PANDEMIC CHALLENGES

In relation to the first research strand, our findings show that the capabilities designer-entrepreneurs exhibit include responsiveness to change and willingness to explore, adapt, seize opportunity and take risks. They also include connecting people and building networks, communicating to diverse audiences, building teams and managing relationships with a wide range of stakeholders – all in addition to having practical industry and business skills.

The onset of the pandemic brought to the fore many of the agile qualities of MSEs, including the ability to be flexible and responsive in rapidly changing circumstances, their small and flat organisational structures enabling rapid deployment of people and resources, in-house production facilities enabling fast prototyping, plus strong networks and relationships with suppliers and manufacturing partners increasing supply chain resilience during crises. For example, direct knowledge and experience of making (in a craft sense) in their own studios and manufacturing (within both small workshop and factory settings) enabled a group of designers to quickly collaborate and mobilise their making teams to create much needed "scrubs" (protective clothing) for NHS workers during the first wave of the pandemic and again in early 2021 as pressures once more increased (Figure 9.5, right).

Pheobe English and Bethany Williams (two MSEs in the FSP study), together with Holly Fulton and Cozette McCreery, all London-based fashion designers, set up the Emergency Designer Network (EDN) in March 2020, acting extremely rapidly and nimbly to help overcome problems with personal protective equipment (PPE) supplies. Using their own trusted networks, the EDN put together teams and raised funds through crowdsourcing and other donations to provide materials and pay workers. With the assistance of the Make it British organisation and lobby group Fashion Roundtable, 150 factories and individual makers went into production locally and across the UK delivered 5–7000 reusable sets of PPE weekly to hospitals. The EDN volunteer activities were recognised in the UK Parliament and honoured in the 2020 British Fashion Awards (UK Parliament 2020; Vogue 2020); an acknowledgement to the commitment of the group whilst caring for the workers and ensuring the survival of their businesses.

CONCLUSIONS

These innovative sustainable fashion MSEs examine new ways of doing business in fashion that tackle the major issues of overproduction and overconsumption, and value the contribution of different skills and disciplines. The collaborative and interdisciplinary mindset of many enterprises enables a new focus on sufficiency with appreciation for social and cultural values identified by the consumers, even when struggling during the pandemic.

Our findings show these fashion design MSEs often have relationship-based, direct-to-consumer business models which enable them to educate customers about sustainable fashion, teach sustainability-related skills and encourage behavioural change through experiential opportunities, resulting in an informed and loyal customer base. Their business practices also rely on strong relationships, especially with local suppliers, collaborators and manufacturing partners to deliver sampling and/or production. These relationships are driven by a desire to improve social equity and contribute to local job creation, for example, by paying the living wage to those making clothes, and by providing skills training and employment for disadvantaged groups. These instances of best practice, including public education through clear messaging and engagement opportunities, demonstrate designer-entrepreneurs' transparent working practices and non-conventional measures of business success.

The cases demonstrate a new ethic in design wherein the role of designer-entrepreneur is expanded from a focus on sales and profit to a wider prosperity and an economy that values people and their creativity in achieving business ambitions, and contributing to community alongside maintaining financial viability.

A culture of sufficiency is evident amongst the case studies. The implications for the wider industry are clear: the urgent adoption of circular material flows and an end to speculative and wasteful overproduction are essential if Net Zero targets are to be met. A move to actual demand-driven fashion by manufacturing products to order or in small batches can create a renewed relationship between consumers and their clothes, giving them lasting pleasure underpinned by quality, transparency and social justice.

As the COVID-19 crisis triggered a wider discourse in a re-assessment of values, foregrounding green renewal, new quality-of-life indicators (Harvey 2020) and implementation of a well-being economy (OECD 2020; Wellbeing Economy Alliance 2017), purpose-driven fashion MSEs provide exemplars of future prosperity that value diversity, balance human and environmental well-being and benefit both local and global communities through their positive influence and relationship-building skills, based on transparency and trust, that extends to supply chains further afield. Such smaller, agile, purpose-led enterprises exemplify a redefinition of what sustainable fashion business is and what it can be in future, presenting viable pathways to building towards a sustainable prosperity for all involved.

ACKNOWLEDGEMENTS

Research funded by the Arts and Humanities Research Council (AHRC) Grant no AH/R006539/1. 'Rethinking Fashion Design Entrepreneurship: Fostering Sustainable Practices' (Oct 2018–March 2021) was led by Centre for Sustainable Fashion (a University of the Arts London research centre, based at London College of Fashion), in collaboration with Middlesex University Centre for Enterprise and Economic Development Research and the Open University Design department.

NOTES

1 At the 2015 Paris Climate Conference (Conference of the Parties COP21) 189 signatories agreed to limit global warming to 1.5°–2° and publish targets for reduction of their greenhouse gas emissions see https://www.diplomatie. gouv.fr/en/french-foreign-policy/climate-and-environment/2015-paris-climate-conference-cop21/cop21-the-paris-agreement-in-four-key-points/ (Accessed 10.1.21). The 2021 conference COP26 held in the UK reconfirmed this target.
2 "The crisis is a catalyst that will shock the industry into change – now is the time to get ready for a post-coronavirus world.… The pandemic will bring values around sustainability into sharp focus, intensifying discussions and further polarising views around materialism, over-consumption and irresponsible business practices." BOF and McKinsey & Co. (2020a: pp. 8, 18).
3 Statement made by UN Secretary-General António Guterres 9.08.2021 on the publication of the Intergovernmental Panel on Climate Change (IPCC) Sixth Assessment Report. See www.un.org/en/delegate/global-warming-'unequivocally'-human-driven-ipcc (Accessed 8.10.22).
4 EU Document 32003H0361 (2003) defines micro businesses as having 0 to 9 employees, small 10–49 employees, medium 50–249 employees, as used by the UK Office for National Statistics. https://eur-lex.europa.eu/legal-content/EN/TXT/?uri=CELEX:32003H0361.
5 Eurostat 2020: 'Volume of retail trade sales July 2020 compared to February 2020' shows Textile, Clothes, and Footwear sales fell by 22% from February to July 2020, far more than any other sector, the next largest fall was automotive fuel at 9%. (Accessed 16.1.21) https://ec.europa.eu/eurostat/statisticsexplained/images/1/13/Retail_sales_June2020–03.jpg.
6 The campaigning organisation Fashion Revolution was set up in direct response to the 2013 Rana Plaza disaster in Bangladesh, and has activated consumer- and industry-facing campaigns globally in more than 90 countries. See www.fashionrevolution.org.
7 See https://payupfashion.com.

REFERENCES

BFC (British Fashion Council). 2020. Evidence Submitted to the UK Government Environmental Audit Committee (13 Nov 2020). Available at https://committees.parliament.uk/writtenevidence/15152/pdf/ (Accessed 10 Oct 2022)
BFC and CFDA (Council of Fashion Designers of America). 2020 (21 May). Available at www.instagram.com/p/CAdiVo.jw0y/
Black, S. 2008. *Eco Chic the Fashion Paradox.* London: Black Dog Publishing.
Black, S., ed. 2012. *The Sustainable Fashion Handbook.* London and New York: Thames and Hudson.
BOF (Business of Fashion). 2020. *Rewiring Fashion.* www.rewiringfashion.org
BOF (Business of Fashion) and McKinsey & Co. 2020a (April). *The State of Fashion 2020 Coronavirus Update.* Available at: www.businessoffashion.com/articles/global-markets/the-state-of-fashion-2020-coronavirus-update-download-the-report/
BOF (Business of Fashion) and McKinsey & Co. 2020b (Dec). *The State of Fashion 2021.* Available at https://cdn.businessoffashion.com/reports/The_State_of_Fashion_2021.pdf

Fletcher, K. 2008. *Sustainable Fashion and Textiles, Design Journeys*. London and Sterling VA: Earthscan.

Fletcher, K. and Tham, M. 2012. *Fashion and Sustainability, Design for Change*. London: Lawrence King.

Harvey, F. 2020 (10 May). "Britons Want Quality-of-Life Indicators to Take Priority Over Economy." *The Guardian*. Available at: www.theguardian.com/society/2020/may/10/britons-want-quality-of-life-indicators-priority-over-economy-coronavirus

OECD (Organisation for Economic Co-Operation and Development). 2020 (5 June). *Building Back Better: A Sustainable, Resilient Recovery after COVID-19*. Available at https://oecd.org/coronavirus/policy-responses/building-back-better-a-sustainable-resilient-recovery-after-COVID-19-52b869f5/

Open Letter to the Fashion Industry. 2020 (May). Available at https://forumletter.org

PEC (Creative Industries Policy and Evidence Centre), Julie's Bicycle and BOP Consulting. 2022. *Creative Industries and the Climate Emergency: The Path to Net Zero*. Available at https://pec.ac.uk/research-reports/creative-industries-and-the-climate-emergency

Steffen, W., Richardson, K., Rockström, J., Cornell, S. E., Fetzer, I., Bennett, E. M. et al. 2015. "Planetary Boundaries: Guiding Human Development on a Changing Planet." *Science* 347 (6223): 1259855:1–10

UK Parliament. 2020 (8 June). Early Day Motions. "UK fashion industry during the covid19 outbreak." Available at https://edm.parliament.uk/early-day-motion/57073/uk-fashion-industry-during-the-covid19-outbreak

Vogue. 2020 (3 Dec). "The 2020 Fashion Awards Winners Share Their Hopes For The Industry." Available at https://www.vogue.co.uk/news/article/2020-fashion-awards-winners

Warrington, S. 2022 (5 August). "Drapers Independents Awards 2022 finalists revealed." Available at www.drapersonline.com/news/drapers-independent-awards-2022-finalists-revealed

Wellbeing Economy Alliance. 2017. *Wellbeing Economy Policy Design Guide*. Available at https://wellbeingeconomy.org/wp-content/uploads/Wellbeing-Economy-Design-Guide_Mar 17_FINAL.pdf

Part IV

Case studies: values-based entrepreneurs

10 Desserto®: cactus fibre as leather substitute

Sandy Black

Desserto is the brand name for an innovative leather substitute fabric created using cactus fibre. The co-founders Adrián López Velarde and Marte Cázarez Duarte began to develop it in 2017 and officially launched the fabric in October 2019. Both their company Adriano di Marti, based in Guadalajara in Mexico, and the Desserto fabric, are gaining in profile and have won a number of awards including a Green Product Award 2020, and an LVMH Innovation Award. The company is working in collaboration with a number of partners in the fashion industry, including adidas, Givenchy, Karl Lagerfeld and H&M to create bags, shoes, boots, outerwear and other products. Adriano di Marti has also developed an automotive upholstery fabric branded Desserttex and has key partners in the automotive industry, including BMW and Mercedes, all seeking a more sustainable alternative to use of animal leathers (Figure 10.1).

BACKGROUND AND MOTIVATION

Although both founders are from Mexico, Marte and Adrián first met in 2011 in Taiwan, when each was working in materials research and development (Research and development) and sourcing, especially for leather and synthetic "leathers," Adrián working in the automotive industry and Marte working in fashion. They started to discuss the environmental impact of these materials, lack of transparency regarding their sources, and the working conditions and pay of people producing them. Following their return to Mexico, Marte and Adrián started

DOI: 10.4324/9781003272878-14

Figure 10.1 Adrián López Velarde and Marte Cázarez Duarte with cactus and Desserto fabric. Courtesy Adriano di Marti

to research more deeply into the Mexican leather industry, especially in the town of Leon, where they saw "scary" practices, such as workers chrome-tanning leather with their bare hands, using toxic chemicals, and "washing their bodies with noxious chrome-loaded water." They say 90% of leather produced in Leon was chrome-tanned, and further research showed similar usage of chrome-tanning in many countries worldwide. Based on their observations and the impending climate crisis, Marte and Adrián started to look for alternatives to leather, but most concepts they found were at the lab stage and highly fragile – there were no scalable solutions at the time, although progress is now being made with other materials such as mycelium from fungi.

RESEARCH AND DEVELOPMENT

Adrián and Marte dreamt of creating their own material and hit upon the idea of experimenting with the Nopal cactus ("prickly pear") – a highly abundant crop in Mexico, and also a symbolic plant (used on the country's flag) that could resonate culturally with people. During intensive research, they discovered that the cactus had a high protein and organic fibre content that could facilitate adhesive properties. It was already used as an additive in concrete and was highly water resistant. The sustainability credentials of the cactus were encouraging, and analysis of its environmental impact revealed advantages over other plant-based products in the way it could be grown and extracted. For example, no irrigation or agro-chemicals (pesticides, fertilisers) are required to enable plant growth; the cactus has great capacity to sequester CO_2 (becoming a carbon sink) and the ability to restore soil quality whilst growing on semi-arid land, not suitable for other crops. Cactus had been grown for decades in Mexico for both human and animal consumption, especially as an emergency animal feed when no grass was available. However, Adrián says that according to the Federal government, over the last eight years, 50% of Mexico's cactus plantations had been lost due to fluctuation in prices in the food industry and changes in land use. Prices had fallen so low to only US$1 per 1 kg of cactus at retail.

Adrián and Marte recognised an opportunity to step in and incentivise farmers to grow cactus again for new applications, without causing conflict between using land for food or materials, as the cactus crop could help restore land deteriorated from intensively growing other crops. They started to work in the Zacatecas state in central Mexico – the region that has the most abundant concentration of Nopal cactus in the world, both farmed and wild, due to its altitude. An agreement was made with one farmer to use 14 acres of previously abandoned land, and to offer him a direct price of US$7–8 to grow and process the cactus. After two years of research and development, the Desserto brand was launched in 2019. Collaborations with major fashion businesses have been brokered by Adrián and Marte (including with LVMH and adidas); however, these companies' complex auditing conditions required a change of mindset for the farmer to comply with all of their social and environmental requirements; Adrián and Marte helped him to navigate this complexity.

An important aspect of growing and harvesting the cactus plants is that only the mature leaves are picked, leaving the rest of the plant to continue growing in an ongoing process of harvesting every 6–8 months, each plant continuing to be productive for up to eight years. The harvested cactus leaves are sun-dried, processed and baled on the farm then transported to the Desserto Research and development Lab in Mexico City, where the proteins are extracted and fibres separated to make bio-resins, and final formulations of the bio-polymers are made, tailored to individual customers' needs for organic content and final surface effects. Adrián says: "In the end you want the material to perform ... it has to be customisable, resistant, compliant to all technical parameters the customer needs, and has to replace an existing material" (Figure 10.2). Bulk production of Desserto material is made via a network of commercial partners in a value chain of perhaps 350 people from farm to manufacturing, all in

Figure 10.2 Backpack by Fossil using Desserto textured fabric. Courtesy Adriano di Marti

Mexico and controlled by Adriano di Marti, which as a company consists of 11 people.

Adriano di Marti has a wide range of clients from micro to large businesses, all with different fabric needs depending on application. The company produces a unique range of materials designed to meet different performance requirements. The baseline Desserto fabric contains 20–30% organic content, combined with other non-toxic chemicals (a patented process), and is manufactured on standard industrial machinery that coats the bio-resin material onto a textile substrate, facilitating the scaling up of production. According to customer requirements, the textile substrate can be made from either new or recycled polyester or cotton, and the Desserto fabric is therefore said to be "partially biodegradable" because of its complex formulation. This standard fabric is their cheapest, costing around the same as cow's leather, with no minimum order quantities, thus removing a barrier to low-volume users and students. It is available in a range of colours

Figure 10.3 Bag by Karl Lagerfeld using Desserto fabric. Courtesy Adriano di Marti

and textures, is breathable and does not stain or crack, and can last up to ten years. It is however possible for more sophisticated (and more expensive) versions of Desserto fabric to be made on demand, that can contain up to 90% organic content from the cactus fibre and protein. The cotton substrate used as a backing can also be "infused with cactus" (Figure 10.3). There have been some criticisms that the standard fabric contains only 20–30% organic material. Adrián believes these critics may be judging too quickly, citing the company's positive early stage life cycle assessment (LCA) figures that compare favourably with leather.[1] He explains the biodegradability potential for Desserto fabrics if they are in landfills:

the way we design the material allows it to biodegrade in part, depending on the type of material and the different percentages of organic content. In thermophilic conditions – at higher temperatures of 45°C – the bacteria that grows is capable of eating more elaborate carbon structures, there are landfills that give us those conditions and need no additional process for the material to biodegrade.

This means there are existing conditions in which the material will break down, albeit not completely. As their company grows, Adrián also envisages the business eventually setting up an "end of life" take-back system "to collect everything and apply certain conditions to maximise the biodegradability of products and even incorporate recycling techniques." The logistics involved here would of course be complex and such a system would need good infrastructures in place.

Compared with cow's leather "where one of the fundamental problems of the industry is the link to deforestation for grazing" even the basic Desserto material has been shown to be much more sustainable. A commissioned LCA by an EU partner has corroborated the company's significant reductions on water use, energy use, greenhouse gases impact, carbon emissions and chemical usage, compared with leather and polyurethane, published on the company website. The Desserto product and components have achieved several certifications including OekoTex 100 and USDA Certified Bio-Based Product (65%), USDA Organic (for the cactus) and also Vegan certification by V-label for the finished product. Desserto has also been awarded the USDA BioPreferred® Program Champion Badge, signifying a "long-term commitment to using renewable materials, reducing reliance on petroleum, supporting the bioeconomy, and bettering the planet."

FUTURE BUSINESS AND CHALLENGES

With regard to developing the range of materials, Adrián states: "The range and possibilities of materials we can make is great and I think a [*sustainability*] solution has to have flexibility."

As 80% of Desserto product is currently exported to main markets in Asia, Europe and America, the company is looking at expanding overseas – setting up teams that can work in the same time frame as customers. Logistics present an ongoing challenge: overseas operations would help to reduce carbon emissions from logistics, cut shipping costs and spread the benefits from the supply chain more widely. Thinking of ways to reduce carbon footprint and bring down costs is a constant challenge. Desserto fabric is in competition with much cheaper synthetic "leathers" made from Polyurethane or PVC, but as a new innovation, cannot currently compete with these on price. In the two years since launch, the business has created materials using a range from 20% to 80% organic cactus content. It might be possible to make a 100% organic material and offer it to the market, but "there would be no point if was not resistant enough to be useful." As a recent start-up business and product, the Desserto technology still has to continue its development and be "acceptable in terms of price, performance, volume, and capacity of manufacturing."

There is no doubt that Marte and Adrián will continue the material innovation towards greater sustainability. They plan to continue improving their sustainability scores from both the product LCA and business perspectives, including encouraging their production factories to change to solar energy to reduce carbon emissions, so the focus is holistic and not just on materials. To this end, they also want to eventually apply for B Corp certification for the entire business.

The co-founders have recently embarked on developing another new material from the cactus fibre – this time working to create a yarn that can be woven or knitted into a sustainable textile. Initial trials and prototypes are promising and "looking fantastic" according to Adrián.

Indeed, their vision for the next five years is passionate and ambitious – to become a "leading international bio-material supplier and developer with labs and production lines in different parts of the world; being a major supplier to the automotive industry and growing the part of the business in fashion."

Adrián identifies that the automotive industry is in the throes of a major paradigm shift for sustainability: that is, the transition to electric (and hydrogen) vehicles. However, it is the transition away from leather upholstery, which wastes up to 45% of the raw materials due to irregularly shaped hides, that provides a great opportunity for Desserttex fabrics.

KEY ISSUES FOR ACCELERATING SUSTAINABILITY

According to Adrián, key issues to be addressed in order to accelerate sustainability in both automotive and fashion industries are:

1) *Price.* This is the main factor and barrier to brands using more sustainable materials – volumes of leather produced and consumed are huge, so potential impact is great. However, it is difficult for a company to transition from a materials price of around US$3 per metre for bovine-based leather to US$20–$30 for sustainable material alternatives. This cannot be done quickly; it takes time to

transform business practices and scale towards using such sustainable materials. Adrián and Marte do not want to make their materials viable only for certain luxury fashion collections – they aim for them to be viable for everyone.

2) *Consumer awareness and communications.* The end consumer has to be more and more aware of the consequences of their choices. Getting a clear message out is very important to help people understand which labels and information to look out for regarding sustainability. Explaining this to the general public creates pressure for the industry but as demand grows, supply will grow. Reducing consumption also plays an important part. Adrián and Marte therefore spend time visiting universities and talking to the media because the more people understand how noxious synthetics and leather are for the environment and people, the more consciousness there is to transform the market and industry.

3) *Sustainability as the norm.* The COVID-19 pandemic accelerated the consciousness of industry – everyone became more aware and careful of processes. There is genuine desire within businesses to transform many industries towards sustainability at all levels including senior management of companies. Although not an instant process, the mindset shift is now evident, but everyone needs to work together to make it happen. Those who do not address sustainability will be substituted in the market by those who do.

It is clear from the case of Adriano di Marti and their Desserto material innovation that new ways of creating materials can be viable and can address major environmental and societal issues. The shift accelerated by the pandemic must be capitalised on, in order to accelerate sustainability across all industries. In the words of Adrián Lopez Valarde:

Sustainability is no longer seen as a luxury, no more simply a story you can tell customers. Sustainability is seen now as it should have been seen from the beginning, a matter of security and a matter of wellbeing for everyone. From now on things are going to be very different.

ACKNOWLEDGEMENTS

Adrián López Velarde and Marte Cázarez Duarte are Co-Founders and Co-CEOs of Adriano Di Marti S.A. de C.V. and are thanked for their support for the preparation of the case study.

NOTE

1 These early stage LCA figures give comparative environmental impact savings of Desserto fabric compared with leather and polyurethane, and follow ISO 14040 and 14044 LCA guidelines according to the Desserto website E-LCA (desserto. com.mx) (accessed 12 Oct 2022).

11 DePloy: customisation for 360° sustainability

Sandy Black

BACKGROUND AND MOTIVATION

DePloy is a fashion house based in London producing clothes for women's wear that has operated from an ethos of "360° Sustainability" since its inception in 2006. As well as deploying a sustainability lens, the name DePloy is also a play on words, signalling that trend-driven fashion and other consumer industries are tantamount to a form of scheme or ploy, driving overconsumption, that must be derailed and disrupted or "de-ployed". Bernice Pan, DePloy's entrepreneurial founder and Creative Director, set up the business to provide well-designed, high-quality, well-fitting tailored clothing styles to women of all ages, and boasts a clientele ranging from 14 to 94 years. Born from a desire to demonstrate that fashion could be done differently, the business is consumer-driven, foregrounding personal service (especially regarding fit and customisation) and strong customer relations, creating long-term loyalty from its clients. The business operates from its base in London, and for ten years, had a physical store in the prestigious Marylebone area, that closed in 2017. DePloy also has a branch office in Taipei and sells internationally, taking its offer on tour with events and pop-up stores taking place across 12–14 cities worldwide each season. In 2022, DePloy certified as a B Corp[1] (Benefit corporation) with an exceptionally high score of 150 against the standard of 80 points.

Bernice Pan came to fashion through a non-traditional route, having decided to study architecture rather than fashion design at university, but always maintaining a strong interest in fashion. After her degree, she gained initial fashion experience with a New Generation designer at London Fashion Week, and then worked in New York's fashion industry,

DOI: 10.4324/9781003272878-15

where she was design director for a luxury women's wear brand with direct retail stores. There, she dressed many celebrities and VIPs, managed all parts of the process, extending beyond design to production, marketing and communications, to wholesale and distribution. A "baptism of fire", the role gave her invaluable experience and intimate knowledge of how the industry worked. Observing the industry's exploitative nature, in relation to garment workers, for example, fuelled ideas about what needed to change, and how she might do it.

Interested in fashion as a system, Bernice returned to the UK to complete her architecture Masters, with a thesis on how to reconnect London's East End rag trade with its glittering West End persona. The fashion system she had observed was very "tunnel minded" and she notes

> if you're a merchandiser all you care about is the numbers and your assortment, if you're a designer all you care about is fabric prices and millions of different variety of similar dresses, because if you're a dress designer all you do is design dresses, not even trousers.

To develop her ideas for a new way of doing fashion, and to link academia and industry, Bernice embarked on a PhD, whilst continuing to work in the fashion industry to finance her studies. The plan was to research the concept for a new customised business model and then if feasible, to start the business "because I can't prove anything only by theory, and I can't change the industry by just joining another big business".

APPROACH AND BUSINESS MODEL

On completion of her PhD in 2005, Bernice started DePloy, selling direct to consumers through pop-up shops (not a term in common use then), before opening her own DePloy store in Marylebone, London, having long recognised that "wholesale was a sunset industry". As with many businesses, the first few years were "a struggle", but the concept proved workable and the business saw year-on-year growth. Two key aspects drove the business:

(1) the "360° Sustainability Compass", which is "never about just sourcing organic or environmentally or recycling, because that's just the beginning and end of the chain, and the middle part is also a big problem – every single step is critical" (Figure 11.1); (2) people – the end consumer. "Until I see the consumer/customer putting our clothes on, being delighted with their purchase and wearing it for the next 10 years, I don't consider my job done, or done well in any way".

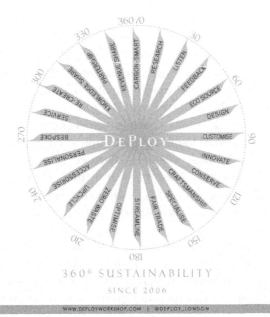

Figure 11.1 DePloy's 360° Sustainability Compass as the company DNA since its founding in 2006. It is the compass for its circular fashion brand ethos, business model, supply chain processes, product-service-experience offering and social-educational-corporate partnerships

The DePloy e-commerce website offers five key components of their approach: "exquisite fabrics, fine-tailoring, functional versatility, lasting style and fit perfection". One of the unique selling points (USPs) of the business is the development of multifunctional garments, using minimum resources to create maximum flexibility. For example, a military-inspired jacket that changes to a cropped bolero jacket via removable lapels and hem; or a four-way coat that can be detached and worn as a dress, and as jacket and skirt separates. Many pieces are designed to be reversible to prolong interest and useful life (Figures 11.2 and 11.3).

The DePloy business model is founded on personal service, offering four different levels of customisation. First is **self-customisation** using the inherent multi-functionality of many styles, as described above. Second is **custom alterations** – any garment can be tailored to individual preferences (such as length), even if bought in a sample sale. Thirdly, DePloy offers a **full bespoke service**, custom designed and made to order starting from scratch with customer's own wishes and DePloy's in-house tailors. The fourth level is **after-sales service**: even if a garment was purchased ten years before, the customer can bring it back to be re-tailored if their fit has changed, and the company offers repairs and refurbishment services.

Figure 11.2 Classic line multifunction suit-dress in jet black 100% gabardine tropical wool available throughout the year. This piece is wearable as a coat, a dress (as seen on right), a cropped jacket (as seen on left), a skirt, or as a double-breasted jacket with an additional peplum hem attached

Figure 11.3 Signature multifunction trench coat in 100% cotton waterproof, a classic best seller over the years. This piece is wearable as a trench coat (as seen on left), a biker dress (as seen in the centre), as a bolero separately, or as a trench cloak with a separate cape attached for in-between seasons

From an initial team of two – Bernice and her original co-founder, now exited – the business currently comprises three directors responsible for creative and sales, production and accessories and brand and marketing, with the complete team totalling ten people. The company is profitable and due to its business model, managed to remain profitable through the COVID-19 pandemic, despite shrinkage in turnover. Pre-pandemic, small batches of garments would be produced, but the business has now transitioned to a completely make-on-demand model.

Bernice is inspired by people to challenge and change the industry, stating "I believe until you really change people's heart and mindset, you can't change their behaviour and lifestyle, therefore you can't change the environment, so it has to start from the impact on people directly".

Although DePloy has been recognised by the industry and media, Bernice says her proudest achievement is being

> one of the few designers who has personally dress-fitted thousands of customers directly, that is the completion of my job, not design something, send it to production, quality control it, sell it – and people give us feedback all the time, that's how we continuously gain insights, find inspiration, fine-tune products and improve processes.

She is also proud that in 15 years of direct-to-consumer relationships, there have been fewer than ten returns in person, a strong track record. Similarly, online sales have only produced a handful of returns across the past five years.

DESIGN DEVELOPMENT

Bernice considers herself a "clothing architect", rather than a fashion designer, who combines couture craftsmanship and customisation expertise with a sustainability ethos to problem-solve. Consumer needs, functionality and fit are crucial: for example, almost all DePloy dresses have pockets (unlike many other brands). Normally, a maximum of 25–30 styles per season are designed and tailored directly on the dress stand, with minimal sampling, a figure that was reduced to around 15 styles during the pandemic. About a third of the collection are classic pieces that remain in the range throughout the year and may be updated, meaning customers can always find something to match a previously bought item. Standard "fit models" are never used, rather garments are tried on and wear-tested by different people in the studio. This is to perfect fit for a wide range of clients, so customers will feel good and wear the pieces for a long time. Focus is on natural fabrics and all fabric offcuts are kept and re-used for trims or accessories. Unusually, the small London-based production houses used by DePloy also return all offcuts with finished merchandise for sorting and re-use.

No garments are ever thrown away, and they are not only provided to wealthy people. Of note is DePloy's work with charities, where for example, garments may be provided (anonymously) for trafficked or disadvantaged women who wish to re-enter the workplace. Where pop-up shops are located in cities around the world, and new clients found through local customers and word-of-mouth, there is always a collaboration with a local charity to give 10% revenues from the popup and/ or event generated from that city to its community. This for Bernice is a key part of the closing of the 360° Sustainability circle – "where we reap, we sow".

CHALLENGES

With a deliberate policy of no external investors, DePloy's directors have full autonomy to make their own decisions, an ethos in common with many other small and micro sustainability-focused businesses. Key challenges include scaling up the impact of DePloy's "strategic action plan" and finding ways to collaborate with bigger businesses to share knowledge and tools and thereby encourage change in the wider system. By changing bigger businesses' processes, starting with efficiencies (both economic and within the workforce), the sustainability impact can be greatly increased, cutting overproduction, waste and human resource exploitation. A different challenge for the business lies in finding ways to combine DePloy's craftsmanship and personal service ethos through technology and e-commerce to enable greater exposure and sustainability benefits, whilst maintaining their personal service and relationships with clients. Reaching and interacting with new customers is challenging because DePloy aims to influence how they shop, as well as what they buy, promoting sustainability without preaching to their customers. Bernice says, "I believe you can't actually preach fashion to other people, you can only service them better to make them change".

During the pandemic, when face-to-face personal service was impossible, DePloy created a new distance sales strategy, sending a hand-picked selection of garments to their VIP customers at home, who could schedule a zoom or face-time fitting appointment with the design team, and usually bought 80% of the package, and returned the rest. Importantly, they also spread the word by introducing new customers. There is still much scope for research and investment in technology as an enabler for their e-commerce, but this in Bernice's view will not include virtual try-on systems, as customers place too much importance on feeling the characteristics of the cloth and the garment's drape and fit, particularly around their different life stages – "circular fashion for us is a circular economy of a personal life cycle as well as an environmental life cycle".

FUTURE OF THE INDUSTRY AND ACCELERATING SUSTAINABILITY

Questioned on the key issues facing accelerating sustainability in the fashion industry, Bernice cites the vast overproduction of clothing – up to 100 billion pieces produced annually, and cumulatively, for a global population of under eight billion people. The key challenge is to make less:

> making less doesn't equate to de-growth with less money and less profit, it's being smarter about it and that's again what DePloy is trying to prove – that we can make more with less and we can actually be more efficient and profitable with fewer garments.

She also cites the overproduction inherent in many fashion brands' processes of developing a range, where hundreds of initial design samples can be generated and then eliminated and discarded, calling for better design management. Bernice also believes the education and training of designers and other industry professionals is critical for the industry's future, so current practices can be radically changed: "education would play the biggest role in terms of changing the methodology and practice of the current generation of creative directors and merchandising directors – then that can start to filter through to the design and production teams". Materials development is another major challenge. In Bernice's opinion, progress is ultimately too slow. There are still many questions to be answered on the environmental impact of both natural and synthetic materials as well as their garment care (e.g. dry clean only), and the proportion of certified fabrics available at key trade fairs is still very small. DePloy sources mostly environmentally certified materials, but ultimately aims to use the most durable and high-quality materials that are eventually biodegradable after a very long life.

Despite the shock for many industries due to the pandemic, Bernice does not see this as having positively affected the fashion industry overall, with little impact of accelerating sustainability initiatives, saying: "the impact is still really limited until legislation is actually put in place and enforcement is duly activated, and I see that as the only real way to make a systemic change".

As a person of great conviction, Bernice Pan demonstrates core business values that aim to accelerate sustainability in the fashion sector. DePloy's combination of product-service knowledge and experience puts the company in a good position to grow its influence beyond the mentoring of other start-up fashion businesses currently taking place. Bernice particularly wants fashion business executives to look beyond servicing only shareholders' interest to value other stakeholders in the system and is currently marshalling her ideas into a potential book on new value systems. DePloy's philosophy could soon be more accessible and its influence greatly magnified.

ACKNOWLEDGEMENT

Bernice Pan, Founder and Creative Director of DePloy is thanked for her cooperation in developing this case study.

NOTE

1 B Corp is an internationally recognised certification that requires businesses embody a wide range of sustainability criteria (social and environmental) within their statutes.

12 TOBEFRANK: transparency in practice

Martin Charter

INTRODUCTION

Frankie Hewitson (previously Phillips) began her career as a designer for a fashion supplier in London, working with high street names. In 2014, she moved to Asia to work for the high street chains Jack and Jones, and Next. It was there that Frankie first saw the devastating effects that fast fashion has on the environment and communities. She realised how small changes could be implemented that could massively reduce environmental impacts such as using cold water in the dying process to significantly reduce energy costs.

After seeing the side effects of badly managed fashion production, Frankie became passionate about transparency within fashion and began working with factories and suppliers to ensure that they were more ethically responsible from source to customer. However, as she says,

> My efforts were often rejected by the big brands that I worked for, so I began working on my TOBEFRANK (TBF) concept, creating a unique framework designed to track and improve transparency and the impact that fashion has on the environment, people and communities.

In 2018, Frankie launched TBF as an e-commerce business that promoted a more transparent, environmentally friendly approach to providing clothing while selling at attainable price points. The brand moved from producing jeans and t-shirts made from post-consumer waste to adding casual wear made from organic fibres and coats and

DOI: 10.4324/9781003272878-16

dresses made from reclaimed fabrics. "I wanted to grow our impact, so I also launched The Rubbish Fashion Company (TRFC) in 2020", she explained. TRFC was created to manufacture and supply clothing at the same standard as TBF but also for other brands and retailers.

Frankie found it difficult to balance the profit demands from her shareholders with her uncompromising focus on sustainability and left her two companies to move into consultancy. Both companies were run by Frankie until the beginning of 2022, when she decided to refocus her energy on developing The Frank Impact Company (TFIC). Both TBF and TRFC are still being run by a successful clothing supplier in London. Frankie reflected

> I had a strong management team and shareholders within TOBE-FRANK and The Rubbish Fashion Company, so it felt like the natural evolution was to pass the baton to them and for me to focus on consulting which could potentially lead to a bigger impact.

TFIC was launched in late 2021 as a hybrid consultancy providing manufacturing support based on robust data collection and analysis methods, as well as significant supply chain and innovation experience. TFIC core consultancy services are mapping out supply chains, highlighting 'red flags' and then implementing "hands on" improvement solutions. The consultancy works directly with brands and retailers as a bridge between them and suppliers. TFIC's approach is to first benchmark a company's current situation and then work with them to reduce their impact. "For example", says Frankie,

> If we are focusing on a fabric type and want to reduce polyester, and replace it with tracked viscose, actions cannot just be made by the buying team but need to be discussed with the entire supply chain to reduce any retaliation, unrealistic cost hikes and production delays. Decisions need to be made with supply chain actors as equal partners, for production to run smoothly.

Politics, money and climate are all part of the issues that need to be balanced in the fashion industry. Changing fashion is not just about changing a fabric, because such a change may well have a political link. For example, polyester pellets made from petrochemical production required to manufacture polyester yarn may be ultimately traced back to Russian oil; or viscose made from wood pulp may be derived from unregulated forestry that causes deforestation. Understanding supply

Figure 12.1 Water treatment workers in Chennai, India

chains is central to TFIC's consulting model. Having built relationships with suppliers over the last decade means that there is a better understanding of issues related to any sourcing decisions. TFIC takes account of these complexities when it engages with people in different parts of the supply chains (Figure 12.1). Supply chain actors worldwide are experts in their area, and it is important to ask them about solutions instead of presuming the answers. "Sustainability isn't about perfection, it's a journey, a messy journey. But by working directly with brands we can help them navigate the messiness, help them implement more innovation, be more responsible and therefore be more resilient as a business".

Starting a business is about finding a gap in the market and creating a solution to fill it. But for Frankie, it has also been about doing good and evolving with the market. Frankie highlighted that her most enjoyable experiences in both TBF and TRFC related to problem-solving.

> The most rewarding parts of both businesses were the moments I felt I'd got through to the buyers, the moment the penny dropped, and I wasn't needed anymore. In those moments I really felt like I'd done my job, I'd made a difference.

BACKGROUND

When Frankie had worked as an employee in the fashion industry, she found it difficult to convince leadership teams to reduce environmental and social impacts in overseas supply chains and production. In response to this, Frankie launched TBF in 2010 but decided quickly that the conditions were not right at the time to take the business forward and re-focused on learning. In 2018, TBF was relaunched with the full focus on transparency, workers' rights and fabric responsibility, working in partnership with supply chains primarily in India and Turkey. Being involved in all the sourcing and working closely with textiles and garment factories meant that TBF could achieve full transparency as there was a documented journey of each product produced. This was presented to the customer as visual journeys using photos and videos.

> The first version of TBF was launched in 2010 at London Fashion Week (LFW) with a focus on creating transparent supply chains. I showed at LFW for four years but was repeatedly told by buyers that 'People don't care where their clothing comes from'. I decided that it was the wrong time to expand the concept, so I paused it and focused my energy on learning. I didn't give up on TOBEFRANK as I wanted to prove that fashion didn't have to be evil.

JUMPING OVER HURDLES

On returning to the UK from Asia in 2018, Frankie began to set up TBF again. After initial discussions with various investors, she got a government loan and started to develop her first collection made from other brands' recycled fabric cuttings and metal trim moulds. Frankie's supply chain collected the fabric cuttings – which would normally went to landfill – from other brands' production tables and sent them to a recycling unit to break down the fibres and then re-spin and weave into new fabric. This fabric was used to make t-shirts and then later to make jumpers and dresses. In 2019, one month after TBF launched its first collection, Frankie got her first investor on board. She then continued to expand her supply chain. The brand started with one factory in Chennai, India and three in Istanbul, Turkey. By 2022, the company was working with more than seven factories and eight fabric mills.

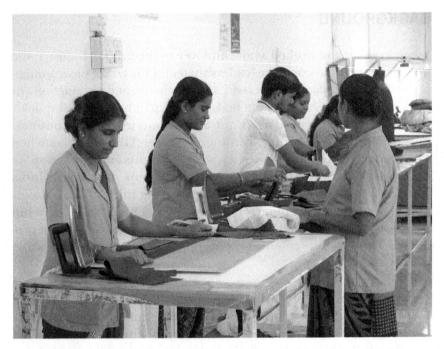

Figure 12.2 Garment workers in Chennai, India

In February 2020, TBF returned to LFW and presented a catwalk show and exhibition with celebrities and industry leaders supporting the brand. TBF collaborated with a luxury designer to produce a fashion show to prove that sustainability could be considered in each market sector of fashion. The collection was traceable right down to its core materials, the factories, mills and cotton farm sources that were used to produce the garments. But as LFW concluded, the COVID-19 pandemic began, and fashion buyers stopped taking any orders for the new season.

The pause gave Frankie and her team time to evaluate what was important to them. She temporarily closed the TBF online shop and worked on adding more educational material to the website. The change made her think of the bigger picture. "Making one fashion brand responsible isn't going to change the world, but by working with other brands, we could have a chance".

During COVID-19, many in the industry had stopped or changed what they were doing and started to think more about the social and environmental impact of fashion (Figure 12.2). Frankie commented,

Before the pandemic we got requests from huge retailers asking for sustainable production support. They wanted to see how we were producing and even wanted us to produce collections for them. This increased during the pandemic, so it made sense to say "yes" to working with them. Sustainability is about collaboration, after all.

A DIFFERENT KIND OF SUPPLIER

As mentioned earlier, Frankie launched TRFC in 2020 to try and make a bigger impact.

TRFC's supply chain was, essentially, an extension of TBF, using the same factories and mills for both operations, with the same team managing the production in Turkey and India. Innovations such as food waste dyes, cold water washing and use of recycled metal trims were offered to TBF customers as well as being offered to other brands. The only difference was that TFRC added commission onto the orders for other retailers to cover the management costs.

As TRFC and TBF shared the same supply chain, from cotton spinning to logistics, it made sense to merge the two companies with TBF becoming a brand of TRFC. "Using only factories and suppliers who were regularly audited, made it possible to build trust with supply chain partners", Frankie says.

Frankie had established a small office based in Istanbul, where most of the garments were produced and this was a vital move in building trust and strong relationships with suppliers. All India and U.K. production was managed through Frankie's London office.

> I had worked for suppliers for most of my career. I can't honestly say it was a goal of mine to run a supplier myself, but financially we needed to evolve to keep going, and using the opportunity to make a big impact was too appealing to say "No". I just needed to make sure it was different and didn't compromise what I believed in.

The supply chains were built with the focus on providing living wages to factory employees. Frankie used the Global Living Wage Coalition (GLWC)[1] published living wage benchmarks created by the Anker Research Institute (ARI)[2] as a guide. The ARI benchmarks are built on a transparent methodology and their data is available free of charge for all suppliers. Living wages are vital to a thriving community and business so it was important that this was incorporated into the factory's financial accounting processes.

The TRFC approach required increased transparency on wages from suppliers coupled with the provision of improved data on environmental performance. By calculating the CO_2 impact from a normal production run, TRFC was able to work on solutions to reduce this by looking at factory locations, energy use and water usage. For example, a normal t-shirt can use 60–200 litres of water in the dying process, but by using a food waste dye innovation that requires no synthetic chemicals and by using cold water, the water usage could be reduced to as little as 2.9 litres per t-shirt and then be reused in the next production. "This may sound like an easy solution but it's more complex than that. It's hard to manage".

The food waste dye innovation was developed by Mehmet Guner, Frankie's Sourcing Director in Turkey, and chemistry experts at the mill. The innovation was a breakthrough in chemical development as it proved that 100% natural dyes could be used in production. The natural dyes were derived from waste from the food industry, e.g. pomegranate seeds, walnut shells and lavender leaves. In the past, marketable natural or vegetable dyes had been mixed with synthetic

Figure 12.3 Fibre recycling unit in Istanbul, Turkey

chemicals to meet industry washing standards which technically could not be classed as "natural". The environmental impact of using natural dyes instead of conventional dyes was significantly lower. For example, by using the natural dye on one TRFC order of 17,000 t-shirts, the water used in the dying process was reduced by three million litres (Figure 12.3).

GREENWASHING IS THE DEVIL

"Greenwashing – aka lying – has been the 'go to' strategy used by too many in the sector", says Frankie. "It is endemic in the industry, but change is being forced by environmentally focused organisations and consumers".

Greenwashing and a lack of good supply chain data are two issues that Frankie has experienced in the sector. Greenwashing relates to false environmental claims but the broader ethical issue behind every environmental claim, e.g. payment of "living wages" is equally important. For example, some brands may be told a fabric is recycled, but with some product prices being so low, it is extremely unlikely that the suppliers are paying people fair wages. Highlighting one sustainability strength but hiding other unethical issues is also greenwashing. Knowing the suppliers' audit history and what to look for on a fabric certificate is the first step to finding out what is true or false. There is a range of misrepresentations being perpetuated by suppliers from the provision of fake "organic cotton" certificates to the use of forced labour in farms during cotton picking season.

> Some brands greenwash unintentionally due to a lack of understanding, but some do it intentionally as a catch-all marketing strategy. Some brands love making a claim, even if they can't back it up, and some knowingly weigh up the financial pros and cons of the risk of wrongly green marketing,

On the client-side, Frankie experienced meetings with retailer's leadership teams who had stated that they would rather pay the fine for false advertising than risk loss of sales without the marketing. Frankie remembers being told by a retailer that "There's no point in changing, because people don't care". However, increased consumer and media pressure is resulting in several retail leaders recognising that increased consumer loyalty can be generated by being open and expecting transparency in their supply chains.

CHALLENGES AND LESSONS LEARNT

Frankie's personal values have meant that she has had to make some tough decisions: being "right for the planet" is not necessarily always financially good for the business. As a businessperson, she found it hard to say "no" to orders, especially when her shareholders were pushing her hard to on profit maximisation. However, in various cases, she decided that it was more important to stick to her values than to take the orders.

> I had to say "no" to some big orders because the people placing them were not doing it for the right reason. Some companies pushed so aggressively on prices and had no interest in the impact it would have on workers' lives. One company gave me such a big order, that it would have changed my life, but they wanted prices which would have resulted in workers being paid below the minimum wage. They even suggested I move production to Bangladesh because the factories were so desperate for orders due to the pandemic, that they would agree to the lower prices. I told them that this was human exploitation and said a loud "no" to their order.

TRFC's main challenge – as a manufacturer working with other brands and retailers – was knowing when and how to compromise when trying to persuade companies to be more sustainable. Because TRFC paid living wages, the company was rarely the most price-competitive option for buyers. Instead, it had to look at other ways to win orders, such as through highlighting its sustainability and innovation competences. However, even when the order had been won, managing the order in the most responsible way was challenging, and compromises sometimes had to be made.

For example, many retailers do not pay for their orders in advance or even pay a small percentage upfront, meaning the factories need to take loans out to cover the costs of the production, and only get paid back when the job is complete. Frankie adds,

> Personally, I think it's wrong that a company in the West expects a supplier on the other side of the world, often in developing countries, to finance its business. But sadly, it's the way it's been done for so many years, it's hard to change such an embedded way of working.

Depending on the lead time, the lack of upfront payment can result in factories not getting paid for over 12 months. In some cases, during COVID-19, orders were cancelled by the retailer, and the factories

Figure 12.4 Models wearing organic cotton, food dyed denim with recycled metal trims, made in Turkey. Photographed by Kyle McGurk

didn't get paid at all, putting them into debt. This is not a sustainable –
or ethical – way of trading as it puts the factories in vulnerable financial
situations which limits their ability to grow, provide a decent working
environment or even pay their workers (Figure 12.4).

> It was important to me that we worked with our factories in a very
> different way, which meant that we shared the burden. If the retail-
> ers placing the order with us refused to pay a deposit, TRFC would
> pay the factory 50% of the costs upfront so factories didn't need to
> take out loans with banks. We got our money back when the retail-
> ers eventually paid.

FUTURE ISSUES

Consumers are now more aware and concerned about issues such as
the need to reduce textile-garment pollution in developing countries.
However, fair wages and working conditions continue to be a major
issue in the sector. For example, printed t-shirts are being exported
from China at about £1 with shipping included, made at less than
minimum wage.

Fast fashion is still a huge problem that needs to be tackled as it is
based on a less-than-minimum-wage culture, low sourcing standards and
lack of accountability. "Fast fashion needs to be regulated, retailers need
to take the liability for the orders they make, and that includes traceability and all the other issues that arise in supply chains", Frankie says.

She had hoped that fast fashion would be reined in by higher costs,
fabric shortages and consumer pressure, but Black Friday events and
low-cost companies continue to support and promote fast fashion.

> These companies lower my hopes. But I do think the retailers are
> changing and will help to reverse fast fashion. Having said that, my
> worry is that a lot of the fast fashion retailers aren't in business for
> the long haul, they're there for a short time to make money quickly,
> to see how much they can make and then move on.

The fast fashion consumer needs to be provided with better fashion
insight and advice to increase awareness and understanding and their
change buyer behaviour.

> However, no matter how much the media reveals the devastat-
> ing facts of fast fashion, some retailers and even consumers are

not listening. Celebrities supporting greenwashed fast fashion brands are now moving centre stage, with retailers influencing consumers to pay for the experience of buying something new endorsed by celebrities, whilst not paying the full environmental and social costs.

Frankie highlighted four key issues that need to be addressed by the fashion and clothing sector:

• Fair wages

Paying living wages instead of minimum wage and understanding local labour laws and rights. Fair wages and working contracts lead to healthier, happier workers and increased product quality. Employers acting in a more environmentally responsible manner often aligns with paying fair wages. During price negotiations with buyers, labour costs are often reduced as it's not a fixed cost like shipping. This is particularly problematic in countries where there is no legal minimum wage. If retailers would treat worker's wages as non-negotiable costs such as energy or logistics, this would change lives.

• Water usage: reduce it and clean it.

"It's a well-known phrase that the next colour trend in fashion is forecasted by the colour of the rivers in China. It is sad but true". Cleaning water is expensive, so, factories which cannot afford to pay the cleaning bill, pour the dirty water into streams and rivers, polluting drinking water, damaging crops and killing wildlife. All supply chains approved by any retailer should have an approved water treatment centre and the retailer should be aware of the process and help with the cost.

• Authenticity of raw materials.

There is a need for thorough checks on the origin of the raw materials, including tracking from source to factory. Most brands don't track where their fabric comes from or what it's made of. For example, not knowing where the cotton staple has come from could result in poor quality short yarn fibre or finding out that forced labour has been used on the cotton farms.

• Managing the "end of life".

Many retailers and even suppliers do not care or monitor a product's life cycle or consider what will happen to that product when its use is over. Retailers who place orders should be liable for the products they sell. "If retailers were fined for each product that used a material damaging the environment such as polyester, you would then see a quick decline in polyester in the market", says Frankie.

ACKNOWLEDGEMENT

Frankie Hewitson, Founder of The Frank Impact Company is thanked for her time in preparation of this case study.

NOTES

1 https://www.globallivingwage.org/about/.
2 https://ankerresearchinstitute.org/.

13 MUD Jeans: denim with circularity

Sandy Black

MUD Jeans is a pioneering denim jeans brand trading for ten years that established its business model from the outset on circular materials principles, aiming to transform the way jeans are made and used. By offering a focused non-seasonal range of products (jeans and jackets), taking back used jeans and encouraging a leasing model of consumption, the business has provided an alternative to fast fashion, with consideration for people and planet at the heart of its operations (Figure 13.1).

BACKGROUND AND MOTIVATION

Bert van Son, founder and CEO of MUD Jeans has worked in the fashion industry for over 30 years, gaining much knowledge and insight into global clothing manufacturing and its complex supply chains, particularly in Asia, but witnessing the negative consequences of fashion on both workers and nature. He was able to reflect on the deteriorating social and environmental practices he observed in the industry with the evolution of fast fashion, cheaper and cheaper clothing and production moving around different countries in the so-called "race to the bottom".

Bert was strongly motivated to create change from within the industry and resolved to set up a fully sustainable business. He selected the denim jeans market, as one of the largest volume businesses in clothing (citing two billion pairs of jeans sold in 2017), but also one of the most polluting areas of fashion, in its conventional manufacturing practices. So, MUD Jeans was born in 2012, self-funded by von Son himself for its first four years, thereby giving him full control over his products and processes. MUD Jeans was set up with the ethos of implementing a circular economy model from the start "aiming to be as close to perfect

DOI: 10.4324/9781003272878-17

Figure 13.1 MUD Jeans in stretch fabric. Courtesy MUD Jeans

as possible in every step". MUD Jeans' mission is "for the fashion industry to be driven by circular production and conscious consumption". The operating principles of the business include paying fair wages to garment workers, using sustainable materials such as certified organic cotton and importantly post-consumer recycled denim, developing non-toxic processes in manufacturing and finishing, plus innovating a leasing model as an alternative to purchasing in order to encourage sufficiency.

APPROACH AND BUSINESS MODEL, PRODUCT AND PROCESSES

MUD Jeans became a leader in sustainable denim by "doing jeans differently" based on circularity and transparency, and a focus on one main product that is fashionable, featuring a small range of styles that remains mostly constant – a truly slow fashion model. Bert says:

> What was most exceptional was we wanted to be responsible for both what we make and for the raw materials, and we would like to take the jeans back – so that's where we really brought something totally new into the garment industry.

Several innovations, particularly in materials, have created this leading position. Since 2013, MUD Jeans' business model has allowed customers to either buy outright, or lease their jeans for a year via a monthly payment (totalling the equivalent to the full price), at which point the jeans can be (1) returned (with an incentive of €10 or a month lease discount on a new pair); (2) swapped for a new pair to lease; or (3) kept. The company collects used jeans (by mail or in retail outlets) in order to either repair and resell as vintage, or mechanically shred them to make new denim fibre and yarn, which is combined with new organic cotton and woven into recycled denim material – a truly circular process. All MUD Jeans are made from a combination of certified organic cotton and recycled denim, in one of two main formulations: the first being 40% recycled denim, and 60% organic cotton, and the second 23% recycled denim, 75% organic cotton and 2% elastane, giving a stretch fabric. A third type of fabric combines 69% organic cotton with 31% Tencel®.[1] MUD Jeans also accepts old jeans from other brands, if they have a minimum of 96% cotton, thereby contributing to an increase in the overall circularity of denim. For a production volume that has now reached close on 100,000 pairs of jeans a year, the company's supply chain is remarkably short, based on only five main partners, from the raw cotton to the finished product and distribution. The recycled denim fibre is produced by Recover, spun by Ferre and their denim fabric manufactured by Tejidos Royo, all in Spain; the jeans are manufactured by Yousstex International in Tunisia and shipped to Marseilles for distribution. These partner businesses share the same circular and sustainability ambitions and seek to minimise environmental impact at all stages. For example, Bert cites three key areas for MUD Jeans:

1. Their manufacturing process uses 94% less water than conventionally made jeans, including the growing of the organic (rain fed) cotton in Turkey and India.
2. Their innovative indigo dyeing process uses foam instead of large amounts of water.
3. The denim surface finishes are achieved not through harsh chemicals (chlorine) or sand blasting, but by ozone and laser treatment processes (Figure 13.2).

Similar gains are claimed in their 2021 Life Cycle Assessment report on carbon footprint: 75% less CO_2 is produced per pair of jeans, and MUD Jeans is overall carbon positive as a company, due to its carbon offsetting strategies. Their jeans also incorporate recyclable components, such as 100% steel buttons and rivets and water-based printed labels (Figure 13.3).

Figure 13.2 MUD Jeans in different washes, creating a range of shades. Courtesy MUD Jeans

Figure 13.3 Printed labels. Courtesy MUD Jeans

In keeping with the principle of transparency, MUD Jeans publishes all the data behind these figures and their processes. To achieve this, the business has appointed a Corporate Social Responsibility Officer who produces an annual life cycle assessment report with EcoChain and an annual sustainability report, both available from the company website.

The management team consists of four people, plus eight more direct employees, so is categorised as a small business. With the help of some external finance (for example, from the North Netherlands Province), in the ten years MUD Jeans has traded, the business has grown fairly fast (increasing its turnover from €1.1 million in 2019 to its current €4 million) and sells through 300 stores in 30 countries as well as directly from its website. Direct sales now account for 50% of that turnover, partly because of the COVID-19 pandemic which stimulated a doubling of visits to the MUD Jeans website, where people stayed longer, resulting in increased sales. MUD Jeans customers are what Bert calls

> conscious explorers – the people that want to find out the thoughts behind the brand instead of only the beautiful pictures. Little by little people are more and more interested to see the story behind the brands ... it gives us faith and belief to continue.

The company strives to keep costs as low as possible to maintain a relatively affordable retail price for its jeans, with strategies such as minimal marketing spend, agile production and low stock levels.

ACHIEVEMENTS AND CHALLENGES

Bert van Son is justly proud of some of his company's achievements, particularly being the first in the Netherlands to gain B Corp accreditation[2] (requiring the company statutes to embody a wide range of sustainability criteria), and then being awarded the Best for the World environmental score – out of 4200 other B Corp-certified businesses worldwide. MUD Jeans also holds several other certifications including Cradle to Cradle for indigo dye, Organic Content Standard, Oekotex 100 and Global Recycling Standard for fabric. An increasing number of jeans has been collected and recycled each year, with a figure of 11,500 for 2021 and 39,000 in total since 2016.

MUD Jeans initially utilised 20% recycled denim content in their jeans, and then fully achieved 40%; however, in the spirit of constant improvement the goal of using 100% recycled fibre has long been a target. Although this internal challenge – termed the "Road to 100" – presents complex problems, and involves new processes including both chemical and mechanical recycling, it has now been achieved at prototype stage. Working in collaboration with Saxion, a Dutch university, jeans made from 100% post-consumer recycled denim content have been developed and are being analysed for strength and durability, and the process of securing intellectual property rights is underway. Successful production with the Road to 100 projects would seal MUD Jeans' unique and pioneering position in the circular denim sector.

MUD Jeans is always open to ideas, and several collaborative projects have been undertaken. Based on his successful reputation, Bert was approached by furniture giant IKEA in 2019 to help them produce a circular denim cover for one of their popular sofas, manufactured in Europe, and the resulting product became a best seller despite a much higher price point. MUD Jeans has contributed to awareness-raising projects such as donating 800 pairs of used jeans to the artist Billie Achilleos who, in partnership with the Waterbear platform,[3] created a denim sculpture of the mythical Loch Ness monster, installed in London's Grosvenor Square for the duration of the 2021 COP26 climate conference in Scotland. More significantly, MUD Jeans is partnering with Justdiggit,[4] an African climate action organisation that digs "bunds" – holes that trap rainwater – to regenerate and "re-green" the soil with plants. For every pair of jeans returned to the company, MUD Jeans donates the money needed to regenerate one tree.

One challenge the company has overcome relates to retail stores, where customers would go and try on jeans and then buy or lease online from MUD Jeans to the detriment of the store sales. A new business model was recently set up bringing stores into the leasing programme, by supplying what Bert calls a "fit kit". The stores can offer customers the full range of available choices and then get a commission if the customer leases jeans, rather than purchasing, at the same time reducing the stock that stores must hold as leasing gains traction.

However, competition in the circularity space from the large brands such as G-Star or Levi's has recently grown, so MUD Jeans needs to invest in marketing to maintain their leading position and get their message out to more people in a succinct manner, as there is much to communicate, and it becomes harder for MUD Jeans to stand out.

FUTURE OF THE INDUSTRY AND ACCELERATING SUSTAINABILITY

MUD Jeans has pushed boundaries by challenging consumers' need to possess garments and demonstrates a different way of consuming by leasing jeans, offering repair services, re-selling used leased jeans and ultimately recycling used jeans into new jeans. Although they recognise they are in the fashion business, the company does not produce fashion collections every six months, instead focusing on selling affordable products with a 100% sustainable sourcing and production strategy, so each pair of jeans is "made by happy people" and worn for a long time.

As far as the fashion industry is concerned, there are still many issues to be resolved in terms of legislation. Bert von Son believes the current laws do not fit circularity. For example, in MUD Jeans' case, there should be a 40% discount on the VAT levied on each pair of jeans, as this tax has already been paid once in the previous life of the recycled fabric. Such legislation would create key incentives for utilising waste and upcycling materials. He identifies issues requiring new legislation including:

- levelling the playing field between those who are actively managing change towards circularity and those who are not
- providing incentives to businesses for operating sustainable practices
- tackling greenwashing by legislating to make unfounded sustainability claims more difficult, with clear penalties
- implementing clear eco-labelling for clothing, like the rating systems in the electronics industry, a task requiring much work.

Developing such legal infrastructure would impact the shift to more circular materials economy and influence consumer behaviour towards more sustainable consumption through accurate marketing and sourcing information.

Bert von Son says, "we work on slow fashion and hope that that a lot less fashion will be bought one day."

ACKNOWLEDGEMENT

Bert van Son, Founder, MUD Jeans International bv is thanked for his cooperation in the preparation of this case study.

NOTES

1 Tencel is the brand name for a regenerated cellulosic fibre, lyocell, made by Lenzing, Austria, in a virtually closed loop viscose process, using non-toxic solvents.
2 B Corp = Benefit Corporation – global certification using business as a force for good.
3 https://waterbear.com a video platform for climate action awareness.
4 https://justdiggit.org/what-we-do/landscape-restoration/fmnr-kisiki-hai/.

14 SXD: working with climate refugees

Martin Charter

INTRODUCTION

Ahmed Fardin began his journey into sustainability in the fashion industry in 2018–2019 through his MPhil in Engineering for Sustainable Development at the University of Cambridge, where his research focused on quantifying carbon emissions from manufacturing in the sector. His field work in Bangladesh led him to an unforeseen opportunity to set up a pilot project producing upcycled denim jackets made by climate-displaced women.[1] In 2021, Ahmed merged his project activities into Shelly Xu Design (SXD)[2] – a zero-waste fashion women's wear brand based in the US, where he became the Manufacturing and Operations Lead. The upcycled jacket design is now marketed online by SXD and Iceland-based Katla[3] amongst others.

BACKGROUND

In 2019, Ahmed visited Bangladesh to complete field research for his MPhil thesis. As part of the research, he visited clothing factories in Chittagong, Bangladesh, and saw first-hand, the huge amount of waste being produced in the industry.

> One factory would be making perhaps a million pieces of denim jacket per annum. Every piece of offcut would be standardised in similar size and shapes, and a lot of materials such as denim, would be discarded as unwanted offcuts.

Ahmed also identified that a few workers in the garment factories were climate change victims. Many had lost their homes in the delta regions

DOI: 10.4324/9781003272878-18

of southern Bangladesh due to floods and rising sea levels and were forced to migrate to large cities like Chittagong to make a living.

Research had identified that there was a lack of manufacturing waste recycling in Bangladesh clothing sector.

> My research had indicated that less than 5% of waste material in factories in Bangladesh was being recycled or upcycled (Fardin, 2019). That was a shock, but in some respects but not a surprise, because it has been "normal practice" for a long time to totally discard offcuts.

After completing his degree, Ahmed returned to Bangladesh for a holiday in early 2020. But soon after, Covid struck, and he was unable to get back to the UK. But this provided him with the time and opportunity to work further on the ideas and insights he developed in his thesis.

While back in Bangladesh during Covid, Ahmed saw a potential opportunity to produce upcycled clothing using the offcuts from the production of the denim jackets. He discussed the idea with friend Tahmid Kamal Chowdhury, Chairperson, Youth World Foundation and a director at Frank Group of Companies (a large manufacturer based in Chittagong producing denim clothing for large brands like Tommy Hilfiger and American Eagle). The Circular Cradle project was then born and started in a small room at the Frank Group with four climate refugees employed part time. As neither Ahmed nor Tahmid were designers,

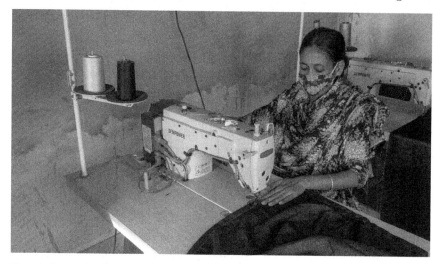

Figure 14.1 Kulsum, one of the climate refugee employees, working on the very first jacket in the small room at Frank Group factory

they used Google/Pinterest to learn about creating upcycled products. The workers then started producing samples of different types and designs of jackets from the offcut denim waste.

SOCIAL NETWORKING

As part of test marketing, in late 2020, Ahmed shared the designs and story of the upcycled jackets made by climate refugees with his social network and this began to gain traction with a range of interested people. He worked with a small network of people he knew from Cambridge, his family and a group of friends in Bangladesh to get the project moving and to acquire orders. He used email marketing, LinkedIn and WhatsApp to connect with his network, receiving very positive reactions to the concept of upcycled garments made by climate change refugees. "People were very, very receptive of the concept of a sustainable fashion initiative that had social impact by helping to support climate refugees".

As a result of the social media activity, Shelly Xu – founder of Shelly Xu Design in the US – expressed interest in the garments and that she wanted to collaborate. Shelly Xu had started her zero-waste fashion design brand in 2019, selling via her website to the luxury end of the market. Shelly wanted to manufacture her zero-waste jackets designs in Circular Cradle's sustainable manufacturing facility Ahmed had built. Shelly's fashion industry experience aligned with Ahmed's sustainable manufacturing know-how, provided an excellent platform for collaboration.

CHALLENGES FROM DESIGN TO SAMPLE TO BULK

Once they received interest from Shelly to collaborate, Ahmed and Tahmid knew that they had to produce the garments in bulk. However, they quickly identified a lack of supply of standardised waste materials from the Frank Group factory. The factory did not have enough waste of a specific fabric type to make bulk products. Neighbouring factories were approached to supply the waste offcuts, but they already had contracts with local brokers who sold these offcuts as fuel in local brick kilns. These brokers had set up a syndicate to control the offcut waste market and would not negotiate any contracts. Accessing the waste offcuts became a major issue. They solved that logistical problem eventually by forming formal partnerships through contracts with neighbouring factories so that they had their pick of wastes before the local brokers.

Next came the technical challenges. Even if the waste came from the same type (and colour) of fabric, it may have slightly different shades of the same colour depending on their production. The difference in shade is absent in a traditionally made garment where every component of the garment comes from the same "batch" of the fabric. But in an upcycled garment, the different components may come from any number of different batches and hence the may shades clash. This problem was solved in two ways: (1) they treated the garment through special washes to remove the shade difference; (2) they acknowledged this to be a feature of the upcycled product instead of a problem, which made the products look more authentic.

Another technical challenge had to do with the alignment of the fabric grain. If all the pieces of the offcuts in a particular garment did not align in one direction, the garment would not stretch similarly in all directions, making it uncomfortable to wear. In addition, washing might cause different pieces to shrink ununiformly, ruining the look of the garment. This issue was solved by carefully planning the alignment of the fabric during the manufacturing process.

> We learned that it was easy to make one sample from waste, but to make hundreds or even thousands is a challenge. A lesson learned is that it's relatively easy to scale up if you're not working with waste material. But if you're working sustainably, with waste materials, sourcing the right kind of waste takes time. That needs time and attention to sort through and get it right, increasing costs significantly.

SUSTAINABLE PRICING

"A denim jacket for a big high-street retail brand costs about US$10 to make in a large 'sweat shop' factory", Ahmed added. "In Bangladesh not every factory pays a fair wage. We pay our climate refugees a fair wage – three times the mean wage of a regular garment worker".

However, the upcycled jacket made by workers paid the 'fair wages' costs about US$60 per item to just manufacture. This cost also reflects the significant supply chain distortion, and the social and technical challenges that need to be overcome to manufacture these upcycled products.

Although SXD operates on the expensive luxury end of the market, Shelley and Ahmed's collaboration led to a mid-level pricing of US$150 for the upcycled jacket with the aim of targeting a larger market.

Figure 14.2 The SXD "Climate Refugees Reverse Climate Change" jacket on models

> We decided that if the retail price was too low, the garment would be treated as just another throwaway item, and the company would also not be able to cover its costs. Therefore, we decided on a mid-range price. As customers equate quality with higher prices and tend to hold on to a garment for longer which is more sustainable in the long term.

Though this was their first project together, they were able to break even with the margins of that middle-level pricing once all the other associated costs were factored in. The first batch of the product was sold out via pre-orders.

CLIMATE REFUGEES EMPLOYED IN THE MANUFACTURING

Ahmed highlighted the importance of regular stable orders.

> It was a difficult time in the early days of the project, because we needed to generate orders for the project to move from a pilot to a business that became financially sustainable. If we weren't manufacturing 1000 to 5000 pieces in every order, the business would cease

to exist and then we could not continue to support and employ the climate refugees. That was a huge pressure.

The partnership with SXD delivered more regular orders and the Circular Cradle facility started to grow. In 2021, Circular Cradle was merged into SXD after collaborating on a few projects and Ahmed now manages manufacturing and supply chain of the upcycled garments under the SXD brand. Given how well they worked together, it was the natural outcome of the collaboration. Ahmed described the merger as "a marriage of complementary strengths, Shelly Xu's in design, and mine in manufacturing and the supply chain". SXD has now completely shifted its manufacturing to Bangladesh.

At any one time, the SXD manufacturing facility (previously Circular Cradle) has now moved to a larger room in a factory within the Frank Group in Chittagong and is employing around 20–40 part-time climate refugees, almost exclusively female. Tahmid is managing the manufacturing on the ground in Bangladesh and Ahmed is co-ordinating the supply chain and quality assurance, quality control and sample production.

The workers can switch to working on other clothing projects, for other retailers in the neighbouring larger factory (Frank Group) if the order numbers drop. This way, climate change refugees continue to be employed and earning money for themselves and their families.

> When I hear from the climate refugee employees that even the small amount of extra money they have earned has made a difference to their lives e.g. it allows them to send their children to school (instead of sending them to someone's house as help) and enables them to assist ageing relatives in their retirement, it makes me very proud of what we are doing.

Bangladesh with a vision can empower the climate-displaced women in Bangladesh.

CUSTOMERS AND STAKEHOLDERS

A big push is coming from the market for sustainability. SXD is potentially over-delivering compared with other brands, by using (a) innovative zero-waste design; (b) sustainable materials; (c) sustainable manufacturing processes; and (d) providing fair wages.

Demand for upcycled sustainable clothes is increasing. This is good for business, but it creates problem in terms of scaling. As indicated above, the right kind of waste is not always available and securing a supply chain with the right kind of waste is sometimes impossible. Logistically there are a series of issues that need to be tackled that include: how much waste is to be collected; where to collect it from; and how much production capacity is needed; or what volume of extra waste materials for contingency is required. "But it's a good problem to have, because it means there is lot of demand in the pipeline and we can continue to support our climate refugee employees."

Sustainability challenges in the sector are a 'Wicked Problem'.

> For example, one major challenge is not to deceive people and say it's easy to produce garments from waste offcuts. However, many companies are indeed doing this – deceiving people. They're greenwashing. Transparency is a huge issue, resulting in the customer being unaware of the fact that what they are buying is not what they think it is. The ultimate challenge is to stay true to yourself as a business and to the customers you are serving.

Ahmed explained:

> What we did and are still doing is to help break the cycle of burning offcuts for fuel or dumping them in landfill. Some of the discarded offcuts are downcycled for filling mattresses. It is not the best use of the fabric, but it is still better than burning them.

CIRCULAR ECONOMY

To help eliminate fashion manufacturing waste, a zero-waste algorithm is now being developed based on the learning from the MPhil research and this is now being aligned with the SXD design methodology. The algorithm aims to be able to create zero-waste designs with minimal human input. SXD has recently raised US$1.2 million in an oversubscribed pre-seed round of funding to develop the artificial intelligence (AI)-based algorithm.[4]

Creating resilience in an upcycled product design is a key issue for SXD, because it means that garments don't have to be returned for repair. It means that every part of the garment should be durable and resistant to tearing of the seams. SXD decided that return for repair didn't make sense from a carbon footprint point of view. Extending

Figure 14.3 A zero-waste laptop sleeve made by SXD for Harvard Innovation Labs

product lifecycle through repair would involve significant transport emissions of garments returned from Western markets to Bangladesh.

In the future, the SXD upcycled jackets may be designed for modularity, to enable customers to complete self-repair. This will eliminate the carbon footprint associated with sending the entire garment item back and forth for repair. "Established clothing companies aren't thinking about such modularity in design and manufacturing at all, making it another differentiator for niche upcycling brands like SXD", says Ahmed.

LESSONS LEARNT AND ISSUES TO BE TACKLED

When the pandemic started, there were a huge number of cancelled orders. That left a lot of factories in Bangladesh without any money. A lot of people had to be laid off. Those people were already living 'pay cheque to pay cheque', with nowhere to go for work. The pandemic showed that brands should take more responsibility in terms of caring for the people who make their clothes. Brands were cancelling orders without any thought for these people. On the other hand, other factories that had received orders re-opened too early, with thousands of people working in crowded and cramped spaces in unpleasant and unsafe conditions.

On the positive side, consumers in the West have become margin-
ally more aware of the negative effect brands can have on the workers. There was a huge backlash by the consumer, saying that "hey,
you're cancelling orders which means people will die from not having food on the table".

SUMMARY

This case study has illustrated that there are a number of key issues that
still need to be addressed by the sector including:

* Working conditions and fair pay
    Tackling working conditions and fair pay in factories in the gar-
    ment supply chain
* Quantity in the market
    There is too much overproduction: people need to buy fewer
    clothes to help reduce waste, emissions and over-use of natural, hu-
    man and other resources
* Circular design
    Design with circularity in mind: products should be designed and
    made to deliver zero waste e.g. through increased durability: at pres-
    ent, up to 20% of the fabric is wasted (Fardin, 2019) – ending up in
    landfill or being burned

ACKNOWLEDGEMENT

Ahmed Fardin, Manufacturing and Operations Lead at SXD is thanked
for his time in the preparation of this case study.

NOTES

1 https://www.shellyxu.design/sxd-x-climate-refugees/.
2 https://www.shellyxu.design/.
3 https://katla.com/collections/sxd.
4 https://www.hbs.edu/environment/blog/post/climate-stories-Xu.

REFERENCE

Fardin A. A. H (2019). Single Material Analysis of Garment Factories, Master of Phi-
    losophy thesis, Centre for Sustainable Development, Department of Engineering,
    University of Cambridge (August 2019)

Part V

Consumers, culture and ecosystems

15 Clothing 2050: garment scenarios to drive circular material systems

Rebecca Earley

INTRODUCTION

This chapter looks ahead – using a framework of circular materials – through the eyes of consumers, at a range of garments and how they might be created, purchased, used, recirculated, recreated and regenerated. Designers working with creative futures thinking can contribute to ideas that lead to scalable ventures if their thinking is underpinned by systemic material knowledge and they make decisions in collaboration with users and other experts.

This chapter offers visions – 'garment scenarios' – for clothing that could be circular, lower in impact and ethically produced whilst meeting everyday needs of different, imagined households. These visions show how circular fashion textiles innovations can enable new ways to enjoy clothing. These may flow within material systems and be supplied via new business models. Recycled polyester, regenerated cellulose and compostable non-wovens are the materials systems used in the scenarios.

In Part 2 of the chapter, the context of the climate emergency, environmental and socio-economic concerns are highlighted, along with the material groups used for the scenarios, which challenge our understanding of current biological and technical cycles. In Part 3, the range of design research and practice methods used for prototyping with these materials is presented; specific materials and prototypes resulted from three large international consortia projects are discussed. Part 4 presents the scenarios for three different households, demonstrating

DOI: 10.4324/9781003272878-20

how framing user needs with circular material systems can provide inspiration for new design challenges.

SOCIO-ECONOMIC CIRCULAR MATERIALS FOR FASHION

Whilst much more is now known about the environmental and social pros and cons for all kinds of materials (Roos, Okcabol & Rex 2019; Textile Exchange 2020; WRAP 2021; Ellen MacArthur Foundation 2017), better understanding and use of emerging circular (recyclable) options, each with environmental and socio-economic impacts, remains under-developed. The UN's Sustainable Development Goals[1] provide a set of targets both material and clothing stakeholders can aim for. It is, however, necessary to prioritise investment in materials and clothing that can build new industry infrastructures and innovation approaches, whilst contributing throughout the supply chain to the wellbeing of people, animals, planet, climate and culture. In a circular economy, materials and products are "designed in such a way that they can be reused, remanufactured, recycled or recovered and thus maintained in the economy for as long as possible" (UNEP 2019).

Whilst biological and technical material cycles thinking gave designers more clarity around the natural and synthetic monomaterial options available to them, the fashion/textile field continues to make 'monstrous hybrids' (blends, e.g. cotton mixed with polyester). There are also materials that cross between the biological and technical cycles through processing; for example, milk can become acrylic fibre[2] and natural resources such as food waste can be synthesised into fibre. These need to be treated as technical materials rather than biological ones: what starts as natural can become synthetic. Some naturals may be able to compost safely – but are the nutrients reclaimed of value? After virgin materials have been processed, their value may well lie in their ability to be cyclically regenerated time and time again (Goldsworthy 2021).

It is also paramount to think carefully about future feedstocks to ensure fibres such as cotton grown on land contributes towards regenerative agriculture and does not take away from future food production capacity. As fossil fuels for transportation and energy use get phased-out, reuse of existing polyester and use of bio-based polyester will become necessary. In a recent report by Biofabricate and Fashion for Good (2020), bio cellulose and bio polyesters – whilst coming from natural resources – are shown as new sub-categories within the man-made materials sphere. Mapping and classifying emerging materials enables the understanding of how they might be best used. This information and transparency is important as confusion and greenwashing persists, often generated by marketing departments of brands/retailers who seek to sell manmade materials as 'naturals' to consumers, by and large ill-equipped with the necessary knowledge to decipher and identify differences in fibres, materials and sources.

RESEARCH PROJECTS AND PROTOTYPES

Approach

Emergent material systems cannot be created by any single stakeholder and require exploration through ambitious partnerships. The projects and prototypes in this chapter have used a range of methods, which all centre on collaborative practice-research approaches, including design-driven material innovation[3] (DDMI) (Tubito *et al.* 2018). Novel materials, exhibition and production prototypes represent the key outcomes from these efforts, which are derived from workshop models, design tools and reports.

The TEN[4] – a set of design strategies developed in the Textiles Environment Design group (a forerunner of CCD) in 2010 – were evolved in 2020 into a new framework for training designers in circular design. This approach maintains the range of values established in sustainable design but guides stakeholders towards how to build materials and products into future circular flows, allowing not just product longevity, but for a multitude of 'circular speeds', in recognition of the wideranging patterns and habits of clothing use that different people have (Earley 2017; Goldsworthy & Politowicz 2019).

Whilst both sustainable design and circular design approaches require collaborative efforts around lifecycle frameworks to enable diverse stakeholder engagement, they differ because circular design demands that the material be regenerated into new resources. (In other words, a product can be sustainable, with careful consideration given to all its lifecycle stages, but may not necessarily be able to be circular as well.) Workshops and discussions with users, producers, policy makers, designers, engineers and others generated holistic insights for future design briefs. All participants were physically placed around a lifecycle worksheet. Participation in science and industry panels and discussions helped to build a broader knowledge around new material fields and future user behaviour, which could be modelled into future design and engineering propositions (Earley 2020).

The fictional users in the scenarios have been created by projecting forward 30 years by reading forecasts about 2050 and aligning the demographic to Generations X and Z[5] and Generation Alpha (McCrindle 2018). This was achieved by a combination of reflecting on primary research from the three projects described in the next part of this chapter and being informed by the future-focused writings of Jonathan Porritt (2013) and Figueres and Rivett-Carnac (2021).

Design strategy and lifecycle speeds in the Mistra Future Fashion Programme

The Mistra Future Fashion[6] Programme began in 2011 and was co-ordinated by Research Institutes of Sweden. In the first phase a training programme using The TEN was created for designers at H&M's head office in Stockholm. The process led the New Development team through product redesign tasks, taking best-selling products and finding ways those products could be improved, scoring them before and after using the Higg Index[7] (Earley et al. 2016). In 2014, back in London, materials and prototypes were made by the CCD researchers in order to understand more about some of the ideas around product lifecycles conceived during the training.[8] How materials and fashion products of different life spans could be designed to move at different speeds was explored. In the second phase of the research (2015–2019),[9] material scientists were paired with lifecycle assessment experts and design researchers in order to produce and evaluate circular fashion prototypes that were both ultrafast (Paper Leather Jacket, Figure 15.3, right) and super-slow (Service Shirt, Figure 15.1, left). Through a residency with Filippa K, a luxury fashion label, a recyclable rPET raincoat (Eternal trench, Figure 15.3, left) and a disposable (domestically compostable) 'paper' dress was made by the designers at the brand (Throwaway Dress, Figure 15.1, right).

Figure 15.1 Service Shirt (left) by Rebecca Earley (2018) Photo by Jelly Luise for UAL; Zero° Shirt (middle) (Trash-2-Cash project 2018) Photo by Cathryn Hall for UAL; Throwaway Dress (right) by Filippa K (2018) Photo by Frida Vega Salomonsson

Prototyping with waste cotton and polyester in the Trash-2-Cash Project

The aim of the Trash-2-Cash project[10] was to develop a DDMI within the context of circular textiles (Tubito *et al.* 2018). Working with 17 partners across ten countries, the partners took waste textiles (hospital bed sheets, other service industry products and polyester clothing) at the end of their useful lives and made new materials with added functionality. The final six prototypes highlighted the opportunities of using chemical regeneration processes to create waterproofing, wicking (ReAct Mid-layer, Figure 15.3, middle) and alternatives to polyester fleece for kid's wear (ReBorn ReWorn, Figure 15.2, middle). In one of the prototypes, blue cotton bedding from hospitals was used to make a pale blue shirt in lyocell,[11] designed with a zero-waste pattern and a business model that included an overprinting service, where dyestuff would be printed on top of used products (Zero Shirt, Figure 15.1, middle).

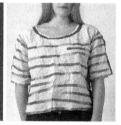

Figure 15.2 'Sports Coat' (left) Parkour Parka by Rebecca Earley and Truman Hickey (2019) Photo by the author; 'Baby Jacket' (middle) (ReBorn ReWorn Jacket from the Trash-2-Cash project 2018) Photo by REIMA; 'Kids Costume' (right) Paper Tee by Kay Politowicz (2012) Photo by Aaron Tilley for UAL

Figure 15.3 Eternal Trench (left) by Filippa K (2018) Photo by Frida Vega Salomonsson; ReAct Mid-layer (middle) (from the Trash-2-Cash project 2018) Photo by REIMA; Paper Leather Jacket (right) by Kay Politowicz (2018) Photo by Jelly Luise for UAL

Developing scenario concepts for bio-based materials in the Herewear Project

The Herewear Project[12] started in 2020 and uses agricultural waste (seaweed, manure, straw) to make new biomaterials for localised, extended-life circular clothing contexts. The research facilitated the understanding of how new bio-based garments can be produced in microfactories to work in using loops via service models: rented, shared, swapped, repaired, reused, re-purposed, upcycled and recycled. Material Portraits[13] were created by mapping bio-based materials, tracing their routes through harvesting, to processing, to use applications and to end-of-life options.[14] This last aspect of the project has informed the garment scenarios below.

GARMENT SCENARIOS

The projects above have all contributed to an understanding around sustainable and circular design approaches, new materials and flows, low-impact production and finishing for textiles, the design, cut and construction of clothing, and the potential for new business models.

The garment scenarios below were created to align to three different household types. A summary of the key attributes of each garment scenario is presented in Table 15.1, framed by the material systems. Each garment scenario has been developed by thinking about how the garments were:

- Created – what are the clothes made from? How were they made?
- Purchased – how were the clothes acquired?
- Used – how are the clothes worn, used, cared for and stored?
- Recirculated – how are the clothes reused?
- Recreated – how are the clothes made into new products?
- Regenerated – how are the materials in the clothes made into new materials?

Generation A: young entrepreneurs and professionals

In this house, two couples split the rent and have developed multiple ways to share resources and keep their environmental impacts as low as possible. Co-habitation has become a desirable way to live after the 2020 pandemic; places where small communities could rely on each other within larger frameworks.

Table 15.1 Generational Profiles, Regenerative Material Systems and Garment Scenarios

Generational Profiles/ Regenerative Material System	Recycled Polyester	Regenerated Cellulose	Tencel & PLA/ Non-Woven
Generation Alpha: Entrepreneurs & Professionals			
Born early 2010s to late 2020s In 2050, they will be 21–39 years of age	**Service Shirt** • Made from rPET • Extended by overprinting and remanufacture • Recycled into interiors	**Zero° Shirt** • Lyocell shirt made from blue cotton waste • Extended by overprinting • Recycled into viscose process	**Throwaway Dress** • Made from Tencel and dyed with waste vegetables from restaurants • Recycled into domestic compost
Generation Z: Future Family			
Born 1997–2012 In 2050, they will be 38–53 years of age	**Sports Coat** • Made from rPET • Extended by repair, reuse, customisation • Recycled into public transport interiors	**Baby Jacket** • Made from red cotton waste • Extended by repair and reuse • Recycled into viscose process	**Kids Costume** • Made from PLA and decorated with compost safe marker pens • Recycled into domestic compost
Generation X: Retired Roamers			
Born early 1965 to late 1980 In 2050, they will be 70–85 years of age	**Eternal Trench** • Made from rPET • Extended by repair and reuse • Recycled into material for brand's supply chain	**React Mid-Layer** • Made from cotton waste • Extended by repair • Recycled into viscose process	**Paper Leather Jacket** • Made from paper and PLA and dyed with walnut • Extended by repair • Recycled into industrial compost

The Service Shirt (Figure 15.1, left) is made from rPET, and is designed to be over-printed by a small brand in the town. Two people in the house share the shirt and enjoy being able to plan its next look. Through the prints they choose, they can make it more formal, or more casual, depending on their needs. They know it will ultimately end up being remade into textile jewellery by local crafts people, long after its useful life. Eventually, it will be regenerated into materials for train interiors. For them, it makes sense to reuse the immense amounts of polyester that earlier generations refined from fossil fuels.

One person in the house has a Zero Shirt (Figure 15.1, middle). It's their go-to garment for work. They like that it's been robustly made from waste cotton garments, and the soft lyocell makes it comfortable against the skin. They do repairs themselves, but if too busy, they use a local tailoring service. After the shirt finally becomes unwearable – stained, snagged, pilled – it goes to a local digital microfactory where it can be overprinted or recreated and then recirculated in a number of ways. The owner has the shirt as part of a subscription service, so a fresh one is delivered as the old one is collected.

The fourth person in the house has a very active social life. They like to go out a lot, and they often like to experiment with their look. Rather than have a fixed set of clothes, this user owns fewer things, but also borrows, rents and swaps on a monthly basis. Occasionally, when they want to try a very new look out, they buy paper-like garments, like the Throwaway Dress (Figure 15.1, right), which they can wear a few times and then bury in the garden. The act of exploring a new aspect of themselves, having new experiences, and then letting go is something they find beneficial to their sense of identity and mental health.

Generation Z: future family

Future families, like those today, have needs that change rapidly and tight financial budgets. They are interested in products and systems that give them variety; they understand and enjoy being part of a series of services and systems that ensure needs are catered to.

In 2050, recycled polyester is still in use – its lightweight yet durable properties mean that it stands the test of time in clothes that get used a lot. The Sports Coat (Figure 15.2, left) is a unisex jacket that was used for sporting events in its first-use phase. When dirty and stained, the jacket was overprinted at home by the kids, using an iron and a bespoke pattern. How the industry uses polyester really changed in the years leading up to 2050. After decades of being the cheapest fibre, taxation and regulations ensured that it became used for performance and high-end clothes. Low-cost polar fleece, common in kids clothing, was replaced by soft, brushed finish regenerated cellulosic materials.

The Baby Jacket (Figure 15.2, middle) was made from used cotton from hotel and hospital bedding. Kids clothes are still swapped and exchanged; a host of new services are available to parents to get a return on purchased clothes or replacement pieces in bigger sizes and different colours.

As ever more diverse cultural moments are celebrated as part of daily life, the paper-like blank costume – Kids Costume (Figure 15.2, right) – can be used, reused, adapted, drawn on and even taped up, to create hundreds of playful and celebratory looks to last a brief moment in a lifetime.

Generation X: retired roamers

In this house, three people – the Retired Roamers – are co-habiting. In their mid-70s, these singletons have found new ways to grow old together. They are fashion philanthropists and travellers – picking up rental clothes from train station boutiques and booking Airbnb apartments complete with wardrobes made available to them. They are interested in spending their time and money well and looking after themselves, and each other.

The Eternal Trench (Figure 15.3, left) is made from vat-dyed rPET pellets. One of the Roamers invested in this classic piece 30 years ago. Over time it has been repaired by the brand, and re-waterproofed by the owner at home, using an organic spray. It is now ready for recycling – the resulting pellets will be used to make high-end wallcoverings. The owner will trade the coat in for points, which they can use for international train travel.

Another Roamer is still very fit, and spends hours cycling. The Peloton creates domestic energy and cycling outside is easy and safe because of the widescale investment in cycleways that transformed cities 20 years ago. The ReAct Mid-layer (Figure 15.3, middle) is made from regenerated cellulose – in this case using local agricultural waste (straw) – which has been used to create fibres that have natural sweat-wicking properties physically engineered-in at the extrusion stage. Thousands of small brands across Europe make such clothing using a network of digital microfactories; local waste is used to make local fibres and clothing, using local businesses – made economically efficient by software that links all the stakeholders across the circular supply chain.

The Paper Leather Jacket (Figure 15.3, right) is a purchase from a company that uses paper and textile waste to make lightweight but strong non-woven materials for short-life fashion. These garments are sold across European cities in vending machines; these garments replaced much of the impulse buying that was so common with fast fashion in the first part of the 21st century. These garments can be worn several times, never washed and then composted at home or in designated places in public parks.

CONCLUSION

Making low-impact long-life circular clothes that don't get worn because they are unattractive, undesirable or impractical is a waste of an immense level of resources. It is vital that we design for future needs, anticipating ways to offer clothing that enables and supports a diversity of lifestyles.

The key takeaways for the stakeholders involved in the ideas presented through the garment scenarios in this chapter are:

- Offering clothing with different lifecycle speeds can enable us to reduce the impact from waste, overproduction and overconsumption, by creating garments that better suit user needs and diverse, ever-changing lifestyles.
- Existing polyester can be recycled into products that don't need to be put in a washing machine (and add to microfibre fibrillation impacts), interior products and hard surfaces for public transport, for example.
- Regenerated cellulose processes can provide an opportunity to use end-of-life cotton, pre-industrial waste and agricultural waste for engineered fibres.
- Compostable non-wovens may provide solutions for short-life clothing that are currently overlooked in the industry.
- New business models can support the sharing economy for clothing, offering mending and alterations, making, swapping, renting and subscriptions, etc., in physical and digital formats.

This chapter brings together the work of many researchers, in order to propose, through creating scenarios, how circular fashion textile systems can work together or in parallel, offering future users a variety of clothing options. It draws together different user needs, materials, technologies and economic contexts, exemplifying that circular design is deeply collaborative; it is about connecting up activities so that circles and loops are able to scale-up more easily. As we seek to change current extractive and exploitative industry practices, design researchers can bring divers stakeholders together to explore new ideas in order to create proposals for imagined futures. These can serve as inspiration and as proposals for further inter- and trans-disciplinary exploration.

ACKNOWLEDGEMENTS

Thank you to: colleagues at CCD, in particular Laetitia Forst, Rosie Horn-buckle, Kay Politowicz and Kate Goldsworthy; industry and academic partners on projects including Mistra Future Fashion, Trash-2-Cash and Herewear. The Trash-2-Cash and Herewear projects received funding from the European Union's Horizon 2020 research and innovation programme, under grant agreement Nos.646226 and 101000632 respectively.

NOTES

1 https://sdgs.un.org/goals.
2 Casein / Milk fibre, https://ecoworldonline.com/what-is-milk-fiber-yarn/.
3 The DDMI methodology won an EU Innovation Radar award in 2019.
4 The TEN, https://www.circulardesign.org.uk/research/ten./
5 Categories for generations, https://www.beresfordresearch.com/age-range-by-generation/.
6 Mistra Future Fashion Programme website, http://mistrafuturefashion.com/.
7 Higg Index, https://apparelcoalition.org/the-higg-index/.
8 Textile Toolbox, http://www.textiletoolbox.com/.
9 Project report, http://mistrafuturefashion.com/wp-content/uploads/2019/10/K.-Goldsworthy-Circular-Design-Speeds-project.-mistra-future-fashion.pdf.
10 Trash-2-Cash project, https://www.trash2cashproject.eu/.
11 Lyocell is a semi-synthetic fabric; a processed cellulosic fibre often made from wood pulp.
12 Herewear project, https://herewear.eu/.
13 Material Portraits, https://herewear.eu/category/material-portrait/.
14 For details of what end of life material processes are currently available, see https://creacycle.de/en/the-process.html.

REFERENCES

Biofabricate and Fashion for Good (2020). *Understanding 'Bio' Material Innovations: A Primer for the Fashion Industry.* Online at https://www.biofabricate.co/resources.
Earley, R., Politowicz, K., Goldsworthy, K., Vuletich, C., & Ribul, M. (2016). *The Textile Toolbox: New Design Thinking, Materials and Processes for Sustainable Fashion Textiles. Mistra Future Fashion Project Report.* MISTRA: Sweden. [Online] Available at: http://textiletoolbox.com/research-writing/mistra-textile-toolbox-report-20112015/.

Earley, R. (2017). Designing Fast & Slow: Exploring Fashion Textile Lifecycle Speeds with Industry Designers. *The Design Journal*, vol. 20, Design for Next, pp. 2645–S2656.

Earley, R. (2020). Circular Fashion 2070: Clothing and Textile Cycles, Systems and Services. *The Bridge*. Washington USA: National Academy of Engineering, pp. 44–47. [online] URL: https://www.nae.edu/244832/The-Bridge-50th-Anniversary-Issue.

Ellen MacArthur Foundation (2017). *A New Textiles Economy: Redesigning Fashion Future*. [Online] Available at: https://www.ellenmacarthurfoundation.org/assets/downloads/A-New-Textiles-Economy_Full-Report_Updated_1-12-17.pdf.

Figueres, C., & Rivett-Carnac, T. (2021). *The Future We Choose*. London: Manilla Press.

Goldsworthy, K. (2021). *Material Ages*. Commissioned Article for Viewpoint Magazine, Issue 09; Spirit of Nature, Metropolitan Publishing, London, pp. 140–147. Available online from https://ualresearchonline.arts.ac.uk/id/eprint/16458/.

Goldsworthy, G., & Politowicz, K. (2019). Fast-Forward: Proposals for a Light and Restorative Fashion Alternative. Futurescan 4: Valuing Practice, Post-Conference Proceedings. Bolton University.

McCrindle, M. (2018). *The ABC of XYZ: Understanding the Global Generations*. McCrindle Research. ISBN: 978 0 9924839 0 6.

Porritt, J. (2013). *The World We Made: Alex McKay's Story from 2050*. London: Phaidon.

Roos, S., Okcabol, S., & Rex, D. (2019). *Fibre Bible Part 1: Possible Sustainable Fibers on the Market and their Technical Properties, Mistra Future Fashion Report*. [Online] Available at: http://mistrafuturefashion.com/wp-content/uploads/2019/03/Roos-D2.1.1.1-Fiber-Bible-Part-1_Mistra-Future-Fashion-2019.02-1.pdf.

Textile Exchange (2020). *Preferred Fiber & Materials Market Report 2020*. [Online] Available at: https://textileexchange.org/wp-content/uploads/2020/06/Textile-Exchange_Preferred-Fiber-Material-Market-Report_2020.pdf.

Tubito, C., Earley, R., Ellams, D., Goldsworthy, K., Hornbuckle, R., Niinimaki, K., Ostmark, E., Sarbach, V., & Tanttu, M. (2018). *Applied DDMI: A White Paper on How Design-Driven Material Innovation Methodology Was Applied in the Trash-2-Cash Project*. Project Report, Trash-2-Cash. Stockholm: Research Institutes of Sweden.

United Nations Environment Programme (2019). *Emissions Gap Report 2019*. UNEP: Nairobi. Available at: https://wedocs.unep.org/bitstream/handle/20.500.11822/30797/EGR2019.pdf?sequence=1&isAllowed=y.

WRAP (2021). *Textiles 2030 Circularity Pathway: Transforming our Industry for the Planet*. [Online] Available at: https://wrap.org.uk/sites/default/files/2021-04/Textiles%202030%20Circularity%20Pathway.pdf. 2021.

16 Shifting the needle: can we build the next generation of consumer activism and advocacy for sustainable fashion?

Oliver Bealby-Wright and Helena Leurent

The process of recovery is not a simple one. We cannot be satisfied merely with makeshift arrangements which will tide us over the present emergencies. We must devise plans that will not merely alleviate the ills of today, but will prevent, as far as it is humanly possible to do so, their recurrence in the future.

Frances Perkins, National Radio Address, February 25, 1935
(Perkins, 1935)

One of the human stories in the early days of consumer advocacy tells of Frances Perkins. Frances was first inspired while at Mount Holyoke college with a speech given by Florence Kelley, consumer activist and the founder of the National League of Consumers. By 1911, Frances became Executive Secretary of the Consumers League of New York, advocating in particular for improved food safety and labour conditions. On March 25th of that year, Frances personally witnessed the Triangle Shirtwaist tragedy, in which 146 garment workers as young as 14 lost their lives from fire, smoke inhalation, or falling or jumping to their deaths. In the subsequent effort to reform working conditions, galvanised by labour pioneers, safety advocates, community leaders, and ordinary workers, Frances was asked to head the new Committee on Public Safety for New York City. Within a few years, the city and state adopted what were, at the time, the United States' most comprehensive labour rules and

DOI: 10.4324/9781003272878-21

public-safety codes. Two decades later, Frances was appointed Secretary of Labour, becoming one of the architects of Roosevelt's New Deal, the series of programmes established during the Great Depression that aimed to restore prosperity to Americans. She later called March 25, 1911 the day the New Deal began (The Economist, 2011).

Now, more than a century on, with a fashion industry immeasurably larger and spanning the globe, and with social and environmental tragedies on a scale those early advocates could not imagine, is there scope for a new wave of consumer activism and leadership to change the modern apparel system for the better?

CHANGING ATTITUDES AND BEHAVIOURS

In 2022, consumers across the globe are increasingly concerned about the climate crisis. In a recent survey spanning 17 countries, more than 60% of respondents considered climate change to be a "very serious" problem (GlobeScan, 2021). Consumers also increasingly recognise the fashion industry as a source of environmental and social harm. A 2018 survey across five cities revealed that a majority of consumers, and particularly younger shoppers, supported the concept of sustainable fashion (KPMG, 2019). The pandemic has not slowed this trend: a McKinsey & Co. study in 2020 found that in the UK and Germany, 65% of consumers are planning to purchase more durable fashion items and 71% are planning to keep items for longer in response to the COVID-19 crisis. Changing consumer sentiment is also reflected in the emergence and success of grassroots campaigns. Most recently, the 'PayUp' campaign has seen consumers demand that companies 'Pay Up' the wages owed to garment workers, and provide transparency in response to key questions, such as: "Who made my clothes?", "Who made my fabric?" and "What's in my clothes?"[1]

Though recognition of the problem and desire for change may be growing, consumer behaviours are trailing. Even for the most concerned consumers, the gap between intention and action remains high – and may even be widening. This is not because consumers are lying – or 'Thunberging' (the growing phenomenon of dating profiles which advertise environmental concern) – when they say they want to live more sustainably (Strong et al., 2021, p.11). Rather, they face real and consistent barriers which prevent them from acting on their good intentions, such as a lack of information or necessary infrastructure. Individual and collective consumer actions, such as purchasing more sustainably produced items, responsible wear and care, or end-of-life actions like swapping, upcycling, and reselling, hold huge potential to accelerate sustainable fashion (Danish Fashion Institute and BSR, 2012, p.4). But nothing short of a fundamentally redesigned system, in which the sustainable behaviour is made the easy one, is needed to unlock these shifts.

CONSUMER RIGHTS FOR SUSTAINABLE FASHION

The purpose of modern consumer associations everywhere is to represent people's intrinsic needs in the marketplace and help re-shape systems around consumer protection and empowerment. As of 2022, Consumers International members – all independent consumer advocacy organisations – exist in 100 countries around the world. They are well recognised and trusted in their own countries, with close alliances with other not-for-profits, academics, and national standards bodies. They are also regularly granted legal standing in courts and engage in policymaking and standards-setting processes (UNCTAD, 2020). With direct connections to consumers through different channels, including complaints-handling systems, these organisations grasp the multiple pressures consumers face, on issues of food, finance, energy, mobility, and more. Significantly, sustainable consumption has become a core strategic issue for all such organisations: 94% of consumer advocacy organisations say that environmental sustainability is now of key importance to their organisation, and most have updated their organisational strategy to reflect this (Consumers International, 2021a).

The global consumer movement was pivotal in the adoption of the United Nations Guidelines for Consumer Protection in 1985, which list 11 legitimate consumer needs for all sectors and marketplaces (UNCTAD, 2016). Consumer advocates consider these needs to be essential rights.

Consumer rights are increasingly useful as a basis for a vision of a sustainable fashion industry. Let's take just two. 'Protection from hazards to health and safety' is a recurring concern for fashion consumers. Consumers increasingly – and rightly – connect the personal benefits of safe and quality clothing with the societal and environmental benefits of responsible production (GlobeScan, 2019, p.7). Consumer organisations reflect this sentiment by carrying out testing for chemicals in clothing products and measuring the extent of microplastic shedding.[2] They also put pressure on businesses and governments for systemic solutions, such as the mandatory requirement of filters in washing machines and

Figure 16.1 The 11 legitimate consumer needs
Source: Consumers International

wastewater treatment plants, robust and harmonised chemical management standards, improved chemicals traceability and disclosure, and the introduction of taxes or bans restricting the use of hazardous chemicals.[3] These interventions have the potential to create a fashion marketplace that is safer both for people and for planet.

Equally important is the consumer right to be informed. A lack of clear and reliable information on the impacts of their choices is a consistent barrier to consumers shopping more sustainably (Deloitte, 2021). The number of clothes and accessories described as "sustainable" quadrupled among online retailers in the US and UK from 2016 to 2020 (Indvik, 2020). And yet a sweep of randomly selected websites found that 40% of green claims could be misleading (Competition and Markets Authority, 2021). Consumer advocates are calling for governments to introduce and effectively enforce guidelines on "greenwashing", and to adopt new regulatory models such as pre-approval schemes for green claims to guarantee credibility (Gautier, 2021).

Consumer advocates directly facilitate, collaborate over, and advocate for the provision of a range of easy to understand and reliable informational tools for consumers. These include third-party verified product labels, digital traceability and transparency tools, accessible educational resources, transparent brand-level disclosures, and trustworthy sustainability marketing.[4] In fashion, this means ensuring that industry standards for measuring and disclosing product-level environmental and social impacts, such as the Sustainable Apparel Coalition's Higg Index or the Responsible Business Coalition's Impact Index, have scientific backing and incorporate third-party verification systems. Consumer advocates participate directly in standards development to help ensure that consumer priorities are not forgotten; that use-phase impacts (such as water and energy consumption during laundering)[5] and product durability and repairability are featured appropriately; and that standards cover the full product lifecycle, to prevent misleading cherry-picking.[6]

CONSUMER ADVOCACY CASE STUDIES IN FASHION

The global consumer advocate's toolkit holds a range of interventions to drive consumer behaviour changes and actively re-shape the marketplace. These include:

- Awareness campaigns at regional, national, and global levels[7]
- Providing consumer information through multiple channels and as a result of reliable product testing[8]
- Undertaking research into consumer attitudes and systemic barriers[9]
- Influencing policy and standards for the consumer interest[10]
- Pursuing class and collective action lawsuits in reaction to marketplace malpractice[11]
- Actively reconfiguring value chains through collective buying and switching schemes.[12]

The following examples, all drawn from members of Consumers International, show how consumer advocates today are approaching sustainable fashion, and where there is potential for replication and scale-up.

Case study 1: Danish consumer council
Tackling clothing waste through circular solutions is on the top of the agenda for many consumer advocates, and for good reason: the most sustainable resources are always those already in use.[13] The Danish Consumer Council's campaign demonstrates the potential of the consumer advocacy toolkit to unlock pathways that combine consumer, government, business, and civil society-led transformation. First, the Council leveraged its grassroots membership in a campaign for consumer behaviour

change. The Council provided instructions and advice for clothing repair and correct care, loaning, swapping, donating, buying second-hand, and buying 'less but better' (Gonzales, 2020). Counter-acting consumer misunderstandings about which behaviour changes are most impactful (Ipsos, 2021), the Council's pyramid of priority actions for consumers is now featured in stores across Denmark (Forbrugerrådet Tænk, 2020a). As well as encouraging consumers to take more responsibility, the Council's campaign has sought to make consumers more aware of their rights: consumers who are aware of two-year legal warranties, for example, are more likely to contact retailers if a garment develops a fault (Carlsen, 2022).

The second pressure point addressed by the campaign was the reputations of apparel companies. Research commissioned by the Council found that on average in the period 2018–2020, 677 tonnes of new clothes were destroyed a year by the Danish private sector (including retailers, supermarkets, department stores, warehouses) – equivalent to three million t-shirts every year (Petersen and Ebbesen, 2020). The Council channelled deep public concern towards corporate actors – nine out of ten Danish consumers surveyed did not think it was fair for new, unsold clothes to be burned – and since 2020, the Council has secured a public commitment from over 170 companies to stop destroying new clothes (Damkjær, 2022).

Ultimately, to put an end to bad practices, governments must act to remove perverse incentives which make donation more expensive for companies than incineration. The Danish Consumer Council are leading a broad alliance of civil society voices calling for the creation of a National Action Plan on clothing waste (Forbrugerrådet Tænk, 2020b). Plans include policy interventions based on consumer rights principles. For example, Extended Producer Responsibility legislation, which makes companies financially or directly liable for the collection, sorting, and recycling of textiles waste, can help to realise the 'polluter pays' principle in the fashion industry.

Case study 2: Verbraucherzentrale Bundesverband (vzvb), Germany

In 2013, the collapse of the Rana Plaza garment factory just outside Dhaka caused the death of 1,100 workers, with many more facing lifelong, debilitating injuries (FCO & DFID, 2014). Verbraucherzentrale Bundesverband (vzvb), the national umbrella organisation for German consumer associations, felt compelled to push for more comprehensive standardisation and regulation of textile supply chains. vzvb began from the principle that it is not in the hands of individual consumers to change production conditions, but that change begins with companies taking responsibility for their supply chains.

One of the main barriers to sustainability for consumers is the tangle of sustainability standards used by fashion brands. In addition to drawing consumer attention to the most reliable ecolabels, consumer advocates often participate directly in their development. In their surveys of German consumers, vzvb uncovered a disconnect between consumer expectations and the true coverage of the government's Green Button standard for sustainable fashion. Consumers, for example, assumed that the standard covered all aspects of the supply chain (including material and fibre use, spinning and weaving) and involved the payment of living wages to workers (vzvb, 2021b). vzvb successfully argued from the consumer rights perspective that the standard needed to be expanded to avoid giving a misleading impression.

Consumer attitudes also drove vzvb's successful campaign to introduce a national Supply Chain Due Diligence Act, which was passed in 2021 and is due to come into force in 2023. Eighty six percent of consumers surveyed by vzvb said that textile companies should be liable for human rights violations in their supply chains, while 84% felt textile companies should be obliged to avoid environmental damage in overseas production (vzvb, 2021a). These findings underscored vzvb's advocacy for a stronger Act that would cover the entire supply chain (and not just direct suppliers), apply to all textiles companies (not just the largest), and include an obligation to avoid environmental risks. In this case, consumer rights principles, together with labour rights, created the basis for a holistic supply chain campaign. "When lobbying German politicians to legislate on global supply chain issues", explains vzvb's sustainable consumption spokesperson Kathrin Krause, "I had the sad feeling that consumer advocacy has an advantage. If the German consumer is an object to protect, rather than only the garment worker in India, there is greater chance of action".

Case study 3: Citizen Consumer and Civic Action Group (CAG), India

The Citizen Consumer and Civic Action Group (CAG) is a powerful champion for sustainable consumption in Tamil Nadu, India. Since 2019, CAG's behaviour change campaigns have confronted the linked problems of hyper-consumption and mounting clothing waste in urban areas, while also addressing gender empowerment and poverty reduction.

CAG shone a spotlight on two desirable consumer behaviours: swapping used clothes and upcycling textile waste. The team targeted younger, urban consumers through 'sharing groups' in secondary colleges. Competitions helped reduce the social stigma around second-hand clothes and challenged over 400 consumers to reuse old clothes creatively. Women from low-income communities were trained in how to turn textile waste into products such as bags, purses, and doormats, and equipped with the skills and tools to supplement their livelihoods through the sale of upcycled products. During the pandemic, CAG continued this programme virtually with a step-by-step video, which reached over 1,000 consumers.

Although relatively small in scale, CAG's campaign demonstrates one of the key strengths of consumer advocacy campaigns: using local knowledge to achieve impact. It also demonstrates the potential for this impact to be global in its reach. While CAG is a regional membership organisation which mobilises local networks and partners with local civil society, the project was supported by a global fund (administered by Consumers International) and part of an annual global campaign on sustainable consumption, Green Action Week (Consumers International, 2021b). Similar textiles upcycling and clothes sharing campaigns were simultaneously initiated elsewhere in Tamil Nadu by the Consumers Association of India, in Rajasthan by the Consumer Unity & Trust Society, and in Gujarat by the Consumer Education and Research Society. Together these campaigns prefigure an alternative mode of consumption in fashion.

EMERGING OPPORTUNITIES

New opportunities for consumer advocacy are opening up. There are a myriad of ways in which the global consumer advocacy' toolkit can be better harnessed to accelerate sustainable fashion. With their internal testing capacity and reputation for trustworthy advice, consumer advocates are in an ideal position to call time on false solutions. Next-generation fibres and new applications, such as nanotechnology and GMOs, should be thoroughly investigated to ensure they deliver the projected environmental benefits and pose no hazards to human health (Peachman, 2019). Consumer advocates champion responsible innovation, not innovation at all costs.

The urgent need to shift to a more circular apparel system has led to widespread demands for new business models which decouple revenue streams from resource use (Ellen McArthur Foundation, 2021). According to Bain & Company's 2021 luxury growth report, by 2030, a high-end fashion brand could be generating 20% of its revenues from resale, increasing per-product revenue by 65% (D'Arpizio et al., 2021). There is significant potential for consumer advocates to work with innovators to help scale pilots into sustainable business models. A circular future – whether shaped by resale, rental, repair, remaking, or other models – will involve industry actors engaging consumers in entirely new and unfamiliar ways. Consumer advocates can bring deeper, evidenced understanding of consumer priorities and motivations required to guarantee sustained participation. They can also become a watchdog, ensuring that consumer protections are developed in tandem. The Consumers Association of Singapore's actions over recent years in protecting consumers against unfair commercial practices of online subscription-based fashion retailers, suggests that non-traditional models will bring their own consumer protection challenges, especially since existing consumer protections are focused on new sales (Competition and Consumer Commission Singapore, 2020).

NEXT-GENERATION CONSUMER ADVOCACY

We started this chapter with an example of how one consumer advocate's actions at the start of the 20th century not only shaped the local market, but rippled out and down the ages. The story of Frances Perkins, the National and New York Consumer Leagues, and the multiple organisations fighting for social justice at the turn of the century, tells of how like-minded individuals, networks, and organisations can create systemic change. The role of consumer advocacy in that tale was just one thread in the larger pattern – but a significant one.

The apparel industry has globalised in orders of magnitude much greater than in the time of Perkins, and our emerging understanding of systemic issues now encompasses a host of environmental and social justice issues. We are at a point in history where new marketplace models, deeper stakeholder responsibilities, and different forms of agile governance are essential if we are to reach our collective sustainable development goals by the end of this decade.

Consumer advocacy has an important role to play – though different to the consumer leagues and unions of the past. Consumer advocates must continue to work to their proven strengths: helping to voice consumer concerns about our marketplace, building visibility and transparency around issues, and creating long-term pressure for better standards and regulation. But we must also find new ways to shift the needle, whether through using technological tools to inform consumers and track the market, innovating to support different models of sustainable consumption and production, or building unusual partnerships for impact at speed. Perhaps a global, connected, innovative, and mobilised consumer advocacy movement can help build the new 'deal' we need for a safe, fair, and sustainable marketplace for the future.

NOTES

1 See the Pay Up and Fashion Revolution campaigns.
2 The CLEAN project, carried out by consumer organisations in Italy, Spain, Belgium, and Portugal, found that that fibre shredding from clothing is the main source of microplastics in wastewater as a consequence of washing cycles.
3 For example, Sweden introduced a tax in 2022 on clothing and footwear that contain chemicals designated "Substances of Very High Concern" under REACH.
4 Leading examples of fashion communicators and marketers pushing more sustainable consumption cultures include the Great Fashion for Climate Action campaign, aimed at using fashion innovation to "encourage the world to 'see things differently'", Purpose Disruptors' Good Life 2030 campaign, an effort by advertising professionals to shift perceptions of what 'a good life' looks like away from material growth, and Canopy's Circular Chic campaign, which provides messaging around the brands prioritising next-gen solutions.
5 Research suggests that energy and water consumption during the laundering process varies greatly depending on fibre content of the garments (Laitala et al., 2018).
6 Such as Cradle To Cradle's Certified Product Standard (Cernansky, 2021).
7 Between 2015 and 2019, for example, six consumer advocacy organisations in India significantly increased awareness of sustainable products in six low-income communities through interventions from puppet shows to community and school consumer rights groups.
8 Consumer Reports in the US and Which? in the UK have recently introduced green choice designations into their product testing and recommendations, for example for washing machines. UFC-Que Choisir in France has developed a free app "QuelProduit" that allows consumers to check the ingredients of over 200,000 food, household, and cosmetics products.
9 In 2021, for example, a group of nine consumer advocates across the world carried out coordinated research into the true recyclability of plastic packaging (Consumers International, 2021c).
10 Consumers International members proposed, worked on, and even drafted the first version of an international standard on improving the delivery of energy services to consumers. The standard was approved by ISO in August 2016 – the first time that a standard proposed by an NGO has become an ISO international standard.
11 In 2020, German consumer group Verbraucherzentrale Bundesverband (vzbv), representing more than 400,000 consumers, reached an out-of-court settlement to compensate people affected by the 2015 Dieselgate emissions scandal.
12 Centro para la Defensa del Consumidor in El Salvador launched an online service "Consumer Lo Que Produzco" linking local consumers to farmers with sustainable agriculture practices. Multiple consumer associations in Europe such

as Consumentenbond in the Netherlands, Altroconsumo in Italy and Zveza Potrošnikov Sloveije in Slovenia have managed collective consumer switching campaigns for better energy prices.
13 The Renewal Workshop (2021) suggests that brands can reduce carbon emissions by 51.5% on average by renewing an existing product instead of producing a new one.

BIBLIOGRAPHY

Carlsen, M.V.S. (2022) *Warranty: Here are Your Rights*, Forbrugerrådet Tænk, Available at: https://taenk.dk/raadgivning/reklamationsret-og-garanti/reklamations-ret-her-er-dine-rettigheder (accessed 31 January 2022)
Cernansky, R. (2021) *Can an End-To-End Sustainability Standard Change Fashion?*, Vogue Business, Available at: https://www.voguebusiness.com/sustainability/can-an-end-to-end-sustainability-standard-change-fashion (accessed 17 January 2022)
Competition and Consumer Commission Singapore (2020) *E-Commerce Retailer Fashion Interactive Ordered to Cease Unfair Trade Practices and Stop Using "Subscription Traps"*, 17 January 2022, Available at: https://www.cccs.gov.sg/media-and-consultation/newsroom/media-releases/fashion-interactive-court-order-17-jan-2020 (accessed 20 January 2022)
Competition and Markets Authority (2021) *Global Sweep Finds 40% of Firms' Green Claims could be Misleading*, Available at: https://www.gov.uk/government/news/global-sweep-finds-40-of-firms-green-claims-could-be-misleading (accessed 17 January 2022)
Consumers International (2021a) *Global COP26 Membership Survey*, [unpublished].
Consumers International (2021b) *Green Action Fund*, Available at: https://www.consumersinternational.org/what-we-do/sustainable-consumption/green-action-fund/ (accessed 31 January 2022)
Consumers International (2021c) *The Consumer Lens on Packaging 2021*, Available at: https://www.consumersinternational.org/media/368767/packaging-research-project-040521.pdf (accessed 17 January 2022)
Damkjær, J. (2022) *Clothing waste: These Brands Don't Burn Clothes*, Forbrugerrådet Tænk, Available at: https://taenk.dk/aktiviteter-og-kampagner/toejspild-toejet-laenge-leve/toejspild-disse-maerker-braender-ikke-toej-af (accessed 17 January 2022)
Danish Fashion Institute and BSR (2012) *The NICE Consumer Framework for Achieving Sustainable Fashion Consumption Through Collaboration*, Available at: https://www.bsr.org/en/our-insights/report-view/nice-consumer-framework-for-achieving-sustainable-fashion-consumption (accessed 17 January 2022)
D'Arpizio, C. et al. (2021) *LuxCo 2030: A Vision of Sustainable Luxury*, Bain & Company, Available at: https://www.bain.com/insights/luxco-2030-a-vision-of-sustainable-luxury/ (accessed 17 January 2022)
Deloitte (2021) *Shifting Sands: Are Consumers Still Embracing Sustainability?*, Available at: https://www2.deloitte.com/uk/en/pages/consumer-business/articles/sustainable-consumer.html (accessed 17 January 2022)
Depop and Bain & Company (2020) *Futureproof: How Gen Z's Empathy, Awareness and Fluidity are Changing Business as Usual*, Available at: https://depopxbainreport.depop.com/empathy-and-awareness (accessed 17 January 2022)

Ellen MacArthur Foundation (2021) *Circular Business Models: Redefining Growth For A Thriving Fashion, Industry*, Available at: https://ellenmacarthurfoundation.org/fashion-business-models/overview (accessed 17 January 2022)

Forbrugerrådet Tænk (2020a) *Avoid Clothing Waste: Download the Consumer Council's Waste Pyramid*, Available at: https://taenk.dk/aktiviteter-og-kampagner/toejspild-toejet-laenge-leve/download-toejspildspyramide (accessed 17 January 2022)

Forbrugerrådet Tænk (2020b) *Stop Wasting Clothes*, Available at: https://taenk.dk/aktiviteter-og-kampagner/toejspild-toejet-laenge-leve (accessed 17 January 2022)

Foreign & Commonwealth Office (FCO) and Department for International Development (DFID) (2014) *Case Study: The Rana Plaza disaster*, 10 April 2014, Available at: https://www.gov.uk/government/case-studies/the-rana-plaza-disaster (accessed 13 March 2022)

Gautier, P. (2021) *Getting Rid of Green Washing: Restoring Consumer Confidence in Green Claims*, Bureau Européen des Unions de Consommateurs (BEUC), Available at: https://www.beuc.eu/publications/beuc-x-2020-116_getting_rid_of_green_washing.pdf (accessed 17 January 2022)

GlobeScan (2019) *Empowering Consumers Through Transparency: Report on Global Consumer Research*, Available at: https://3ng5l43rkkzc34ep72kj9as1-wpengine.netdna-ssl.com/wp-content/uploads/2021/04/GlobeScan-SAC-Research-Report-Empowering-Consumers-Through-Transparency-1.pdf (accessed 17 January 2022)

GlobeScan (2021) *BBC-GlobeScan Poll on Climate Change*, Available at: https://3ng5l43rkkzc34ep72kj9as1-wpengine.netdna-ssl.com/wp-content/uploads/2021/10/2021BBC_GlobeScan_Climate_Polling_Oct21_Press-release.pdf (accessed 17 January 2022)

Gonzales, L. (2020) *Clothes: How to Achieve More Sustainable Consumption*, Available at: https://taenk.dk/test-og-forbrugerliv/ferie-og-fritid/toejspild/toej-baeredygtigt-forbrug (accessed 17 January 2022)

Indvik, L. (2020) *Sustainable Fashion? There's no Such Thing*, Financial Times, Available at: https://www.ft.com/content/d174e7d7-97c4-43fc-8765-95075e5fcce7 (accessed 17 January 2022)

Ipsos (2021) *Perils of Perception 2021*, Available at: https://www.ipsos.com/sites/default/files/ct/news/documents/2021-04/Environmental%20Perils%20of%20Perception%202021_0.pdf (accessed 17 January 2022)

KPMG (2019) *Sustainable Fashion: A Survey on Global Perspectives*, Available at: https://assets.kpmg/content/dam/kpmg/cn/pdf/en/2019/01/sustainable-fashion.pdf (accessed 31 January 2022)

Laitala, K. et al. (2018) 'Does Use Matter? Comparison of Environmental Impacts of Clothing Based on Fiber Type', *Sustainability*, 10(7), doi:10.3390/su10072524

McKinsey and Co. (2020) *Survey: Consumer Sentiment on Sustainability in Fashion*, Available at: https://www.mckinsey.com/industries/retail/our-insights/survey-consumer-sentiment-on-sustainability-in-fashion (accessed 17 January 2022)

Peachman, R.R. (2019) *Meat Gets a Makeover*, Consumer Reports, Available at: https://www.consumerreports.org/nutrition-healthy-eating/meat-gets-a-makeover/ (accessed 17 January 2022)

Perkins, F. (1948) '*Social Insurance for U.S*', Social Security Administration, 25 February 1935, Available at: https://www.ssa.gov/history/perkinsradio.html (accessed 17 January 2022)

Petersen, C. and Ebbesen, E.R. (2020) *New Clothes in the Waste: Prepared for the Consumer Council,* Available at: https://dokumentation.taenk.dk/sites/default/files/rapport_om_nyt_toej_i_affald_2020_forbrugerraadet_taenk_econet.pdf (accessed 31 January 2022)

Strong, C. et al. (2021) *Addressing the Sustainability Say-Do-Gap: Leading the Way To Activate Consumer Behaviour Change,* Ipsos, Available at: https://www.ipsos.com/sites/default/files/ct/publication/documents/2021-07/Ipsos-Views_Addressing-the-Sustainability-Say-Do-Gap.pdf (accessed 13 March 2022)

The Economist (2011) *The Birth of the New Deal: A Blaze that Galvanised the Labour Movement,* 29 March 2011, Available at: https://www.economist.com/united-states/2011/03/17/the-birth-of-the-new-deal (accessed 15 March 2022)

The Renewal Workshop (2021) *Leading Circular 2021: The Climate Crisis, Carbon and Circular,* Available at: https://renewalworkshop.com/pages/leadingcircular (accessed 17 January 2022)

UNCTAD (2016) *United Nations Guidelines for Consumer Protection,* Available at: https://unctad.org/system/files/official-document/ditccplpmisc2016d1_en.pdf (accessed 13 March 2022)

UNCTAD (2020) *Report on Consumer Associations,* Available at: https://unctad.org/system/files/official-document/ditcclp2019d2_en.pdf (accessed 17 January 2022)

vzvb (2021a) *Consumer Survey on Corporate Responsibility in Supply Chains,* 20 May 2021, Available at: https://www.vzbv.de/pressemitteilungen/umfrage-verbraucher-fuer-starkes-lieferkettengesetz (accessed 17 January 2022)

vzvb (2021b) *State Textile Seal: Consumer Opinions,* 9 September 2021, Available at: https://www.vzbv.de/meldungen/gruener-knopf-muss-versprechen-halten (accessed 17 January 2022)

17 Crafting connections with clothing: values, influence and relationships

Carra Santos, Kadian Gosler and Ann Marie Newton

INTRODUCTION

This chapter proposes how brands and customers can work together to cultivate sustainable fashion behaviours.

There is a disconnect between customers in the Global North (Millstone, 2017), where the world's largest fashion brands are based, and the clothing they procure, which is produced predominantly in the Global South. Readers are introduced to this disconnection that has developed over time due to an increasingly market-driven fashion system, resulting in devalued clothing and customers adopting the role of passive 'consumer'.

Next, the significance of individual agency and choice within the system is explored, highlighting how brands can improve customer access to *materials*, *competences* and *meaning* to transform their behaviour from passive 'consumers' to active 'participants'. Craft and social media are examined as tools for brands to connect, collaborate and empower customers throughout the product lifecycle, by involving them in design decisions pre-production, providing manufacturing comprehension and extending the life of garments post-salé.

Subsequently, a case study of eco-conscious lingerie brands is carried out to understand their applied approach to marketing sustainability while using social media to cultivate a sense of product value for both the maker and wearers.

DOI: 10.4324/9781003272878-22

Overall, a future-thinking system of meaning and value creation through creative empowerment and collaborative relationships is proposed as a desirable future for fashion.

DISCONNECTION

Almost all goods are made apart from the life of those who use them: we are not responsible for them, our will has had no part in their production...
(Morris, in Adamson, 2018: 148)

The above quote was first recorded in 1888 by William Morris, a polymath and pioneer of the Arts & Craft movement in Victorian Britain. Although the quote is over 100 years old, his concerns are still relevant today. Morris highlights a facet of the industrialised process and later mass production that is interesting to consider; the physical, intellectual and emotional separation that results in customers having no idea where, how or by whom clothing is made. It is difficult to comprehend the number of decisions, steps, processes, locations, logistics and people involved in clothing production. This means that customers cannot appreciate what goes into making a garment and, as Morris stated, have no responsibility for the item. There is a lack of connection and relationship with the item, resulting in devaluing clothing beyond the price, aesthetic and tactile qualities.

This is a part of the market system which became prominent during the 18th and 19th centuries in Europe. Morris commented "people have to 'make do' within a system that is not of their choosing" (Gauntlett, 2018: 49). The marketplace was, and largely still is, set up so that a company presents goods, essentially what *the company* anticipates people will buy, in a *'take it or leave it'* way. There is no involvement of the customer from the initial concept through manufacturing to the end product. The first customer contact with mass-produced clothing is at the point of purchase, rental or other acquisition.

A lack of knowledge and responsibility links with ethical and environmental concerns (Harris, Roby & Dibb, 2016). Not knowing how and by whom fashion clothing is made makes it difficult for 'consumers' to make considered, responsible choices. Nothing is known about the physical and social effects of making a piece of clothing; from aspects such as water, energy and chemical use through to the livelihoods and working conditions of the many people involved. These are unknown not only to the end 'consumers', but also to the brands or retailers selling the items – especially beyond the initial tiers of the supply chains.

One organisation working to make the unseen seen is Fashion Revolution,[1] which started in 2013 following the Rana Plaza garment factory collapse in Bangladesh. This non-profit created successful global
campaigns focusing on "Who made my clothes?", showcasing people
involved in clothing production, and, more recently, "What is in my
clothes?" highlighting the importance of what is used to make clothing.

As with many concepts, the idea of consumption has changed over time.
Mid-19th century economists WS Jevons, Carl Manger and Leon Walras
argued that *consuming*, rather than labour, created *value* (Trentmann,
2016: 3). This perspective shift towards value creation is significant, making it dependent on price, as opposed to manufacturing. This is reflected
in the dramatic increase in fashion clothing production. Consider how,
in the early 1900s, new fashion collections were presented in two 'seasons'
a year, namely Spring/Summer and Autumn/Winter, so becoming the
key commercial selling opportunities of the traditional fashion system.
In line with fashion theory, this allowed time for design inspiration to
'trickle down' from the catwalk (Veblen, 2009 [1899]) while preserving
craft skills at various levels, for example, via bespoke commissions, made-
to-measure and hand-making (Thomas, 2019). However, as industrialisation increased in the 20th century, and 'fast fashion' brands emerged in
the 1980s and 1990s, the two key selling seasons of Spring/Summer and
Autumn/Winter increased to four, then eight, until 'micro-seasons' were
introduced at up to 52 a year (Global Fashion Agenda, 2020).

New designs now reach stores within days, making fashion more
accessible, but also cultivating a mindset that it is 'chic to be cheap'.
This pace and mindset has arguably created the 'consumer' practice of
'buy, wear, bin' (Ellen MacArthur Foundation, 2020), which questions
whether certain aspects of industry are not meeting growing demand,
but creating it, and sustaining it, for corporate profit (House of Commons Environmental Audit Committee, 2019). If so, this strategy may
have sparked unsustainable fashion purchasing behaviours that people
cannot control or easily change because the behaviours have become
standard practice.

ANALYSIS: SOCIAL PRACTICE THEORY

This part examines the practice of fashion purchasing using Practice
Theory, a type of socio-cultural theory which contemplates individual
and structured roles in society. In particular, Social Practice Theory ar-
gues that an individual's behaviours and practices are not always based
on their values, but on the dominant social structure that surrounds

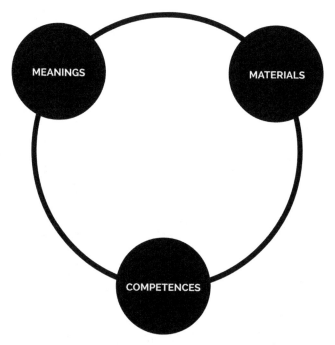

Figure 17.1 Circulation of Elements in a Social Practice model, adapted from Shove, Pantzar and Watson (2012)

them (Shove, Pantzar & Watson, 2012). In fashion consumption, this theory can help ascertain how much or little agency people have over their purchasing habits, whether they are 'active' or 'passive'. And, if 'passive', where agency could be restored.

The Circulation of Elements in a Practice model (Figure 17.1) portrays the core activities of a social practice within three linked Elements: *materials, competences* and *meaning*. Certain queries arise when these Elements are considered alongside fashion production and consumption (Table 17.1).

In theory, if customers are largely disconnected from the three Elements, then focusing on individual behaviour is insufficient, as society as a whole is 'locked in' to the 'social practice' of passive fashion consumption (Figure 17.2). Individuals' attempts to keep clothes for longer are quickly hampered, for example, by the quality of today's garments being too poor to repair; a trends-led culture where clothes are quickly discarded for upcoming styles; or the decline of craft and sewing skills practised or taught within schools and families, which hinders good intentions to repair or repurpose clothes. This is one reason why 300,000 tonnes of textile waste go to landfill or incineration annually (House of Commons Environmental Audit Committee, 2019).

Table 17.1 Definition of Elements in a Social Practice (Adapted from Shove, Pantzar & Watson, 2012), with Contextual Interpretations

Social Practice Theory Definition (Shove, Pantzar & Watson, 2012: 14)	*Contextual Interpretation for Fashion Consumption Practice (Author elaboration)*
Materials	
Access to things, technologies, tangible physical entities and the stuff of which objects are made	Access to the physical materials considering type, quality, durability, production methods, affordability and origin
Competences	
Access to skills, know-how and techniques	Access to the skills, know-how and techniques associated with producing, caring for, customising, altering and repairing clothing
Meanings	
Symbolic meanings, ideas and aspirations	Cultivating value and appreciation for the materials, processes, craft and creativity behind clothing design and production

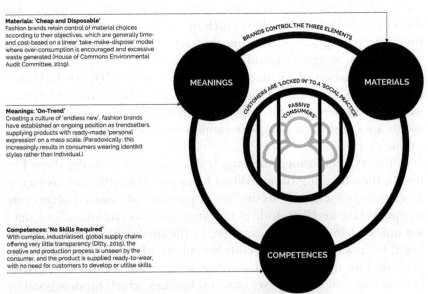

FASHION CUSTOMERS AS PASSIVE 'CONSUMERS'

Materials: 'Cheap and Disposable'
Fashion brands retain control of material choices according to their objectives, which are generally time- and cost-based on a linear 'take-make-dispose' model where over-consumption is encouraged and excessive waste generated (House of Commons Environmental Audit Committee, 2019).

Meanings: 'On-Trend'
Creating a culture of 'endless new', fashion brands have established an ongoing position as trendsetters, supplying products with ready-made 'personal expression' on a mass scale. (Paradoxically, this increasingly results in consumers wearing identikit styles rather than individual.)

Competences: 'No Skills Required'
With complex, industrialised, global supply chains offering very little transparency (Ditty, 2015), the creative and production process is unseen by the consumer, and the product is supplied ready-to-wear, with no need for customers to develop or utilise skills.

BRANDS CONTROL THE THREE ELEMENTS

CUSTOMERS ARE 'LOCKED IN' TO A 'SOCIAL PRACTICE'

PASSIVE 'CONSUMERS'

MEANINGS   MATERIALS

COMPETENCES

Figure 17.2 Circulation of Elements in a Social Practice, adapted and interpreted from Shove, Pantzar and Watson (2012) by Carra Santos, to examine the role of fashion customers as passive 'consumers'

RE-CONNECTION

Theory

Addressing a social practice requires weakening or breaking the links between Elements (Figure 17.1) to make space for more sustainable behaviours (Hargreaves, 2011; Shove, Pantzar & Watson, 2012). Notably, there are active attempts by sustainability-minded customers to reconnect to the three Elements themselves (Figure 17.3). Efforts include 'thrift-flipping' – the restyling and reselling of second-hand clothes – that has significant coverage on social media and emerging resale apps such as Depop[2] and Vinted.[3] Millennials[4] and Generation Z[5] are increasingly addressing socio-environmental concerns by purchasing from smaller or lesser-known brands, renting and buying second-hand (Cameron, 2021; Deloitte, 2021). These behaviours are often connected to creativity, uniqueness and reducing demand for new items. Community groups such as the Repair Café movement[6] support such efforts by offering access to free skills. However, according to a recent McKinsey & Company report (2020), nine in ten Generation Z customers believe companies should address sustainability issues. This indicates a growing expectation that responsible brands should meet

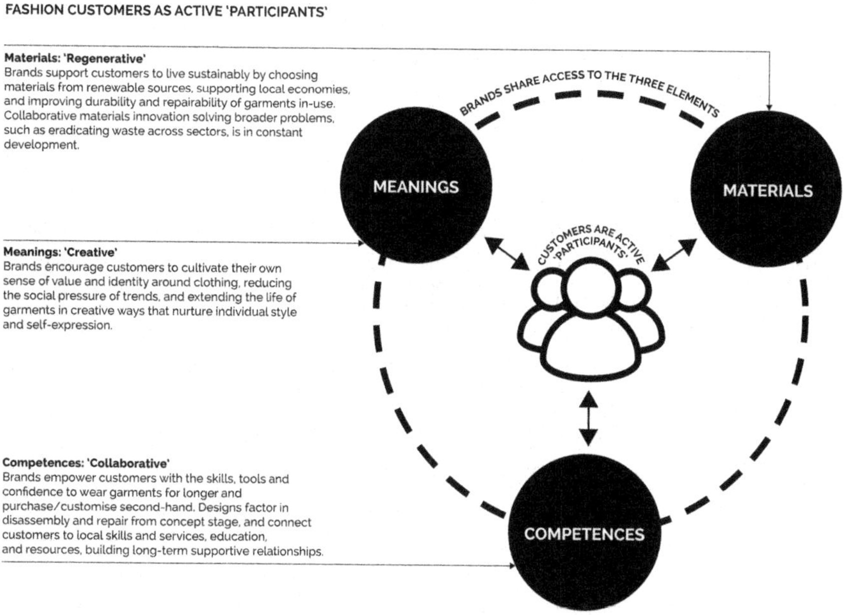

FASHION CUSTOMERS AS ACTIVE 'PARTICIPANTS'

Materials: 'Regenerative'
Brands support customers to live sustainably by choosing materials from renewable sources, supporting local economies, and improving durability and repairability of garments in-use. Collaborative materials innovation solving broader problems, such as eradicating waste across sectors, is in constant development.

Meanings: 'Creative'
Brands encourage customers to cultivate their own sense of value and identity around clothing, reducing the social pressure of trends, and extending the life of garments in creative ways that nurture individual style and self-expression.

Competences: 'Collaborative'
Brands empower customers with the skills, tools and confidence to wear garments for longer and purchase/customise second-hand. Designs factor in disassembly and repair from concept stage, and connect customers to local skills and services, education, and resources, building long-term supportive relationships.

BRANDS SHARE ACCESS TO THE THREE ELEMENTS

MEANINGS

MATERIALS

CUSTOMERS ARE ACTIVE 'PARTICIPANTS'

COMPETENCES

Figure 17.3 Circulation of Elements in a Social Practice, adapted and interpreted from Shove, Pantzar and Watson (2012) by Carra Santos, to examine the role of fashion customers as active 'participants'

customer and community efforts to reconnect to the three Elements, by inviting their participation throughout the process of development and use.

Craft

One conduit for people to demonstrate sustainable behaviours is crafting, which is a process of connecting as illustrated in this quote from sociologist David Gauntlett:

> When one is not just a consumer guzzling thing after thing, but also a producer, going through the necessarily slower and more thoughtful process of making something, one becomes more aware of the details and decisions which underpin everyday things and experiences, and therefore more able to gain pleasure and inspiration from the appreciation of things
>
> (Gauntlett, 2018: 71)

Participation in making something – holding materials, and manipulating them – not only offers knowledge about that specific material, but also understanding of the material aspect of life. Craft takes time and is thoughtful. Taking part in craft processes builds appreciation for things and how they might be made. Appreciation is one way that craft can help to connect people with the things of everyday lives, including clothes, and start to restore their agency.

Reconnecting with clothes through crafting is not restricted to the physical activities in the post-production phase such as repair. It could also have intangible effects on people's relationships with the surrounding world, and very importantly where material resources come from. As such, craft processes can aid the *meaning* aspect of social practice theory. According to furniture maker Peter Korn (2013), to participate in a craft is to take part in a continuous feedback loop – the more one makes, the greater the appreciation of how things are made in general, and what goes into the making, which is unseen when acting purely as a 'consumer'. This extends beyond familiar materials to a general appreciation of the world. Korn proposed that: "The holistic quality of craft lies not only in engaging the whole person, but also in harmonizing his understanding of himself in the world" (Korn, 2013: 56). Participation in craft is one method for brands to shift customers' relationship with clothing, thereby elevating its *meaning* and *value*.

ENABLING PARTICIPATION

Certain brands are experimenting with customer participation, from factoring longevity, disassembly and repairability into design considerations pre-production, to rental, re-commerce, remaking and repair processes post-production. These practices demonstrate key hallmarks of the circular fashion economy (Ellen MacArthur Foundation, 2017). Here, the focus becomes the long-term brand/customer relationship rather than the transaction, supported by local partnerships and purpose-led engagement. UK brand TOAST,[7] for example, operates both TOAST Circle, an in-store clothes-swapping initiative, and TOAST Renewal, a free repair service, engaging specialist experts in invisible and visible mending and traditional techniques such as Sashiko repair.[8] This localised 'skills and service' model prolongs the life of garments, values skills and encourages society to develop a relationship with clothing through participatory processes.

Crafting provides an alternative route for sustainability. It is also a useful means to reach customers that mainstream fashion has neglected. Maker groups and talented individuals supply the materials, skills and community for those who may be 'sized out' or priced out of fashion. Crafting is made widely accessible via social media, reinforcing the notion that 'craft values social engagement and knowledge sharing' (Hur and Beverley, 2013: 40). Examples are evident in YouTube channels such as Ela Orsini's 'Shine with new skills' on bra-making aiding those in-between bra sizes (Orsini, 2021) and Pinterest boards featuring quick and simple mending techniques and tutorials. Social media has emerged as a bridge facilitating a design space where people can acquire new *competences*, learn about responsible fashion practices and connect with a community of craftspeople and brands.

Social media

With over 3.78 billion daily active users (Mosin, 2021), social media is optimal for brands to engage with customers directly. Recent findings indicate that 54% of shoppers research products via social media (Beer, 2018), and 49% rely on influencer[9] recommendations prior to purchasing (Osborne, 2019). Before launching, brands – niche to high end – create several accounts across various platforms, as each provides a different format to establish a presence. However, rather than marketing to customers, brands have an opportunity to connect with them – transforming them into active 'participants' – by bringing them into design decisions, teaching making, mending and caring skills and establishing dialogue on evolving brand meaning. Opportunities lie in partnering with influencers[10] or brands like Clothes Doctor,[11] which specialises in cleaning, protecting, repairing and alterations to extend the garment use.

Despite all its faults, social media (such as Reddit, Facebook, Pinterest and Instagram) also offers a space for inspiration, education and community for many people, including bra wearers who make their bras, due to difficulties in finding long-lasting, well-fitted, comfortable bras. Most bra wearers purchase three to six bras a year on average, often keeping older worn bras – extending usage. The bra's intricacy and functional necessities require much research and time to design and develop. This has resulted in larger manufacturers avoiding the development of sustainable bras or enquiring into alternative circular business models. The lingerie sector possesses nuances[12] requiring alternative sustainable approaches, such as designing bras for physical and emotional durability and recyclability. A case study on smaller eco-conscious lingerie brands identifies their utilisation of social media as a pathway to reshape customer experiences focused on connection, collaboration and education – supporting passive 'consumers' to become active 'participants'.

CASE STUDY: SUSTAINABLE LINGERIE BRANDS

A small-scale qualitative study on five eco-conscious lingerie brands[13] utilised Instagram to investigate their sustainable marketing strategies (Gosler, 2021). Instagram has a high interaction rate (Ahmed, 2017), enabling brands to market products and engage through two-way dialogue (Prahalad and Ramaswamy, 2004), fostering trust and building relationships (Strähle and Gräff, 2017). From November 2019 to 2020, 926 images, videos and Stories from the five brands' Instagram accounts were collated, coded and analysed. Table 17.2 illustrates the selected brands and their Instagram statistics during that one-year period.[14]

These brands' marketing strategies cultivate a sense of value by generating a relationship and educating on various sustainable aspects. Brands brought customers into the design process, engaging them in fabric and colour selections through polls in Instagram Stories. Additionally, they provided behind-the-scenes production videos facilitating transparency and information on bra manufacturing. These actions educate customers on the materials, processes and skills necessary to produce sustainable bras, cultivating value and meaning.

Table 17.2 Sustainable Lingerie Brands and Instagram Profile Analysis

Brand Name & Instagram	Instagram Profile	Followers	# of Posts Nov 19'–Nov 20'	Hashtags	Hashtags Usage
Pact @WearPact	Earth's favourite™ clothing, organic cotton clothing, sustainably and ethically made	112k	260	#organicallyme #wearpact	79.7%
Organic basics@ organicbasics	Eco-friendly underwear, activewear and essentials, ethically made in Europe	260k	259	#organicbasics #sustainablefashion #ethicalfashion #conciousfashion #slowfashion #slowliving #veganunderwear #ecofashion #ethicalclothing #ecofriendlyfashion (plus 19 more used)	91.2%
Underprotection@ underprotection	Sustainable lingerie, loungewear and swimwear, organic, recycled and eco-friendly fabrics, fair production	61.8k	504	#sustainablefashion #ethicallingerie #sustainablelingerie #recycledpolyester #recycledmesh #recycledlace	93.7%
Lara intimates@ laraintimates	Underwear made in London from deadstock fabric	22.5k	223	#teamlara #larafactory #ethicalfashion #sustainablefashion #zerowaste #ethicalfactory	9.3%
Uye Surana@ uyesurana	Handmade with artistic and modern appeal	43.1k	342	#WeloveUye #LoveUyeFirst #UyeSurana #TheRealUye	26.9%

The brands tagged and reposted customers in their marketing to further engender relationships and enhance emotional durability. This method often gains many 'likes'; however, Instagram influencer models receive noticeably more interaction. Utilising a range of influencers, the brands incorporated lingerie bloggers and models, sustainability influencers and activists within social sustainability. Selecting the right influencer for the brand is imperative. For example, Organic Basics utilised an influencer to promote the environmental aspect of sustainable living. However, this influencer's pro-life views conflicted with the sustainability and inclusivity beliefs of the brand's followers. The brand therefore apologised and removed the influencer as its model. This scenario validates that brands' relationship with customers must work both ways, and together they shape the brands' sustainability values.

Demonstrating an awareness of overconsumption, these brands limited posts directing followers to purchase products. Instead, they lean towards education, exploiting Stories and posts to inform their followers about their sustainability efforts. Some brands focused on informing about the recycled materials used, the quality and physical durability of the designs, and prolonging usage through care suggestions like how to wash consciously.

With bras designed for longevity, easier recyclability, and inclusivity, these pioneering brands highlight innovative ways of utilising social media to showcase and extend sustainability practices.

CONCLUSION

The disconnection between people and clothing production caused by industrialisation and globalised mass production has forged an unsustainable fashion system. This disconnection generates many challenges regarding sustainable development. However, reconnection methods also offer opportunities for customers to be involved throughout the process, where good environment, ethical and social practices are a shared goal. Using Social Practice Theory as a framework for analysis, this chapter illustrates how access to *materials, competences* and *meaning* can restore agency, supporting people from being passive 'consumers' into active 'participants' throughout the product lifecycle.

Social media presents an opportunity for brands to inspire passive 'consumers' to become active 'participants'. As shown with eco-conscious lingerie brands, Instagram enables brands' connection, communication, education and engagement with their followers, creating and maintaining a two-way relationship. The various social media platforms encompass features that allow brands to introduce followers into the product design process by aiding in the selection of material and creative elements; thus emphasising transparency in production practices and providing tutorials to learn making or mending craft skills. Purposeful utilisation of social media empowers brands and their followers to co-create and maintain the brands' sustainable values and meanings.

On the whole, it is suggested that a sustainable fashion system relies on brands and customers working together. The most innovative brands will support society towards a more sustainable future, where the fundamental human need for creativity, personal expression and practical skills is recognised, valued and revived. Such brands will look beyond the fashion industry and business itself to identify long-term sustainable behaviours, and enable them through business models that reduce production and consumption, and restore quality, craft and creativity to everyday life. Collectively, these focused efforts will accelerate the necessary systems-shift within fashion, and contribute to more sustainable futures overall.

NOTES

1 https://www.fashionrevolution.org/.
2 https://www.depop.com/.
3 https://www.vinted.co.uk/.
4 https://www.oxfordlearnersdictionaries.com/definition/english/millennial_2?q=millennials.
5 https://www.oxfordlearnersdictionaries.com/definition/english/generation-z.
6 https://repaircafe.org/en/.
7 https://www.toa.st/.
8 https://www.toa.st/blogs/magazine/sashiko-repair.
9 An influencer is a person with a large (micro, mid-tier, and macro) social media following who shares their skills, recommendations and opinions in a specific area such as fashion design, art, or craft.
10 On Instagram, influencers like @visible_creative_mending and @mindful_mending teach repair and mending skills leveraging hashtags such as #visible-mending and #makedoandmend, which yields over 100,000 posts. The high volume of posts indicates a thriving craft community.
11 Clothes Doctor is a brand that educates and empowers people to maintain their garments and offer related local services – notably, partnering with Net-a-Porter and Harrods in 2019. Instagram @ClothesDoctorUK. Https://clothes-doctor.com/.
12 Although resale, rental, repair, and remaking may work for some garments, it poses a challenge for others like intimate apparel. A person may rent a dress for a special occasion or purchase a preloved jacket from a charity shop, not so much underwear. Bras, like shoes, require a level of expertise that may not easily lend itself to remaking or repair by non-specialists.

13 The sustainable lingerie brands are Pact, Organic Basics, Underprotection, Lara Intimates, and Uye Surana.
14 At the time of writing this, it is noteworthy that Organic Basics and Underprotection are some of the few bra providers certified B Corp. Pact Instagram has changed to @_pact_, and Lara Intimates is no longer operating.

REFERENCES

Ahmed, T. (2017) 'Instagram Follower Growth Is Now Lagging Behind Facebook Page Likes Growth', *Locowise Blog*, 18 April. Available at: https://locowise.com/blog/instagram-follower-growth-is-now-lagging-behind-facebook-page-likes-growth (Accessed: 20 December 2020).
Beer, C. (2018) 'Social Browsers Engage with Brands', *GWI*, 13 June. Available at: https://blog.gwi.com/chart-of-the-day/social-browsers-brand/ (Accessed: 20 December 2020).
Cameron, I. (2021) 'Young Adults Rejecting Fast Fashion for Pre-Loved Clothes in Eco Boom', *Charged Retail Tech News*, 31 December. Available at: https://www.chargedretail.co.uk/2021/12/31/young-adults-rejecting-fast-fashion-for-pre-loved-clothes-in-eco-boom/ (Accessed: 14 April 2022).
Deloitte (2021) *A Call for Accountability and Action. The Deloitte Global 2021 Millennial and Gen Z Survey*. Available at: https://www2.deloitte.com/content/dam/Deloitte/global/Documents/2021-deloitte-global-millennial-survey-report.pdf (Accessed: 13 January 2022).
Ellen MacArthur Foundation (2017) *A new Textiles Economy: Redesigning Fashion's Future*. Available at: https://ellenmacarthurfoundation.org/a-new-textiles-economy (Accessed: 15 April 2020).
Ellen MacArthur Foundation (2020) *Vision of a Circular Economy for Fashion*. Available at: https://www.ellenmacarthurfoundation.org/assets/downloads/Vision-of-a-circulareconomy- for-fashion.pdf (Accessed: 11 February 2021).
Gauntlett, D. (2018) *Making is Connecting: The Social Power of Creativity, from Craft and Knitting to Digital Everything* (2nd edition). Cambridge, UK: Polity.
Global Fashion Agenda (2020) 'The Increase in Seasons', Global Fashion Agenda, (no date). Available at: https://designforlongevity.com/articles/the-increase-in-seasons (Accessed: 11 February 2021).
Gosler, K. (2021) 'The Sustainable Bra: Analysis of Lingerie Brand's Communication on Instagram', *Sustainable Innovation 2021*, 23rd International Conference, Online, pp. 155–171. Available at: https://www.researchgate.net/publication/351068933_The_Sustainable_Bra_Analysis_of_Lingerie_Brands_Communication_via_Instagram (Accessed: 16 January 2022).
Hargreaves, T. (2011) 'Practice-ing behaviour change: Applying social practice theory to pro-environmental behaviour change', *Journal of Consumer Culture*, 11(1), pp. 79–99.
Harris, F., Roby, H. and Dibb, S. (2016) 'Sustainable clothing: challenges, barriers and interventions for encouraging more sustainable consumer behaviour', *International Journal of Consumer Studies*, 40(3), pp. 309–318.
House of Commons Environmental Audit Committee (2019) *Fixing Fashion: Clothing Consumption and Sustainability* (HC 1952). Available at: https://publications.parliament.uk/pa/cm201719/cmselect/cmenvaud/1952/1952.pdf (Accessed: 15 April 2020).

Hur, E.S. and Beverley, K.J. (2013) 'The Role of Craft in a Co-Design System for Sustainable Fashion', In: *Making Futures: The Crafts in the Context of Emerging Global Sustainability Agendas*. 15–16 September 2011, Dartington Estate, Devon, UK

Korn, P. (2013) *Why We Make Things and Why It Matters: The Education of a Craftsman*. Boston, MA: David R. Godine Publisher.

McKinsey & Company (2020) *Survey: Consumer Sentiment on Sustainability in Fashion*. Available at: https://www.mckinsey.com/industries/retail/our-insights/survey-consumer-sentiment-onsustainability-in-fashion (Accessed: 11 February 2021).

Millstone, C. (2017) *Frugal Value: Designing Business for a Crowded Planet*. London: Routledge.

Morris, W. (2018) 'The Revival of Handicraft', In: Adamson, G (ed.), *The Craft Reader* (2nd edition). London: Bloomsbury. pp. 146–155.

Mosin, M. (2021) '10 Social Media Statistics You Need to Know', *Oberlo*, 5 April. Available at: https://www.oberlo.com/blog/social-media-marketing-statistics (Accessed: 18 December 2021).

Orsini, E. (2021) *Shine with New Skills*. [YouTube] 7 May. Available at: https://www.youtube.com/c/ElaOrsini (Accessed: 20 December 2021).

Osborne, O. (2019) 'To #ad or not to #ad – Insights on Influencer Marketing', *Four Communications*, 18 February. Available at: https://fourcommunications.com/insights-on-influencer-marketing/ (Accessed: 18 December 2021).

Prahalad, C.K. and Ramaswamy, V. (2004) 'Co-creation experiences: The next practice in value creation', *Journal of Interactive Marketing*, 18(3), pp. 5–14. https://doi.org/10.1002/dir.20015

Shove, E., Pantzar, M. and Watson, M. (2012) *The Dynamics of Social Practice: Everyday Life and How It Changes*. Los Angeles, CA: Sage.

Strähle, J. and Gräff, C. (2017). 'The Role of Social Media for a Sustainable Consumption', In: Strähle, J. (ed.), *Green Fashion Retail*. Singapore: Springer, pp. 225–247. https://doi.org/10.1007/978-981-10-2440-5_12

Thomas, D. (2019) *Fashionopolis: The Price of Fast Fashion - and the Future of Clothes*. New York: Apollo.

Trentmann, F. (2016) *Empire of Things: How We Became a World of Consumers, from the Fifteenth Century to the Twenty-First*. UK: Penguin.

Veblen, T. (2009 [1899]) *The Theory of the Leisure Class*. Reissue, New York: Oxford University Press Inc.

18 Unheard voices: reclaiming fashion sustainability

Elizabeth Bye, Paige Tomfohrde, Lisa Nel, and Sage Davis

INTRODUCTION

The lack of ethics and agency in the fashion industry contributes to the depletion of earth's resources (Walker 2017). Globally, Black, Indigenous, and people of color (BIPOC) who have been oppressed by colonialism and capitalism are not free to take action or exert power needed for change in the fashion industry, yet they provide the labor and resources that perpetuate unsustainable growth. The experiences of these individuals are marginalized, but solutions to this crisis require diverse voices and sources of wisdom. Consumerism and the reduced opportunity for individual and cultural expression are core to the lack of agency in the fashion industry. The wisdom and practices of Indigenous peoples survive over time and offer strategies to realign our relationship with the earth. Considering the barriers that individuals in underrepresented BIPOC groups face in supporting sustainable fashion can enable a deeper understanding of how to address challenges such as lack of visual representation and cultural integration. Ethics of care as the moral lens aims to address the oppression of underrepresented groups and emphasizes relationships, connection, and community (Jaggar 1992). Societies are responsible for the harm caused by pollution, such as toxic wastewater and oil pipelines that leak into the land. Thus, ethics is a compelling tool to protect the environment (Ehrlich & Ehrlich 1996) and foster democratic responsibility. Individuals have fundamental human rights to equal consideration (Hamington 2019; Nel 2018; Shrader-Frechette 2012); however, utilitarian principles do not always provide ethical conduct guidelines, a concept that raises

DOI: 10.4324/9781003272878-23

the possibility of shifting from consumerism towards a paradigm that supports environmental, human, and economic flourishing and sustainability through more inclusive ethical approaches (UCLA 2022).

PROBLEMS OF LEARNING, REPRESENTATION, AND AGENCY

The problems of learning

Indigenous people worldwide have advocated for protecting the earth and her resources in response to colonization. The western world does not listen to and learn from core Indigenous values of gratitude and reciprocity but instead embraces the anti-ethical perspective of consumerism (Bye & Davis 2021). Daily traditions and practices that show appreciation for the natural world and recognize the wealth of our ecosystems have been forgotten (Bowers 2016; Fletcher 2019; Petheram et al. 2010). Governments have restricted the exploration of Indigenous-driven climate change initiatives (Nursey-Bray et al. 2019) and undervalued Indigenous perspectives, which prevents Indigenous voices from being heard. In the words of Indigenous activist Lewis Grassrope during the protest against the Dakota Access Pipeline: "We don't have a voice. We don't have a standing. We don't have influence, but as you can see here, we are the tip of the spear" (Estes 2019:36–37). This oil pipeline directly connects to valuable, finite resources used in the fashion industry in the form of synthetic fibers and dyes.

Indigenous peoples have a cultural drive to survive, honoring stories that uphold the principles of "we should do what we do well" (Yohe & Greeves 2019:37). Beaded pieces made by Indigenous designers are considered heirlooms (Bye & Davis 2021) and cultural meaning is conveyed in the specific colors, shapes, and patterns of the design (Monture 1993). Unfortunately, the product of consumerist fashion is unsustainable because there is little appreciation for the materials, talent, and time invested in the production, and there is a lack of inherent cultural meaning and values. Bye and Davis (2021) argue that we must learn to express gratitude and reciprocity for nature's resources and the individuals who make our clothes to shift to a sustainable fashion paradigm.

The problems of representation

BIPOC voices continue to be unheard in the fashion industry. Otto von Busch (2018:322) points out the exclusionary state of the sustainable fashion industry, where "the discourse around sustainable fashion often lacks a socio-political perspective on who and what kinds of consumerism should be sustained and for which social groups". The current fashion industry often neglects to understand how differences in social position and power shape the identities and access of global customers who increasingly lead lives unrepresented in the white, western-dominated fashion industry. The multitude of identities that customers inhabit is reflected in the barriers they face toward participating in sustainable fashion purchase behavior.

The barriers faced by consumers, regardless of identity, include style, price, availability, and knowledge (Eder-Hansen et al. 2012). However, in their US-based study, Tomfohrde and Bye (2021) found that plus-size individuals with non-white racial identities may experience these barriers differently or experience different barriers altogether. For instance, due to lack of style options, plus-size female racial minorities in the US often purchased items that did not fit their style because nothing else was available in their size. For these women, experiences of discrimination decrease the likelihood of purchasing from a brand, while seeing more diverse visual representation in advertising and inside stores increases purchase intention. One participant in Tomfohrde and Bye's study explained: "I would be more willing to buy something if I saw myself in those clothes" (2021:291), while other participants stated that hiring more minority women in leadership positions would help improve the sustainable fashion industry by adding representation and perspectives that could enable more inclusive engagement (Tomfohrde & Bye 2021). Ahiaveh and Mawire (2020) showed that racial diversity in fast fashion advertising matters to consumers, especially racial minorities, indicating that it likely matters in sustainable fashion as well. Gardetti and Rahman (2016) discussed how incorporating Indigenous cultures can result in items being more valuable to the wearer. Regarding politics, racial minorities are increasingly interested in seeing greater commitment to causes that matter to them, such as politically divisive organizations like Black Lives Matter (Tomfohrde & Bye 2021). Plus-size female racial minorities in the US feel disenfranchised from the sustainable fashion industry, mainly because of the lack of available plus-size options. Understanding these barriers and the individuals who experience them is a critical and often unaddressed part of bringing more subjectivity to the conversation around sustainable fashion.

The problems of agency
The term "agency" refers here to the role-players in the fashion industry who demonstrate positive, active engagement in a company's

success as opposed to stakeholders with unchecked, exploitive power to profit (Kaiser 2012; Nel 2018). In a world dominated by capitalist models, individuals need satisfaction, such as representation in their socio-cultural context, learning from each other in a community, and the agency to construct cultural identities and meet financial goals (Fletcher & Grose 2012). However, these needs are disrupted by exploitative social pressure from retailers in their desire to profit from consumers (Nel et al. 2021). For example, there is social pressure to fit in with current fashion as a visual form of identity expression and group belonging (Kaiser 2012). Brands and media target these social needs to achieve profit margins, not to satisfy them (Craik 2009). The social pressure to stand out often conflicts with the need to fit in. The global proliferation of western fashion trends capitalizes on these conflicting needs while marginalizing individual and cultural expression (Nel 2018). The fashion industry faces economic pressures under a model of growth and consumerism, often at the expense of the environment (Nel et al. 2021, The fashion sustainability index 2020). The problem is that the fashion industry is driven by profits that exploit the individual agency of role-players to meet capitalist business needs (Kaiser 2012).

Kaiser's (2012) circuit of style-fashion-dress represents a circular value chain with interconnected domains and movements that flow in multiple directions. Each circuit concept is a process in the fashion supply chain. The processes (regulation, consumption, distribution, and production) intersect with cultural paradigms and practices through subject formation. Kaiser (2012) describes subject formation as '**subject**ion', as being subjected to something structured by others, or '**subject**ivity', as having the agency to express one's way of being. Nel adapts the circuit to illustrate how each process offers intervention points by contextualizing the place of the agents in the system (Figure 18.1).

In the circuit, fashion and media teams promise customer satisfaction by promoting less ethical "fast" fashion instead of products that encourage sustainable behaviors (Nel et al. 2021). Similarly, textile and apparel producers prioritize production efficiency, not ethical needs (Descatoires 2017; Lehmann et al. 2019). Fashion marketing teams drive excessive consumption behaviors that lead to individuals' discontent and the exploitation of raw materials needed to make fashion goods (Crane 2000; Ehrenfeld 2008). The lack of ethics in the fashion industry is linked to the waste and destruction of our natural resources (Walker 2017), emphasizing the urgent need for ethical redirection from a paradigm of consumerism to one that recognizes that our resources are finite.

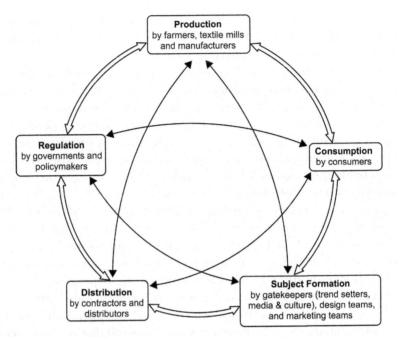

Figure 18.1 The agents in the circuit of style-fashion-dress. (Adapted from Kaiser 2012, by Nel)

SOLUTIONS OF LEARNING, REPRESENTATION, AND AGENCY

Solutions through learning

Garment production has the highest impact in the fashion supply chain (Muthukumarana et al. 2018). As a counterbalance, Indigenous practices can actively guide engagement in reciprocity "through gratitude, through ceremony, through land stewardship, science, art, and in everyday acts of practical reverence" (Kimmerer 2015:190). During interviews with US and Canadian Indigenous fashion designers, Bye and Davis (2021:73–74) learn how the values of gratitude and reciprocity are implemented in garment production. Designers share the importance of relationships, connection to the land, spirituality, and community to their design process. Relationships with relatives, past and present, are essential to the designers' lives and making practice. The Indigenous fashion designers discussed the sentiment that connecting with the youth and encouraging them to keep Indigenous traditions alive honors the past and future. According to this community's belief system, even the land is considered a relative. One apparel designer highlights humanity's responsibility for the earth by explaining a common belief that "everything comes from the earth and the earth gives us life. I give thanks to it every day".

Pexa (2019) describes "response-ability" as attuning to the world beyond oneself. The concept of gift-giving, or reciprocity, is essential to living in an ecosystem. As one beadwork artist shares, "knowing the commercialism and mass production of fashion, it's important to me not [to] create what is not needed so as not to waste" (Bye & Davis 2021:74) Harjo (2019) describes community knowledge as a key component to becoming independent of the colonized mindset. In this way, the voices of these Indigenous designers can guide us to a more sustainable and balanced relationship with the earth. Actions to support agency include:

- Take time to build, nurture, and respect inclusive personal and professional relationships that encourage growth, health, and the common good.
- Slow down and be intentional in our stewardship of the earth's resources to support a sustainable fashion future through reciprocity.
- Connect to nature with gratitude.

There is a purpose to every element in the ecosystem, and each decision impacts our agency to be heard and represented equitably in fashion's sustainable future.

Solutions through representation

Developing sustainable solutions requires a deeper understanding of our current conditions. When companies approach customers empathetically, aware of how they interact with apparel, they can embrace practices to enhance sustainability. Part of this process requires readily offering equitable sizing. Customers are doing their part by building communities around fashion sharing, swapping, and donation (Albinsson & Yasanthi Perera 2012). Customers have the agency to co-create solutions with companies to increase the sustainability and equity of apparel options. However, companies must be willing to listen and create space for equitable improvements.

In Tomfohrde and Bye's (2021) US-based study, the plus-size, female, BIPOC participants have broad-ranging ideas about increasing fashion's human and economic sustainability, including:

- Implementation of sliding scale payments for garments
- "Buy one" – "give one" models

- Clothing grants for the underprivileged
- Expanded size range
- Removal of gender categories
- Authentic backing of social and political causes by brands.

The hope is for the system to be ethically refashioned to prioritize people over capitalism. Companies can champion these ideas instead of exploiting them. Universal Standard,[1] a fashion brand that focuses on modern, elevated essentials for women, champions extended sizing. MADI Apparel[2] produces sustainably and ethically made underwear and apparel basics and donates underwear to women in need at shelters internationally for each purchase made. Unfortunately, many brands still exclude underrepresented groups. Developing inclusive sustainable models built on an ethical foundation are critical to people and the planet.

Solutions through agency

Nel, Munro, and Smal (2021) argue that many of the fashion industry's ethical deficits can be countered through an ethic of care using Tronto's (1993) four moral dynamics: attentiveness, responsibility, competence, and responsiveness. These care dynamics can be applied to ethical deficits, such as the lack of inclusivity, gratitude, and reciprocity. Integrating care into the circuit of style-fashion-dress provides ways of reactivating positive agency (Nel 2018). The following are four such examples.

- The element of production from the ethical lens of 'attentiveness' can counter 'ignorance', resulting in clothing sized to fit a wide range of body measurements and shapes to improve inclusivity.
- Applying the element of regulation in the circuit from the ethical lens of 'responsibility' can counter 'obligation', resulting in a fashion brand that intentionally rejects the appropriation of Indigenous cultures and enables reciprocity.
- In the care-giving and care-receiving domain, 'competence' contrasts with the problems of "imposed competence", such as the assumption that brands know what consumers need and how to provide it.
- The notion of empathetic 'responsiveness' contrasts with 'condescending responsiveness'. By designing uncompleted or anti-media products (Fuad-Luke 2009), designers can enable customers to participate in the production and branding process as they customize products to express their personal style, thereby enabling the agency for self-expression (Nel 2018).

Using a combination of care ethics and design thinking (Hamington 2019; Nel et al. 2021), the fashion industry can consider ethical, empathetic strategies in addition to productivity. Tronto's ethics of care elements offer approaches to counter the exploitation of individual agency in the fashion industry by countering 'subjection' with 'subjectivity' in ways that can lead to more ethical and sustainable decisions.

CONCLUSION

Ethics of care is identified as a moral foundation to assess whether an approach is ethically grounded, and as a tool to uncover strategies that intersect with Kaiser's (2012) circuit of style-fashion-dress. It is crucial for industry leaders to listen to a diversity of unheard voices and support equitable representation in our journey to reclaim fashion sustainability. For example, collaboration with BIPOC groups can allow for diverse visual forms of identity expression and better need satisfaction. Respecting and learning the ways and ideas of people who move us past the status quo and making an effort to understand each other's experiences supports the subjectivity and agency of all. Indigenous cultures can model how to move away from growth mindsets at the expense of a flourishing community and environment. Agents can reclaim this collective power by integrating care ethics in the circuit of style-fashion-dress to challenge the fashion industry's subjectiveness and develop ethical strategies. Agents in the circuit can thereby reclaim moral dynamics, such as inclusivity and reciprocity, that have been silenced by consumerism towards building an ethical and sustainable fashion industry.

NOTES

1 https://www.universalstandard.com/.
2 https://www.madiapparel.com/.

REFERENCES

Ahiaveh, A.N. and Mawire, M., 2020. Exploring the mediating impact of identity on perceptions of racially diverse fast fashion advertisements: Evidence from millennial individuals. Master's Thesis, University School of Economics & Management.
Albinsson, P.A. and Yasanthi Perera, B., 2012. Alternative marketplaces in the 21st century: Building community through sharing events. *Journal of Consumer Behaviour*, 11(4), pp. 303–315.

Bowers, C.A., 2016. Digital Detachment: How Computer Culture Undermines Democracy (1st ed.). Routledge. https://doi.org/10.4324/9781315643540.

Bye, E. and Davis, S., 2021, March 21. *Gratitude & reciprocity: Foundational values for a sustainable apparel future*. Presented at Sustainable Innovation 2021: Accelerating Sustainability in Fashion, Clothing, Sportswear & Accessories. Virtual.

Craik, J., 2009. *Fashion: The key concepts*. Berg Publishers.

Crane, D., 2000. *Fashion and its social agendas: Class, gender, and identity in clothing*. University of Chicago Press.

Descatoires, E., 2017. *I shop, therefore I am: The meaning of fast and slow fashion consumption*. Auckland University of Technology. [Unpublished master's dissertation of business in marketing]. [Online]. Available: https://pdfs.semanticscholar.org/2b14/1fbfcf6a7a2d83af39f2e5f9497b0465b7f1.pdf [28 February 2019].

Eder-Hansen, J., Kryger, J., Morris, J., Sisco, C., Bang Larsen, K., Watson, D. and Burchardi, I., 2012. The NICE consumer: Research summary and discussion paper. *Danish Fashion Institute*.

Ehrlich, P.R. and Ehrlich, A.H., 1996. *Betrayal of science and reason: How anti-environmental rhetoric threatens our future*. Island Press.

Ehrenfeld, J.R., 2008. *Sustainability by design*. Yale University Press.

Estes, N., 2019. *Our history is the future: Standing Rock versus the Dakota Access Pipeline, and the long tradition of indigenous resistance*. Verso.

Fletcher, K. and Grose, L., 2012. *Fashion & sustainability: Design for change*. Laurence King Publishing Ltd.

Fletcher, K., 2019. Clothes that connect, in Resnick, E. (ed.), *The social design reader* (pp. 229–240). Bloomsbury Publishing.

Fuad-Luke, A., 2009. *Design activism: Beautiful strangeness for a sustainable world*. Earthscan.

Gardetti, M.A. and Rahman, S. (eds.), 2016. *Ethnic fashion* (pp. 1–18). Springer.

Hamington, M., 2019. Integrating care ethics and design thinking. *Journal of Business Ethics*, 155(1), pp. 91–103.

Harjo, L., 2019. *Spiral to the stars: Mvskoke tools of futurity*. University of Arizona Press.

Jaggar, A.M., 1992. Feminist Ethics, in Becker, L.C. and Becker, C.B. (eds.), *Encyclopedia of ethics*: A - K, 362. Routledge.

Kaiser, S.B. 2012. *Fashion and cultural studies*. London and New York: Berg.

Kimmerer, R.W., 2015. *Braiding sweetgrass: Indigenous wisdom, scientific knowledge and the teachings of plants*. Milkweed Editions.

Lehmann, M., Arici, G., Boger, S., Martinez-Pardo, C., Krueger, F., Schneider, M., Carrière-Pradal, B. and Schou, D. (eds.), 2019. *Pulse of the fashion industry update*. Global Fashion Agenda, The Boston Consulting Group, Sustainable Apparel Coalition. Accessed 10 August 2020: https://csr.dk/sites/default/files/Pulse_of_the_Fashion_Industry_2019_Update.pdf.

Monture, J., 1993. *The complete guide to traditional Native American beadwork: A definitive study of authentic tools, materials, techniques, and styles*. Collier Books.

Muthukumarana, T.T., Karunathilake, H.P., Punchihewa, H.K.G., Manthilake, M.M.I.D. and Hewage, K.N., 2018. Life cycle environmental impacts of the apparel industry in Sri Lanka: Analysis of the energy sources. *Journal of Cleaner Production*, 172, pp. 1346–1357.

Nursey-Bray, M., Palmer, R., Smith, T.F. and Rist, P., 2019. Old ways for new days: Australian Indigenous peoples and climate change. *Local Environment*, 24(5), pp. 473–486.

Nel, L., 2018. *Revaluing commodity fetishism to facilitate fashion sustainability.* Supervised by Munro, A. and Smal, D. [Unpublished master's dissertation]: Central University of Technology, Free state, South Africa.

Nel, L., Munro, A. and Smal, D., 2021, March 17. *Ethics of care disrupting unsustainable fashion design: Radical change and innovation methodologies.* Presented at Sustainable Innovation 2021: Accelerating Sustainability in Fashion, Clothing, Sportswear & Accessories. Virtual.

Petheram, L., Zander, K.K., Campbell, B.M., High, C. and Stacey, N., 2010. 'Strange changes': Indigenous perspectives of climate change and adaptation in NE Arnhem Land (Australia). *Global Environmental Change,* 20(4), pp. 681–692.

Pexa, C.J., 2019. *Translated nation: Rewriting the Dakhóta Oyáte.* University of Minnesota Press.

Shrader-Frechette, K., 2012. *Values and ethics for the 21st century: Ecology and environmental ethics.* The manifesto for global economic ethics. BBVA. Vol. 4, pp. 309–337.

The Fashion Sustainability Index. 2020. [Online] Available: https://www.fashionrevolution.org/about/transparency/

Tomfohrde, P. and Bye, E., 2021, March 17. *Accelerating racial equity in sustainable apparel: Barriers to entry for racial minorities.* Presented at Sustainable Innovation 2021: Accelerating Sustainability in Fashion, Clothing, Sportswear & Accessories. Virtual.

Tronto, J., 1993. *Moral boundaries: A political argument for an ethic of care.* Routledge.

von Busch, O., 2018. Inclusive fashion—an oxymoron—or a possibility for sustainable fashion? *Fashion Practice,* 10(3), pp. 311–327.

UCLA. 2022. *What is sustainability?* [Online] Available: https://www.sustain.ucla.edu/what-is-sustainability/ [30 August 2022].

Walker, S., 2017. The object of nightingales. Design values for meaningful material culture, in Chapman, J. (ed.), *The Routledge handbook of sustainable product design.* pp. 53–68. Routledge.

Yohe, J.A. and Greeves, T. (eds.), 2019. *Hearts of our people: Native women artists,* University of Washington Press.

19 Regions, communities, and localism

Miguel Ángel Gardetti, Rawan Maki, Shalini Gupta, and Sara Cavagnero

INTRODUCTION

Within sustainability discourse, engagement with and inclusion of local, transparent, and ethical practices is crucial. Local paradigms have the potential to inform global responses and efforts towards sustainability whereas fashion sustainability as a discipline has centred on a Western understanding of fashion systems, practice, and language. Current trends tend to reflect this status quo, where solutions are often inadequate, struggling to scale against goals of constant profit growth. In activist circles and within academia, the colonial history of fashion has been asserted and is widely acknowledged (Rabine, 1997; Rovine, 2009; Horning, 2014; Semaan, 2018; Bramwell, 2020; Mayer, 2020). Within fashion sustainability, the voices of marginalized, indigenous, and non-Western groups (predominantly from the Global South) often remain in the periphery.

Through examples discussed in this chapter, we explore the added value of local resources and skills, to enrich 'sustainability' with localized and plural 'sustainabilities'. We argue that: first, it is vital to examine the ways in which different geographies and communities approach sustainability. Artisans and makers, for instance, as flagbearers of localized practices and crafts, define success using both conventional benchmarks like profit and revenue and intrinsic values like personal gratification and capability to perpetuate craft traditions (Paige & Littrell, 2002).

In our discussion of place-specific knowledge, we draw on three key examples. The first social practice is surrounding fashion in Bahrain.

DOI: 10.4324/9781003272878-24

This case emphasizes that local social and cultural practices, as well as local socio-politics, are integral to the notion of fashion localism. The second and third examples illustrate experiences and learnings with artisans from India and indigenous people from Argentina respectively, focusing on craft-based products and drawing in voices from the periphery. Both of these examples explore methods of working with artisanal or indigenous communities, and how to bring voices from the periphery into the centre within fashion. Finally, the last part investigates potential geographical indications (GIs) for fashion sustainability, and how this legal tool could help strengthen place-specific know-how and reputational links to each place of manufacture.

THE LIMITS OF WESTERN FASHION SUSTAINABILITY DISCOURSE FROM AN ARAB PERSPECTIVE: THE CASE OF BAHRAIN AND THE GULF

Looking at fashion systems and practice in Bahrain reveals a local fashion ontology, which prioritizes social practice – such as a strong local tailoring sector – a "mall", "souq", and "sharing" culture, and the niche role of local bespoke designers. This ontology emerges within a unique regional context where per capita income is high (despite local income inequality), labour conditions for vulnerable migrant workers are often exploitative (Gardner, 2012), and local customs blend historical fashion practice – including tailoring, mending, informal sharing economies – with modern fast fashion consumption.

From the example of Bahrain and the Gulf, several aspects of a local fashion ontology emerge. First, it is essential to place a geography, like the Gulf, within its global context, in terms of power, labour dynamics, and trade. Second, it is paramount to keep local social practice and local notions of materialism at the centre of an analysis. Without such an approach, exporting notions of sustainability in any design discipline from a Western understanding may re-enforce neo-colonial dynamics, where progress is measured by Western standards.

Another crucial aspect of current fashion sustainability discourse is how consumerism and fast fashion, a global phenomenon, are manifested locally. Put simply, the economic mammoths of global fashion have local supply chains around the world, but the way in which social, cultural, and material systems are organized around the presence of these multi-national corporations varies from locality to locality. For instance, for Bahrain and the Gulf, consumerism manifests culturally

Figure 19.1 One of Bahrain's prominent weavers, Mohammed Saleh Abdul-Ridha Jaffar, in the Bani Jamrah weaving workshop
Source: Photo by Maki Rawan

as "mall culture", an "Instagram culture", and the decline in "sharing culture" – a practice of sharing garments among women of the same household, or at times the neighbourhood (Figure 19.1).

The history of craft, and the economic and political trajectory of craft-workers and communities in Bahrain over the past decades, is also key to its fashion sustainability. Different geographies and communities have approached the survival of their craft, and often livelihoods, in different ways. For instance, Bahrain – an island with a long history of textile weaving – has seen a sharp decline in weaving, which is in part due to its participation in the globalized fashion economy, and in part to local socio-politics. Today, local tailoring in Bahrain remains a strong cultural facet, particularly for traditional designs. However, local designers often use imported fabrics within their designs, with a limited number of (socially driven or craft-preserving) designers using locally woven fabrics.[1]

The example of Bahrain shows that social systems must be considered when defining fashion "sustainability" at a local context. Further, it suggests that differences in fashion ontology and everyday lived experience impact what could be considered true "sustainability innovation", and frames a methodology applicable to other non-Western contexts. For example, while an emphasis on local tailoring is now considered 'sustainable' in Western locales today, in the case of Bahrain and the Gulf, local tailoring is part of the status quo. This means that modifications to the process of local tailoring must emerge from the Gulf's unique challenges (e.g. labour relations, reliance on fabric imports) and its assets (e.g. local tailoring networks, accessibility within neighbourhoods, traditions of weaving).

MAIN STAKEHOLDERS AND FRINGE STAKEHOLDERS: THE CASE OF CRAFTSMANSHIP IN INDIA AND ARGENTINA

Epistemologically speaking, Adamson in his book, *Thinking Through Craft* posits that 'craft is not an explicit practice but a way of reflecting on and encapsulating various practices' (Adamson, 2016). As such, a craftsperson's expression of local fashion sustainability is shaped by traditions, necessity, and climate and actively contributes to responsible practices both for communities and the environment. This is well-demonstrated by the Indian and Argentinian cases in this part wherein strategies for highlighting the value of handcrafted clothing and textiles and, at the same time, drawing in voices from the periphery are discussed.

INDIA

Craft is ubiquitous in India, emerging as the second largest sector of employment locally (Bhat & Yadav, 2016). In their fashion editorial, Gage and Pasricha have stated that "craftmanship and sustainability go hand in hand in the context of rich craft traditions and cultural heritage of India" (Gage & Pasricha, 2020) and drew attention to Sass Brown's speech at the PLATE Conference,[2] where she declared that "in a globalized, branded world, the true luxury of the future is handcrafted, indigenous and heritage crafts, re-interpreted into high end fashion" (Brown, 2019).

"Raising Awareness of Value (RAV): Women and Crafts in India",[3] a British Council-funded pilot project, reported here, set out to support the livelihoods of five female and two male craft makers, producing complex indigenous and place-based textiles in Gujarat, India. The RAV project was planned as a series of 16 online workshop sessions of two hours each. The intention was to co-create brand narratives using still and moving images. The workshops examined the potential power and agency of the image. An important outcome from the project was the improved use of imagery, as seen in the composition by participant and Bandhani (tie dye) artisan designer Zakiya Khatri after learning how to use the rule of thirds in photographic composition (Figure 19.2), drawing viewers into their ecosystem and facilitating the value allocation of their products.

Figure 19.2 Zakiya Khatri modelling her own creation of Bandhani, as part of the photography workshop

The group of craft makers, having learnt photography, image making, and digital marketing, felt confident using social media platforms to engage with their customers and communicate the value of their crafts. They were able to re-frame the narrative on their terms and build awareness of their unique, local, ecologically sensitive, and community-led practice.

The impact of the workshops was mapped, examining, and recording the participants' Instagram feeds before and at regular intervals after the intervention, as seen in the screenshots of the brand BairRaj, by participant Zakiya Khatri (Figures 19.3–19.5). It is evident that the brand's followers increased from 116 to 630 over this period.

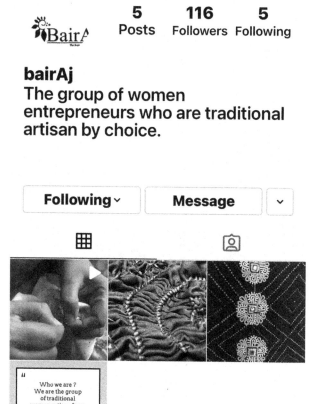

Figure 19.3 Screenshot of BaiRaj Instagram Feed before the workshops

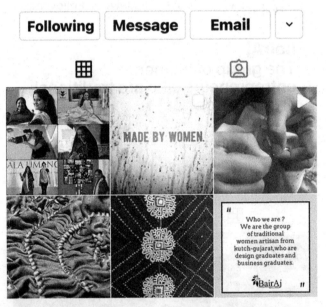

Figure 19.4 Screenshot of BaiRaj Instagram Feed three months after the workshops were completed

The RAV project, through its examination of the evolution of Instagram usage by the artisans, proposes that 'voice' today, is not what is spoken and heard only, but instead, it extends to what is seen and felt through images. Therefore, facilitating visibility and the voice of the artisans through social media channels could potentially help foreground

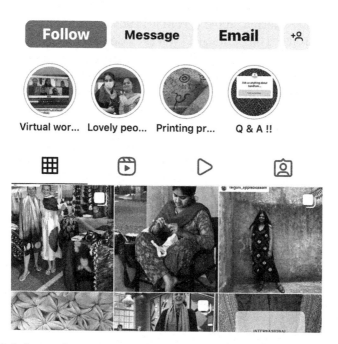

Figure 19.5 Screenshot of BaiRaj Instagram Feed on 16 July 2022

the symbiotic dichotomy between the traditional and the modern, and unlock possibilities for co-creation and collaboration between the traditionally trained craftspeople and the formally trained designers. A collaborative project titled 'The Craftisan Project' run in May 2021 between Pearl Academy, India and Manchester Metropolitan University, UK, is an example of such co-creative sharing and production.

The project facilitated collaboration between the students at both universities and a group of textile artisans from Gujarat, India, where they together, through a community of praxis, created branding and marketing material for the artisanal brands.

ARGENTINA

In Argentina, local indigenous communities often provide the labour behind craft products, i.e., they are the skilled hands producing the products, but remain on the periphery or "fringe" of mainstream fashion practice. Hart and Sharma built on Freeman's definition of stakeholders – i.e., any natural or legal person who can affect or is affected by the objectives of a company – and elaborated the notion of "fringe stakeholders" – namely, those affected with less voice, power, and urgency (Hart & Sharma, 2004; Freeman, 1984).

The project "The unheard voices", developed in Santa María (Catamarca, Argentina), was based on interviews with people of ancestral community descent in the aforementioned locality mainly through listening to and documenting their narratives. Some of the objectives of this project were: integration of knowledge, beliefs, identities through coexistence to allow opportunities, capacities and potentialities to emerge in order to achieve sustainability; from the Andean cosmovision, make a contribution to the United Nations Sustainable Development Goals; and include the indigenous world view in pedagogy and in the development of curricula in undergraduate and postgraduate courses related to fashion and textiles.

Some initial conclusions from this experience are that the indigenous people have a deep understanding of nature and are integrated with it. It is important to understand – in order to achieve sustainability – the spiritual sphere that surrounds these indigenous communities and the meaning they give to each garment. Clearly, these communities retain practices passed down from their ancestors, and their way of living, consuming, and interpreting the world is very different from that of Western society.

As Luis Enrique Maturana, a descendant of indigenous people, puts it:

> I give myself to my supreme beings. There is a mother, Mother Earth, Pachamama... it is a higher state in which I am inserted. We are all children of Mother Earth. Nothing is small and nothing is supreme in the context of nature.[4]

Reconciling different visions and attitudes necessarily requires a wider set of capabilities, to embrace a concept that can be summarized with the expression of "being native". These capacities could be summarized as openness to cultural diversity and "being one within the community". Achieving these capacities involves a learning process.

The connection to nature and a more sustainable way of life can be learnt by brands for the achievement of a sustainable industry. This could be achieved if brands develop "cultural appreciation" rather than cultural appropriation. This could be achieved if the voices of these peripheral communities were integrated into university careers in textiles and fashion. In this way, the future professionals would have knowledge of the inherited worldviews and practices of indigenous communities.

STRENGTHENING LOCALISM AND SUSTAINABILITY THROUGH GEOGRAPHICAL INDICATIONS

Building on the previous case studies, this part addresses how the value of local or indigenous know-how and crafts could be brought to a wider audience, from a legal perspective.

Currently, despite the lack of a harmonized legal definition, the term "artisanal" is widely used by fashion players at the global level, not only to emphasize exquisite craftsmanship, but also to address consumers' growing interest in product origins (Bhaduri & Stanforth, 2017). Similarly, the "made in" concept (e.g., "Made in Italy") is often framed in sustainability terms (Clarke-Sather & Cobb, 2019) although origin-marking legislation responds solely to trade and customs requirements, with no direct associations to sustainability credentials.

From an intellectual property (IP) perspective, the joint promotion of culturally related and sustainable fashion production could be achieved through GIs. GIs are defined in international IP treaties as signs that identify a good as originating from a specific territory, region, or locality, which possess a certain reputation, quality, or other characteristic by virtue of that place of origin (Article 22(1) TRIPS Agreement). A GI typically includes the name of the place, which can be used by all entities from the area, provided that they manufacture the given product in a prescribed way (Figure 19.6).

Several authors emphasized that GIs can foster rural development, reach marginalized communities, and contribute towards craft dignity, by stimulating the growth of niche markets, strengthening intergenerational knowledge transfer, promoting cultural heritage preservation,

Figure 19.6 Geographical Indications schemes in the European Union
Source: https://ec.europa.eu/info/food-farming-fisheries/food-safety-and-quality/
certification/quality-labels/quality-schemes-explained_en

and endorsing regional centres for artisanal craftsmanship (Calboli, 2015; Covarrubia, 2019).

The three geographic areas outlined in the case studies above exemplify both the pitfalls and benefits of the current non-harmonized international regulatory framework. Several States – including Bahrain (Law 16 of 2006) – do ensure recognition of foreign GIs and prohibit misappropriation or misuse of words or symbols that may suggest a geographical origin, but have not established any internal registration mechanisms. Other countries, such as Argentina (Decree No. 556/2009 of May 15, 2009), limit the scope of protection to foodstuffs, wines, and spirits. Conversely, the Indian GI system (Act No. 48 of 1999) is well-known for covering more handicrafts than agricultural items (Marie Vivien, 2015).

Against this background, the following case example will take the Kutch province, in the Gujarat state, where the aforementioned "RAV" project was conducted, as a reference for outlining the potential for GIs to create value for sustainable crafts. The two GIs retrieved in the Indian Registry refer to the "*Kachchh Shawls*" and "*Kutch Embroidery*".

An analysis of the product specifications shows the prominence of some features that embody the "ontology" of fashion in the territory: place-specific knowledge and culture. The Kutch Embroidery links to the history of embroidery in India and dates back to 2.500–1.500 BC. The traditional production methods use local resources such as the "*desi*" wool for the Kachchh Shawls and incorporate the traditional "*kori*" pattern or "*dholki*" motif. Influences of climate, geographical, and historical features traceable from the techniques, patterns, colours, and raw materials used in the Kutch Embroidery and the Kachchh Shawls are amplified by the art of handloom weaving.

The analysis of the owners revealed public-private cooperation between local entities, manufacturers, and national institutions.[5] This confirms that the GI voluntary regime supported by public entities has the potential to provide assurances on the origin and characteristics of the products, as per propositions of previous studies (Pai & Singla, 2017).

There are however, some drawbacks that emerged from the use of GIs. Firstly, the location of the raw material sourced is not precise or is un-confirmed, and traceability and lifecycle considerations are not addressed. Secondly, internal and external checks and balance mechanisms to verify product specifications and compliance are yet to be established. Nevertheless, these pitfalls can be turned into opportunities if additional measures are developed and put in place. On the one hand, the use of technology to track the products and certify quality may assist producers in monitoring the manufacturing processes of the GI-denominated products. Furthermore, the establishment of inspection structures, with Codes of Conduct and periodic audits, can ground the claims regarding products' sustainability, quality, and reputation. This, in turn, could increase consumers' trust and make traditional crafts more recognisable in the international arena.

Thus, despite the limitations, GIs are an option worth considering for groups seeking to ensure the cultural appreciation of traditional fashion, support the authenticity and values-communication for marginalized communities, and to designate and promote sustainable apparel productions related to a specific territory and knowledge.

CONCLUSION

Current approaches underpinning sustainable development, shaped by Western scholars and businesses, fail to address the root-cause of the problem: a hegemonic paradigm that heavily depends on one economic system, grounded on assumptions of infinite growth and on entrenched human-centred symmetries. The examples of Bahrain, India, and Argentina illustrate the importance of including local, social, cultural, and political considerations when assessing fashion 'sustainability' from a non-Western perspective. These examples also infer that by exploring the sustainability discourse around local, social practice, and knowledge, less harmful commercialized strategies could be replicated. However, further studies will need to be conducted to substantiate this argument.

Expanding the lens of fashion sustainability beyond its hegemonic narrative can start with an examination of local, social, and cultural practices and working methodologies in many marginalized communities around the world, with a practical exploration of their unique legal assets which can bolster quality-led, place-based systems.

NOTES

1 According to Hussain (2011), the number of weaving workshops in Bahrain has dwindled from fifteen to one, over the course of the past three decades. The last one is located in the village of Bani Jamrah. An additional workshop for weaving in al-Jasrah was funded by the government with the aims of craft preservation.
2 The 3rd international PLATE conference (Product Lifetimes and the Environment), held in Germany in 2019 addresses product lifetimes in the context of sustainability.
3 The principal investigators of the project were Shalini Gupta (Pearl Academy, India) and Alison Welsh (Manchester Metropolitan University, UK). The other members of the team included Dr. Fiona Hackney, PhD Student Jackie Morris (MMU UK), Sabbah Sharma, Varun Goel, and Amitesh Singhal (Pearl Academy, India) and independent artist and designer Lokesh Ghai. Nine artisans living in Kachchh, a district in northwest Gujarat, participated in this project. These professional artisans specialized in refined methods of hand-weaving, tie-dye, or complex embroidery work, specific to each of their communities.
4 In the same vein, the Sustainable Development Goals (SDGs) viewed from the community worldview: the cosmovision of the Indigenous People of Latin America and the Caribbean, represent an opportunity to bridge different intercultural development models, in the pursuit of sustainability. Starting from the garment, this unique vision embraces the broader concept of harmony between human beings and nature, where the development proposal must be understood as a new form of social and environmental coexistence.
5 KAMIR and Ministry of Textiles for Kutch Embroidery; the Kutch Weavers Association and Ministry of Commerce & Industry, UNCTAD, DFID for Kachchh Shawls, respectively.

REFERENCES

Adamson, G. (2016) *Thinking Through Craft.* London/Newyork: Bloomsbury Academic.
Bhaduri, G. & Stanforth, N. (2017) 'To (or not to) label products as artisanal: Effect of fashion involvement on customer perceived value', *Journal of Product & Brand Management*, 26(2), 177–189. https://doi.org/10.1108/JPBM-04-2016-1153
Bhat, J. & Yadav, P. (2016) 'Handicraft sector: The comforting sector of employment review', *Management Studies and Economic Systems*, 3, 111–117.
Bramwell, L. (2020) 'Eco-colonialism: How Bangladesh is burdened by the impacts of fast fashion', *The Meridian.* Available at: https://meridian-magazine.com/eco-colonialism-fast-fashion-in-bangladesh/ (Accessed: 14 January 2021).
Brown, S. (2019) 'Can global craft and artisanship be the future of luxury fashion', *PLATE Product Lifetimes and the Environment.* Available at: https://www.plateconference.org/can-global-craft-artisanship-future-luxury-fashion/.
Calboli, I. (2015) 'Geographical indications of origin at the crossroads of local development, consumer protection, and marketing strategies', *IIC - International Review of Intellectual Property and Competition Law*, 46(7), 760.
Clarke-Sather, A. & Cobb, K. (2019) 'Onshoring fashion: Worker sustainability impacts of global and local apparel production', *Journal of Cleaner Production*, 208(1), 1206–1218. Available at: https://doi.org/10.1016/j.jclepro.2018.09.073.

Covarrubia, P. (2019) 'Geographical indications of traditional handicrafts: A cultural element in a predominantly economic activity', *IIC - International Review of Intellectual Property and Competition Law*, 50. Available at: 10.1007/s40319-019-00810-3.

Freeman, R. E. (1984) *Strategic Management: A Stakeholder Approach*. Boston, MA: Pitman.

Gage, K. & Pasricha, A. (2020) 'Editorial-Fashion in India', *Fashion Practice*, 12(2), 163–171.

Gardner, A. M. (2012) 'Why do they keep coming? Labor migrants in the Persian Gulf States', in M. Kamrava and Z. Babar (eds) *Migrant Labour in the Persian Gulf*. London: Hurst.

Hart, S. L. & Sharma, S. Y. (2004) 'Engaging fringe stakeholders for competitive imagination', *The Academy of Management Executive*, 18(1), 7–18.

Horning, A. (2014) 'Clothing and colonialism: The Dungiven costume and the fashioning of early modern identities', *Journal of Social Archaeology*, 14(3), 296–318. DOI: 10.1177/1469605314539580.

Hussain, H. M. (2011) *The Occupation of Weaving in Bani Jamrah: Its History, Description, and People [translated, Arabic: mihnat al-naseej fi-bani jamrah: tareekhaha wa-wasfaha wa-rajalaatuha]*. Manama: Al-Wasat Publishing.

Marie Vivien, D. (2015) *The Protection of Geographical Indications in India: A New Perspective on the French and European Experience. In (Vol. 2)*. Beaverton: SAGE Publications.

Mayer, A. (2020) 'Sustainability must mean decolonization', *State of Fashion*. Available at: https://www.stateoffashion.org/en/intervention/intervention-2-origins/longread-2-aditi-mayer/ (Accessed: 14 January 2021).

Pai, Y. & Singla, T. (2017) '"Vanity GIs': India's legislation on geographical indications and the missing regulatory framework," in I. Calboli & W. L. Ng-Loy (eds) *Geographical Indications at the Crossroads of Trade, Development, and Culture: Focus on Asia-Pacific*. Cambridge: Cambridge University Press, pp. 333–358.

Paige, R. C. & Littrell, M. A. (2002) 'Craft retailers' criteria for success and associated business strategies', *Journal of Small Business Management*. 40(4), 314–33.

Rabine, L. W. (1997) 'Not a mere ornament: Tradition, modernity, and colonialism in kenyan and western clothing', *Fashion Theory*, 1(2), 145–167. DOI: 10.2752/136270497779592101.

Rovine, V. L. (2009) 'Colonialism's clothing: Africa, France, and the deployment of fashion', *Design Issues*, 25(3), 44–61.

Semaan, C. (2018) 'Understanding sustainability means talking about colonialism', *The Cut*. Available at: https://www.thecut.com/2018/02/understanding-sustainability-means-talking-about-colonialism.html (Accessed: 14 January 2021).

Zhan, X. & Walker, S. (2009) 'Craft as leverage for sustainable design transformation: A theoretical foundation', *The Design Journal*. 22(4), 438–503.

WEBSITES

Chonnabot Mudmee Thai Silk, ASEAN GI Database: http://www.asean-gidatabase.org/gidatabase/sites/default/files/gidocs/THGI0000052100058-en.pdf (last accessed 25 March 2022).

Cochinilla de Canarias, EU GI Database: https://ec.europa.eu/info/food-farming-fisheries/food-safety-and-quality/certification/quality-labels/geographical-indications-register//pdf/ec_food_14421.pdf (last accessed 25 March 2022).

EU Quality Schemes: https://ec.europa.eu/info/food-farming-fisheries/food-safety-and-quality/certification/quality-labels/quality-schemes-explained_en (last accessed 6 July 2022).

Kachchh Shawls, Indian GI Registry https://search.ipindia.gov.in/GIRPublic/Application/Details/174 (last accessed 24 January 2022).

Kutch Embroidery, Indian GI Registry https://search.ipindia.gov.in/GIRPublic/Application/Details/103 (last accessed 24 January 2022).

Shetland Wool, EU GI Database: https://eur-lex.europa.eu/legal-content/EN/TXT/HTML/?uri=CELEX:32011R1121&from=EN (last accessed 25 March 2022).

LEGISLATIVE SOURCES

1994 Agreement on Trade-Related Aspects of Intellectual Property (TRIPS), World Trade Organization (WTO).

Argentina, Decree No. 556/2009 of May 15, 2009, on the Implementation of Law No. 25.380 and its amendment, Law No. 25.966 which established the Legal Regime for Geographical Indications and Appellations of Origin of Agricultural and Food Products in Argentina.

Bahrain, Law No. 16 of 2006 on Amendments to Law No. 16 of 2004 on the Protection of Geographical Indications.

Declaración Universal de los Derechos de la Madre Tierra. From World People's Conference on Climate Change and the Rights of Mother Earth, Cochabamba, Bolivia, 22 April – Earth Day 2010.

India, The Geographical Indications of Goods (Registration and Protection) Act, 1999 (Act No. 48 of 1999).

Part VI

Circular economy

20 Circular economy in the textile and apparel sector: an overview of global trends, challenges and opportunities

Lis Suarez-Visbal, Claudia Stuckrath and Jesús Rosales Carreón

INTRODUCTION

The textile and apparel (T&A)[1] sector symbolises the epitome of the linear business paradigm, characterised by the take-make-waste model. Globally, only 20% of clothing waste is collected for reuse and recycling (Jacometti, 2019). Additionally, it is estimated that less than 1% of all textiles worldwide are recycled into new textiles (Ellen MacArthur Foundation, 2017). The sector holds asymmetrical environmental and social interests across different stakeholders. Most of the impacts related to the consumption of clothing in developed countries occur in developing countries where most of the production occurs, affecting the environment and livelihood of close-by communities. At the same time, while the sector is known for its often-questionable working conditions, it employs more than 300 million workers globally along its value chain (Ellen MacArthur Foundation, 2017).

The Circular Economy (CE) could help the sector become more sustainable by increasing efficiency, decreasing pollution, using more renewable and safely recycled inputs, and reducing the extraction of raw materials (PACE, 2021). However, critics highlight that those circular

DOI: 10.4324/9781003272878-26

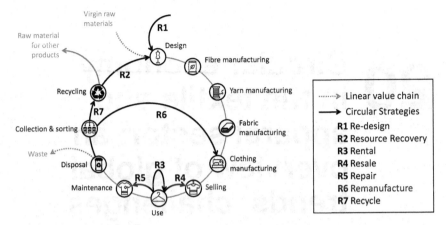

Figure 20.1 Highlights seven of the most used circular strategies in the global textile and apparel value chain, which stages of this chain they comprise

strategies (CS) based on reuse loops may reduce production, thus displacing employment in production countries. Other criticisms gravitate around the weak social dimension of CE, which only mention the number of jobs created without elaboration on the quality of these jobs and the impact of CS in communities where they are applied (Dufourmont & Goodwin Brown, 2020). Therefore, targeted efforts are needed to ensure the transition is just and inclusive.

CS close the loop of materials with different processes where the shorter the loop, the higher the product value retention (Kirchherr et al., 2017). The R-framework (see Figure 20.1) presents these CS in a hierarchical order (Blomsma & Brennan, 2017).

This chapter looks at circularity in the T&A sector from a global perspective. It includes a review of global trends, policy challenges and opportunities. Also, it uses the CS shown in Figure 20.1 as an anchor to highlight the complex and multi-layered ties between actors and organisations in different countries.

GLOBAL TRENDS

Even though circularity interest in the T&A sector has grown among businesses, policymakers and academics in the last ten years, its implementation is still in its infancy (Barrie & Schröder, 2021). The global COVID-19 pandemic has had substantial economic and social repercussions on the sector, manifesting the power imbalance between big global brands and manufacturers in emerging markets (Anner, 2020).

However, post-COVID-19 has been seen as an opportunity for a sustainable recovery where the CE can play a significant role. Although reshoring some of the manufacturing processes represents high costs, it has become an alternative for businesses to create local jobs, reduce risk and have a better compliance with regulations and similar levels of enforcement (Charter & Cheng, 2021). Additionally, consumer behaviour has played a role in making sustainability relevant, with more than 70% of European consumers interested in circular business models (European Environment Agency, 2019).

Market trends

The different CSs shown in Figure 22.1 have specific market trends associated with them. For example, the resale (R4) market is projected to double in five years to reach US$77 billion in the US (ThredUp, 2021), while in the EU, it is expected to grow to €30 billion by 2030 (Neerman, 2021). Also, the global online clothing rental (R3) market is projected to increase by 8.7% from 2019 to 2024 (Mordor Intelligence, 2021). The global recycled (R7) textile market is anticipated to generate US$7.6 billion by 2027, with Asian countries such as Vietnam, Turkey, India, Malaysia, Indonesia and Bangladesh taking a significant role (Prasad, 2021).

Africa presents a potential case for remanufacture (R6) and recycle (R7) CS. On one side, it has a large influx of second-hand clothing coming from developed countries, where currently unsold clothes end up in landfills and water bodies; on the other side, the continent's production is growing, given the manufacturing knowledge, capacity and relatively cheaper labour available (Ellen MacArthur Foundation, 2021). Finally, Latin American countries are differentiating themselves from low-cost Asian production countries by introducing biomaterials and circular supplies such as organic alpaca and recycled textiles (R2) (Garcia Jarpa & Halog, 2021).

Multilateral initiatives related to circularity and the T&A sector

Multilateral collaborations play a critical role in accelerating the CE. They differ in scope, direction and level of engagement, but they share the creation of aligned agendas and principles among actors. However, critics of large multilateral collaborations state that they often lack enforcement mechanisms, particularly for the participation of the least developed countries in trade and policy negotiations directly affected by these arrangements. This problem is particularly true in the T&A sector, characterised by a global deployment where production mainly happens in developing nations (Barrie & Schröder, 2021).

Alliances such as the G7 and G20 align interests around CE's take up (Charter & Cheng, 2021). However, there is no specific focus in the T&A sector. More circularity-specific multilateral alliances have been formed at the global, regional and city levels in the last few years. At the global level, some examples are the Global Alliance for Resource Efficiency and Circular Economy (GARECE) and the Platform for Accelerating the Circular Economy (PACE). Specific to the T&A sector, PACE is one of the few global alliances targeting the sector, with textiles being part of its five action agendas.

PACE has also helped to develop regional coalitions in Africa and Latin America. The African Alliance on Circular Economy (AACE) was founded by Rwanda, Nigeria and South Africa, in 2016 and the Latin American and the Caribbean Circular Economic Coalition launched in 2021. Both alliances promote textiles' PACE Circular Economic Action Agenda (PACE, 2021).

Other regional industry collaborations are present in Asia, mainly Bangladesh and India. One of these alliances is The Circular Fashion Partnership which facilitates circular collaborations between textile and garment manufacturers, recyclers and fashion brands operating in Bangladesh (Global Fashion Agenda (GFA), 2021).

At the city level, there are many examples around the globe. One worth mentioning is #WearNext. In this initiative, the New York City Department of Sanitation (DSNY), the New York City Economic Development Corporation (NYCEDC) and the Ellen MacArthur Foundation joined forces to promote circularity in the fashion industry in New York City (Ellen MacArthur Foundation, 2019). In February 2021, New York State enacted a regulation that stipulates that any business with more than 10% of its waste comprising textiles is obligated to send all the textile waste for recycling (Mizrachi & Tal, 2022).

POLICIES

In Europe, more than 33 national CE roadmaps have been launched (Barrie & Schröder, 2021). The European Union (EU) has ambitious CE policies related to the T&A sector. They are contained in the European Green Deal, the Circular Economy Action Plan (CEAP), the Sustainable Products Initiative and the recent European Textile Strategy (Lazarevic & Valve, 2017). The EEA has put together a set of policy tools recommended to accelerate circularity for the sector. These tools include, among others[2] extending producer responsibility (EPR) for textiles. To date, EPR for textiles has only been adopted in France and Sweden (Bettin, 2022). It is essential to highlight that for an EPR scheme to help the circular transition, it should be governed collaboratively, while goals should be formulated to promote high-ranked CS in the R-hierarchy (OVAM et al., 2021).

The leading T&A manufacturing countries in Asia are China, Bangladesh, and India. China has recently released its five-year Development Plan for Circular Economy (2021–2025), promoting green design (R1), clean production and recycling (R7), which will have a direct effect on their manufacturing industries (Chipman Koty, 2021). Even though Bangladesh does not have a CE plan, it has aligned political and financial support from the Netherlands and other countries for its transition (SAM, 2020). Since 2019, India has created a national plan for the CE. However, it does not prioritise textiles as a focus sector (Niti Aayog, 2021). In Japan, the Ministry of Economy, Trade and Industry (METI) formulated the Circular Economy Vision in 2020, where textiles are one of the key areas to be targeted (METI, 2021).

In 2021, the US launched the National Recycling Strategy (R7) to support the CE transition highlighting that textiles targeted the waste stream (Environmental Protection Agency, 2021). Additionally, some cities took the leadership on circular policies and regulations within their control. Charlotte in North Carolina, is one of the first cities to adopt the CE as a public sector strategy that includes textiles as a prioritised resource stream (Gladek et al., 2018).

In Canada, every jurisdiction has a different CE ambition with varying waste collection, management and recycling standards (R7). There is no national CE plan nor EPR scheme at a national level (Chatham House, 2020). In terms of textile waste, only British Columbia, Quebec and Ontario have recycling systems that are well-established and funded by industry through EPR programmes (Environment and Climate Change Canada, 2020).

Latin American countries, including Colombia, Chile, Mexico, Ecuador, Peru and Uruguay, have CE roadmaps or strategies (Schröder et al., 2020). Also, EPR schemes have been introduced by Chile, Mexico, Costa Rica and Brazil (Fernández Ortíz & Eberz, 2019). However, only Chile has included textiles as a prioritised waste stream in its EPR legislation (Molina Alomar, 2021).

In Africa, the Durban Declaration in 2019 marked the first Pan-African policy related to African CE ambitions (African Ministers for the Environment, 2019). Rwanda, Gabon, Uganda and Tunisia have integrated the promotion of some circular principles in their sustainable development policies and legislation. Moreover, South Africa, Kenya, Namibia and Tanzania have put the CE at the core of their plans (Desmond & Milcah, 2019). Additionally, several African countries are currently discussing banning or increasing tariffs on second-hand clothing imports to protect local industries (World Economic Forum, 2021).

CHALLENGES

CE lacks systemic, traceable and enforceable laws and regulations generally and specifically in the T&A sector (Lazarevic & Valve, 2017). Furthermore, harmonising and standardising policies are critical for governments across borders, as the T&A sector comprises countries with different levels of development, infrastructure, knowledge and capacity, making it problematic to implement CE opportunities (UNEP & IRP, 2020). This mitigates the chances of a fair circular transition for all stakeholders and countries involved (Barrie & Schröder, 2021).

Also, policy instruments such as import tariffs, gate fees and taxes make some CS expensive for manufacturing and remanufacturing (R6) businesses. For example, a 19.2% global average import tariff for remanufacturing textiles abroad makes this process a less desirable option (The Observatory of Economic Complexity (OEC), 2020). Additionally, there are minimal or no waste disposal fees in many countries, which facilitate the common practice of garment-textile waste disposal and incineration by brands and retailers (Jia et al., 2020).

Furthermore, there is little mention of CE in current international trade instruments applied to the T&A sector, such as free trade agreements (FTAs) and World Trade Organization (WTO) provisions, technical standards, subsidies and sustainability clauses. This results in a limited CE uptake in the T&A sector (Barrie & Schröder, 2021).

Finally, another common challenge is the lack of organised textile collection, sorting and recycling infrastructure (Ellen MacArthur Foundation, 2017). In many countries, these collection systems are informally organised, with high health and safety risks and poor working conditions for workers (PACE, 2021). Also, across different geographies, there is a lack of an effective incentive mechanism for companies to initiate and sustain circular design changes (UN Environment Programme, 2020).

OPPORTUNITIES

Circularity in the T&A sector can bring potential new business opportunities, as companies can combine multiple CS by developing collaborations with local partners. For instance, extended services such as rental (R3), resale (R4) and repair (R5) have a significant potential to be deployed together, maximising opportunities for businesses and consumers too.

CS such as remanufacture (R6), repair (R5) and recycle (R7) are labour-intensive practices, and they have the potential to develop new jobs paired with new reskilling programmes. However, the quality of jobs created is often unclear. Thus, the need to have comprehensive and specific social impact assessment frameworks to monitor the working conditions and the T&A sector and provide insights into where conditions should be improved (Suarez-Visbal et al., 2022).

Digitalisation and advanced recycling technologies paired with strong business collaborations can help develop regional and/or local hubs (R7) to increase the output of recycled materials that can be reintroduced into the value chain and incentivise the adoption of recovered material (R2). At the same time, this consolidation can help develop local circular T&A value chains by reshoring. Furthermore, collaborations bring more knowledge and better tracking of materials and resources, allowing more efficient use of materials. Additionally, the consolidation of digital platforms has and can further enable CS, such as rental (R3) and resale (R4).

In terms of policies, new proposed regulations such as the European Textile Strategy are critical leavers for the development of more hierarchical CS such as redesign (R1), reduce (R2) and repair (R5), which are now prioritised by this plan. Redesign (R1) involves a systemic change where collaboration is needed along the whole value chain. Also, reduced value-added tax for second-hand products (R4) and rental services (R3) is an opportunity to encourage consumers to support different circular business models and purchase more circular apparel products. Additionally, with a harmonised systemic approach, fully maximised CE can also promote traceability and transparency, which are critical for consolidating integration and collaboration amongst stakeholders of the T&A sector (Potting et al., 2017).

Finally, the CE is a promising way to reduce environmental impacts (PACE, 2021). As raw material extraction for fibres and fabric manufacturing is an essential contributor to the carbon footprint of clothing (Peters et al., 2015), reducing the utilisation of virgin raw materials by resource recovery (R2) has the potential to reduce this impact. Also, minimising textile waste is a clear opportunity for CE. By using CS related to waste management, such as recycle (R7), combined with redesign (R1), waste can be designed out of the ideation of the product.

CONCLUSION

Given the size and complexity of the global T&A value chain and the tension between local and global CE approaches from production and consumption countries, harmonising policies and strategies for circularity in the T&A has been challenging. Efforts by governments and multilateral alliances should focus on orchestrating incentives across jurisdictions with the countries that are part of the T&A value chain. National and regional policy tools and their impacts should be discussed and negotiated with businesses and other relevant stakeholders in the value chain (such as workers and suppliers), ensuring their participation in existing multilateral alliances concerned with circular textiles. Ideally, both the CE agenda and the social agenda (especially related to employment) should also work in tandem; across jurisdictions to avoid the trade-off between different segments of the T&A value chain.

In addition, funding mechanisms from the government and private investors should be coordinated, as they can reduce the high up-front investment costs of a circular business model. This funding should be available in developed and developing nations, targeting start-ups, scale-ups and consolidated businesses such as circular suppliers, manufacturers, resale-rental platforms and recycling businesses. It could be done, for example, through an international trade-aid mechanism and regional bodies such as the EU.

Finally, CE in the T&A sector presents clear opportunities to tackle sustainability issues from the triple bottom line: economic, environmental and social. Although the economic and environmental opportunities are well-studied, social opportunities should be further explored, as many CS are labour intensive and could amplify pre-existent poor working conditions in the sector.

NOTES

1 In this research, the textile and apparel (T&A) sector includes manufacturing textiles and fabric from raw materials and transforming these fabrics into clothing.
2 Other policy tools include Green Public Procurement, reduced VAT on repair and labour subsidies, reuse targets, reduced VAT on second-hand products, separated collection obligation, recycling and recycled targets, the quality requirement for recycled fibres, taxes and bans on textile incineration and landfill, resource taxed in new fibres, consumer awareness campaign, circular economy training and education in schools and higher education (European Environment Agency, 2019).

REFERENCES

African ministers for the environment. (2019). Draft Durban Declaration on taking action for environmental sustainability and prosperity in Africa. *African Ministerial Conference on the Environment*, Durban, South Africa, November 15, 2019.

Anner, M. (2020). *Abandoned? The Impact of COVID-19 on Workers and Businesses at the Bottom of Global Garment Supply Chains.* https://www.workersrights.org/wp-content/uploads/2020/03/Abandoned-Penn-State-WRC-Report-March-27-2020.pdf

Barrie, J., & Schröder, P. (2021). Circular economy and international trade: A systematic literature review. *Circular Economy and Sustainability, 0123456789.* https://doi.org/10.1007/s43615-021-00126-w

Bettin, L. (2022). *Textile EPR: Recycling Laws for Fashion E-Commerce Across Europe.* E-Commerce Germany News.

Blomsma, F., & Brennan, G. (2017). The emergence of circular economy: A new framing around prolonging resource productivity. *Journal of Industrial Ecology, 21*(3), 603–614. https://doi.org/10.1111/JIEC.12603

Charter, M., & Cheng, I. (2021). The G20: accelerating the transition to a global circular economy. In N. Edizioni (Ed.). *Global Governance at a Turning Point: The Role of the G20* (pp. 115–154.).

Chatham House. (2020). *Policies|Circular Economy. Earth.* https://circulareconomy.earth/

Chipman Koty, A. (2021). *China's Circular Economy: Understanding the New Five Year Plan.* China Briefing. https://www.china-briefing.com/news/chinas-circular-economy-understanding-the-new-five-year-plan/

Desmond, P., & Milcah, A. (2019). Accelerating the transition to a circular economy in Africa. In *The Circular Economy and the Global South Project: The Circular Economy and the Global South.* https://doi.org/0.4324/9780429434006-9

Dufourmont, J., & Goodwin Brown, E. (2020). *Jobs & skills in the Circular Economy.*

Ellen MacArthur Foundation. (2017). A new textiles economy: Redesigning fashion's future. In *Ellen MacArthur Foundation.* https://www.ellenmacarthurfoundation.org/publications/a-new-textiles-economy-redesigning-fashions-future

Ellen MacArthur Foundation. (2019). *City and Industry in Collaboration to Save Clothes from Landfills.* http://www.ellenmacarthurfoundation.org/our-work/activities/circular-economy-in-cities

Ellen MacArthur Foundation. (2021). *Circular Economy in Africa: Examples and Opportunities. Fashion and Textiles.*

Environment and Climate Change Canada. (2020). *Circular North America: Accelerating the Transition to a Thriving and Resilient Low-carbon Economy.*

Environmental Protection Agency. (2021). *National Recycling Strategy: Part One of a Series on Building a Circular Economy for All.*

European Environment Agency. (2019). *Textiles in Europe's Circular Economy.*

Fernández Ortíz, J. C., & Eberz, G. (2019). *Responsabilidad Extendida del Productor: Estudio Regional sobre la figura REP en Latinoamérica en comparación con Alemania y España bajo el Marco Legal de la Unión Europea.*

Garcia Jarpa, S., & Halog, A. (2021). Pursuing a Circular and Sustainable Textile Industry in Latin America. In *Sustainable Fashion and Textiles in Latin America* (pp. 105–130). Springer Nature.

Gladek, E., Kennedy, E., & Thorin, T. (2018). *Circular Charlotte: Towards a Zero Waste and Inclusive City.* https://www.metabolic.nl/publications/circular-charlotte-pdf/

GlobalFashionAgenda (GFA). (2021). *Scaling Circularity: Lessons Learned from the Circular Fashion Partnership for Building Pre-competitive Collaborations to Scale Upstream Circular FashionSystems.*https://www.globalfashionagenda.com/circular-fashion-partnership/cfp-overview/

Jacometti, V. (2019). Circular economy and waste in the fashion industry. *Laws*, *8*(4), 27. https://doi.org/10.3390/laws8040027

Jia, F. P., Yin, S., Chen, L., & Chen, X. (2020). The circular Economy in the textile and apparel industry: A systematic literature review. *Journal of Cleaner Production*, *259.* https://doi.org/https://doi.org/10.1016/j.jclepro.2020.120728

Kirchherr, J., Reike, D., & Hekkert, M. (2017). Conceptualising the circular economy: An analysis of 114 definitions. *Resources, Conservation and Recycling*, *127*, 221–232. https://doi.org/10.1016/j.resconrec.2017.09.005

Lazarevic, D., & Valve, H. (2017). Narrating expectations for the circular economy: Towards a common and contested European transition. *Energy Research & Social Science 3, 31*(1), 60–69.

UNEP and IRP. (2020). *Sustainable Trade in Resources: Global Material Flows, Circularity and Trade.* United Nations Environment Programme, Nairobi, Kenya. https://wedocs.unep.org/bitstream/handle/20.500.11822/34344/STR.pdf?sequence=1&isAllowed=y

METI. (2021). *Study Group on Sustainability of Textile and Apparel Industry.*

Mizrachi, M. P., & Tal, A. (2022). Regulation for promoting sustainable, fair and circular fashion. *Sustainability 2022, 14*(1), 502. https://doi.org/10.3390/SU14010502

Molina Alomar, J. (2021). *Incorporación de la ropa a la Ley REP: El camino que ya se está trazando para regular los residuos de la industria textil en Chile.* Pais Circular. https://www.paiscircular.cl/consumo-y-produccion/incorporar-la-ropa-a-la-ley-rep-el-camino-que-ya-se-esta-trazando-para-regular-los-residuos-de-la-industria-textil/

Mordor Intelligence. (2021). *Online Clothing Rental Market - Growth, Trends, COVID-19 Impact, and Forecasts (2022–2027).*

Neerman, P. (2021). *These are Europe's Most Sustainable Marketplaces.* RetailDetail. https://www.retaildetail.eu/en/news/fashion/these-are-europes-most-sustainable-marketplaces

Niti Aayog. (2021, March 18). *Govt Driving Transition from Linear to Circular Economy.* Government of India. https://pib.gov.in/PressReleasePage.aspx?PRID=1705772

UN Environment Programme. (2020). *Sustainability and Circularity in the Textile Value Chain-Global Stocktaking.* Nairobi, Kenya. https://wedocs.unep.org/20.500.11822/34184

OVAM, EEB, EuRIC, & EuroCommerce. (2021). *Exploring EPR for Textiles: Taking Responsibility for Europe's Textile Waste.*

PACE. (2021). *Circular Economy Action Agenda: Textiles.*

Peters, G., Svanström, M., Roos, S., Sandin, G., & Zamani, B. (2015). Carbon footprints in the textile industry. *Handbook of Life Cycle Assessment (LCA) of Textiles and Clothing*, 3–30. https://doi.org/10.1016/B978-0-08-100169-1.00001-0

Potting, J., Hekkert, M., Worrell, E., & Hanemaaijer, A. (2017). *Circular Economy: Measuring Innovation in the Product Chain.* PBL Netherlands Environmental Assessment Agency, The Hague. https://www.pbl.nl/sites/default/files/downloads/pbl-2016-circular-economy-measuring-innovation-in-product-chains-2544.pdf

Prasad, E. (2021). *The Global Recycled Textiles Market by Type.* Allied Market Research. https://www.alliedmarketresearch.com/recycle-textile-market

SAM. (2020). *The Netherlands to assist Bangladesh in a Circular Economy.* South Asia Monitor. www.southasiamonitor.org/cooperationtrade/netherlands-assist-Bangladesh-circular-economy

Schröder, P., Albaladejo, M., Ribas, A., Macewen, M., & Tilkanen, J. (2020). *The Circular Economy in Latin America and the Caribbean: Opportunities for Building Resilience.* Chatham House, London, UK. https://www.chathamhouse.org/sites/default/files/2020-09-17-circular-economy-lac-Schr%C3%B6der-et-al.pdf

Suarez-Visbal, L., Stuckrath, C., & Rosales Carreón, J. (2022). Assessing through a gender-inclusion lens the social impact of circular strategies in the apparel value chain: The Dutch case. In V. Pál (Ed.), *Social and Cultural Aspects of the Circular Economy.* Routledge. https://www.routledge.com/Social-and-Cultural-Aspects-of-the-Circular-Economy-Toward-Solidarity-and/Pal/p/book/9781032185804

The Observatory of Economic Complexity (OEC). (2020). *Used Clothing.* https://oec.world/en/profile/hs92/used-clothing

ThredUp. (2021). 2021 Fashion Resale Market and Trend Report | thredUP. In *ThredUp.com.* https://www.thredup.com/resale/#resale-industry

World Economic Forum. (2021). *Five Big Bets for the Circular Economy in Africa: African Circular Economy Alliance.* https://90156329-3689-4baa-b686-cfc78b14a040.filesusr.com/ugd/056cf4_9ef0689c02154ce68ba801c1c2731be1.pdf

21 New forms of governance to accelerate circular textiles in the Netherlands

Jacqueline Cramer

INTRODUCTION

Circular textiles sector is one of the key priorities of the Dutch circular economy policy programme. Because of this priority, those engaged in sustainable textiles in the Netherlands often use the term circular textile. Both sustainability and circular economy are essentially global in their nature, and position system-level changes at their very core. Sustainability, however, is more open-ended and includes a multitude of goals, depending on the actors and their interests. Circular economy focuses on moving from linear to circular flows, ideally eliminating all resource input and leakage out of the system (Geissdoerfer et al., 2017). This latter view lays the foundation for the circular initiatives in the Dutch clothing and fashion sector.

To realise the transformation to a circular textile industry is a tremendous challenge. The Dutch clothing and fashion sector is highly globalised, competitive and geared towards fast, cheap production. Major brands dominate the market, which makes it hard for newcomers with circular products to scale up. Consumers have got used to throwing away their clothes and buying new ones; often they are unaware of the environmental and social impact of their behaviour. Thinking in terms of slow fashion, directed at extended clothing utilisation, is still in its infancy. Similarly, hardly any attention is yet paid

DOI: 10.4324/9781003272878-27

to phasing out substances of concern and plastic microfibres' release (Dris et al., 2017), using renewable inputs and radically improving re-use and recycling.

No one actor can realise this complex system change to a circular textile sector alone. Actors in the textile chain and other relevant stake-holders need to collaborate in networks that are willing to implement circular initiatives. To govern this change, the Dutch government has been inspired by the notion of 'transition management' (Hekkert and Negro, 2009; Loorbach et al., 2017; Cramer, 2020a; Simons and Nijhof, 2021). Transition management is a governance approach which seeks to adopt a multi-actor, long-term and systems thinking perspective and focuses on learning (Loorbach 2007). Dutch experiences with transi-tion management have led to learning that public governance will not be enough to effectively implement system changes. This conventional type of governance is insufficiently connected to the actors who are sup-posed to help realise such complex changes. Therefore, network govern-ance has been proposed as complementary to conventional governance (Cramer, 2020a). This new form of governance is about building co-alitions of partners: people willing to contribute to transformational change and who need each other to realise this. Networks of partners can perform successful circular initiatives, which are the building blocks for the circular economy (Cramer, 2020b). When such initiatives are scaled up and ultimately become mainstream, the linear economic system is successively broken down and the circular system is built up (Loorbach et al., 2017). Thus, in creating a circular textile sector, net-work governance and public governance should go hand in hand. We need public governance, because the national government—as guard-ian of the common good—is responsible for clear circular economy policies to which all actors should adhere. To put these policies into practice, we need network governance in which actors, including the national government, jointly realise the desired objectives.

This chapter analyses the way in which the Dutch government has implemented both public and network governance to build a circular textile sector in cooperation with a variety of stakeholders. It describes the interaction between national policies, the national not-for-profit Dutch Circular Textile Valley and the initiatives taken at regional level in networks of partners, and the benefits that have been achieved to date. The chapter concludes that although public governance remains crucial to enhancing a circular clothing and fashion industry, circu-lar textiles will be accelerated by concurrent goal-oriented network governance.

PUBLIC POLICIES ON CIRCULAR TEXTILES

Dutch government policies focused on the negative environmental impact of textile date back to the late 1980s. The first initiatives focused on the collection of discarded clothing from households, which generated a market for second-hand clothes. The next step, taken in the 1990s, was the promotion of eco-design, an environmentally friendly approach to designing products that could be applied to various product categories, including clothing (Brezet and van Hemel, 1997). This policy was followed in the 2000s by the introduction of chain-oriented materials policies (such as the reuse of discarded, non-wearable textiles, for example, for insulation) (Cramer, 2014). Building on these past experiences, an ambitious government-wide circular economy programme was launched in 2016 (Dutch government, 2016), in which circular textiles sector has been selected as one of the focal points. Since then, the focus is on transforming the linear textiles sector into circular ones. To codify this policy, the Dutch government issued a document formulating ambitious policy objectives to steer the clothing and textile industry in a more circular direction (Ministry of Infrastructure and Water Management, 2020). The main focus of this policy is on high-value recycling and the use of eco-friendly materials, but with little coverage of steps higher on the ladder of circularity (e.g. refuse, redesign and reuse) and on promoting slow fashion. The objectives set by the Dutch government is that by 2025, 25% of material in textile products should be eco-friendly or recycled content and 30% of all marketed textile products should be recycled. By 2030, 50% of all marketed textile products should contain at least 30% recycled content or consist of eco-friendly materials (20%), while 50% should be recycled. The government's intention is to meet these ambitions in close cooperation with the sector, for example by implementing an Extended Producer Responsibility (EPR) policy in 2023 (Dutch government, 2021).

Besides these national policy initiatives on circular textiles, a wide variety of business initiatives have recently been launched, covering specific elements of the clothing product chain. Frontrunners in the fashion industry have introduced more eco-friendly product lines, for instance Flocus (using kapok fibres), Patagonia (outdoor clothing with organic, recycled and upcycled fibres) and Jackalo (organic play clothes for kids).[1] Newcomers, both startups and scale-ups, have developed a range of slow fashion alternatives as a response to the fast fashion trends in the mainstream market, for instance Unrecorded (a new wave of unisex brands) and Hacked by (using residual materials and unsold and over-produced garments from the fashion industry as a resource).[2] Instead of producing more clothing, newcomers such as MUD Jeans and Dutch Spirit[3] promote the idea of buying less and sharing and leasing clothing. Besides the traditional outlets for second-hand clothing, new second-hand concepts have been introduced, including online marketplaces, for instance United Wardrobe (in 2020 taken over by Vinted) and The Next Closet.[4] The recycling of discarded, no longer wearable textiles – which represents about 50% of the clothing discarded in the Netherlands via municipal textile collection – has also gradually got off the ground. A good example is the Denim Deal initiative,[5] which focuses on blending virgin cotton with recycled fibres from discarded denim. Similarly, companies reusing recycled fibres in new workwear also gained market share, for instance Schijvens and van Puijenbroek.[6] Finally, some mainstream brands already take back and resell second-hand clothing, anticipating EPR legislation in 2023, for instance Zeeman, H&M, Zalando and Hilfiger. Although progress had been made, most circular initiatives still represent standalone projects and lack scaling opportunities.

FLAGSHIP PROJECT DUTCH CIRCULAR TEXTILE VALLEY (DCTV)

To bundle and strengthen circular initiatives, the not-for-profit organisation 'Het Groene Brein' (The Green Brain) and the government-led 'Versnellingshuis' (Acceleration house) joined forces with Modint, the trade association for fashion, interiors, textiles and carpets.[7] By aligning the circular initiatives, they expected to create greater synergy throughout the entire clothing chain. This led to the establishment of DCTV in May 2019.[8] The initiative has been heralded as a flagship project for the circular economy programme by the government.

DCTV is a not-for-profit foundation. Some of its staff have dedicated expertise; the Board, consisting of representatives of the various chain initiatives governs DCTV.[9] To kickstart the initiative, the Ministry of Infrastructure and Water Management provided €700,000 euros in funding from 2019 to 2021. From 2022, new sources of funding are being sought, which are likely to become available when the EPR policy has been implemented in 2023. Until then, DCTV needs to mobilise extra budget, of which €70,000 euros has already been received. The flagship project aims to turn a collection of individual, worthwhile and predominantly small-scale initiatives into a widely supported movement towards the circular economy in the textiles sector in regions of the Netherlands. The idea is that circular initiatives should gain leverage and fashion brands and retailers will follow them. Besides lowering environmental impact, the aim is also to create job opportunities and develop innovative technologies and strategies that can be marketed abroad. DCTV's primary target groups are circular startups and innovative businesses; proactive fashion brands and retailers; and textile collection, sorting and recycling companies. They have been selected because of their drive to promote circular textiles. Other target groups that can support new initiatives have also been invited to participate, for example research institutes, the financial sector, governments, consumers and commercial customers and supply chain partners. DCTV aims to support the primary target groups in the implementation of their circular solutions, while the other actors are being targeted to help create the market.

DCTV's objective is to establish a circular textile chain by 2030 which closes the loops of products, materials and resources, and utilises new business models. To achieve this goal, DCTV mobilises the combined strength of innovative companies in four regional hubs: Twente Area, Tilburg Area, Province of Gelderland and the Amsterdam Metropolitan Area. These hubs reflect past and present-day economic strengths connected to textiles, fashion and clothing. Each hub is characterised by a specific focus.

FOUR DUTCH REGIONAL TEXTILE HUBS

In the Twente Area, high-value textile recycling attracted interest in the 1990s, which was not surprising considering the city's rich textile manufacturing history. Twente now has a pilot production capacity for high-value recycling, with a focus on innovations in mechanical and chemical recycling. The six partners participating in the initiative are the companies SaXcell (chemical recycling), Frankenhuis (mechanical recycling), Enschede Textile City Innovation (production of materials with recycled fibres), Regional Textile Sorting Center Twente,[10] the University of Applied Sciences Saxion and the regional government Twente Environment (collection of textiles). The initiators are seeking funds to scale up the pilot together with designers and manufacturers. These new funds should go hand in hand with large-scale collection, comprehensive sorting and the application of recycled fibres in design and production (see Chapter 24).

In the Tilburg Area, the hub efforts first concentrated on the separate collection of workwear, the fiberisation of the workwear materials and the reuse of recycled fibres in new workwear. The companies Van

Puijenbroek and Schijvens, both established in the Tilburg region, are considered frontrunners in this field. Furthermore, Wolkat – a family-owned group of innovative, international textile recycling companies – collects, sorts, recycles and re-creates recycled products for the fashion, car and furniture industries.[11] Recently, the hub has also extended its activities towards circular design in cooperation with the Textile Museum in Tilburg that has a unique textile knowledge center. Midpoint Brabant (a regional public-private partnership) and the municipality of Tilburg actively support the hub initiatives.

In the province of Gelderland, the hub focuses on innovators for circular textiles and the manufacturing of new biomaterials for textiles, such as mycelium and 'fruit leather', and bacterial and algal dyes. It is a partnership between ArtEZ (University of the Arts) Future Makers, KIEMT (a proactive network organisation of innovative entrepreneurs) and the Wageningen University Circular Fashion Lab. The hub is one of the spear heads of the circular economy action programme of the province of Gelderland.

In the Amsterdam Metropolitan Area, various initiatives have been combined into two main themes: circular aesthetics[12] and high-value use of post-consumer textiles. The aim of the circular aesthetics theme is to link a variety of slow fashion startups and scale-ups to interested clothing labels, many of which are located in this region. In addition, the aim of circular aesthetics theme is to inspire interested clothing labels to embed circular design and new business models in their strategies and create consumer awareness for slow fashion, with initiators being the companies Brightfiber Factory, ByBorre and Exota (King Louie).[13]

Under the umbrella of the second theme 'use of post-consumer textiles', various initiatives have been taken. One example, which had already gained traction before the DCTV launch, is the House of Denim located in Amsterdam.[14] House of Denim started blending virgin cotton with recycled fibres from discarded denim. Large-scale adoption of recycled content is hindered by its higher effort/price point and low demand. House of Denim has sought cooperation from the company Wieland in Zaanstad, as another flagship project in the Amsterdam region. Wieland has succeeded in sorting non-wearable clothing using new scanning techniques, working closely with the Salvation Army's clothing collectors and Loop. A milestone came with the signing of the Denim Deal on 29 October 2020[15] by 30 parties in the fashion and textile industry, the Ministry of Infrastructure and Water Management, the municipalities of Amsterdam and Zaanstad, the Amsterdam Metropolitan Area and the Amsterdam Economic Board. This was the first time that parties ranging from manufacturers, brands and retailers to collectors, sorters, cutters and weavers had joined forces to achieve more circular denim clothing.

Besides the Denim Deal, a second initiative has emerged in the COVID-19 crisis that focused on protective aprons in hospitals, six million of which are currently discarded per week in the Netherlands. The initiative aims to replace them with circular aprons, so that their use can continue after the crisis. These aprons, made from discarded laboratory coats, shirts and overalls, are suitable for nursing staff, care practitioners and doctors in care homes and rehabilitation centres.

In addition, various other high-value recycling and reuse initiative were developed in the context of the hub. For example, the company Loop.a life[16] produces new clothes from recycled wool fibres and Patagonia has set up the Makers Unite Repair Center for integrated repair of clothing and re-commerce solutions. Furthermore, various hotels in Amsterdam now focus on procurement of long-lasting hotel bed linen with a growing amount of recycled content.

REFLECTION ON CIRCULAR TEXTILE VALLEY

Three years after the start of DCTV in 2019, the board of DCTV decided to review the results achieved to date. This pause for reflection was fruitful because it led to a redirection of the strategy and working method. DCTV concluded that various positive results were achieved. In the first preparatory phase (2019–2020), the four regional hubs were set up and/ or strengthened with the support of DCTV and many circular textile initiatives were implemented. In the second building phase (2020–2021), projects were carried out, rather separately from the four hubs. For instance, a circular textile exhibition was organised and new business models were developed for re-commerce. The hubs continued their work, each with their own complementary focus. Despite these positive results, DCTV observed that the four hubs had been operating independently of the coordinating national DCTV team and vice versa, which was not considered desirable. The shared opinion was that the orchestration of DCTV should be improved. If all DCTV partners were to join forces, they would be able to achieve much more than had been possible with everybody working separately. Additionally, it was stated that DCTV could also boost the regional initiatives by helping to formulate the necessary policy instruments in cooperation with the government and other relevant parties (e.g. financiers) in alignment with the EPR policy being developed. To carry out these activities, some changes have occurred in the composition of the team.

Utilising the network governance approach developed by the author of this chapter (Cramer, 2020a), the DCTV network has been formalised and made more goal-oriented. The roles and responsibilities of those involved have been defined as follows. The national DCTV team focuses on coordinating the existing and new regional hubs to ensure 'added value' and in connection with national policies. Each hub orchestrates a regional multi-stakeholder network in which companies, local government, research institutes and/or the local community cooperate in concrete circular initiatives. The overall aim of the hubs is to cover jointly all steps of the 10 R-ladder of circularity, starting with initiatives that refuse and reduce raw material use, then prioritise the redesign of products and product use in view of circularity, finally focusing on high-value recycling (Cramer, 2017; Figure 21.1).

The national DCTV team will draw up a roadmap establishing where initiatives are still lacking and initiate searches for possibilities to fill the gaps. The hubs will subsequently develop various circular initiatives. Where successful, these will be scaled and finally mainstreamed. The hubs will not be able to implement the scaling alone but will need the support of the national DCTV team and the government. Additionally, it is seen as crucial to obtain finance for an innovation programme to enable the development of circular materials, new business models

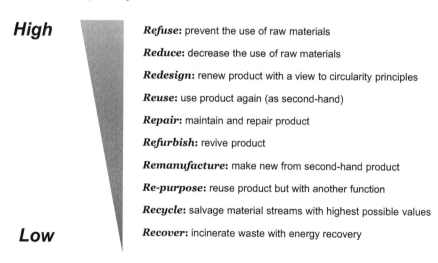

Order of priority

High

Refuse: prevent the use of raw materials

Reduce: decrease the use of raw materials

Redesign: renew product with a view to circularity principles

Reuse: use product again (as second-hand)

Repair: maintain and repair product

Refurbish: revive product

Remanufacture: make new from second-hand product

Re-purpose: reuse product but with another function

Recycle: salvage material streams with highest possible values

Low   **Recover**: incinerate waste with energy recovery

Figure 21.1 Levels of circularity: 10Rs

and new initiatives, targeting all steps on the 10R-ladder of circularity. Therefore, DCTV aims to mobilise innovation funds through the funding associated with the EPR for the Dutch textile chain.

In the coming years, these activities will be further enhanced, showcasing the possibilities of a circular textile chain. Collaboration between innovative companies, retailers and fashion brands will make new circular concepts and business models more mainstream, which will also lead to more employment in circularity tasks amongst various actors. However, if these expectations are not fulfilled, central government will need to play a more stringent role in relation to the targets it will set.

IMPORTANCE OF CONCURRENTLY APPLYING PUBLIC AND NETWORK GOVERNANCE

The above description of the development of circular textiles in the Netherlands shows the importance of the parallel application of both public and network governance. There is a need for public governance, because central government is responsible for formulating circular economy policies and the accompanying legal, economic and social government instruments. However, to implement these policies, we need network governance in which stakeholders, including central government, join forces. DCTV and the four hubs have put network governance into practice, which has helped the implementation of the circular economy policy for textiles formulated by the Dutch government. The Dutch public governance on circular textile primarily focuses on the use of recycled content and eco-friendly materials and recycling. This is a good first step, but the government also needs to develop instruments that promote initiatives higher on the 10 R-ladder of circularity. Based on examples (e.g. the implementation of new business models, circular designs, reuse concepts and slow fashion models), the hubs can indicate which specific policy measures stimulate the latter initiatives. The transition brokers employed by the hubs can align proactive companies with other relevant stakeholders to accelerate the change into the desired direction. The national DCTV also acts as transition broker by playing an orchestrating role between the hubs and acting as a liaison between the hubs and the national government. When the transition brokers are given the mandate by the stakeholders involved to fulfil this leadership role, the preconditions for successful implementation can be more easily realised. Therefore, it is concluded that although public governance remains crucial to enhancing circular textiles, the circular economy is empowered concurrently by setting up goal-oriented network governance.

NOTES

1 www.flocus.pro; www.eu.patagonia.com; hellojackalo.com.
2 www.unrecorded.co; www.shop.hackedby.nl.
3 www.mudjeans.nl; www.dutchspirit.info.
4 www.vinted.nl; www.thenextcloset.com.
5 www.amsterdameconomicboard.com.
6 www.schijvensmode.nl; www.vpcapital.eu.
7 www.hetgroenebrein.nl; www.versnellingshuisce.nl; www.modint.nl.
8 www.dutchcirculartextile.org.
9 Modint, ABN AMRO, independent Cradle to Cradle (C2C) expert, Wageningen University (hub Arnhem-Nijmegen), Het Goed (hub Twente), Schijvens (hub Tilburg) and independent chair (hub Amsterdam Metropolitan Area).
10 www.saxcell.com; www.frankenhuisbv.nl; www.tekdeeps.com; www.twente.com.
11 www.wolkat.com.
12 Circular aesthetics focuses both on circular design and production and on a new consumer attitude of slow fashion.
13 www.eurofiber.com; www.byborre.com; www.kinglouie.nl.
14 www.houseofdenim.org.
15 C-233 Green Deal on Circular Denim "Denim Deal", report issued by the Dutch government, October 29, 2020.
16 www.loopalife.com.

REFERENCES

Brezet, H., and Van Hemel, C. (1997), *A Promising Approach to Sustainable Production and Consumption*, The Hague: Rathenau Institute.

Cramer, J. (2014), *Milieu (Environment)*, Amsterdam: Amsterdam University Press.

Cramer, J. (2017), The Raw Materials Transition in the Amsterdam Metropolitan Area: Added Value for the Economy, Well-Being and the Environment, *Environment*, Vol. 59, No. 3, pp. 14–21.

Cramer, J. (2020a), *How Network Governance Powers the Circular Economy; Ten Guiding Principles for Building a Circular Economy, Based on Dutch Experiences*, Amsterdam: Amsterdam Economic Board.

Cramer, J.M. (2020b), Practice-Based Model for Implementing Circular Economy: The Case of the Amsterdam Metropolitan Area, *Journal of Cleaner Production*, Vol. 255, No. 120255, pp. 1–9.

Dris, R., Gasperi, J., Mirande, C., Mandin, C., Guerrouache, M., Langlois, V., and Tassin, B. (2017), A first Overview of Textile Fibers, Including Microplastics, in Indoor and Outdoor Environments, *Environmental Pollution*, Vol. 221, pp. 453–458.

Dutch Government (2016), *A Circular Economy for the Netherlands by 2050: Government-WideProgrammeforaCircularEconomy*,TheHague.https://www.government.nl/documents/poli- cy-notes/2016/09/14/a-circular-economy-in-the-netherlands-by-2050.

Dutch Government (2021), *Towards an EPR for Textile; Progress Report Circular Textile, Letter to Parliament*, The Hague: Dutch Government.

Geissdoerfer, M., Savaget, P., Bocken, N., and Hultink, E.J. (2017), The Circular Economy—A New Sustainability Paradigm? *Journal of Cleaner Production*, Vol. 143, pp. 757–768.

Hekkert, M.P., and Negro, S.O. (2009), Functions of Innovation Systems as a Frame-
    work to Understand Sustainable Technological Change: Empirical Evidence for
    Earlier Claims, *Technological Forecasting & Social Change*, Vol. 76, pp. 584–594.
Loorbach, D. (2007), *Transition Management; New Mode of Governance for Sustainable
    Development*, Utrecht: International Books.
Loorbach, D., Frantzeskaki, N., and Avelino, F. (2017), Sustainability Transitions
    Research: Transforming Science and Practice for Societal Change, *Annual Review
    of Environment and Resources*, Vol. 42, pp. 599–626.
Ministry of Infrastructure and Water Management (2020), *Beleidsprogramma Circu-
    lair Textiel 2020–2025 (Policy Programme for Circular Textile 2020–2025)*, The Hague:
    Dutch Government.
Simons, L. and Nijhof, A. (2021), *Changing the Game: Sustainable Market Transforma-
    tion Strategies to Understand and Tackle the Big and Complex Sustainability Challenges of
    Our Generation*, London: Routledge.

22 Accelerating circularity in textiles: lessons learned from a regional perspective

Jan Mahy and Jens Oelerich

INTRODUCTION

The "low countries", roughly extending from northern France (region "Hauts de France"), Belgium (mainly "Flanders" region) and the Netherlands (mainly eastern part centred around region "Twente") have a centuries-old tradition in yarn spinning and textile weaving. Materials of bio-origin such as wool, hemp, flax and increasing production capacity in cotton weaving have led to world famous interior (curtains, carpets) and clothing textile manufacturing and related crafts. These regions, among others, have been frontrunners in the transition from a "craft" to an "industry" in the 19th century, with large-scale spinning and weaving mills. After World War II, increasing labour costs and a shift to manmade cellulose fibres (rayon, viscose), synthetic fibres (polyester, polyamide) and cotton have caused an accelerated transfer of textile production outside Western Europe.

The legacy of this industry has led to excellent vocational and academic education centres and a network of industries in the low countries founded on fibre and polymer technology, including commercially successful products of high performance fibres such as aramid (Twaron®), carbon (Tenax®) and ultra-high molecular weight polyethylene (UHMWPE, Dyneema®) from large industrial conglomerates such as Akzo Nobel and DSM (Toeters, 2019). While a dwindling

DOI: 10.4324/9781003272878-28

fashion-manufacturing industry resulted in a massive loss of vocational skills and academic expertise in the Netherlands towards the end of the 20th century, a dynamic and highly automated carpet and technical textile industry as well as a strong global fashion design and retail industry has remained. This has, for instance, led Amsterdam to be baptized as the "Denim capital" because it is the location of many global and local brand owners, fashion designers and a young urban fashion-conscious population, even though no denim is woven and hardly any clothing is being manufactured in the Netherlands.

More recently, the reuse of textiles through secondhand clothing shops and online platforms as well as the installation of fibre processing of *post-consumer recycled* (PCR) textile has resulted in a renewed interest in crafts and skills in the region. Next to reuse of clothing, national legislation and European policies for the transition to a *circular economy* (CE) has driven innovation in new recycling technologies such as polyester, polyamide and cellulose based natural fibres. Furthermore, sustainable (biobased) raw materials as alternatives to fossil-based (e.g. synthetic polymer) fibres are increasingly used in textile products. However, many innovative biomaterials and their products are at a lower "Technology Readiness Level" (TRL), i.e. laboratory and pilot stages (TRL 3–5), requiring substantial investment and involving significant risks towards industrial upscaling.

The transition from a highly globalized and logistically complex "linear" textile economy towards a "closed-loop" (i.e. textile-to-textile) CE is now entering the stage of industrial scale-up (Luiken & Brinks, 2020). For instance, closed-loop mechanical recycling of PCR textile and chemical recycling of fossil-based raw materials in carpets and interior textiles has led to the development of promising technologies at higher TRL levels (>5). In the Netherlands, the introduction of "Extended Producer Responsibility" (EPR) legislation in 2023 (Kort, 2021) and an increasing amount of locally available PCR textile material, potentially well over 300 kilotons annually (Bakker et al., 2020), requires an accelerated industrial scale-up of such recycling technologies.

TOWARDS A "CLOSED-LOOP" CIRCULAR TEXTILE ECONOMY: TWENTE CASE

Collecting end-of-life clothing and interior textiles in the Netherlands is typically local activity, i.e. on a *municipal* scale, carried out by waste collectors, nonprofit organizations or commercial initiatives, with relatively modest volumes of collected textiles. By 2025 however, national regulation will require that all discarded textiles must be collected separately from residual waste, thus allowing for more reuse and (mechanical or chemical) recycling. This goal is ambitious, as currently over 50% of such textile waste is still incinerated together with residual waste (Ellen MacArthur, 2017). However, due to the economy of scale involved, mechanical recycling is *regionally* organized, typically processing thousands of tonnes of discarded textiles annually, whereas using recycled fibres as feedstock for yarn spinning is economically viable on much larger scales. Contrary to plastics chemical recycling, such as for polyamide, cotton-based textile mixtures are mainly mechanically processed, with chemical processing currently available at a pilot scale only. This is due to the complex composition of textile input streams, which may include other polymers, finishes, dyes and metals, which can adversely affect chemical processing (Oelerich, 2017; Luiken & Brinks, 2020). Preferably, the raw material streams (from PCR textiles to fibres to yarns and back to textiles) should be connected in order to avoid complex logistics.

Since a "closed-loop" textile-to-textile CE typically starts with local initiatives, this chapter considers such *local* ecosystems of circular value-chain partners as crucial building blocks for the CE transition. The region Twente, with its legacy of textile manufacturing skills is well-equipped for this transition with a population of over 600,000 people, consisting of urban communities in a rural area, boasting a strong academic presence (Saxion University of Applied Sciences) and an entrepreneurial culture of innovation (Twente Board, 2021). Moreover, the largest mechanical recycling plant in the Netherlands, Frankenhuis BV, as well as the pilot plant for cotton fibre (SaXcell™) chemical recycling and a sustainable weaving mill, Enschede Textielstad BV, all operate in this region. Twente is the recycling technology "hub" for the *Dutch Circular Textile Valley* (DCTV) initiative, the role of which is elaborated in Chapter 23 (Cramer, 2022).

These industrial partners, along with the main secondhand clothing and sorting organization (Regionaal Textielsorteercentrum Twente, RTT), the regional waste collector (Twente Milieu) and Saxion UAS have founded "TexPlus", a nonprofit foundation acting as *regional ecosystem for textile recycling technology*, were together nominated in 2020 as "best practice" by the EU Committee of the Regions (EU CoR, 2020).

A "TRIPLE-HELIX" PARTNERSHIP

The "regional" organization of value-chain partners in "TexPlus" is considered a key feature, as well as the "systemic" nature of required collaboration for CE: Academic research and innovation, entrepreneurial initiatives and regional policies together facilitate this collaboration make for a so-called "triple-helix" partnership. This model of innovation refers to a set of interactions between academia, industry and government (Stanford University Triple Helix Research Group, 2011).

The circular value-chain partners work in a fundamentally different and partly experimental, ecosystem compared with established linear value chains. For example, the TexPlus "hub" of DCTV contributes to the piloting of systemic innovations and modelling of a circular textile ecosystem in order to promote the overall circularity of textile products and materials in the Netherlands. Circular design concepts and novel (possibly disruptive) circular business models are being established to enable more effective use of clothing (e.g., in terms of longer lifespan, number of wears per user and reuse). The "systemic" nature of the innovation creates value for the industry *system as a whole*. However, the value creation has been explored to a limited extent only. Therefore, there is a need for designing and piloting circular systems, including business models, products and materials to cover the entire value chain in scope, in order to test and demonstrate systemic innovation towards a CE.

CHALLENGES FOR THE ECOSYSTEM

Several behavioural, technological, economic and regulatory challenges need to be dealt with in order to create a working circular ecosystem.

1. "Behavioural" refers to the way the region's inhabitants, i.e. the consumers' awareness of the effect of purchasing fashion products, their use, reuse and disposal in a proper way at the end of their serviceable life. The rapid growth of "fast fashion", i.e., cheap, short-lived, low-quality clothing items indicates that this awareness is not visible in terms of behaviour. EU consumers use their clothes for a relatively short time (Ellen MacArthur Foundation, 2017) and discard about 11 kg of textiles annually (EEA, 2019). By developing, testing and implementing new, circular business models as well as *regulatory* (preferably EU-wide) policies, consumers are expected to become more aware of sustainability and circularity. TexPlus partner Twente Milieu works with field labs (named "Texlabs") to stimulate consumer behaviour in this way.

2. This requires better, more effective *technologies* than those currently available. Although innovative sorting equipment, particularly near-infrared (NIR) technology for characterizing textile items or clippings is available, their accuracy and efficiency is insufficient to

deal with large-scale fibre processing (Van Duijn, 2019). Therefore, faster and better sorting technologies, most likely a combination of instrumental and chemometrical (data analysis) methods, are urgently needed.

3. *Economic and regulatory* challenge: The consumption of clothing by EU households was 6.4 million tonnes (ECAP, 2017) which represented €483 billion (Euratex, 2019) in 2014. By 2018, the consumption had increased by 7% to €520 billion. Furthermore, currently less than 1% of total discarded material is recycled back to high-value textiles (Ellen MacArthur Foundation, 2017). These numbers indicate that there is a huge loss of *economic* value in the current system, which could partly be recovered by a transition to a CE. TexPlus partners Enschede Textielstad and Frankenhuis are developing circular business models and identifying new application markets for high added-value products respectively. This development activity requires network funding.

When raw materials from PCR textiles can be identified and sorted into uniform material streams, technologies for mechanical and chemical recycling can be scaled-up to industrial scale. For instance, from chemical recycling of cotton, a high-quality pulp can be prepared, leading to higher-quality fibre material as basis for yarns spinning for use in textile weaving mills.

In a regional ecosystem, the material streams collected would preferably be in the proximity of further process steps such as sorting, recycled fibre production, yarn spinning and weaving. By connecting the material streams, a "textile recycling hub" is likely to attract key role players e.g. sustainable fashion designers, repair and secondhand clothing shops and other stakeholders who play key roles in the transition to CE. Establishing education programmes in such "hubs" will help to develop vocational and academic skills and knowledge for future generations from across material, commercial and design perspectives.

Funding innovative ideas to develop lab-scale prototypes of processes and products involves substantially lower investments and hence lower financial risks. But this is not enough. Successful initiatives must be further developed to higher TRL levels (5–8) to scale-up promising technology to industrial scale. The initial work at Saxion UAS in the development of a proprietary chemical recycling process for post-consumer cotton (TRL 3–5) has led to a start-up company, SaXcell BV. This initiative resulted in creating a cellulosic material – SaXcell™ – and bringing the production process from laboratory to an industrially viable scale (TRL 8). The result of the process is high-quality pulp for the wet spinning of post-consumer manmade cellulose fibres (Oelerich et al., 2017; Brinks et al. 2019).

Making a circular textile ecosystem to meet the above challenges is the objective of the founding partners in TexPlus in the region Twente. To that end, a number of tangible goals have been agreed upon (Twente Board, 2021), the results of which are hoped to be achieved by the end of 2023. A summary of this work is presented in the next paragraphs.

TEXPLUS GOALS: DISCARDED TEXTILE COLLECTION, SORTING, PROCESSING IMPROVEMENTS

As a *consumer-behaviour goal*, Twente Milieu organized "Texlabs" among various communities in the region, including schools. New ideas on how to discard used clothes, e.g., by separating "waste" from "clothes" collection, are submitted, tested and implemented with community members. For instance, positioning textile containers separately from other waste containers, with clear labelling is contributing to the 2023 goal of doubling the volume of sorted textiles, from 1,400 tonnes in 2019 to 2,000 tonnes in 2021.

As *technological goals*, sorting and fibre-processing technologies need innovative development. The fraction of discarded textiles which is not fit for reuse is typically sorted manually into roughly similar material streams (e.g. based on fibre mixture, colour, knitted or woven fabric, etc.) before being cut into clippings. Non-fibre parts (e.g. zip, button, adhesive labels) are removed and the resulting fabric is torn into fibres. This raw fibre material can be processed into (acoustical and thermal) insulating blankets in automotive and other industries, i.e. reused for "open loop" applications. A significant obstacle for converting mixed fibres into yarns for "closed-loop" textiles is the non-uniformity of the composition as well as the inferior mechanical properties of the resulting fibre as compared with virgin fibres. The development of fast, accurate and sensitive textile and fibre identification technology, followed by semi-automated sorting into well-defined and uniform material streams is required in order to process large amounts of materials for closed-loop applications.

While the uniformity is expected to improve through the development and use of innovative sorting technology, better fibre properties require fibre processing equipment. Together with TexPlus partners, new applications and markets are being explored for higher added-value raw materials. By 2023, the total volume of processed material in Twente is targeted to increase from 7,000 tonnes to 15,000 tonnes annually, while substantially increasing the "closed-loop" fraction to over 25% by 2025. A possible outlet for this fraction is for denim textiles from Amsterdam-based brand owners who are demanding substantial amounts of high-quality mechanically recycled PCR cotton raw materials. The government's *Dutch Denim Deal* (2021), of which TexPlus is a contract partner, is regarded as one of the most forward-looking initiatives of its kind across the fashion industry. It includes global brands in addition to recyclers, manufacturers and local authorities, ensuring that representatives from all parts of the circular product value chain are represented.

From an economic and regulatory point of view, governments need to provide incentives for industry and funding network partners in order to transition towards circularity. As an example, an "Extended Producer Responsibility" (EPR) will be introduced in the Netherlands as of July 2023 (Dutch Government, 2023), following the example of other EU countries. A further incentive could be achieved by creating a different levy for "virgin" and "PCR content" textile products, supporting the industry to increase the amount of recyclate, as proposed in a report from the Copernicus Institute for Sustainable Development (Vermeulen et al., 2021). In this way, circular value-chain partners such as sorters and fibre-processing plants can sell their products in a level playing field without undesired competition with suppliers of virgin material.

GOALS BEYOND 2023: TOWARDS A SUSTAINABLE EUROPEAN ECOSYSTEM

In the previous paragraphs, a number of regional and national initiatives and goal-oriented networks have been described, which are considered important building blocks for the transition to a circular textile economy. An important question is whether the resulting patchwork of ecosystems, a collaborative network and related policies are sufficient for a CE, in line with the goals issued by the European Commission (*Green Deal*, 2019)? These goals refer to medium- to long-term targets in 2030 up to 2050, when Europe aims to be the first climate neutral continent with circular solutions helping to reduce the industry's carbon footprint. Some considerations are proposed, which may help to consolidate the CE in Europe.

In an analysis of the transition to circular textiles in the Netherlands, recommendations for accelerating the demand for recycled content are provided (Hekkert et al., 2021, p. 4)

> in order to be able to meet the demand, it is important that mechanical recycling facilities improve and scale up, and that chemical recycling technology is introduced to the market and quickly scales up afterwards. For this to happen the innovation ecosystems that drive these developments need to perform better. Key challenges are the lack of financial resources, knowledge exchange, coordination of innovative activities and building new supply chains.

For the TexPlus partners, the recommendations above have been a strong guideline in setting the goals for 2023 and beyond. Chemical recycling technology at SaXcell for cotton is now at its pilot stage (tonnes per year) and expected to upscale to pre-industrial scale by the end of 2024 (> 3000 tonnes annually) for a wide range of textiles made from cotton, polyester and their blends. The entire range of pilot scale spinning technologies, starting from cellulosic pulps from processed fibres and textiles into prototype fabrics for testing and finishing, has been available at Saxion UAS since 2022. Additionally, innovative weaving technology is being developed by TexPlus partner Enschede Textielstad, and this will enable the production of sustainable textile fabric to meet industrial scale. It is expected that by having all relevant technologies and the supply of well-sorted materials streams in proximity, including fibre-processing, recycling, weaving and laboratory facilities, new designs and compositions will emerge to identify new applications. By embedding these facilities next to point of sale for used clothes and discarded textile containers, awareness among citizens is expected to be heightened, and in turn change consumer behaviour in the local community to steer away from "fast fashion"!

ACKNOWLEDGEMENTS

The authors wish to thank the TexPlus Foundation (www.TexPlus. eu), the Twente Board and Province of Overijssel in the Netherlands for providing the financial support, as well as Messrs Anton Luiken (Alconadvies) and Ger Brinks (BMA Techne) for their valuable input.

REFERENCES

Bakker, A. et al. (2020) RoyalHaskoningDHV(2020) "Beleidsprogramma Circulair Textiel". https://www.rijksoverheid.nl/documenten/rapporten/2020/04/14/beleidsprogramma-circulair-textiel, [Accessed 17-05-23].

Brinks, G. J., Bouwhuis, G. H., Agrawal, P. B., Gooijer, H., & Oelerich, J. J. (2019). "Method for producing regenerated cellulose fibers from cotton containing textile waste", International patent publication Nr. WO 2017/135816.

Cramer, J., (2022) see Chapter 23 of this book.

Dutch Government (2020) Contract C-233 "Green Deal on Circular Denim, 'Denim Deal'" https://www.government.nl/documents/reports/2020/10/29/c-233-green-deal-on-circular-denim-denim-deal

Dutch Goverment (2023) "Besluit van 14 april 2023, houdende regels voor uitgebreide producenten verantwoordelijkheid". https://zoek.officielebekendmakingen.nl/stb-2023-132.html [Accessed 17-05-2023].

ECAP (2017) *European Textiles & Workwear Market*. http://www.ecap.eu.com/wp-content/uploads/2016/09/ECAP-Workwear-Report-Pt-1-def-final.pdf

EEA (2019) *Textiles in Europe's Circular Economy*. https://www.eea.europa.eu/themes/waste/resource-efficiency/textiles-in-europe-s-circular-economy

Ellen MacArthur Foundation (2017) "A New Textiles Economy: Redesigning Fashion's Future", http://www.ellenmacarthurfoundation.org/publications.

EU *Action Plan for the Circular Economy* (2019) https://ec.europa.eu/environment/circular-economy/

European Commission *Green Deal* (2019) https://ec.europa.eu/info/sites/info/files/european-green-deal-communication_en.pdf

EU Committee of the Regions (2020) "Green Deal Going Local: Twente Circular Textiles Programme", https://cor.europa.eu/en/news/Pages/Green-Deal-Going-Local-call-for-best-practices.aspx

EURATEX (2019) *Statistica Household Consumption* https://www.statista.com/statistics/417674/eu-european-union-textile-clothing-household-consumption/

Hekkert, M. et al. (2021) "Transition to Circular Textiles in the Netherlands: An innovation systems analysis", Copernicus Institute of Sustainable Development, University of Utrecht.

Kort et al., Tauw & Rebel, M. Kort et al. (2021) "Naar een UPV voor textiel" https://www.rijksoverheid.nl/documenten/rapporten/2021/05/20/bijlage-5-eindrapportage-upv-textiel-rebel-group [Accessed 17-05-2023].

Luiken, A., & Brinks, G.J. (2020) "A Primer On Textile Recycling", EU Horizon 2020 project "Reflow" (grant agreement 820937), https://reflowproject.eu/wp-content/uploads/2021/05/REFLOW_BOOKLET_TEXTILE_WHEEL-compressed.pdf.

Oelerich, J., Bijleveld, M., Bouwhuis, G. H., & Brinks, G. J. (2017) "The life cycle assessment of cellulose pulp from waste cotton via the SaXcell™ process". In *IOP Conf. Ser Mater. Sci. Eng.* (Vol. 254, 192012). https://iopscience.iop.org/article/10.1088/1757-899X/254/19/192012 [Accessed 17-05-2023].

Toeters (ed.) (2019) "Unfolding Fashion Tech: Pioneers of Bright Futures", ISBN 978-94-93148-14-7, Language English, Release date 15/08/2019.

Twente Board on Circular Textile (2021) https://www.twente.com/twente-board/circulairtextiel

Van Duijn (ed.) (2019) Circle Economy "Interreg NWE project Fibersort" https://www.nweurope.eu/media/8244/fibersort-52-policy-recommendations-20191030.pdf

Vermeulen, W.J.V., Backes, C.W. de Munck, M.C.J. Campbell-Johnston, K. Rosales Carreon, J. Boeve, M.N., & de Waal, I.M. (2021) "Pathways for Extended Producer Responsibility on the Road to a Circular Economy", Utrecht University, Circular Economy and Society Hub, Utrecht. ISBN: 978–90–6266–600–3, www.uu.nl/en/research/copernicus-institute-of-sustainable-development/reports

23 Biomimicry, biomaterials and textiles

Veronika Kapsali and Carolina Roberte de Oliveira

INTRODUCTION AND BACKGROUND

The influence of biology within the context of key challenges of the 21st century is wide reaching. The first examples of systematic study of biological phenomena for engineering applications can be traced back to 1920s Northern America (Harkness, 2004). From the 1960s, biology transcended the natural science into social science and the humanities (Kapsali, 2022). Events leading to the first fuel crisis in 1973 highlighted the scale of our dependence on fossil fuels and their contrasting finite nature. By 1969, an interdisciplinary group of scientists founded the New Alchemy Institute to seek alternative paradigms and demonstrate the possibility to live within a society whose infrastructure did not rely on fossil fuels and other polluting industrial practices such as the use of pesticides in modern agriculture. The group drew on the transdisciplinary framework of general systems thinking (Von Bertalanffy, 1950) and extended it to concepts from ecology (a branch of biology that studies the relationship between organisms and their physical surroundings). The resulting ecosystem model informed a pioneering set of strategies (such as renewable energy and organic farming) that enabled small communities to survive with minimum reliance on fossil fuels (Wade, 1975).

At a similar time, iconic industrial designer Victor Papanek considered how design could contribute to this discourse. In his seminal book *Design for the Real World: Human Ecology and Social Change*, Papanek & Fuller (1972, pp. 186–214) maps out opportunities for biology to inform

DOI: 10.4324/9781003272878-29

ecological strategies for industrial design. Although this is not an exhaustive review of the discourse within the subject of environmental sustainably in the 1960s and 1970s, pioneering ideas emerged via interdisciplinary actions that traverse every academic domain and stimulate new paradigms. This provided a new lens from which to view resource flows within modern society and shaped manifestos such as Cradle to Cradle (Braungart & McDonough, 2002), regenerative design (Wahl, 2016) and the Circular Economy (Ellen MacArthur Foundation, 2013).

This chapter touches on key barriers preventing the scaling of sustainable materials technologies emerging from the intersection of textiles and biotechnology: these include terminology, complex manufacturing processes, policy and investment.

TERMINOLOGY

Interdisciplinary practice that draws on biology for ideas and inspiration informs a spectrum of activity, the outcomes of which span artistic practice such as by Stelarc[1] and Anne Dimitriu,[2] to new economic models i.e. circular, regenerative, sustainable, etc. A novel range of terminology emerged organically to support the communication of these new intellectual spaces (Vincent, 2001; Harkness, 2004; Pecman, 2014). However, terminology containing the prefix bio- (such as *bio*mimetics, *bio*mimicry, *bio*design, *bio*nic) is difficult to navigate, especially by the non-scientific sectors.

The presence of diverse meanings for a small number of terms (polysemy) is a systemic issue reported by scholars from both scientific disciplines (Lepora et al., 2013; Vincent, 2014; Vincent et al., 2006) and the humanities (Wahl, 2006; Iouguina, 2013; Kapsali, 2016). Kapsali (2022) conducted a review of five contemporary biologically informed textile practices and mapped the practice against the academic domains that informed them. Initial observations revealed two distinct areas of practice where textiles intersect (a) biotechnology and (b) material science (see Figure 23.1). The most established space is the former, where practice draws on the tools, materials and methods of biotechnology to create alternative materials for textile products, e.g. using mycelium to create sheet material from agricultural waste streams as an alternative to leather. The report *Understanding 'bio' material innovations: a primer for the fashion industry*, produced by Lee et al. (2020) provides a comprehensive overview of bio-based material innovation for the fashion/textile sector. The latter (biology + material science) refers to the nascent space where knowledge of the structure of

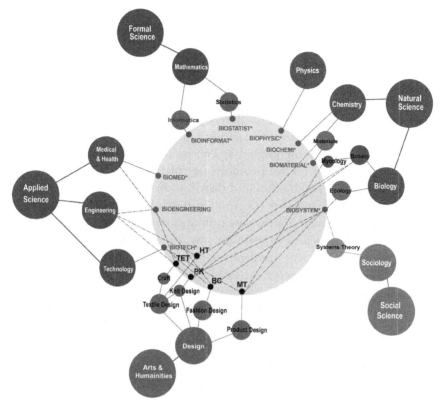

Figure 23.1 Map of Bio-Inspired Design (BID) landscape including five textile design-based case studies mapped according to the BID disciplines that informed the practice: TET=Tissue Engineered Textiles, PK= Programmable Knit, BC= Biocouture, HT= Hygroscopic textiles, MT= Mycelium Textiles. The map highlights a distinction between textile practice informed by either (materials) engineering or biotechnology.
Source: Kapsali, V (2022)

biological materials and its lessons are implemented into textile design via a material science lens (Kapsali & Hall, 2022). This chapter focuses on material and processing innovations at the intersection of textiles and biotechnology.

Lee et al. (2020) define *bio-based* materials as an umbrella term that includes everything from conventional as well as non-animal "leathers" that contain fruit or vegetable waste combined with natural and/or synthetic fibres. *Biofabricated* specifically refers to material components or building blocks for both natural and synthetic polymers produced by microbes. *Biosynthetic* materials include the production of chemicals from bio-derived materials or processes for synthetic polymers such as nylon and polyester. Lastly, *bioassembled* materials include materials grown by mycelium, bacteria or mammalian cells (Lee, Suzanne et al., 2020).

CONTEXT

The global bio-based materials market size was valued at US$14 billion in 2020 with expectations of reaching US$87 billion by 2026.[3] On July 2, 2021, the Directive on Single-Use Plastics took effect in the European Union (EU). The directive prohibits petroleum-based single-use[4] plastics, as well as the production and distribution of a specific list of products within the EU markets (i.e. food and drink containers).[5] This new legislation set the agenda for research and development of alternative bio-based materials and investment priorities within the EU.[6] Despite environmental concerns underpinned by government regulations driving the growth in this sector, the fashion and textile industry (F&TI) has yet to benefit significantly from the growth and investment in this space. Despite many independent developments in textile bio-based materials, these tend to fall short of meeting the industry's requirements. This chapter focuses on *scalability* – other factors such as *flexibility*, influenced by seasonal demands on production volumes and changing trends (Rex, Okcabol and Roos, 2019) are outside the scope of this chapter.

CARBON FOOTPRINT AND TEXTILE PROCESSING

The environmental impact of industrial processes is measured in terms of carbon footprint and expressed as units of mass (e.g. gr, kg, tonnes) of CO_2. Factors across the life cycle of a product affecting the carbon footprint include the *energy* source used to power industrial processes and the *distance* between adjoining points in the supply chain but also *fibre production* methods. Although the calculation protocols are problematic (Matthews et al., 2008; Laurent et al., 2012; Salo et al., 2019), this is the main measure for comparing and evaluating impacts. Niinimäkiet al. (2020) estimate that the F&TI global production emits 2.9 Gt[7] of CO_2, of which two-thirds is associated with the manufacturing process (fibre-garment production). Accurate calculation of such complex and nuanced systems is far from simple and often conflicting; this is highlighted in the case of cotton fibre production, and conventional cotton can produce 3–5 times more CO_2 than organic cotton due to the heavy carbon footprint of the pesticides used; however, organic practices require more water than conventional farming, so which one is optimal? Such paradoxes create a landscape within the F&TI that is highly susceptible to misinformation and *greenwashing*.

In principle, materials produced using the tools and methods of biotechnology are likely to produce significantly less CO_2, compared with conventional natural and manmade materials (e.g., cotton, viscose); however, these claims lack a rigorous evidence base. For example, MycoWorks (USA) produce biofabricated sheet material using mycelium and local agricultural waste, as an alternative to animal-based leather. The company estimates the process to be carbon neutral; this means that the balance between CO_2 input and output are equivalent, thus resulting in net zero CO_2 emissions. Desserto (Mexico) is another example of bio-based sheet material innovation;[8] the product is composed of 40% organic cactus fibre and 60% polyurethane. Preliminary results from a life cycle analysis commissioned by the company suggest that every kilogram of Desserto material produces 1.39 kg of CO_2 compared with animal leather processing, which produces 27.30 kg of CO_2 (*Early Life Cycle Analysis*, n.d.).

Vegatex (Hong Kong) is a leather-like material produced using plant-based waste streams from local apple juice and beer production industries that can be coated onto a backing textile for use in footwear and accessories. The resulting composite incorporates 66% bio-based content and contains nominal values of ($\leq 0.01\%$) volatile organic compounds (VOCs) such as benzene, toluene, ethylbenzene and styrene. VOCs are used in several textile processes for the application of dye as well as functional finishes such as crease resistance and easy care (formaldehyde), antistatic (oxy-ethylated polyamide) and fire resistance (flame retardants). These chemicals are known to cause a wider range of environmental and health problems that can be catastrophic; to this effect many countries have introduced limits to the number of VOCs permitted within a particular product category; however, this is incredibly difficult to monitor.

Textile wet processing

The textile industry uses over 15,000 chemicals such as lubricants and solvents (Niinimäkiet al., 2020). Wet processing refers to the step usually between textile production and garment/product manufacture that can include sizing, mercerizing,[9] dyeing and finishing. These processes rely on the use of toxic substances such as heavy metals (dyes), wax/fats/lubricants (from scouring) and VOCs that remain present in the wastewater (Babu et al., 2007) and find their way into the environment (Gunay, 2013).

The extraction and processing of natural dyes from plants is an ancient craft-based practice that could provide an alternative to synthetic dyes. However, obstacles preventing scale up include the consistency of raw materials, testing and durability of colour. Brazilian start-up SUI Biotecnologia launched a collection of plant-dyed T-shirts using pigment extracted from locally sourced organic agricultural waste. Preliminary studies conducted by the SUI team suggest that the novel shirt production and colouring processes used 70% less water compared with a conventional dyeing process (SUI, 2020). Keracol (UK) have developed textile colourants by extracting natural pigments from blackcurrant skin, a waste sourced from local fruit juice industry. The team evaluated the pigments on silk and wool textiles; although colouration was successful, colourfastness was poor (Tidder et al., 2018).

Examples of less-polluting alternatives to dyeing are observed in the activities of companies such as Faber Futures (UK) and Living Colour X PUMA (NL) invest in biotechnology informed methods for producing coloured pigments for textiles without the use of harmful chemicals and significantly less water. Similarly, Modern Synthesis (UK) collaborated with bioengineer Markus Walker to engineer self-dying bacteria capable of producing cellulose fibres embedded with natural melanin (pigment). The coloured material can be processed via 3D printing into products. The presence of colour within the material does not require additional processing normally required to introduce colour to the product. Despite the gap in data related to actual CO_2 input and output, we observe a significant drop in hazardous substance and water use from preliminary studies and reports in addition to any energy savings achieved by reducing the processing steps of the production process.

SCALING UP

The *Technology readiness level* (TRL)[10] is the standard framework used to assess the maturity of a particular innovation in terms of trajectory to commercialization, the scale ranges from 1 to 9 (see Table 23.1). During the period 2016–2021, the European Commission invested 350,000,000 in alternative plastic research for the packaging sector; as a result, bio-based technologies are at TRL9. In contrast, relevant innovations in the F&TI are estimated at TRL4 (Lee et al., 2020). This disjuncture suggests that the sector has yet to benefit from the wider context of investment in bio-based plastics.

TRL4–5, referred to as the 'valley of death', is a critical point for any innovation. The significant investment required to scale by the manufacturing sector, coupled with the high risk of failure, deters investment from the private sector. Figure 23.2 illustrates Research and development

Table 23.1 Technology readiness levels and descriptors

Level	Description
TRL1	Basic principles observed, the start of scientific research
TRL2	Technology concept formulated, none or little experimental proof of concept
TRL3	Experimental proof of concept conducted
TRL4	Technology validated in the laboratory
TRL5	Technology validated in relevant environment
TRL6	Technology validated as fully functional prototype in relevant environment
TRL 7	System prototype demonstrated in operational environment
TRL8	System complete and qualified
TRL9	Actual system proven in operational environment

Source: *Horizon Europe*[11]

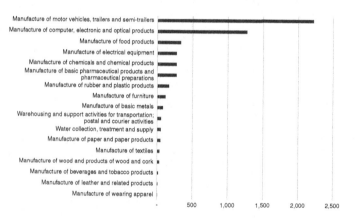

Figure 23.2 Research and development expenditure (£ million) per U.K. manufacturing sector in 2020
Data source U.K. Office of National Statistics

expenditure per U.K. manufacturing sector in 2020 (Business Enterprise Research and Development – Office for National Statistics, 2021) and highlights that overall, the F&TI invest the least in Research and development suggesting that these industries lack agility to contribute to Research and development in this space.

However, private investment is not necessarily the solution; for example, alternative protein material research, motivated by the food industry in search of animal-free meat substitutes, raised US$3.1 billion in 2020, a three-fold increase compared with sums reported in 2019 (Tubb, 2021). Estimated at TRL4–5, several U.S. companies (e.g. Bolt Threads, Modern Meadows) have received several rounds of investment from U.S. venture capital and private funds to scale material production.

However, the nature of funding directly impacts the sharing of research findings. Data related to the performance of these materials, as well as findings related to scale-up barriers are not subject to the same dissemination efforts as a project in receipt of public funding. This results in an inefficient ecosystem where different groups independently tackle the same or similar technical problems.

CONCLUSION

The bio-based materials sector is new and still evolving with biosynthetic plastics leading the mission to replace single-use plastic packaging. Despite significant investment in this material space, the world's second most polluting industry[12] has yet to benefit substantially from advances made in early stage Research and development for bio-based materials. This chapter can only touch upon key issues pertaining to terminology, complex manufacturing processes, policy and investment. Although not exhaustive, we demonstrate that bio-based technologies operate within a fragmented F&TI ecosystem that lacks transparency and consistency. The global and complex nature of the supply chain, historic production processes and the limited resource available for Research and development constitute some of the key barriers preventing the scaling of these technologies. We can learn from the trajectory of innovation in the single-use plastic packaging sector regarding investment to underpin a similar bio-based material innovation agenda with a specific focus on the F&TI.

Perhaps a more disruptive approach is needed – biology teaches us that we need to work with the nuances of materials and processes rather than attempt to fit a square peg into a round hole. For example, PUMA's 'design to fade' initiative[13] uses the inferior colourfastness of biofabricated dyes as an opportunity to create new design paradigms specifically for fading colour. Although not a new idea, it is the first time a multinational brand has addressed this topic and raises a very important question: given the complexity of existing F&TI production processes, how can design – rather than material and process – contribute to this discourse?

NOTES

1 Australian performance artist exploring how technology can help extend the body. In 2007, Stelarc had a cell-cultivated ear surgically attached to his left arm.
2 British installation artist who uses the materials and tools of synthetic biology to create artworks.
3 https://www.globenewswire.com/news-release/2021/12/17/2354362/0/en/Global-Bio-Based-Materials-Market-Size-Is-Expected-To-Reach-About-USD-87-Billion-by-2026-at-a-CAGR-of-26-5-Facts-Factors.html.

4 A product that is wholly or partly made from plastic and that is not conceived, designed, or placed on the market to be used multiple times for the same purpose.
5 Art. 5 in conjunction with annex, part B.
6 https://www.verifiedmarketresearch.com/product/bio-based-materials-market/.
7 1 Gigatonne (Gt) = 1 billion tonnes = 1,000,000,000 tonnes.
8 See also Chapter 11 for more information.
9 A textile finishing process giving sheen/lustre to cellulosic yarns and the final fabric especially as in *mercerized* cotton.
10 https://news.un.org/en/story/2019/03/1035161.
11 https://ec.europa.eu/research/participants/data/ref/h2020/wp/2014_2015/annexes/h2020-wp1415-annex-g-trl_en.pdf.
12 https://designtofade.puma.com/.
13 https://ec.europa.eu/research/participants/data/ref/h2020/wp/2014_2015/annexes/h2020-wp1415-annex-g-trl_en.pdf.

REFERENCES

Babu, B. R., Parande, A. K., Raghu, S., & Kumar, T. P. (2007). Textile technology-an overview of wastes produced during cotton textile processing and effluent treatment methods. *Journal of Cotton Sciences*, 11, p. 110.
Bolt Threads. (n.d.). Mylo. Bolt Threads Inc. Retrieved 6 October 2021, from https://boltthreads.com/technology/mylo/.
Braungart, M., & McDonough, W. (2002). *Cradle to cradle. Remaking the way we make things*. 1st edition. New York: North Point Press.
Business enterprise research and development - Office for National Statistics. (2021, November 19). Office for National Statistics. Retrieved 13 January 2022, from https://www.ons.gov.uk/economy/governmentpublicsectorandtaxes/researchanddevelopmentexpenditure/datasets/ukbusinessenterpriseresearchanddevelopment.
Early life cycle analysis. (n.d.). DESSERTO. Retrieved 12 January 2022, from https://desserto.com.mx/e-lca.
Ellen MacArthur Foundation. (2013). *Towards the circular economy: Economic and business rationale for an accelerated transition*. 1. London: Ellen Macarthur Foundation, from https://www.ellenmacarthurfoundation.org/assets/downloads/publications/Ellen-MacArthur-Foundation-Towards-the-Circular-Economy-vol.1.pdf.
Faber Futures. (n.d). Retrieved 12/01/2021 from https://faberfutures.com/projects/project-coelicolor/.
Gunay, Melihh. (2013). Eco-Friendly Textile Dyeing and Finishing. *Intechopen*, 272 p. ISBN: 978-9535108924.
Harkness, J. M. (2004). *An idea man (the life of otto Herbert Schmitt)* doi:10.1109/MEMB.2004.1378631.
Iouguina, A. (2013). *Biologically informed disciplines: A comparative analysis of terminology within the fields of bionics, biomimetics, and biomimicry* (Doctoral dissertation, Carleton University).Kapsali, V. (2016). *Biomimetics for designers*. London: Thames & Hudson. ISBN 9780500518489.
Kapsali, V. (2022). All things bio: A conceptual domain-based approach to mapping research and practice within the landscape of biologically informed disciplines. *The Design Journal*, doi:10.1080/14606925.2022.2058449.

Kapsali, V., & Hall, C. (2022). Sustainable approaches to textile design: Lessons from biology, in Lockton, D., Lenzi, S., Hekkert, P., Oak, A., Sádaba, J., & Lloyd, P. (eds.), *DRS2022: Bilbao*, 25 June–3 July, Bilbao, Spain. https://doi.org/10.21606/drs.2022.199.

Laurent, A., Olsen, S. I., & Hauschild, M. Z. (2012). Limitations of carbon footprint as indicator of environmental sustainability. *Environmental Science & Technology*, 46(7), pp. 4100–4108.

Lee, S., Congdon, A., Parker, G., & Borst, C. (2020). Understanding "Bio" Material Innovations Report [Industry Report]. Biofabricate, Fashion for Good. https://app.box.com/s/amjq9answv8hvwdexoxg6wubes4aaxqa

Lepora, N. F., Verschure, P., & Prescott, T. J. (2013). The state of the art in biomimetics. Bioinspiration & Biomimetics, 8(1), 013001.

Matthews, H. S., Hendrickson, C. T., & Weber, C. L. (2008). The importance of carbon footprint estimation boundaries. *Environmental Science & Technology*, 42(16), pp. 5839–5842. https://doi.org/10.1021/es703112w.

Niinimäki, K., Peters, G., Dahlbo, H., Perry, P., Rissanen, T., & Gwilt, A. (2020). The environmental price of fast fashion. *Nature Reviews Earth & Environment*, [online] 1(4), pp. 189–200. https://doi.org/10.1038/s43017-020-0039-9.

Papanek, V., & Fuller, R. B. (1972). *Design for the real world*. London: Thames and Hudson.

Pecman, M. (2014). Variation as a cognitive device: How scientists construct knowledge through term formation. Terminology. *International Journal of Theoretical and Applied Issues in Specialized Communication*, 20(1), pp. 1–24. https://doi.org/10.1075/term.20.1.01pec.

Rex, D., Okcabol, S., & Roos, S. (2019). Possible Sustainable Fibers on the Market and Their Technical Properties. The Fiber Bible Part 1. Available from: https://refashion.fr/eco-design/sites/default/files/fichiers/The%20fiber%20bible%20part%201%20Possible%20sustainable%20fibers%20on%20the%20market%20and%20their%20technical%20properties.pdf.

Salo, M., Mattinen-Yuryev, M. K., & Nissinen, A. (2019). Opportunities and limitations of carbon footprint calculators to steer sustainable household consumption–Analysis of Nordic calculator features. *Journal of Cleaner Production*, 207, 658–666.

Tidder, A., Benohoud, M., Rayner, C. M., & Blackburn, R. S. (2018, May). Extraction of anthocyanins from blackcurrant (Ribes nigrum L.) fruit waste and application as renewable textile dyes. *In Proceedings of the BIOColours Conference 2018*. Leeds.

Tubb, C. (2021). Can alternative proteins transform textiles? *Textiles*, 48(3), pp. 12–17.

Vincent, J. F. V. (2001). Stealing ideas from nature. *Deployable Structures*, pp. 51–58. https://doi.org/10.1007/978-3-7091-2584-7_3.

Vincent, J. F., Bogatyreva, O. A., Bogatyrev, N. R., Bowyer, A., & Pahl, A.-K. (2006). Biomimetics: Its practice and theory. *Journal of the Royal Society Interface*, 3(9), 471–482.

Vincent, J. F. (2014). An ontology of biomimetics. *Biologically Inspired Design: Computational Methods and Tools*, 269–285.

Von Bertalanffy, L. (1950). The theory of open systems in physics and biology. *Science*, 111(2872), pp. 23–29.

Wade, N. (1975). New Alchemy institute: Search for an alternative agriculture. *Science*, 187(4178), pp. 727–729. https://doi.org/10.1126/science.187.4178.727.

Wahl, D. C. (2006). Bionics vs. biomimicry: from control of nature to sustainable participation in nature. *Design and nature III: comparing design in nature with science and engineering*, 87, pp. 289–298.

Wahl, D. (2016). *Designing regenerative cultures*. Charmouth: Triarchy Press.

24 Reincarnation: waste, reuse, repair and upcycling

Yoon Jung Choi, Jen Ballie and Alka Puri

INTRODUCTION

Globally, consumers miss out on US$460 billion of value each year by throwing away clothing that has potential to be reused, repaired and upcycled (PACE, 2021). Around 30% of clothing in wardrobes has not been worn for at least a year and estimated £140 million worth of clothing goes into landfill (WRAP, 2020). A transformation of the fashion and textiles industry is both urgently necessary and an opportunity-in-waiting. A transition to a circular economy is expected to unlock US$560 billion economic opportunity in the fashion industry globally, by better capturing the value of underutilised and landfilled or incinerated clothes (Ellen MacArthur Foundation, 2017). The circular economy (CE) aims to reduce our impact on the planet by keeping clothing in circulation for as long as possible and out of landfills. It requires a systematic approach to maintain high-quality products and material. The closed-loop cycle offers an alternative to selling significant numbers of low-cost products. In practice, this means exhausting every opportunity for reusing, repairing and re-purposing, and proving that it is possible to generate financial profit while respecting both the environment and society. One of the most environmentally friendly behaviours is to re-use the clothing you already own because it does not require raw material extraction or energy and water for manufacturing. As we are in the transitional stage to CE, appropriate design approaches are needed to address people's sustainable behaviour in dealing with the end-of-use clothing, until the full circular system is established.

DOI: 10.4324/9781003272878-30

As von Busch and Palmas (2016) claim, in order to see changes in the consumption patterns of fashion or the attitudes among consumers, we will have to design systems which include them and take their role in the lifecycle of clothing seriously, yet they require more support. Brands and retailers should guarantee the provision of service for care and mend of any wear and tear for garments they produce or retail. That means designing garments that are possible to repair or designing tools to improve the condition of clothing items over long-term wear and tear. Clothing must be designed to be easy to disassemble; therefore, the worn-out clothing could also become an upgraded or updated form of the garment. Designers and business need to re-think how clothing might be designed, used and cared for in the future and develop ways in which consumers can be part of the circular system to reuse more clothing and create awareness about the value of clothing.

The aim of this chapter is threefold: to (1) understand the consumer's barriers in bringing clothing back to life at the end-of-use stage; (2) acknowledge that raising awareness and design-oriented education are promising intervention to change behaviour (Bhamra et al., 2011); (3) propose design strategies that encourage consumers to take proactive roles in reducing their own fashion waste. Through a participatory research method, four practical design strategies have been established that might contribute towards empowering the consumer in reuse. It will then discuss how design opportunities might encourage the business to re-think clothing reuse in the future.

BARRIERS

The potential barriers which prevent users participating in reuse are discussed under three categories below based on the insight learned from the Reuse study from WRAP (2015).

Lack of knowledge, skills and time

The cost of unused clothing in the wardrobe is estimated to be around £30 billion (WRAP, 2017). As reuse activities can be seen as time-consuming, people tend to hibernate or accumulate clothing at end of use, rather than reuse (WRAP, 2017). The skills for repair are diminishing (Harris et al., 2016) and there is limited knowledge about environmental impact of throw-away behaviour. Additionally, lack of knowledge about service available for repair/upcycle prevents consumers participating in reuse (WRAP, 2015). There are a few websites, including Remake,[1] which enables users to learn upcycle techniques and access repair instructions. Pantagonia[2] is another example of offering repair classes online and in-store workshop. Though these platforms exist, there is a need for a greater variety of accessible and functional platforms to facilitate reuse, upcycle and repair culture amongst consumers.

Lack of availability of service provisions, resources and facilities

The lack of available service provisions, resources or facilitates beyond the point of purchase limits the lifecycle of clothing as it does not orientate consumer behaviour towards reuse or modification. This is largely due to the lack of easily accessible resources or facilities that support consumers to upcycle garments with appropriate and replicable methods to educate and inspire. The high street retailer Zara offers alteration as a bolt on service for altering a hem and H&M retail Do It Yourself kits with iron on patches and embellishments. While there is a lack of local haberdashery shops, clothing repair or alteration services on local high streets, and this makes it difficult to procure the necessary sewing tools, resources or expert knowledge. There is scope to pilot new schemes locally within community centres, or commercially for independent designers to offer innovative solutions or to be sponsored with the support of global fashion brands. While these ideas might offer small-scale solutions, they have the potential to be the catalyst for bolder and bigger ambitions.

Negative associations of upcycled clothing

From a cultural perspective, there is a social risk to consumers in relation to the negative associations with upcycling and repairing of clothing items, where it is typically perceived as an activity from lower social-economic status suggesting the inability to afford new clothes, or reused items may be seen as inferior products, with little guarantee of reliability (WRAP, 2015). A significant proportion that is estimated to be around 70% of textiles collected for reuse is sent overseas (Ellen MacArthur Foundation, 2017). Due to lack of infrastructure and systems for high-quality recycling or other environmentally sound waste management, clothing waste often gets downcycled or improperly disposed of (PACE, 2021). Recently, a new market has emerged in the West where it sources deadstock fabrics that are left unused or discarded textiles from large manufacturers in Bangladesh and China. However, the business and design strategies should work collectively in establishing the local reusing system, to raise awareness for more acceptance of and preference for repaired and upcycled clothing. India based Doodlage[3] is an example where it sources off cut and unwanted fabrics from local manufacturing.

RAISING USERS AWARENESS

Increasing consumers' awareness of the clothing lifecycle and its impacts has been described as "the best hope for sustainability in the fashion industry" (Claudio, 2007). Indeed, raising consumers' awareness of the potential reuse opportunities through education and inspirable design can contribute developing consumer healthier habits around how they care for, use and dispose. By working collectively across business and academia, this can be achieved through making information more visible, whether through organising exhibitions, facilitating talks or media communication, or training and education (Fuad-Luke, 2013). Furthermore, providing accessible facilities and tools for reuse has potential to increase consumers' awareness for prolonging the useful life of unworn clothing. These initiatives would primarily focus on raising consumer awareness on the importance of reusing pre-owned garments. In doing so, it supports knowledge gain and upskilling to drive forward new mindsets, enabling consumers to build their personal confidence in carrying out the upcycling activities and wearing upcycled, reused/ repaired clothes. By extension, they become empowered to act in accordance with this newfound knowledge, awareness and options. Such interventions could contribute towards the reduction in recourse and value loss within the material loop, ensuring that the end-of-use products and valuable material resources contained are retained within the loop and not landfilled, incinerated or lost.

DESIGN OPPORTUNITIES

This chapter presents four practical design strategies that offer the potential to extend the life of clothing including graphical information, toolkits for good maintenance, visible mending and customisation. These strategies can create a vast range of options available users to adapt and maintain clothing, thereby enabling reuse behaviour. They can also support and incentivise businesses and designers to create and innovate for reuse. The four strategies are presented within a live research project, 'Sewing Box for the Future', under the themes of care, repair and customisation, which was accompanied by a pop-up exhibition and toolkit showcased within V&A Dundee – a design museum in Scotland – during the period of February to December in 2020. This exhibition included infographics depicting visually the journey of different fibre compositions from wardrobe to landfill and the time frame for them to decompose. It was also important to showcase the work of designers at the forefront of reuse for circular innovation and a selection of work from Filippa K and the Centre for Circular Design, Celia Pym, Post-Couture Collective and Chloe Patience was exhibited. This pop-up had over 10,000 visitors and distributed 2,000 free repair kits to schools and outreach groups in the local community.

Infographic

The infographic in Figure 24.1 titled 'How long do clothes take to decompose in landfill?' (Young, 2019) was used as an introduction to the 'Sewing Box for the Future' project. It quickly became a powerful tool for prompting conversations around the CE through its interrogation of the material properties of our clothing. As consumers, we are potentially making our clothing obsolete, with each new purchase. Outlining the different timescales for fibres decomposing was therefore central to the messaging of the project, given its pertinence to the realities of waste in the fashion industry.

The project included reference images on caring for clothing and how long different textile fibres might take to decompose in landfill. This infographic also functioned as a tool for consumers to question or consider the textile fibres composition of their clothing at the point of purchase and stimulated personal reflection on their own wardrobe and behaviours. Through facilitated conversations, consumers shared that they were unable to derive the fibre composition by touching and handling their clothing, and that they relied on the labelling to interpret this information. If consumers were educated about textile fibres that make up their own clothing and how long they take to decompose in landfill, they could perhaps make more informed decisions around their own consumption.

Providing maintenance tool and services

The 'Sewing Box for the Future' toolkit included sewing needles, thread, buttons, a darning mushroom and darning needle, alongside ten activity cards with practical remedies for extending the lifetime of

Figure 24.1 How long do clothes take to decompose in landfill? Graphic work by Young (2019)

clothing. This was supported by a pop-up exhibit showcasing the work of designers at the forefront of circular innovation, who had applied their design expertise to add value to existing materials.

This theme of clothing care was evident in exhibition pieces, including an External Trench Coat (see Figure 24.2) designed by Swedish brand Filippa K in collaboration with the Centre for Circular Design, University of the Arts London, which made use of the principles of circular design. The coat comes with a ten-year care guarantee, which means Filippa K will mend any wear and tear for the first ten years. The coat is made entirely from recycled materials and is also in itself 100% recyclable. The intention to extend its longevity was further explored through the curation of a 'Wash and care kit of five products' selected by Flippa K for the

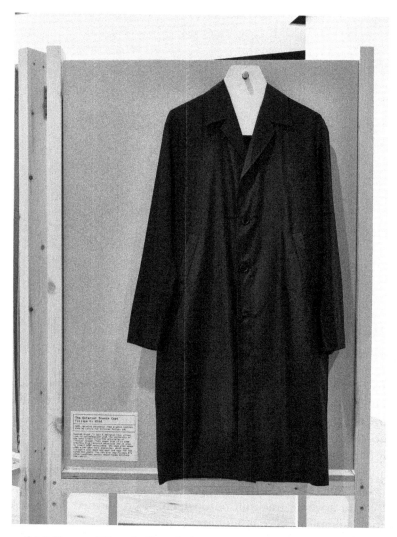

Figure 24.2 External Trench Coat designed by Filippa K in collaboration with the Centre for Circular Design, UAL

maintenance of any garment. The kit included a water-repellent spray that increases clothes' ability to repel water and dirt; a Guppyfriend washing bag that filters out microplastics to stop them reaching rivers and oceans; a clothes brush; a sweater stone; and pocket clothes brush (see Figure 24.3).

Visible mending

In line with the theme of repair, the exhibition also featured a collection of clothing titled, 'Where holes happen map, sweatshirt and socks',

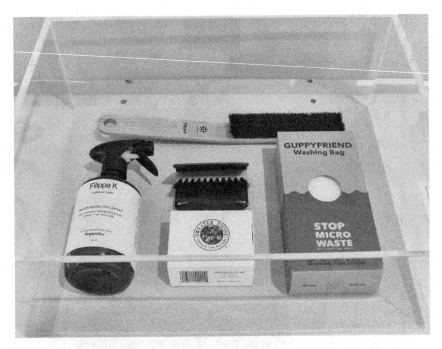

Figure 24.3 Wash and care kit of five products

by textile artist Celia Pym (2018). The collection showcased bold confident darning, demonstrating that clothing repairs do not need to be discreet. The collection was created for the Woman's Hour Craft Prize at the V&A in London in 2017–18. As part of this collection of a 'whole body of garments', comprising a hat, gloves, jumper, trousers and socks, 94 holey garments brought in by members of the public were mended by Celia Pym. The sweatshirt and a pair of socks pictured in Figure 24.4 are part of a whole tracksuit onto which she replicated all 94 repairs, creating a map of where holes happen the most: the right shoulder, elbows, back of the forearms for top and right forefinger pad and thumb and heels for socks and gloves.

Customisation

The theme of customisation was a Modular T-Shirt by Post-Couture Collective (2019) (Figure 24.5), along with a set of garments that could be made and assembled without any sewing at all. Their vision of clothing design breaks with the traditional fashion system and is built on the principles of the open-source movement, whereby companies and/or individuals who share digital designs online can have their garments

Figure 24.4 'Where holes happen map, sweatshirt and socks' by Celia Pym

made by using laser cutting facilities in local Makerspaces. The patterns for each garment design can be downloaded as a complete set and then be made into individual pieces, informed by personal colour and fabric choices. This theme was explored further with the Snake Embellished Denim Jacket by Chloe Patience (2019), a Levi Denim jacket purchased from Depop, embellished using sequins from the Sustainable Sequin Company (see Figure 24.6). This was commissioned to showcase that customising something you already have can be better than buying something new. The decorative detail in the form of a delicate snake for a second-hand denim jacket demonstrated a creative way to add a personal touch to a pre-loved garment.

INSIGHT

The project was evaluated using 243 feedback cards received and participants shared their learning and made a pledge to adopt a new behaviour. The project and the activities with toolkit were thought to be positive and practical. Further resources to be developed were requested in order to support the reuse in the future.

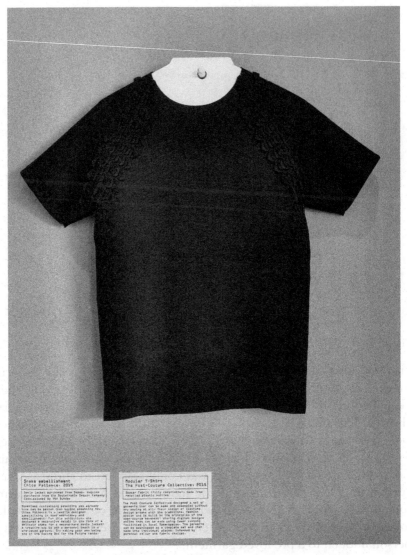

Figure 24.5 Modular T-Shirt by Post-Couture Collective

DISCUSSION

This project explored how we encourage consumers to recognise their unique role and engage them in systemic transformation towards CE through creating a more sustainable and durable connection with our clothes. Although there is no quick-fix or catch-all approach for driving forward a systemic shift in the fashion industry, 'Sewing Box for the Future' provides a series of small-scale and practical steps for individuals to

Figure 24.6 Customised Levi's jacket by Chloe Patience

challenge their own status quo by providing practical activities for them to question, make and reflect, thereby increase their knowledge and skill about behaviour impact. This also mediated intergenerational conversations with a broad audience, evoking a nostalgia around traditional sewing skills that were once commonplace in the home, which help in shifting people's negative view in repair.

The test was set out in a museum environment, yet it can be further extended to industry practice. Four design strategies identified through participatory design approach have potential to offer new business opportunities aimed to reduce consumer barriers. Particularly, integrating creative repair method such as visible mending and customisation into business models will enable consumers to shift their negative perspective of repaired and upcycled clothing, making this option an appealing service, and thereby reaping further potential for businesses. Furthermore, clothing maintenance/repair tools or service should be made widely available in the market, in order to encourage consumers in providing consistent care to garments and prolong their life cycles. Integrating such design strategies in the business model would raise consumer awareness on environmental and social problems, and empower them to self-care, self-repair and self-upcycle their existing garments. The business opportunity can expand on the transformation from customer ownership to usership by introducing monthly subscription, enabling consumer return of clothing for reuse, remanufacturing and upcycling. Consumers can thereby become 'active users' (Tietze and Hansen, 2013). This will allow companies to increase loyalty by customers returning to the company for services and tools, enabling resource efficiency by saving material cost. Consequently, engaging consumers in the system could significantly reduce waste associated with accumulated clothing output, while bringing unworn clothing back to life.

The proposed design strategies should be considered with future development. Developing trimmings made such as thread, buttons and fasteners in recycled or regenerative material to replace petrol-chemical based material must also be considered. Additionally, maintenance tools such as a water-repellent spray or wash bag suitable for different products' technical and biological properties should be designed and offered to enhance product circularity.

CONCLUSION

Business leaders, designers and researchers should reconsider consumers' role as an 'active user' and develop business models to support clothing reuse in the future as part of the circular system. Businesses and designers should investigate how to integrate design-driven reuse strategies into business models, thereby transforming consumers into informed and engaged users that will bring promising change in clothing reuse and offer new fashion experiences in the future. Researchers can work collectively with businesses to develop recycled/renewable material-based trimmings, tools and easily disassembled garments to support repair and upcycle activities for clothing longevity and recyclability.

ACKNOWLEDGEMENTS

We would like to thank Celia Pym, Chloe Patience, Post-Couture Collective, Filippa K and Young who shared their work in this chapter.

NOTES

1 www.remake.world.
2 www.patagonia.com.
3 https://doodlage.in/.

BIBLIOGRAPHY

Bhamra, T., Lilley, D. and Tang, T. (2011). Design for sustainable behaviour: Using products to change consumer behaviour. *The Design Journal.* 14(4), pp. 427–445.

Claudio, L. (2007). Waste couture. Environmental impact of the clothing industry. *Environmental Health Perspectives*, 115(9), pp. 448–454.

Ellen MacArthur Foundation. (2017). A new textiles economy: Redesigning fashion's future. Retrieved from http://www.ellenmacarthurfoundation.org/publications.

Fletcher, K. (2016). *Craft of Use Post-Growth Fashion*, 1st ed. London: Routledge.

Fuad-Luke, A. (2013). *Design Activism Beautiful Strangeness for a Sustainable World*, 3rd ed. London and Sterling VA: Earthscan.

Harris, F., Roby, H. and Dibb, S. (2016). Sustainable clothing: Challenges, barriers and interventions for encouraging more sustainable consumer behaviour. *International Journal of Consumer.* 40(3), pp. 309–318.

PACE. (2021). *Circular Economy Action Agenda Textile.* Hague, Netherland: PACE in partnership with Accenture.

Patience, C. (2019). *Snake Embellished Denim Jacket.* Retrieved from http://www.chloepatience.com/va-dundee

Post-Couture Collective. (2019). *Modular T-Shirt.* Retrieved from https://www.here-now.nl/martijn-van-strien-the post- couture-collective

Pym, C. (2018). *Where Holes Happen Map, Sweatshirt and Socks.* Retrieved from http://celiapym.com/work/where-holes-happen-map/

Tietze, F. and Hansen, E.G. (2013). To own or to use? How product service system facilitate eco-innovation behaviour. *2013 Academy of Management Conference*, 3 April, Orland, p.30.

von Busch, O. and Palmas, K. (2016). Designing consent: Can design thinking manufacture democratic capitalism?. *Organizational Aesthetics*, 5(2), pp. 10–24.

WRAP. (2015). *Barrier to Re-use.* WRAP. Retrieved from https://wrap.org.uk/resources/guide/re-use/barriers-re-use

WRAP. (2017). *Valuing our Clothes: The Cost of UK Fashion.* Banbury, UK: WRAP.

WRAP. (2020). *Sustainable Clothing Action Plan 2020 Commitment.* Oxon, UK: WRAP.

Young, G. (2019). How long do clothes take to decompose in landfill?. In: *Sustainable Innovation 2021* 23rd International Conference 'Accelerating Sustainability in Fashion, Clothing, Sportswear & Accessories, 15–21 March 2021.* Surry UK. pp. 42–50.

Part VII

Education

25 Curriculum: challenges, opportunities, and approaches to increasing sustainability content in fashion and textiles education

Christine Baeza, Samantha Corcoran, and Elizabeth S. Quinn

INTRODUCTION

In a rapidly changing world increasingly focused on ecological and social footprints, the adoption of more socially and environmentally responsible design strategies within the textile and fashion sectors has become a necessity, not only for industry professionals but also for educators teaching the next generation. With pressures being placed on the fashion industry to clean up its supply chains and design practices, the timeliness of upgrading and evolving higher education curricula is critical. Students entering the fashion and textile sectors are conflicted about how to balance securing employment while remaining true to their sustainable aspirations. They need a foundation that focuses on sustainable practices, while also preserving the art form and craft inherent in good design. Fashion design and merchandising curricula may skim the surface of sustainable practices, but largely holds true to David

DOI: 10.4324/9781003272878-32

W. Orr's criticism of higher education: "Modern education has certainly better equipped us to dominate nature rather than dwell in harmony with it and to understand things in fragments rather than think broadly about systems and ecosystems" (Orr, 1992, p. 4).

UNESCO asserts that "Higher education should emphasise experiential, inquiry-based, problem-solving, interdisciplinary systems, approaches, and critical thinking" (UNESCO 2004, pp. 22–23). Spanning research and higher education coursework in both Ireland and America, this chapter explores the exchange of ideas and the intersections linking material and craft, the natural world, and social responsibility to assert the importance of collaboratively addressing how design problems are understood, how solutions will be executed, and how higher education develops the next generation of industry professionals. The three authors, each bringing perspective from different sectors of the industry and academia (merchandising, textile design, and apparel design), offer a glimpse into the collaborative effort, mutual respect, and diverse expertise needed to bring about positive change that is holistically and collectively beneficial.

FUTURE THINKING AND CURRICULUM DEVELOPMENT

Across the world, design educators are exploring what it means to teach in a time of flux and hybridity. How do we transition students into an existing industry while arming them for future systemic change? Educators must first pilot new and innovative curricula and analyse the outcomes before instituting broader adoption. This part examines coursework at the National College of Art and Design (Dublin, Ireland) and Drexel University (Pennsylvania, United States), within fashion design, merchandising, and textiles programmes. These projects aimed to inspire a more future-fit, nutritive, and holistic approach to the design development phase. The authors assert that opportunities for improving and advancing higher education curriculum can be drawn from sustainability-focused pilots, through the lenses of responsible design practice.

National college of art and design coursework
Driven by an urgency of action regarding innovative design research, ideation, and creation of a circular, symbiotic space, a team of educators devised a series of collaborative Design School projects exploring Innovative Material Making & Biophilic Inspired Design (Corcoran, O'Dowd, Tuffy, 2021). As an antithesis to our sterile, technologically consumed, distant,

and often virtual lives, we proposed that a reconnection with biophilia[1] may direct us towards a protective approach for the material future, where human and environmental sustainability become inherently linked to how we design, live, and operate. Diverse, multidisciplinary teams of design students, led by staff across Textile & Surface Design (TSD), Product, and Jewellery Design, were set a range of experiential, reflective, material making challenges to reawaken their connection to "the origin of materials of the earth, land and environment" (Corcoran et al., 2021, p. 116). By connecting students meaningfully to the experience and skill of making alongside a deeper appreciation of material, provenance, ecology, and social-environmental responsibility, we hoped to challenge design thinking and empower students to become transformative fashion, material, and textile designers who designed with integrity and ethics.

Ocean pollution (2017): industrial waste as resource: disruption and rebirth

Responding to environmental degradation students sourced industrial waste and non-recyclable plastics, and prototyped innovative material approaches towards resource second life. "The power of materials and surfaces as experiences which can enhance our lives," beyond their functionality and aesthetics and our emotional human connection to material and the natural world was introduced (Corcoran et al., 2021, p. 117). This encouraged genuine and empathetic design thinking and innovation regarding reuse, reassembly, and reinvention. Rethinking textile print equipment usage to fit new approaches, disrupting and retro-fitting screen print techniques by incorporating industrial waste content within established techniques e.g. industrial ash waste within puff print and non-recyclable foil waste within foil print, created fascinating "Waste Prints."

Short intensive team-based projects pooled resources, knowledge, and time, and encouraged competitive and collaborative peer learning, rapid ideation, and critical decision-making. Diversity of discipline (textiles, product, fashion, jewellery, graphic design) experience, university level (MA and second year undergraduate) and culture expanded design thinking and methodology to help solve complex problems from different perspectives. As Katie Hanlan MA Design graduate, Acting Lecturer in TSD/Fashion Knit, stated:

Each individual approach to solving design problems was one of the most important elements of the project, as we navigated a way of working together to experiment and reach an outcome that met the brief but also reflected each of our practices.

Material futures (2018): nutritive material making:
beneficial to life

This second project evolved with the aim of designing out harmful waste, reducing resource depletion, and advancing towards a sustainable, protective system for all. Enda O'Dowd Lecturer and course coordinator of the MSc Medical Device Design programme, coined the phrase "Nutritive Material Making" with the objective of creating a circular holistic system of materials and textiles, nurturing and nourishing to people and place, throughout its life cycle. Staff questioned "Can Plants Save the World?" and pivoted towards natural plant-based material solutions and biodegradable bioplastics which could shape, protect, and future proof (Corcoran et al., 2021, p. 120).

Students sourced abundant natural waste locally and created hybrid material composites. Designer and consumer ethics and care, regarding material provenance, value, life cycle, and their relationship to the environment was introduced. In contrast to our increasingly virtual world, we embraced a return to the physicality of collaborative and regenerative workshop experimentation. Concepts explored included moulding and baking form without the need for assembly, and creating naturally dyed bioplastics and natural hybrids, designed to disappear non-destructively.

This project challenged us all to find new ways forward to reinvent material making, surface intervention, finish, and colouration to benefit both environment and human health.

Brohwyn Brennan, Product Design graduate and Intern Rosendahl Design Group Copenhagen, Denmark, summarised her learning experience:

> The project taught me that designing and innovating is not always about having a beautifully polished product and perfect renders. It's about trial and error, experimentation, exploration and discovery where 'mistakes' can open up a whole new set of opportunities and realm of further exploration.

Material futures (2020): biophilia: biodegradable materials:
from the earth to the earth

The success of the nutritive materials project reinforced our belief that working with and for nature, to create biodegradable natural material hybrids was an important part of the solution for future material development. A new team member, Rachel Tuffy, Lecturer in Constructed Textiles, identified Irish sheep wool, a by-product of the meat industry,

Table 25.1 NCAD Post Course Reflections

Key Insights	Course Findings and Reflections
Respect and value our connection to nature, individual skill sets, and each other to help drive ambitious design solutions and creative approaches	• Peer learning and communication across (diverse) disciplines is valuable but connecting disciplines should not come at the expense of discipline specific skill sets that inspire future collaborative developments • As Edward O. Wilson states "to the degree that we come to understand other organisms, we will place a greater value on them, and ourselves" (Wilson E.O., 1984, p. 2). Holistic and human connection to nature and each other, awareness, and acceptance of environmental problems alongside the joy of making encourages genuine problem-solving • Sincere connections and synergy between natural collaborators (both staff and students) can help inspire passion to work both individually and collectively towards a common goal
Knowledge-share can be enabled and supported	• While short, intensive collaborative projects can inspire change in values, mindset and drive ambition, considered material/prototype advancement will need further curricular time and support • Real-world change will take time, investment, support, and forward planning: for project development, preparation, upskilling, collaborative conversations, research, knowledge-share, and postgraduate curricular development. Realistic time allocation (timeout/buyout from teaching commitments) and funding must be provided by *Universities* for staff involved • Further ongoing opportunities for accessible global sustainable knowledge-share and research across universities and industry is necessary to drive change
Evaluation of circular systems of design will help design out the harmful cycle of waste and create a more holistic and protective future system	• Sustainable postgraduate courses should be designed, developed, funded, staffed, and equipped, to allow space for the formation and development of innovative research exploration and collaborative research clusters

as a valuable waste resource leading to the inclusion of animal fibres/skins alongside locally abundant plant resources.

In response to the "biological annihilation" (Ceballos et al., 2017) of the natural world, the students were asked to consider the environmental consequences of their design approach.

> As designers, how can we influence and guide a way forward to create and produce in a less wasteful and more considered way? How can we take an earth approach and learn to reconnect, value and treasure our land, animals, biodiversity and local resources?
>
> (Corcoran et al., 2021, p. 122)

Influence from traditional and contemporary techniques were key to the success of creative hybrid innovation produced e.g. carding, felting, embellishing, natural screen printing and dyeing, embossing, moulding, laser cutting, and etching. Nose to tail usage and natural finish was explored, using lanolin extracted from waste wool to naturally waterproof, and experimenting with acacia powder to create a natural gum/grip on wool. Inspirational prototyping with Irish waste wool, peat, and bioplastics echoed a distinctly Irish voice and moved Irish craft, farming, and ecology towards a new material heritage.

The aim for us as design educators, alongside teaching technical skills, was to introduce design students to the joy of innovating, collaborating, and making new discoveries, and to instil in them the confidence and power to know they could make a difference to increase sustainable practices.

Cliona McLoughlin TSD Print graduate explained her personal perspective on the educational significance of the project:

> It instilled a strong sense of responsibility in me to design sustainably. It gave me the confidence to question the ways in which things have always been done and the curiosity to seek out or create better alternatives. Through a safe environment of experimentation I became acutely aware of the positive impact I can make as a critically thinking and curious designer.

Drexel university coursework

Through the exploration of both fashion design and merchandising curricula, two of the authors shared resources, insights, and course outcomes to develop frameworks that address ecological and social impacts incurred during the design development phase. By integrating moments of reflection throughout the product development process and introducing ethical frameworks, students were challenged to make meaningful connections to people and the planet, with and through their designs, and identify the difference between "CAN we make this" and "OUGHT we." Each of the classes below was conducted independently within their respective disciplines, a factor that led the pair to explore a transdisciplinary approach to future work.

Sustainable collection design (2019, 2020): circular practices using pre- and post-consumer textile waste

A key area of focus for the United Nations Fashion Charter for Climate Change is in the commitment to investigate raw materials and "explore the whole life cycle of the fibre to provide for a holistic point of view" (Unfcc.int 2021). By procuring pre- and post-consumer textile waste and experimenting with innovative ways of reimagining and reclaiming materials, fashion design students considered circularity as the foundation for their craft. Using responsible design principles (zero waste pattern-making, upcycling, and de/reconstruction), students worked in pairs to research, experiment, design, and create collections. Challenging the status quo and doing no harm, students ensured that this collaborative effort developed from a foundation of mutual respect and understanding. This approach to design introduced students to the vast potential of creating from waste and reexamining the entire design process. Additionally, students analysed not only how they were making garments, but also why they were creating them in the first place.

Students valued this experimental coursework; however, they also expressed the limitations of this isolated elective course. Lindsay Alshouse, a third-year fashion design student reflected, "These projects grew my awareness of the importance of circularity and innovation within responsible design, but I am not sure how I will translate some of the techniques into my career practice." This feedback reinforces the urgency for this research to continue, expand, and take hold in curricula.

Experimental accessories (2021): biomaterials and the impermanence of fashion

Material innovations that make use of bio-based components and naturally regenerative resources could help put the fashion industry on a path to a more synergistic production model. However, circularity and biodegradability are essential considerations that must be addressed to

Table 25.2 Drexel Post Course Reflections (Design-Focused Courses)

Key Insights	Course Findings and Reflections

Thoughtful designs should communicate purpose and intent	• Students should be challenged during the ideation phase to justify the need for their designs:
	  • "What is the reason for making this product?"
	  • "What need does it fulfil?"
	• Introducing students to the practice of consumer wear-testing and customer feedback sessions are necessary to ensure their design decisions always centre people

Moments of reflection reduce unnecessary and/or overproduction	• Just because students can make a product, should they? Working through this question while in an academic setting provides the backdrop for students to carry this mentality into industry • Designing in the "bubble" of an academic setting gives students the false notion that everything they sketch is worth making simply for its aesthetic value • Training students to have an open mind and critical eye, while also accepting outside criticism ensures that all aspects of a design are analysed, prior to production
Strategic planning of curriculum is a must	• Isolated coursework does not allow for students to develop strong ideation, design, and production methods that centre responsible practices • A sequence of courses incorporating all levels of the academic plan of study and involving an interdisciplinary mix of students and instructors is critical for the projects in these courses to be meaningful and impactful

ensure that new materials stay out of landfills. If brands and designers quickly embrace new bio-based materials before they are part of a circular economy, do these innovations have the potential to do more harm than good?

The focus of this elective course was to look at innovation with an emphasis on material end-of-life. By adapting tools and pedagogy, this course aimed to create a framework in which students could contemplate concepts for radical change and innovation. Through research and experimentation, students developed bio-based and biodegradable materials by cooking common ingredients, such as potato starch, gelatin, agar agar powder, and coffee. Students created materials with varying degrees of flexibility, density, and structure to work outside the norms of what materials can and should be used, and redefine the ways of approaching design. Nina Sajankila, a first-year graduate student, reflected, "My experience challenged me to think in different ways, learn how to use what already exists to create something new, and gave me hope for advances in textile research."

Design, disaster, and impact (2020) – transdisciplinary approach to integrating ethics and social entrepreneurship

In the paper, "Integrating Ethics into the Curriculum through Design Courses," the authors state, "ethics instruction does not address every day decisions" (Civjan and Tooker, 2020). This is reinforced by McGinn's survey results which concluded that student ethical preparation was not sufficient for the dilemmas faced by those in the industry, and asserted that teaching students to internalise decision-making and raise awareness of the multitude of dilemmas they face may be more effective at altering future decisions (Civjan and Tooker, 2020). During the fall of 2020, Christine Baeza from Design and Merchandising and Raja Schaar from Product Design co-taught a course with students from product design, merchandising, and engineering who were introduced to a series of ethics-related assignments. The learner centred pedagogy integrated design fiction, ethics, and social entrepreneurship with the aim of reconsidering the design process (Figure 25.1) by creating moments of reflection to better understand the ethical implications of design proposals. The ethical canvas (Figure 25.2) was adapted from a resource found during the literature review and applied to a variety of activities

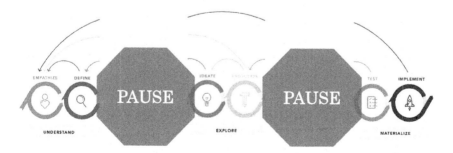

Figure 25.1 Design thinking disruption

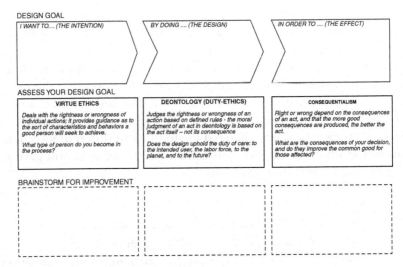

Figure 25.2 Ethics canvas for design evaluation.
Adapted from Gispen, Jet (2017); BBC Ethics; Rand-Hendriksen, M. (2018).

throughout the term, where ethical dilemmas via real-world scenarios were contrasted with sci-fi films and literature. Students were actively engaged with analysis, critical evaluation, and self-reflection. Comments from students revealed that different lenses of ethics brought up unique considerations that created new perspectives which informed adjustments made throughout the design process. Grace Landry, a third-year product design student, commented that, "Our foundation of ethics informed our evaluation of ideas which lead us to identify a meaningful design opportunity."

This course emphasised the importance of an entrepreneurial mindset in giving students the tools to consider sustainability ideas as viable business endeavours, as opposed to its usual basis solely on profitability. Students aligned business, social, and environmental goals using the Ethical Entrepreneurship Canvas tool (Figure 25.3), adapted for this course, in order to create novel solutions that are aligned with ethical decision-making. Landry stated, "We utilised this tool to contemplate how our design could be a sustainable business model. However, due to the constraints of the course, we did not have an opportunity to deeply consider the funding opportunities for this design."

THE FUTURE OF FASHION AND TEXTILES EDUCATION

The curriculum development illustrated above analyses how fashion, textile, and merchandising curriculum offerings equip students with the tools needed to become change agents. Current plans of study prepare

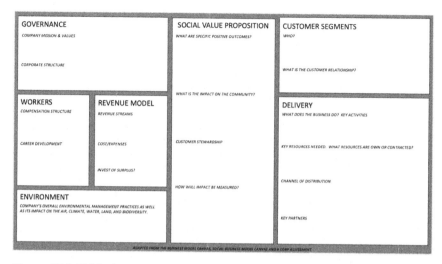

Figure 25.3 Ethical entrepreneurship canvas

Table 25.3 Drexel Post Course Reflections (Design Fiction-Focused Course)

Key Insights	Course Findings and Reflections
Allow more time for each ethical lens	• Pick science fiction clips that align with each ethical lens for use as in-class activities that allow students to develop their awareness of moral and ethical problems related to decision-making
How might we combine the provocations of speculative design to solve the dilemma of environmental and social issues in a collaborative and playful exercise for designers?	• The world-building game, *AfroRithms from the Future* was created to provoke the unfolding of ideas and theories of the student. Not my ideas. Not my interests. The students' • Consider using the game as a propositional and discursive pedological strategy and as an analytical pedological strategy
Allow more time for the Ethical Entrepreneurship Canvas	• Most students felt that they did not have an opportunity to deeply consider the funding opportunities for their final project • Consider how guest speakers or industry mentors could support the students during the development of their Ethical Entrepreneurship Canvas

students with industry skills and knowledge; however, the course reflection tables should encourage educators to integrate more forward-thinking pedagogy and learning outcomes that would ensure graduates are better prepared for longevity in the textile and fashion sectors.

Victor Papanek, designer, educator, and advocate of responsible design, stated, "The main trouble with design schools seems to be that they teach too much design and not enough about the ecological, social, economic, and political environment in which design takes place." (Papanek 2016). It is now imperative for higher education institutions to create opportunities that connect a variety of disciplines and establish creative, collaborative, and real-world learning environments. Additionally, utilising ethical frameworks as the foundation for how students engage with coursework and develop creative thinking is essential.

Summary
Extrapolating how institutions might begin to reshape curricula to be more thought-provoking, experience-based, and collaborative, the authors looked at trends, key findings, and student feedback from the above courses and offer their key insights in Table 25.4.

Ethics in design
It is time to rethink the way design is taught by allowing students to develop their own understanding of how to create better conditions by evaluating the past and future. For centuries, philosophers have grappled with the same questions we now face in various design industries: how to do more good than harm, by way of human responsibility, and how to measure success not just by the economics. Ethics is an often overlooked yet crucial component when discussing sustainable and responsible practices related to design.

"There are at least two possibilities of integrating ethics in design curriculum: (1) Recognition of ethical dilemmas by discussing moral challenges and (2) intuitive understanding through reflective practice, or according to Aristotle, 'developing one's moral and intellectual virtues'" (Keitsch and Ornas 2016).

Experiential learning and transdisciplinary pedagogy
Educators have a moral obligation, to push designers to explore far beyond present-day constraints and encourage the question "what if?" leading to imaginative and novel solutions to both speculated and real problems. Strong grounding in individual discipline enables meaningful knowledge-share across disciplines. Experience of historical and current technical knowhow allows for disruption and hybridising of techniques to conceptualise a new way forward through creative design thinking and experiential making.

Table 25.4 Key Insights and Future Applications

Key Insights	Course Findings and Reflections	Future Course Applications
Practice and Develop Humility	• Positive change comes from respect for, appreciation of, and learning from traditions • Past practices are not always inferior and/or negative; and current/future practices are not always superior and/or positive • Listening and communication are key skills to develop respect for diverse attitudes	• Create a Humility Course Charter • Assign research projects on recent historical innovations to understand how new developments impact the industry, planet, and humans immediately and over time
Create with Intent	• Identify the problem (waste/pollution), make connections and synergies regarding staff and student cohorts, and choose a direction/goal/purpose (material innovation, ecology, sustainability) • Take criticism, be open to change, have conviction for your share, and analyse direction/approach • Test, review, share, and analyse • Think critically about the design industry's roles and responsibilities in all aspects of a product's lifecycle	• Utilise a Lifecycle Analysis Tool • Develop experiential projects that address the needs of the consumer, industry, and community • Identify potential abundant local ingredients/waste to explore, research, and develop key partnerships (e.g., farming, ecology, botany, material science, textile design, biology, and chemistry)
Pause and Reflect	• Moments of speculation are necessary throughout the design process to consider the impact of ideas and actions both in academic settings and in the industry • Exhibit awareness of moral and ethical problems related to decision-making and translate knowledge into solutions for a positive future	• Film clips for in-class discussion • World-Building game play • B-Corp Case Studies • Develop a Purpose-Driven Design Framework to be used throughout the development process • Create opportunities to research and assess technical approaches (e.g., synthetic vs. natural vs. bacterial/microbial, dying, colouration, printing)

(Continued)

Table 25.4 (Continued)

Key Insights	Course Findings and Reflections	Future Course Applications
Holistic Approach to Strategic Planning	• Funding, equipment, training, and time provisions towards research and development of curricular design are important • Recognition that this dynamic, non-prescriptive pedagogy needs expert staff to design and guide • Provision of circular systems (material innovation design laboratories and incubator units) is necessary to develop, test, and commercialise material innovations	• Offer Research Fellowship positions for directed avenues towards sustainable innovation • Empower individual faculty/staff members to contribute unique skill sets and perspectives in reshaping and directing cross-disciplinary curricula

As the fashion and textile sectors contemplate how to better align ecological and social footprints within supply chains and business structures, there has been a growing urgency to reach outside the knowledge and skill sets of individuals working in the industry to gain expertise from a variety of disciplines and sectors e.g. science, engineering, and technology. Additionally, academic institutions must embrace cross-disciplinary approaches to education for students to be well-rounded, critical, and creative. Claire Whelan TSD Print Graduate NCAD who pushed "technical innovation beyond traditional function" in her final year collection, stated that she became conscious that "interdisciplinary collaboration between textiles, fashion and other disciplines such as architecture and science" will be important to drive new discoveries.

The integrated learning model

The following model (Figure 25.4) offers an approach for educators to adapt within their departments and/or programmes, in order to advance the interconnectedness of material and craft, the natural world, and social responsibility. Both instructors and learners are active in the process of constructing meaning and knowledge to inform their design work.

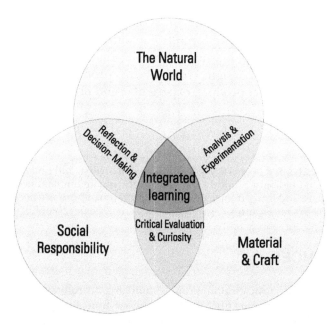

The Natural
World

Reflection &
Decision-Making

Analysis &
Experimentation

Integrated
learning

Social
Responsibility

Critical Evaluation
& Curiosity

Material
& Craft

Figure 25.4 Integrated learning model

CONCLUSION

Recognising and protecting good design practice, skill, and knowledge while incubating future design thinking, experiential making, material innovation, and new business models, with ethics and sustainability at the core, is critical. Gleaning cultural and craft knowledge from material masters, skilled practitioners and cross-disciplinary collaborators, while simultaneously looking at the wider contemporary world and its environmental challenges will bring opportunities to link ideas and form potential new partnerships directed towards positive learning, research, and ultimately, real-world change.

Changing minds will inevitably change actions and using inspirational, emotive, honest, and positive reasoning, and an appreciation of empathy, respect, humanity, and compassion will bring people on the shared journey. The goal for educators is to recognise that mindset development is as important as skill development. Students trained in social entrepreneurship and ethical decision-making may hold the key to solving the world's most pressing issues.

Collaboration between experts in diverse disciplines (design, ethics, biology, science, chemistry, ecology, sociology, and philosophy) who connect on both a personal and professional level is vital to create truly immersive and collaborative learning experiences that inspire potential avenues for positive innovation. We are all connected to each other and the natural environment but only by recognising and respecting our individual disciplinary, human, ecological, ethical, and social differences and values, can we formulate a pathway towards a sustainable system from the inside out. As a society, it's time to redefine our value system in relation to design, creation, and production and prioritise people, quality of life, product, experience, and ecology.

NOTE

1 Biophilia: Defined by social psychologist, psychoanalyst, and philosopher, Erich Fromm and biologist Edward O. Wilson, as the innate human need to connect with nature and living things. Rogers, K. (2019, June 25). *biophilia hypothesis. Encyclopedia Britannica.* https://www.britannica.com/science/biophilia-hypothesis.

REFERENCES

AfroRithms, https://www.afrorithmsfromthefuture.org/, AfroRithms, August 4, 2022.

BBC. (n.d.). Introduction. BBC Ethics. Retrieved from https://www.bbc.co.uk/ethics/introduction/

Ceballos, G., Ehrlich, P. R., and Dirzo, R. (2017). "Biological annihilation via the ongoing sixth mass extinction signalled by vertebrate population losses and declines". Proceedings of the National Academy of Sciences of the United States of America PNAS July 25, 2017, 114(30) pp. E6089–E6096.

Civjan, P. E., Scott and Tooker, Nicholas (2020). Integrating ethics into the curriculum through design courses" *American Society for Engineering Education.*

Corcoran, S., O'Dowd, E., and Tuffy, R. (2021). 'Innovative Material Making & Biophilic Inspired Design', paper presented at SUSTAINABLE INNOVATION 2021 Accelerating Sustainability in Fashion, Clothing, Sportswear & Accessories, The Centre for Sustainable Design, UCA, UK. 15th–21st March 2021, pp. 116–122.

Gispen, Jet (2017). Ethics for Designers. (n.d.). Normative Design Scheme. Retrieved from https://www.ethicsfordesigners.com/normative-design-scheme

Hiort af Ornas, V., & Keitsch, M. (2016). *Ethics in Design Curricula - Teaching Approaches.* Department of Product & Production Development, Chalmers University of Technology. Department of Product Design, Norwegian University of Science and Technology.

McGinn, R. (2013). 'Mind the gaps': An empirical approach to engineering ethics, 1997- 2001. *Science and Engineering Ethics.* 9, pp. 517–542.

Orr, D. W. (1992). The problem of education. In: *The Campus and Environmental Responsibility.* D. J. Eagan and D. W. Orr (eds.). San Francisco, USA: Jossey-Bass, pp. 3–8.

Papanek, V. (2016). *Design for the Real World.* London: Thames & Hudson, p. 291.

Rand-Hendriksen, M. (2018, March 12). Using Ethics In Web Design. Smashing Magazine. Retrieved from https://www.smashingmagazine.com/2018/03/using-ethics-in-web-design/

Rogers, K. (2019, June 25). *Biophilia hypothesis. Encyclopedia Britannica.* https://www.britannica.com/science/biophilia-hypothesis.

UNESCO (2004). *United Nations Decade of Education for Sustainable Development (2005-2014): Draft International Implementation Scheme.* Paris: UNESCO.

Wilson, E. O. (1984). *Biophilia: The Human Bond with other Species.* Cambridge, MA: Harvard University Press, p. 2.

26 Methodologies and tools: incorporating sustainability content in fashion, apparel and textiles educational curriculum through facilitating materials

Ulla Ræbild, Sabine Lettmann and Karen Marie Hasling

INTRODUCTION

This chapter addresses the notion of tools and methodologies advancing design for sustainability in fashion, apparel and textiles educational curriculum. As the need for incorporating design-led sustainability content in education and industry has increased, the question of how to go about the change has risen with it. This has led to a growing interest over the last decade in facilitating teaching and learning materials that can help bridge between sustainability knowledge and fashion design education, and also design practitioners and industry stakeholders in order to build sustainability competencies. Consequently, these materials need to support current and upcoming fashion designers in integrating sustainability in practical and strategic decision-making processes through key competencies related to systems thinking, anticipatory, normative, and interpersonal competencies, user engagement

DOI: 10.4324/9781003272878-33

as well as communication (Wiek et al., 2011; Sumter et al., 2020). These facilitation materials also go under the name 'tools' or 'toolkits' and can contain for example design strategies, sustainability approaches, design and sustainability methodologies or activities. Tools are oftentimes devised in a tangible format that invites user engagement.

Broadly speaking, a tool is something 'that aids in accomplishing a task' or 'a means to an end' (*Tool*, 2022) whereas an approach is about taking 'preliminary steps toward accomplishment' (*Approach*, 2022) and methodology means 'a body of methods' or 'a particular procedure' employed by a discipline (*Methodology*, 2022). Thus, it makes sense that many facilitating materials are conceptualised as tools and processes that can aid in addressing and solving sustainability challenges as well as offer suggestions on methods and strategies in the context of the fashion design discipline and its practices. In this chapter, we will mainly use the term 'tool' as a common denominator for these materials. The term 'fashion education' is similarly used to encompass programmes within fashion, apparel and textiles.

In the chapter, newcomers are introduced to the notion of tools enhancing sustainability in education. The aim is to contribute to the understanding of the need for strategic design support for education in the form of tools and why new tools are continuously developed.

The first part provides background to the topic of tools in the field of fashion, apparel and textiles education including a temporal overview of some of the many tools that have been developed. Two cases then follow to exemplify and contextualise different types of tools for specific purposes: (1) *Material Pathways* (Hasling & Ræbild, 2021b) aims for learning through reflection, awareness and dialogue; (2) *Let's Play Fashion: Circular Design Cards and the Circular Design Matrix* (Lettmann, 2021) targets hands-on action-based learning in practice for non-traditionally educated designers. The chapter rounds off with a reflection on the role of tools and methodologies concerning the acceleration of sustainability in fashion, apparel and textiles and further needs for the future, simultaneously aiming for a multicultural perspective when we develop, share and apply tools in both education and industry.

BACKGROUND

The timeline in Table 26.1 illustrates the many types of tools available for education that have been developed by institutions, organisations and companies. The examples have been sourced from an extensive tool search conducted by Design School Kolding within the

FashionSEEDS project (Riisberg et al., 2021) focusing on the relevance for implementing sustainability into fashion and textiles education. To underpin the selection, we further lean on Baumann et al. (2002) in that the term 'tools' is used to describe design strategies, methodologies or techniques for considering environmental issues or promoting pro-environmental behaviour during design development. Lastly, the selection is framed by the physical scope of the chapter.

Table 26.1 Sustainable Design Tools

Year	Name of Tool	Who	What
2011	TED's TEN www.circulardesign.org.uk/tools/	University Textiles Environment Design University of the Arts London, UK	Toolbox with practice-based sustainable design strategies and Ted'sTen Cards
2011–2019	Mistra Future Fashion http://mistrafuturefashion.com	University Mistra Research Programme University of the Arts London, UK	Website with tools and guides, for example Mistra Textile Toolbox Focus on circular economy in a systems perspective
2013	Sustainable Fashion Bridges https://www.researchgate.net/publication/299576078 https://ahc.leeds.ac.uk/design/staff/301/dr-eunsuk-hur	University University of Leeds Leeds, UK	Ideation Toolkit. Link Co-Design and sustainable consumption and production in the fashion industry with focus on the design process
2013	Fashion Revolution https://www.fashionrevolution.org	Organisation The Fashion Revolution Foundation and FR CIC. Global movement based in the UK	Website with Resources offering educational materials such as booklets. Focus on ethical fashion, production and supply chain

(*Continued*)

Table 26.1 (Continued)

Year	Name of Tool	Who	What
2016	CFDA https://cfda.com/ resources-tools	Organisation The Council of Fashion Designers of America Non-profit trade organisation NY, US	Open-source tools for educators, designers and companies to aid sustainability initiatives and business strategies
2017	Sustainable Design Cards www.sustainabledesign cards.dk	University Design School Kolding Kolding, Denmark	Deck of cards with approaches to sustainability combining circularity and longevity
2017	Circular Design Guide www.circulardesign guide.com	Organisation/ Company Ellen MacAthur Foundation & design consultancy IDEO in collaboration EMF global HQ Isle of Wight UK. IDEO global HQ California, US	Online toolkit. For example, circular strategy cards, super power cards, challenge cards, facilitating sheets and much more
2018	The Wheel https://www. researchgate.net/ publication/ 330702795	University University of Johannesburg Johannesburg, South Africa	A wheel model teaching tool for fashion design students bringing together human centred design with triple bottom line strategies
2019	Fashion Futures 2030 https://www. fashionfutures2030. com/scenarios/ home	University/Company organisation University of the Arts, London College of Fashion, Centre for Sustainable Fashion UK in collaboration with C&A foundation, fashion retail, HQ Zug, Switzerland	Toolkit for exploring possible sustainable fashion futures. Focus on speculative creative thinking and the design process

(Continued)

Table 26.1 (Continued)

Year	Name of Tool	Who	What
2020	Circular Design & Circular Matrix https://www. sabinelettmann.de	Company Sabine Lettmann Creative Consulting Hamburg, Germany	Deck of cards applied within a circular framework fostering circular design while offering general subject knowledge of fashion design
2020	Material Pathways www.materialpathways. dk	University Design School Kolding Kolding, Denmark	Deck of cards. Reflection and dialogue tool on materials' role in design. Bridge social, natural and human knowledge domains
2021	Close the Loop https://www.close-the-loop.be/en	Organisation Flanders DC (District of Creativity) Non-profit organisation for entrepreneurship, Leuven, Belgium In collaboration with Circular Flanders, Mechelen, Belgium. Belgian governmental initiated hub for circular economy	Website with tool to guide fashion entrepreneurs through the basics of a more sustainable way of working with focus on circular approaches
2022	Learning Activity Tool https://www. fashionseeds. org/link-activity-learning-tool-1-2-title-2	University EU project London College of Fashion (UAL) London, UK Design School Kolding, Kolding, DK Politecnico di Milano, Milano, Italy Estonia Academy of Arts, Tallinn, Estonia	Compilation of downloadable 1-pagers. Provides learning activities for fashion tutors to activate existing tools and resources in their teaching

(Continued)

Table 26.1 (Continued)

Year	Name of Tool	Who	What
2022	Fashion Seeds Cards https://www. fashionseeds.org/ link-fashionseeds-cards-title	University EU project London College of Fashion (UAL) London, UK Design School Kolding, Kolding, DK Politecnico di Milano, Milano, Italy Estonia Academy of Arts, Tallinn, Estonia	Set of cards. Centres on the four pillars of sustainability: social, cultural, environmental and economic. Provides guidance, information and references to help tutors build sustainability content and curriculum in teaching and courses

The search on sustainable teaching and learning tools for fashion from which the timeline is sourced shows a predominantly Northern Western hemisphere in its origin. This may be due to the tool search being conducted in English, and thus present a certain limitation to the research aiming at exemplifying design tools developed between 2011 and 2022. Nevertheless, it points towards a growing tradition for tool development beyond the more generic ecodesign tools available and particularly ones applicable in fashion education and industry in this region. The timeline table shows a tentative development wherein tools shift from generic (e.g. introducing circular loops strategies) to more specific purposes, for instance, addressing different target audiences or educational levels. It also shows how tools differ in format and scope from singular teaching assets to large-scale online platforms with multiple types of materials.

The growing body of tools has led to critical reflection on their usefulness to practise. Connor-Crabb (2018) identified several barriers for tool implementation and use e.g. too complex to understand; lack of time to implement; lack of knowledge on how to use them; unsuitable in form and function and "one size fits all" proposals are not applicable. Connor-Crabb concludes that tools must become better at limiting and declaring their specific focus while making clear how they can work in synergy. Overall, it was found that training of users and funding for training activities over time is crucial for successful adoption of the tools in design practice and for building the needed sustainability competencies. However, this is often not the case, as many tools are developed as outputs within research projects where funding ends when the project finalises.

Research into the effectiveness of tools through reviews has helped to clarify strengths and weaknesses and thereby played an important role in tool development. For example, a study by Kozlowski, Bardecki & Searcy (2019) finds that tools work best when they are designed with a specific purpose and are part of a portfolio of other facilitating teaching tools. Furthermore, that tools must show a comprehensive understanding of how designers work and speak their language (p.16). They must also identify the best context for their use and be specifically developed for these contexts. Thus, the designing and development of tools must target specific situations and/or actions in design education or practice to be appropriate for a certain target audience (Lofthouse, 2006); rethinking the role of the designer as more than simply a creator of garments, and work with designers on the variety of circular competencies required within their design practice (Sumter et al., 2020).

Tool evaluations have also been conducted on an individual level. An example is a study by Ræbild and Hasling (2019) that addresses the "potential of the tool as a means for building competencies for sustainability in design practice and education" (p. 438). The study shows that to achieve change, understanding tools in use is as important as developing them, and recommends building customised materials and services that challenge higher levels of innovation beyond product level, with the key question: How might fashion designers increasingly engage in systemic rather than insular initiatives based on people rather than technological involvement? The objective is to first support users' understanding and application of the tool, then help to move their focus from an industry to a society level.

The barriers identified across the studies concerning use and implementation of tools in education and practice are addressed by the recent FashionSEEDS project and platform[1] (2022). New tools developed in the project were made to work in synergy with already existing ones. As an example, the Learning Activity Tool offers concrete teaching activities inspired by Teds Ten, The Circular Design Guide, Close the Loop and many more. The activities translate concepts of sustainability into classroom learning by merging them with hands-on making, experimentation and research. The main aim is to support tutors in implementing design-led sustainability in education whether on beginner or advanced level, suited to and adjustable for many types of institutions and teaching/learning cultures.

Finally, existing fashion design practices such as moodboards, collection building and trend forecasting commonly taught in the curriculum have been researched in industry and education contexts in order to re-conceptualise these practices as tools and methodologies aiding sustainability (Ræbild & Bang, 2018, Raybould, 2018).

MATERIAL PATHWAYS TOOL

Material Pathways is a physical card deck that was launched in autumn 2020 as a follow-up and addition to the Sustainable Design Cards, a card deck developed to facilitate conversations on and decision-making through approaches to sustainable design in design education (Hasling & Ræbild, 2017). The Sustainable Design Cards card deck includes 28 approaches to sustainable design each described through two visual systems: a design compass spanning three lifetime aspects and a product life cycle to emphasise that circularity and longevity can co-exist, be combined and mutually facilitated. The cards also include information sections elaborating on 'What's, 'Why's and 'How's. Examples of cards are Design for Disassembly (Figure 26.1), Embedded Storytelling, Informal Sharing and Heritage and Product Honesty.

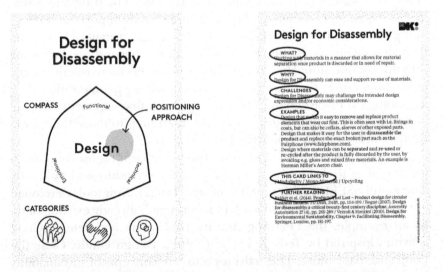

Figure 26.1 Sustainable Design Card example: Design for Disassembly

In a design process, the cards can e.g. be used to inspire and create common ground in groups (Figure 26.2a), to analyse existing businesses by highlighting approaches (Figure 26.2b) and based on that propose alternative strategies or to ideate business opportunities and conceptualise entirely new business models by combining approaches in new ways.

(a)   (b)

Figure 26.2 Examples of the Sustainable Design Cards in use

Introducing the Sustainable Design Cards in workshops for students within Design School Kolding as well as in other institutions and through conversations with design professionals have shown that the Sustainable Design Cards card deck serves as a useful, relevant and applicable means to engage with and tackle issues related to sustainability. This is enabled through outlining concrete approaches that provide users with an easy-to-approach introduction to potential strategies and how these can be combined into design concepts (Ræbild & Hasling, 2019). Furthermore, experience is that the card deck has value for beginners, students and design professionals, when entering the field of sustainable design, but also when gaining more experience as a source of information and overview to return to.

The Material Pathways deck aims to expand on the potential roles of materials in design for sustainability (Hasling & Ræbild, 2021a). The motivation was to go beyond the dominant focus of the environmental impact of resource production and consumption to increasingly recognise the multiplicity of material perspectives from a range of disciplines and how these can inform the field of designing for sustainability.

The Material Pathways deck consists of 22 cards that each describes a position to take, or perspective to have, when considering and challenging material's role in design for sustainability. It builds on the same logic as the Sustainable Design Cards and has a similar layout, so the cards can co-exist and together inform a design process by making explicit possible approaches and positions and connections between concepts such as circular strategies and material approaches.

The card example Material Ageing (changing material behaviours over time) is shown in Figure 28.3. Other examples of cards in the deck are: Living Materials (embracing growth and degradation dynamics of living organisms); Material Circulation (materials as part of circular

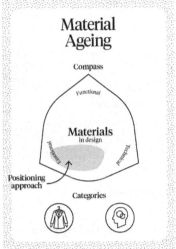

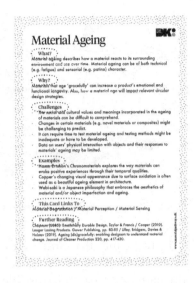

Figure 26.3 Material Pathways example

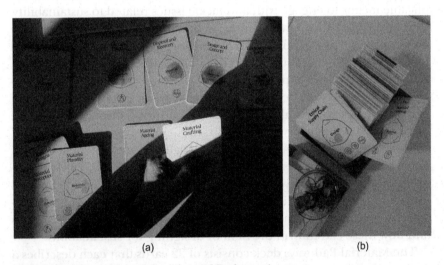

(a)   (b)

Figure 26.4 Examples of the Material Pathways in use

systems), Material Crafting (materials as a means for craft) and Material Geography (materials as geographically determined and influencing entities).

In addition to building on experiences from the Sustainable Design Cards, the Material Pathway cards were developed simultaneously with a new Master's programme in design for sustainability within Design School Kolding. Here the cards have been incorporated in a course in the first semester that has the objective to explore material narratives.

In the final week of the course, students are introduced to the card deck, firstly as a means to make explicit, structure and discuss concepts relevant to the course and secondly, to support reflection on and highlight valuable aspects in student projects. This has shown that while students on the Master's course are generally familiar with the concepts described in the Sustainable Design Cards, the Material Pathways adds a new dimension and supports students in seeing new links between perspectives of projects through the cards (Figure 26.4).

LET'S PLAY FASHION WORKSHOP

The Circular Design Matrix and Cards, designed specifically with entry-level learners in mind is another physical tool. As an underlying framework, the Circular Design Matrix (CDM) aims at embedding strategies based on circular principles such as to design out waste and pollution, or to keep products in use and stay in the loop into overall business structures. The infinite CDM (Figure 26.5) encourages

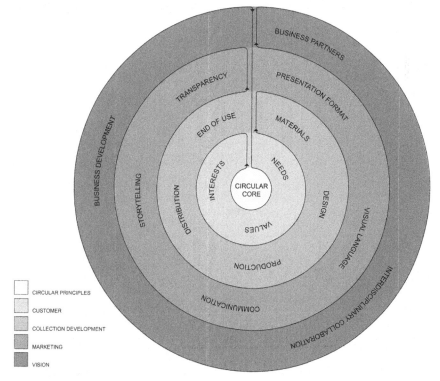

Figure 26.5 Circular design matrix

reflection to ensure the alignment of layers 2–5 with the core circular principles. Selecting individual Circular Design Cards (CDC) within each layer supports an in-depth definition of layer details from material selection to business vision.

CDC comprises 110 cards that are structured in the eight main categories consumer, materials, design, production, distribution, end of use, marketing and vision (Table 26.2) plus subcategories of each with further alternatives such as fibres or surface designs to choose from.

All (sub-)categories are defined as succinct areas with an introductory challenge card instigating the reflection of context. Each individual card discusses specifics such as cultural appropriation, for example; each has general subject information plus an exemplary visual aim at disseminating relevant knowledge to enhance the simulation of design realities with variable overall consequences (Figure 26.6). The cards address supporting a visual learner type in determining possible outcomes and thus, to encourage creative thinking (Ulger, 2018).

As a process, learning through play is connected to imagination and trial creating deeper engagement and understanding (Dieleman and Huisingh, 2006) particularly important at entry learner level as identified for Hamburg brand Inferno Ragazzi. The founder gained

Figure 26.6 Circular design cards

Table 26.2 Circular Design Cards

			Main Categories				
Customer	Material	Design	Production	Distribution	End of Use	Marketing	Vision
Analysis	Fibre (20 cards)	Modularity	Pattern construction (2 cards)	Bricks and mortar	Biological cycle	Transparency	Business partners
Engagement	Surface design/ finishing (10 cards)	Disassembly	Sampling (3 cards)	Online	Technical cycle	Storytelling	Interdisciplinary collaboration
Insights	Type (6 cards)	Usability	Manufacturing (4 cards)	Lease	Take back scheme	Communication	Business development
	Category (5 cards)	Scalability	Location (3 cards)	Sale		Visual language	
Subcategories	Certification (7 cards)	Upcycling		Service		Presentation format	
		Life cycle assessment		Packaging			
		Artificial intelligence					
		Biomimicry/ biodesign					
		Cultural appropriation					
		Reflection					

fashion experience through practice-based learning without formal fashion design education. According to him, the brand currently applies limited sustainable practices due to a lack of subject knowledge, experience as well as time restrictions (Lettmann, 2021). Hence, implementing circular strategies poses a significant challenge that requires complex and holistic training to initiate circular design approaches. Based on an existing contact with the founder, his interest in sustainability and trust in the author's guidance, the author proposed to link hypothetical design ideas with Inferno Ragazzi's collection through using the CDM and CDC in a workshop learning situation. This setting aimed at enhancing sustainability competencies through collaborative, constructive and contextual approaches (Cörvers et al., 2016) while not being business disruptive (Ritzén and Sandström, 2017). The workshop Let's Play Fashion was held with Pinck, the brand's Founder, Head of Marketing and Pattern Cutter in June 2020 (Figure 26.7).

After an introductory presentation about circular fashion design, the CDM and CDC were used collaboratively to identify one collection piece's details leading to its reimagining with the best possible sustainable properties. Removing the implementation actuality enhanced participants' ability to investigate and play with ideas instead, resulting in the opening of their mindsets towards envisioning potential design alternatives considering circular principles. Secondly, the participants evaluated which solutions could be achieved with little effort

Figure 26.7 Workshop 'Let's Play Fashion'

and identified others that required higher resource changes more suitable for long-term goals. Finally, two ideas were developed aiming at embedding circularity in areas such as customer service (Repair Kit) or sales (Clothing Club). Using the tools also enabled gaining confidence in fashion design; Pinck stated they would definitely be able to work creatively without further guidance to implement circular approaches in the future (Lettmann, 2021).

One of the participants' main workshop takeaways was that it was necessary to pay more attention towards embedding circularity into all products and optimise processes, as Pinck saw "potential to apply circular economy principles in all areas from material sourcing to design, production, sales, use and end of use" (Lettmann, 2021). Eager to start implementing sustainable design solutions, participants identified short-term goals as (1) material waste reduction, (2) material blend avoidance, (3) pattern-cutting adaptation and (4) design detail adjustment. Pinck highlighted that adjustments were evaluated as a "benefit for marketing, transparency and credibility, supporting an overall brand transformation" (Lettmann, 2021). Removing the constraints and limitations of actual implementation through focusing on hypothetical solutions enabled the participants to open up their imagination. In accordance with Dieleman and Huisingh (2006), the team understood how systematic approaches can create a holistic, values-driven brand profile aligned with circular principles.

REFLECTION

Both cases raise a number of issues: if tools move towards a narrower focus with increased complexity, it is important to consider the individual case alongside the general context of sustainability. It may be problematic to dive directly into specifics, if there is not enough understanding of the overall context, i.e., how do we make better use of existing or future tools and fine-tune progression in tool development for education? Moreover, as design practice expands and the number of tools increases, how do we make room for a variety of tools in the educational curriculum while securing quality of learning? Similarly, if targeting industry, how can tools help ensure that companies can navigate the broader context of sustainability as well as their own specific case?

Working with an entrepreneur such as the Inferno Ragazzi founder who does not have a formal design education indicates how bridging existing practice with a hypothetical re-design can create a tool-fostered "what-if?" situation in support of envisioning potential future brand goals. Where subject knowledge is lacking, visual tools can enable the imagination of different scenarios to apply sustainable design practice and broaden the user's horizon alongside substantial knowledge learning.

While tools and methodologies do not provide quick fixes for systematic change, they are essential in transforming knowledge into understanding to enable the mindset shift needed for design change at product or concept level. It is essential that educators consider that tools can help to break down the high level of complexity around sustainability and enable the implementation of sustainable, circular principles into practice. However, tools can also prevent learning, if they are seen as descriptive carriers of fixed answers. Tutors must be aware and ensure that tools are used to think with, not relieve the user from the burden of reflection and the nuanced inquiry necessary within each design process, whether in education or business.

This chapter is intended as a call to action: although an increasing interconnectedness of educators around the world allows sharing and participating in different approaches to sustainable fashion design, there are still few research findings that address the application of methodologies and tools in different cultural practices. To foster a multicultural and thus truly sustainable fashion education perspective that shifts from its current Western-centric grounding to span different geographic regions around the globe, it is important that further research, experimentation and practice is carried out. Moreover, only by utilising teaching approaches from other cultures in conjunction with our own can we bridge insular learning experiences and support the development of comprehensive and inclusive curricula to accelerate sustainable fashion in a globally connected world.

NOTE

1 See Fashion Seeds platform https://www.fashionseeds.org.

REFERENCES

Approach. (2022). https://www.merriam-webster.com/dictionary/approach (retrieved January 20, 2022).

Baumann, H., Boons, F., & Bragd, A. (2002). Mapping the green product development field: Engineering, policy and business perspectives, *Journal of Cleaner Production*, 10(5), 409–425.

Connor-Crabb, A. (2018). *A Critique of Design Toolkits for Sustainable Fashion.* Proceedings of Global Fashion Conference 2018, London, England. http://gfc-conference.eu/wp-content/uploads/2018/12/CONNOR-CRABB_A-Critique-of-Design-Toolkits-for-Sustainable-Fashion.pdf.

Cörvers, R., Wiek, A., de Kraker, J., Lang, D. J., & Martens, P. (2016). Problem-based and project-based learning for sustainable development. In H. Heinrichs, P. Martens, G. Michelsen, & A. Wiek (eds.), *Sustainability Science: An Introduction.* Dordrecht: Springer, 349–358.

Dieleman, H., & Huisingh, D. (2006). Games by which to learn and teach about sustainable development: Exploring the relevance of games and experiential learning for sustainability. *Cleaner Production,* 14, 837–847. http://dx.doi.org/10.1016/j.jclepro.2005.11.031.

Hasling, K. M., & Ræbild, U. (2021a). Using material pathways to build sustainable material narratives. *Proceedings of the International Conference on Engineering and Product Design Education.* International Conference on Engineering and Product Design Education, Herning, Denmark.

Hasling, K. M., & Ræbild, U. (2021b). Building sustainable material narratives with material pathways. In *DS 110: Proceedings of the 23rd International Conference on Engineering and Product Design Education (E&PDE 2021),* VIA Design, VIA University in Herning, Denmark. 9-10 September 2021.

Hasling, K. M., & Ræbild, U. (2017). Sustainability cards: Design for longevity. *Proceedings of PLATE 2017 – Product Lifetimes and the Environment,* Delft University of Technology, The Netherlands, 166–170.

Kozlowski, A., Bardecki, M., & Searcy, C. (2019). Tools for sustainable fashion design: An analysis of their fitness for purpose. *Sustainability,* 11(3581), 1–19.

Lettmann, S. (2021). Let's play fashion: Circular design cards and the circular design matrix. *Proceedings of the Sustainable Innovation 2021. Accelerating Sustainability in Fashion, Clothing, Sportswear & Accessories Conference.* 23rd International Conference, London, United Kingdom.

Lofthouse, V. A. (2006). Ecodesign tools for designers: Defining requirements. *Cleaner Production,* 14(15–16), 1386–1395.

Methodology. (2022). https://www.merriam-webster.com/dictionary/methodology (retrieved January 20, 2022).

Raybould, C. (2018). *Trends Forecasting as a Tool for Sustainable Education.* Proceedings of Global Fashion Conference 2018, London, England. http://gfc-conference.eu/wp-content/uploads/2018/12/RAYBOULD_Trends-Forecasting-as-a-Tool-for-Sustainable-Education.pdf.

Ræbild, U., & Bang, A. L. (2018). *The Fashion Collection Recalibrated – a Design Tool Furthering Sustainable Strategies.* Proceedings DRS Conference, Limerick Ireland, 589–599. http://dx.doi.org/10.1080/14606925.2017.1353007.

Ræbild, U., & Hasling, K. M. (2019). Experiences of the sustainable design cards: Evaluation of applications, potentials and limitations. *Fashion Practice: The Journal of Design, Creative Process & the Fashion Industry,* 11(3), 417–442. https://doi.org/10.1080/17569370.2019.1664026.

Riisberg, V., Ræbild, U., Hasling, K. M., & Ravnløkke, L. (ed.). (2021). *FashionSEEDS Handbook of Sustainability Teaching Materials.* Available at https://www.fashionseeds.org/_files/ugd/ed0694_488bb65b79484e3584efcac84e16773c.pdf.

Ritzén, S., & Ölundh Sandström, G. (2017). Barriers to the circular economy – integration of perspectives and domains. *9th CIRP IPSS Conference: Circular Perspectives*

348   ULLA RÆBILD ET AL.

on Product/Service-Systems. Kongens Lyngby, Denmark. https://doi.org/10.1016/j.procir.2017.03.005.

Sumter, D., de Koning, J., Bakker, C., & Balkenende, R. (2020). Circular economy competencies for design. *Sustainability*, 12(4), 1–16. https://doi.org/10.3390/su12041561.

Tool. (2022). https://www.merriam-webster.com/dictionary/tool (retrieved January 20, 2022).

Ulger, K. (2018). The effect of problem-based learning on the creative thinking and critical thinking disposition of students in visual arts education. *Interdisciplinary Journal of Problem-Based Learning*, 12(1). https://doi.org/10.7771/1541-5015.1649.

Wiek, A., Withycombe, L. & Redman, C. L. (2011). Key competencies in sustainability: A reference framework for academic program development. *Sustainability Science*, 6, 203–218.

27 The use of digital pedagogies for accessible and equitable teaching and learning of fashion design for sustainability: a case study

Natasha Bonnelame and Nina Stevenson

FASHION EDUCATION IN A TIME OF ECOLOGICAL CRISIS

We find ourselves in the midst of an ecological crisis, heavy with the all-encompassing knowledge that dominant human activity is breaching our planetary boundaries and perpetuating inequality amongst each other. Societies with the power and the means to do so must re-examine and redesign practices. Education is a leverage point for fundamental shifts in society, and we are at a time when education must facilitate transformative learning, that is: unlearning some established patterns of thinking and behaviour, re-learning sustainable patterns where appropriate, and new learning to be able to recognise, create and engage with necessary alternatives (Sterling 2013).

The modes and methods of designing and delivering teaching and learning in Higher Education settings are under review at local level within individual institutions, such as University of the Arts

DOI: 10.4324/9781003272878-34

London where the authors are located, and more broadly in the Higher Education sector in the UK and internationally, with a focus on accessibility and inclusivity (Qualtiy Assurance Agency for Higher Education 2021, Stevenson & Budd 2021, UNESCO 2021).

> Higher education needs to be a fierce advocate for free and open access to knowledge and science when it comes to academic scholarship, learning materials, software, and digital connectivity, among others.
>
> (UNESCO 2021, p. 75)

Fashion education has a long tradition of serving the industrial practices of fashion (Webb 2021), and the work of UAL's Centre for Sustainable Fashion (CSF) has been challenging this tradition, cultivating relationships between industry and academia built on mutual trust, collaboration and co-design. CSF's partnership with global fashion group Kering (2014–2020) is one example, where tutors, researchers, designers and sustainability experts came together to co-design new models for fashion education through the discipline of Fashion Design for Sustainability, with a shared vision to empower fashion graduates with both knowledge about sustainability and competences for new fashion practices that put human and planetary health first. Kering has demonstrated commitment to sustainability through initiatives such as Environmental Profit and Loss accounting and contribution to the Global Fashion Agenda industry consortium.

Fashion Design for Sustainability involves conceiving, realising and communicating multiple ways in which fashion activities can create prosperity at micro and macro scales whilst consuming less of the earth's finite resources (Williams 2021). It is essential that the teaching and learning of fashion acknowledges our complicity as humans in ecological collapse and social inequity. Through education, fashion design, business and media can be explored safely and radically with the goal of restoring and regenerating our social, economic, cultural and ecological systems.

During a five-year partnership, CSF and Kering co-created a course for fashion students at London College of Fashion, UAL, intrigued by the idea of exploring fashion as a contributor to a nature- and humanity-centred future, welcoming a diverse mix of students from a spectrum of fashion disciplines – communication, business and design, theory and practice. Through a 15-week taught curriculum for master's level students, Empowering Imagination, CSF and Kering sought to develop new fashion expertise and talent, linking knowledge-led aspects of learning about fashion as products, services and business with values-led ones that articulate human dreams and capabilities

(Williams & Toth-Fejel 2016). With students working collaboratively in teams, the ambition was for all involved to become changemakers for fashion. For five years, cohorts of 40 students explored the context of our times from different perspectives, to identify how fashion might transform itself and contribute to transformed societies, cultures and economies.

Due to the success of the partnership and a growing demand for accessible fashion sustainability education outside of Higher Education delivery modes, the course was reviewed and redesigned for a new global audience of online learners. Staged on FutureLearn, the UK digital educational platform,[1] the 15-week taught programme became a six-week digital-only programme using the Massive Open Online Course (MOOC) format and becoming the first fashion and sustainability course to be delivered on the platform. Since its launch it has enrolled more than 83,000 learners from 191 countries.

RECONSIDERING THE MOOC

Whilst the history, nature and structure of MOOCs are controversial, we can trace three elements. The open element derives from the Open Educational Resources movement, a term first coined at a UNESCO Forum in 2002, which places emphasis on creating easier access to free educational material (McClure 2014, p. 272) and MIT's OpenCourse-Ware project launched in the spring of 2001, which became emblematic of the movement. This innovative initiative saw the Institute publish materials from all MIT undergraduate and postgraduate subjects freely and openly on the web for permanent worldwide use (Abelson 2008). Copyright permitting, for the past 20 years, users have been able to access a range of lecture notes, videos, assignments and quizzes. They are expected to create their own learner journeys and the OpenCourse-Ware has been designed as a repository for the publication of course materials as opposed to an interactive learning experience.

The online and course elements of a MOOC can be traced to what is now considered the first MOOC 'CCK08', developed by George Siemens and Stephen Downes in 2008 (Downes 2012). Delivered through the University of Manitoba, the course was free, online and engaged 2,300 students worldwide (Stephens & Jones 2014). The intention was to explore the affordances of digital platforms, and the possibilities held within the notion of networked communities (Downes 2012). Could online networks foster communities of learners who were autonomous; diverse; open; and connected? And if this could be achieved, how would this "connectivist" approach – that asked students to immerse themselves within their environments in order to discover and communicate – change the ways in which institutions approached learning and engagement beyond the traditional campus model? 'CCK08', encouraged students to create content in multiple places online beyond the course site, and explicitly asked them to comment on each other's work and share ideas. What Siemens and Downes were offering in their design of 'CCK08' has now become known as the cMOOC, where the emphasis is the relationship between the course content and a community of learners, as opposed to the xMOOC, based on a more traditional classroom structure and a focus on quizzes and forms of assessments (Stephens & Jones 2014, p. 346). Of interest here, is Siemens' and Downes' emphasis on the community versus the material and the notion that 'the community that forms around the courses or subjects are a lot more important than the content'.

The early excitement around MOOCs steadily gathered pace and by 2012 MOOCs as learning tools were being developed by Higher Education and Cultural institutions alike (Weller 2014). However, the cost of creating and maintaining MOOCs and online learning platforms at scale, the low levels of completion rates and the perceived static nature of MOOCs and large online learning platforms meant that by 2015 this approach to digital learning had quietly disappeared as a viable offer from most HE institutions (Chuang and Ho 2016). Furthermore, there was an unevenness to the range and diversity of courses offered via MOOCs. STEM subjects (Science, Technology, Engineering, Mathematics) had typically dominated the MOOC landscape, but in 2013, art historians Beth Harris and Steven Zucker partnered with a number of art institutions and galleries to create accessible content, allowing global audiences to access collections from leading museums and galleries. Hosted on the Khan Academy platform, this was a concerted effort at creating networked communities specifically interested in the arts and humanities and engaging in learning beyond the quizzes and exams offered on xMOOC platforms.

A particular concern for educators interested in using digital platforms to provide spaces for creative thinking was the pattern of learner engagement typical of MOOCs. MOOCs for the most part were generally short as participants were usually adult learners and these courses functioned as taster sessions. Conversely, arts educators were designing courses that demanded that as the weeks progressed, engagement ramped up. Learners were expected to become more vocal and crucially, be able to share their practice the further they progressed. This also raised questions around how a learner's journey could be scaffolded in the absence of a tutor and if learners were expected to communicate, what would this mean within the context of a global audience engaged with an English language course. These questions were at the forefront of the development process for CSF's MOOC and the ways in which the team approached fashion and sustainability education for a networked community of learners.

FUTURELEARN AND CSF

By the time CSF embarked on designing a MOOC in 2017, online courses delivered at scale had been available for nearly a decade. Yet when the course titled 'Fashion and Sustainability: Understanding Luxury Fashion in a Changing World', launched in February 2018 on FutureLearn, there were only 30 courses in the Creative Arts and Media category; FutureLearn's portfolio of courses at the time numbered 1,000 (Shah 2018). Launched in 2012, FutureLearn had been identified by CSF as the most suitable platform for hosting the MOOC. Research had shown higher than average completion rates than other platforms, and they had expanded to new audiences of users who were older and more female than those in the US (Gibney 2013, Paar 2013). Although FutureLearn encouraged the inclusion of quizzes, emphasis could be placed on the use of discussion forums or engagement on third-party social media sites, and interactive digital platforms, thereby achieving a key ambition of the CSF MOOC and UAL's Creative Attributes Framework; storytelling and the ability to share your learning with a wider audience (UAL 2016).

The MOOC was designed as a free six-week course and participants were encouraged to spend three hours on their weekly studies. Drawing on the connectivist approach, the aim was to provide a platform for informed decision-making, to equip participants to be changemakers through creative design, entrepreneurship and communication skills. A range of topics are explored including:

- Why Sustainability in Fashion? – The environmental, social, cultural and economic imperatives for rethinking fashion's practices.
- Contextualising Sustainability for a Changing World – Theoretical frameworks such as human rights and planetary boundaries; creation of individual learner manifestos.
- Material Dimensions: Sourcing for luxury fashion – Why materials matter; the Materials Innovation Lab at Kering.
- Informed Decision-Making – Tools and methods for measuring environmental profit and loss.

- Creative Possibilities – Design for sustainability methods and processes for ideation.
- Creative Realisation – Revisit, reflect, refine and share a manifesto for fashion and sustainability.

To date, 83,878 learners from 191 countries[2] have explored key sustainability issues, agendas and contexts associated with luxury fashion, and the course is expected to be online until at least 2023. The MOOC received a Green Gown Award in 2018 as part of the Next Generation Learning and Skills category.[3]

The ambition of the MOOC was to empower a new kind of fashion graduate with the skills and capabilities to realise sustainability practices and innovate within the industry. To address the issues concerning language, and engagement, materials to suit a variety of learning styles were developed, such as short form film and audio content; explanatory articles; a diverse range of downloadable materials (text, diagrams, and templates). These materials not only made the learner journey accessible to different learner styles, but users were expected to share these resources beyond their immediate desktop space. In the absence of a shared physical learning space, the materials were a point of tactile connection across a global, digital divide. It was also decided that whilst CSF could not provide a permanent community manager to engage with the users, a light touch approach to moderation, where CSF staff would periodically jump in to engage in discussions would enhance the learner journey.

A debate was staged during week 3 where learners were asked to answer a provocation, and over a 48-hour period were invited to engage in online debate with peers and members of the CSF team. Digital noticeboards (padlets) which redirected users away from the FutureLearn site asked learners to share images and create short form films and audio responses, thereby diversifying the ways in which they could communicate with one another and reflect on their learning.

COLLABORATION AND NEW LEARNING

A key feature, and a potential source of tension of the MOOC was the relationship between the higher educational institution through CSF and the industry partner, Kering. The pedagogic principles of fashion design for sustainability (Williams and Stevenson 2012 cited in Williams. & Toth-Fejel, 2017) which inform the MOOC are a result of ten years of work at CSF. They ensure that learners are learning about sustainability and developing skills and competencies for sustainable thinking and practice. These pedagogies reference the work of UNESCO, Sustainable Development Goals (SDGs), and theorists such as Stephen Sterling and David Orr and foreground the context of planetary boundaries and human equity. The experimental and open-sourced nature of this approach is at odds with the typical industry and academic partnerships which are often based on a service provision model meeting employability needs of an existing industry, rather than preparing for speculative futures. The MOOCs required and indeed demanded a different approach which in this instance took shape in the form of knowledge exchange. An open, trusting, collaborative practice was established and nurtured for all involved from industry and academia. This resulted in a curriculum which offers learners access to leading business insight and practice in relation to sustainability, leading to a values-led critical exploration analysis of fashion and its role in the world through agendas of culture, economy, environment and society. The course could not have been delivered without the mutual trust of both partners through ongoing multi-faceted collaboration, and this informed a best practice case study for how HEIs collaborate with industry (Williams 2016).

The course was designed to not only benefit fashion students, educators and industry professionals, but to offer insights for sustainability-engaged learners from other industries and disciplines. Cross-disciplinary learning is essential in the development of sustainable behaviours and practices; the course demonstrates this point by having established an engaged community of learners from a wide range of vocations and locations with participation across all continents. It was extremely important for all partners to ensure free access to all course attendees. As funding models have changed in the MOOC market, CSF have insisted that the content remains free to access for eight weeks from enrolment, thus ensuring accessibility.

Feedback collated from across the course has indicated that learners are concerned about how to integrate sustainability into their work. Employees and employers have ambitions to instigate operational changes within business that could result in incremental impacts for better practice. By offering a unique space for industry representatives, students and educators to engage in study collaboratively and interactively, the MOOC enables the fusion of different perspectives. This in turn indicates an appetite to enable a breaking-down of hierarchical barriers for systemic and cultural change regarding fashion and sustainability.

In its first run, the MOOC followed an expected pattern. The 10,000 learners who signed up before the course started to drop off by week

2 to 6,222. What was unexpected was the number of active learners who stayed with the course until week 5. These 1,500 participants engaged with the final design challenge. and the reaction from the learners via the online Padlets (digital noticeboards) provided a glimpse into how we might engage this community in affecting change towards sustainability. Whilst Padlet is now a commonly used tool across UAL, in 2018, it was still relatively under used. Its inclusion during the MOOC provided an insight into how we might engage with students beyond the boundaries of a campus setting. We now had a platform that was easily accessible, where users could use a variety of media as alternative ways to engage with and respond to academic discourse.

Back on the MOOC, learners noted that the design challenge process was time-consuming and daunting, yet exciting. They felt empowered to explore creative possibilities for fashion and sustainability and now had an understanding of how they might affect change within their own local and personal environments.

FURTHER EXPERIMENTATION

In 2019/20, CSF further experimented with the MOOC by taking it back into master's courses and piloting a hybrid version making use of in-house digital learning platform Moodle plus face-to-face activities. The six-week MOOC content was extrapolated over 15 weeks, with the addition of in-person group sessions to discuss, collaborate and prototype – a "blended learning" model. The group of 15 students from a range of fashion courses worked in small teams and were tasked to meet weekly to collaborate and develop cross-disciplinary responses to the challenges. The face-to-face sessions took place in non-traditional locations including art galleries and in nature. Sadly, the course was mid-way through when the COVID-19 pandemic interrupted delivery and the teaching and learning landscape changed overnight through necessity. The course shifted to purely online delivery, with limited scope to gather complete data.

Through an internal qualitative review of the Fashion & Sustainability MOOC comments and feedback, a significant limitation was identified in mostly having content contributions from European academics and fashion professionals. If CSF and Kering were to build on this new model, it was important to extend perspectives and debates beyond the Eurocentric viewpoint, and thus better reflect the challenges and experiences of this new global community of fashion and sustainability learners and meet the need for more accessible and inclusive education.

A follow-up portfolio of four MOOCs was launched by CSF in 2021 – Fashion Values, also in collaboration with Kering, offering four-week deep dives into fashion and sustainability through the lenses of Nature, Cultures, Economy and Society. Fashion Values builds on the framework established in the first course, and develops more complex ideas and provocations from an extensive faculty of academics, practitioners, designers, activists and commentators from a range of global locations. This approach was more complex to design and deliver but built on the learnings gained through the first course.

An additional learning from the first course was the need for ongoing administrative and academic review points after the point of delivery. The design of the MOOC allows it to run without a community manager or academic facilitation; however, the continued popularity of the course beyond original expectations has necessitated that CSF undertake regular content and feedback reviews to ensure relevance and accuracy. For example, reflecting and linking world events such as the COVID-19 pandemic and the Black Lives Matter movement to relevant moments in the course.

CONCLUSIONS

New transformative models of fashion education are needed if we are to shift dominant fashion practices away from those that are contributing to ecological crisis, towards those that are restorative and regenerative of planetary health and human equity. These models should be visible across existing education institutions and infrastructure but also within new experimental environments that disrupt the Higher Education sector and nurture lifelong learning.

Digital spaces open possibilities for transformative, accessible and inclusive teaching and learning. The MOOC and the subsequent blended delivery highlighted that not only could engagement happen at scale, but that digital interfaces did not necessarily impede collaboration or meaningful exchange. Developing interactive content for learners in this way proved challenging and exhausting at times for the academic and digital teams developing the course, and the process demanded an iterative approach often at odds with an academic calendar. Yet it has allowed CSF to connect cohorts of learners that would not otherwise learn together. The use of art and design and sustainability pedagogies, and the emphasis on a user journey that was both visual and text based allowed to experiment and challenge traditional MOOC formats, leading to FutureLearn highlighting,

> The approach from CSF contained three key elements that we now know, from our research across the platform, impact the effectiveness of a course: duration, endorsement and social engagement [...] Fashion and Sustainability: Understanding Luxury Fashion in a Changing World used FutureLearn's social learning capabilities to encourage discussion and debate throughout the course [this] has since been studied and has informed FutureLearn's automated social learning prompt to ensure engagement across our courses.
>
> (FutureLearn 2022)

Presence, normally understood the context of attendance sheets and students sat in rows, meant something else now. It wasn't always obvious that participants were present at all, and in some instances the team didn't find out that any kind of impact had taken place until months after the participant had engaged with the community and the content. The MOOC demanded trust and an acceptance that users learn in different ways and that we, the institution, couldn't control every aspect of the learning process.

Industry and academic collaborations should be based on principles of trust, openness and collaboration, establishing supportive environments for co-learning for all participants. When these working principles are put into practice, then new opportunities for fashion education can emerge. Cycles of ongoing action and reflection have cemented a long-term meaningful partnership between CSF and Kering. This has enabled the subsequent Fashion Values partnership with IBM and Vogue Business, launched 2021, further committing efforts towards global models of accessible education.

In summary, the learnings taken forward are as follows:

- MOOCs can offer innovative and accessible transformative spaces for fashion education connecting learners that would traditionally not learn together.
- Industry–Academia collaborations offer opportunities for values-led and technical learning to be co-designed to develop new skills and competencies in fashion design for sustainability.
- Art and design disciplines offer new approaches to digital learning design and delivery not previously seen in delivery of STEM subjects offering higher engagement through the use of creative pedagogies.
- Online faculties and industry examples must be diverse and representative to ensure inclusivity for the global communities of learners created through MOOCs.

NOTES

1 www.futurelearn.com founded in 2012 by The Open University.
2 Learners enrolled between 20 February 2018 and 18 August 2022.
3 Green Gown Awards are an annual programme recognising exceptional sustainability initiatives being undertaken by universities and colleges across the world and coordinated by Environmental Association for Universities and Colleges (EAUC).

REFERENCES

Abelson, H. (2008) 'The Creation of OpenCourseWare at MIT', *Journal of Science Education and Technology*, 17(12), pp. 164–174.

Downes, S. (2012) *Connectivism and Connective Knowledge.* EdTech Books. https://edtechbooks.org/connectivism (Accessed: 15 January 2022).

Chuang, I. and Ho, A. (2016) 'HarvardX and MITx: Four Years of Open Online Courses' Available at: https://ssrn.com/abstract=2889436 or http://dx.doi.org/10.2139/ssrn.2889436 (Accessed: 16 January 2022).

FutureLearn, email interview by N. Stevenson, 18 August 2022.

McClure, M.W. (2014) 'MOOCs, Wicked Problems, and the Spirit of the Liberal Arts', *The Journal of General Education*, 63(4), pp. 269–286.

Parr, C. (2013) 'FutureLearn is go, but it is not quite the finished article', *Times Higher Education*, 4 October. Available at: https://www.timeshighereducation.com/news/futurelearn-is-go-but-it-is-not-quite-thefinished-article/2008347.article (Accessed: 25 August 2022).

Shah, D. (2018) *FutureLearn's 2018: Year in Review. Available at:* https://www.classcentral.com/report/futurelearn-2018-year-review (Accessed: 25 August, 2022).

Stephens, M., and Jones, K. (2014) 'MOOCs as LIS Professional Development Platforms: Evaluating and Refining SJSU's First Not-for-Credit MOOC', *Journal of Education for Library and Information Science*, 55(4), pp. 345–361.

Sterling, S. (2013) *Winning the Future We Want – The Pivotal Role of Education and Learning* commissioned by UNESCO in preparation for the World Conference on Education for Sustainable Development, Nagoya 2014. Available at: How can ESD contribute to (sustainableeducation.co.uk).

Stevenson, N., and Budd, L. (2021) *Education for Sustainability Transformation – Progress Report 2021.* University of the Arts London https://www.sustainable-fashion.com/publications/education-for-sustainability-transformation-%E2%80%93-progress-report-2021.

The Quality Assurance Agency for Higher Education and Advance HE (2021) *Education for Sustainable Development Guidance* https://www.qaa.ac.uk/quality-code/education-for-sustainable-development.

Webb, B. (2021) *Fashion Education Is Future-Proofing Its Curriculum. What Does this Mean for the Industry?* Vogue Business, 8 December 2021 (Accessed: 19 March 2022).

Weller, M. (2014) *The Battle for Open: How Openness Won and Why it Doesn't Feel Like Victory.* Ubiquity Press. Available at http://www.jstor.org/stable/j.ctv3t5r3r (Accessed: 29 July).

Williams, D. (2016) 'Transition and Transformation in Fashion Education for Sustainability', in *Engaging Stakeholders in Education for Sustainable Development at University Level*. London: Springer, pp. 217–232.

Williams, D., and Toth-Fejel, K. (2017) 'The Will and the Skill in Education for Sustainability' in *Handbook of Theory and Practice of Sustainable Development in Higher Education*. London: Springer, pp. 79–94.

Williams, D., Puppart, P., Valle-Noronha, J., Crew, J., Stevenson, N., D'Itria, E., Vacca, F., Hasling, K.M, and Riisberg, V. (2021) *FashionSEEDS: I02 - Framework Document for Design-Led Sustainability Education*, Erasmus + 2018, ISBN 978-1-906908-76-8.

UAL (2016) *Creative Attributes Framework*. Available at: https://www.arts.ac.uk/__data/assets/pdf_file/0012/204330/Creative-Attributes-Framework-OVERVIEW-2020-FINAL.pdf (Accessed: 29 August 2022).

Part VIII

Future and technology

28 A pathway towards future sustainable fashion in 2030

Ichin Cheng and Martin Charter

INTRODUCTION

Fashion, clothing and textiles[1] are a fundamental part of everyday life and an important sector in the global economy. The US\$1.3 trillion fashion industry employs more than 300 million people worldwide along the value chain. After the oil industry, textiles and clothing form the second largest polluting sector in the world. The sector accounts for 10% global carbon dioxide (CO_2) emissions, 25% of chemical usage, and is second only to agriculture as a consumer of water. One kilogram of textile material requires approximately 100–150 litres of water (Carmen Busquets, 2018). The manufacturing process contributes to the sector's poor water record and it is estimated that around 20% of the world's industrial water pollution comes from the treatment and dying of textiles and pesticide usage to grow raw materials. Each year, the fashion industry dyes around 28 billion kilograms of textiles (Ellen Macarthur Foundation, 2018). Plastics, commonly utilised in synthetic fibres, end up in the oceans, contaminating the food chain as micro-plastics. Furthermore, 87% of clothes end up as waste in landfill or are incinerated, while 30% of garments are overproduced and disposed of without being worn even once (European Parliamentary Research Service, 2020). Moreover, it is estimated that only less than 1% of all textiles worldwide are recycled into new textiles (Ellen Macarthur Foundation, 2018).

Despite all this, world fashion industry consumption is projected to rise by 63% by 2030 with significant increases in water consumption (+50%), CO_2 emissions (+63%) and waste generation (+62%) (Kerr and Landry, 2017). There has been growing pressure for brand name

DOI: 10.4324/9781003272878-36

companies and retailers to move away from fast fashion and new initiatives and institutions have been set up to support that transition.

This chapter will use a foresight approach to look into a 2030 sustainable pathway for fashion, clothing and textiles sectors with special focus on technological acceleration, circular design, bio-based materials and new collaborative models. It incorporates a range of examples in emerging technologies, businesses and materials to illustrate what will be more mainstream by 2030, giving a glimpse into the near future.

TECHNOLOGICAL ACCELERATION

Acceleration to 2030

By 2030, on-going technological change will have led to further breakthroughs e.g., internet of things (IOT), artificial intelligence (AI) and machine learning. This technological change will also lead to increased inter-connectivity between people, services, products and information e.g., wearable technologies[2] monitoring personal health and external air pollution levels (WEAR Sustain, 2018); and an increasing blurring of boundaries between consumer electronics, clothing and accessories through wearable technologies and e-textiles. By 2030, designers can expect fashion to be more tightly integrated with wearable devices, particularly those with medical or sporting performance aspects to them.

Smart or/e-textiles are a bridge between wearable technologies and textile design. One example, during COVID-19, as masks became an everyday need, was that companies started to develop smart masks with built-in sensors to monitor air-quality or to avoid COVID-19 virus (BBC, 2021). For example, MASKFONE features replaceable PM2.5 and N95/FFP2 filters, a built-in microphone, and earphones, reducing the need to remove one's mask in public (MaskFone, 2022).

By 2030, smart wearable technology will likely incorporate electronics in fabrics, textiles and clothing. This smart clothing innovation will pose new issues around safety, ethical and environmental issues. Therefore, the fashion sector will need to design to enable disassembly and separation of fabrics, trims and electronics at the 'end of (first) life' to enable product life extension. There will also be increasing questions surrounding the mixing of biological, e.g., natural fibres and manmade materials e.g., polymers-based fibres, and electronics in each item of clothing.

Digital fashion and sustainability

Technological innovation will also lead to the development of smart and virtual design that will enable increased customisation and potentially reduce development, manufacturing and product waste. For example, the largest Japanese online fashion retailer ZOZO uses its measurement technology to reduce waste in design and production. ZOZOSUITs are specially designed using information provided by the consumer through a ZOZOFIT app that precisely measures an individual body in 3D form: the goal is to help customers to better determine the fit of their clothing, which will lead to less wasteful production and logistics. In 2020, ZOZO developed ZOZOSUIT 2 to allow data on more than one million body shapes to be shared with other companies, helping the apparel industry to develop clothing that fits customers more accurately (ZOZO, 2022). Another example of smart clothing measurement is MySizeID, a free app for smartphones that produces body measurements. VOOR is a further example of re-shaping the traditional fashion business model by providing brands with virtual merchandising showrooms. This means designers do not need physical materials to produce fashion samples or prototypes, therefore cutting costs, saving time and reducing material and energy consumption.

In 2020, Microsoft and EON partnered to create 'Connected Products', a platform that aims to bring 400 million products online by 2025. The collaboration introduces an industry-wide digital foundation for a connected and circular economy across fashion, clothing and retail. Connected Products aims to unlock customer insight and enable brands to monetise and scale new circular business models such as rental, resale, digital wardrobing, peer-to-peer exchange, styling services, reuse and recycling (EON, 2021).

Transparency and traceability

Increased transparency and traceability will help drive sustainability in fashion. In a recent survey, around 80% of consumers highlighted that it is important for brands to disclose more information and be more transparent with their supply chains, from raw materials to garments (Changingmarkets, 2019). Technology will play an important part in increasing transparency and traceability. There are several new web-based tools that track and map where products are made e.g., ChainReact and WikiRate, and CERTH has begun to extract data from suppliers' disclosures published by apparel companies (WikiRate, 2021). Blockchain-based applications provide a new level of data flow security across supply chains. In a blockchain network, information is recorded and distributed across a series of devices instead of a single entity, ensuring data is stored securely and accurately in a digital, tamper-proof and accessible database. As brand name companies and retailers start to use blockchain to track their supply chains, traceability data (financial, technical, environmental and social) can be recorded from subcontractors and raw material suppliers as textile products move along the supply chain or network (Heralder, 2020). For example, Lenzing, ARMED-ANGELS and Schneider have partnered with TextileGenesis who have developed a blockchain-based technology for fibre-to-retail traceability pilots for the apparel ecosystem (TextileGenesis, 2021).

CIRCULAR DESIGN AND BIO-BASED MATERIAL

Acceleration to 2030

Material use in fashion industry counts as one of the biggest environmental impacts (SAC, 2022).

As little as a fifth of textile waste is currently estimated to be collected for recycling in EU, while approximately 165 chemicals used to manufacture textiles are classed as hazardous within the European Union (EU) according to a report by the Swedish Chemicals Agency (Pickstone, 2021). The textile industry is also an energy-intensive sector that uses a significant amount of water in the dyeing processes. In recent years, water-free dyeing technologies and techniques have been developed by manufacturers alongside sustainable production processes to reduce water, energy and chemical usage.

New bio-based materials are also being developed. Genetically modified bacteria produce spider silk, which is strong, elastic and waterproof, while bio-leathers are produced by yeast-made collagen, the major component of skin, or bacterial cellulose. Fungi are being engineered to grow novel fibres and to decontaminate textile waste. Pigments produced by algae may partially replace toxic chemical dyes, and enzymes may be used instead of chemical treatment steps to reduce water consumption and provide non-toxic alternatives (European Parliament, 2020).

By 2030, circular design will start to move the industry from a paradigm of waste generation to resource recovery in both biological and technical cycles. Reclaimed, instead of virgin resources can then be fed back into new rounds of reuse and remanufacturing. In the biological cycle, nutrients can be restored into the biosphere to regenerate resources and rebuild natural capital i.e., the planet's natural assets including biodiversity in species, geological formations, soil, air and water. In the technical cycle, products, components and materials can be retained in the economy and society through maintenance, repair, refurbishment, remanufacturing, parts harvesting and materials recycling (Charter & Cheng, 2020).

Bio-based materials

The use of bio-based materials in the fashion industry is not new. Natural materials from cotton, hemp, bamboo, linen, wool and silk to paper have been widely used in many applications in the fashion industry. However, petroleum-based fibres such as acrylic, polyester, nylon and spandex remain in high demand. In 2021, 64% of the world supply of fibres was synthetics, compared with 24% being natural fibres, 6% being cellulosics and 7% being spunlaid (Engelhardt, 2022). As the fashion industry heads towards a future where textile resources are scarce, natural fibres such as cotton, which remains a resource-intensive material, will further increase in price, and petroleum-chemical based fibres will likely remain in high demand.

Various designers and brand houses have already begun research and development into different bio-based materials to replace petroleum-based materials as part of the journey to a sustainable future. Table 28.1 illustrates some of the bio-based fabrics or materials that are already being developed for the sector: these are examples of the types of materials that are likely to become more mainstream in the very near future towards 2030.

Many companies are developing natural fibres and other materials from bamboo, hemp, pineapples, banana, nettles, mushroom roots, algae, coconuts and lotus stems that either be traced back to traditional use in different countries or are derived from new material technologies. Ananas Anam, based in the UK, has developed 'vegan leather' from discarded pineapple leaves. Piñatex® is made of fibre from the waste leaves of the pineapple plant (Ananas Anam, 2021). These leaves are a by-product from pineapple harvest waste and are now incorporated into high-street products, e.g., Boss shoes. Bolt Threads' innovative biomaterial Mylo™ claims to be the world's first commercially available leather grown from mycelium, the root structure of mushrooms. In 2020, the Mylo consortium, comprising Adidas, Kering, Lululemon and Stella McCartney, collectively worked with Bolt Threads with a view to bring this biomaterial innovation into product launches incorporating Mylo™, as vegan leather alternative to traditional leather. Bolt Threads is a US-based biomaterial company that was selected as one of the Global Cleantech 100 in 2018 for their advanced material and production technology. The vegan leather is also being applied to upholstery in luxury vehicles, e.g., Mercedes electric concept car EQXX (Bolt Threads, 2022). To consolidate and provide a home for the plant-based textile industry, Ananas Anam, Bananatex and Circular Systems founded the FIBRAL Material Alliance in 2022. The FIBRAL Material Alliance is an international organisation established by three founders: Dr Carmen Hijosa from Ananas Anam, Hannes Schoenegger from Bananatex® and Ricardo Garay of Regenerate Fashion (Ananas Anam, 2022).

A number of future-ready, innovative bio-based materials are available from different parts of the world, including some from developing countries that have deep roots in bio-based textile traditions. For instance, lotus fibres have been woven into traditional fabrics in Thailand and Myanmar for centuries. Now, new Asian textile companies are using lotus fibre to make high-end fabrics for clothing and lotus leather products (Preuss, 2017; Samatoa, 2021).

Some of the new bio-based materials also claim to have a much lower environmental footprint in the production. Samatoa, a lotus micro-fibre leather social enterprise, which produces lotus flower fabric and leather, claims that its lotus leather generates less than 2 kg CO_2 per tonne compared with virgin polyester, which generates 10 kg CO_2 per tonne. It requires 100 times less water than virgin polyester and 150 times less than organic cotton. In addition, the manufacturing process is generating employment opportunities and long-term economic empowerment for women in rural areas (Samatoa, 2021). Hero's Fashion Pvt has also claimed that their NoMark Lotus shirts, made from lotus fibres, have the performance qualities of stain resistance, less embedded water per unit and higher durability, resulting in longer-lasting clothing items.

AlgaLife, a start-up based in Berlin and Israel, is making progress towards developing algae-based materials for the fashion and textile industries. SmartFiber, a company based in Rudolstadt, Germany, launched a lyocell fibre containing seaweed under the brand name Seacell. It is made from dried and finely grounded seaweed that is incorporated into a lyocell yarn and produced in a closed-loop process by Lenzing in Austria (Sustainable Fashion, 2022).

There is also a group of potentially greener semi-synthetic fabrics that can be produced from agricultural bio-waste such as coffee grounds, sour milk, oyster shells and discarded fish skin. Semi-synthetic fabrics mix natural and synthetic fibres to provide better performance qualities and/or cleaner production benefits. Examples include Singtex (S. Café® and AIRMEM™), a company that creates functional garments from waste coffee grounds. Singtex is based in Taiwan and developed a process to collect and use waste coffee grounds to make a coating in the yarn or fabric finishing processes to provide odour-resistant and quick-drying functions. According to Singtex, their fibres and fabrics consist of recycled coffee grounds which are three times more effective than cotton in absorbing odour. The company has stated that they have secured orders from nearly 100 international apparel brands including American Eagle, North Face and Wacoal (Singtex, 2022). Another Taiwanese company HerMin Textile has also developed a process to convert fish skin waste into a new functional textile (Hermin, 2020). These semi-synthetic materials deliver environmental benefits through the incorporation of waste materials into fabrics. However, some face the challenge of mixing biological materials with manmade, technical materials which will create problems in relation to disassembly for reuse or recycling in the second life and/or at the end of life.

Recycled and reused materials within the industry

Various natural fibres are being recycled or upcycled to fibre and yarns for use in the fashion, clothing and textile industry. For example, the Swedish company, Renewcell developed an innovative recycling method for natural fibres. Renewcell's technology dissolves used cotton fabrics and other natural fibres into a new, biodegradable raw material called Circulose®. It can be turned into textile fibre and fed into the textile production cycle (Renewcell, 2022) (Boer Group Recycling Solutions, 2022). Circulose is claimed to be the only commercially available textile-to-textile recycled natural material of virgin equivalent quality. The European Investment Bank (EIB) invested €30.75 million Renewcell for its first commercial scale factory in Sundsvall in 2021. Fast Company named Renewcell as one of the World's most Innovative Companies 2021. Circulose was also included on *TIME Magazine*'s list of the 100 Best Inventions 2020 (EIB, 2021).

In the fashion industry, one of the most prominent technical fibres is polyester. Also referred to as polyethylene terephthalate (PET), it has represented more than half of total global fibre production for 20 years and continues to grow in consumption and production (The Fiber Year, 2022). Fibre-to-fibre polyester recovery was first industrialised by Teijin (Japan) with EcoCircle in 2006 (Teijin, 2022). Teijin EcoCircle is a closed-loop chemical recycling technology that makes it possible to transform waste PET into new PET. Teijin's technology de-polymerises and re-polymerises polyester waste back into new polymer feedstock equivalent to those newly made from petroleum. Teijin has also developed EcoCircle Plant Fibre, a plant-based polyester which contains 30% sugarcane. Nissan was one of the first companies to use the fabric for the car upholstery in the Nissan Leaf electric car

The most common form of textile made using recycled PET is fleece, a knitted pile fabric often used by outdoor clothing companies to make

Table 28.1 Future-Ready Bio-Based Fabrics and Materials

Name	Bio-Based Fabric and Material	Commercial Status	Application for Designers
Piñatex	A natural textile made from pineapple leaves fibre	Piñatex is commercial ready and is being taken forward by a UK based start-up: Ananas Anam. Hugo Boss launched a range of vegan shoes made from Piñatex	Includes footwear and fashion accessories, clothing, bags, interior furnishing and automotive upholstery
Mylo™	Mylo™ is a leather substitute made from mycelium (mushroom roots) being developed by a US-based start-up: Bolt Threads	Mylo™ is commercial ready and products will be available for purchase in stores and online starting in 2021	Mylo™ can be used like animal or synthetic leather and can take on any colour or finish for the use in bags, shoes and other leather applications
MycoTEX	MycoTEX is a flexible version of mycelium that can be used for textile production	A dress has been produced – as a proof-of-concept – by Dutch textile designer Aniela Hoitink	The MycoTEX fabric can be repaired without it interfering with its look. Additionally, a garment can be built in 3D and shaped according to the wearer's wishes. The length of the garment can be changed
Seacell	Seaweed-based fabric, e.g., kelp and algae. Lyocell fibre containing seaweed	Seacell is produced by SmartFiber based in Germany and is commercial ready. There are other algae/seaweed-based fabrics that are still in Research and development in a number of companies	Clothes, shoes, blankets

(Continued)

Table 28.1 (Continued)

Name	Bio-Based Fabric and Material	Commercial Status	Application for Designers
VITADYLAN™	A garment, using seaweed, beechwood and zinc fibres	Commercial ready technology from GREY Fashion UG from Germany	Fabric and clothes
Musa	A natural textile made of banana waste to fibre	Musa is in the Research and development stage and is working on refining the chemical process necessary to turn the banana waste into fibres. The producer appears to be in the Phillipines	Fabric and clothes
Desserto	Vegan leather and fabric made of cactus	Commercial ready materials produced by Mexico based company Dessertex	Handbags, footwear, furniture, automotive and other fashion industries
NoMark Lotus fabric; Samatoa Lotus Fabric	A natural textile made of lotus stems	Lotus fabrics are commercially ready. NoMark Lotus is produced by Hero's Fashion Pvt in India and Samatoa Lotus Textiles is produced in Cambodia. In 2012, Samatoa was awarded the UNESCO Prize for excellence for its unique lotus flower fabric	Fabric and leather Lotus fibres have been weaved into fabrics in countries like Thailand or Myanmar for centuries

Source: Authors own analysis based on info from Ananas Anam (2021), Preuss (2017), Bolt Threads (2022), HerMin (2022), Desserto (2021), Hendriksz, V. (2018) and Samatoa (2021)

jackets and tops. Patagonia is a pioneer of PET recycling and formed a partnership with Teijin. By using recycled PET fleece, Patagonia claims to have achieved 87% raw materials being made with recycled inputs and is now moving towards 100% renewable and recycled raw materials

(Patagonia, 2022). Likewise, in the UK, major retailers such as Marks & Spencer have also started to use recycled PET in some of their clothing ranges (Textiles Environment Design, 2022).

Craghoppers claim that 70% of their products are made from recycled materials. By the end of 2021, Craghoppers stated that they had recycled nearly 42 million plastic bottles. A Craghoppers Pember jacket is made from 110 recycled plastic bottles and includes recycled content in almost all its elements, including its padding (100% recycled), labels, buttons and zip tapes (Craghoppers, 2022).

COLLABORATION, COOPERATION, CO-CREATION

There is a growing range of sustainability initiatives that have been launched to catalyse cooperation in the sector. This includes establishment of new organisations and new programmes from existing organisations.

New organisations include:

- Ethical Trading Initiative in 1998
- Better Cotton Initiative in 2009
- Sustainable Apparel Coalition (SAC) in 2011
- Fashion Revolution in 2013
- Fashion for Good in 2017

New programmes from existing organisations include:

- Fashion Transparency Index in 2016 (from Fashion Revolution)
- Circular Fibres Initiative in 2017 (from Ellen MacArthur Foundation)
- Positive Fashion Initiative in 2019 (from the British Fashion Council)
- Circular Fashion Pledge in 2020 (from Fashion Revolution)

By 2030, fostering co-creation and cooperation will become key to cross-disciplinary collaboration, in order to empower solution-based sustainable innovation. Environmentally minded designers may wish to move ideas forward by sharing solutions to common problems. Since 2012, Stella McCartney, one of the UK's top fashion designers has redesigned her products, brands and high-street stores using eco-innovation. She is collaborating and co-creating by working with eco-innovative companies around the world including some of the following:

- Bolt Thread and Mylo™ consortium: US company developing vegan leather
- Evrnu: US start-up that has developed a process to recycle cotton into a cellulose-based fibre
- Tipa: Israeli company producing biodegradable plastic
- Colorifix: UK company producing a dye using synthetic biology to engineer bacteria with dye-giving property which uses 1/10th of water in the dyeing process
- Ecotricity: UK company that supplies stores with renewable energy
- Airlabs: UK company that supplies stores with clean air with 95% of pollution removed (Franklin-Wallis, 2019).

Incubators have been established to facilitate sustainable innovation in fashion. Fashion for Good was established by Laudes Foundation (formerly C&A Foundation) to deliver an innovation platform to incubate and scale sustainable technologies and business models aimed at transforming the sector (Fashion for Good, 2022). In 2019, One X One was established as the first incubator programme to integrate deep science and sustainability with high fashion. One X One was organised by the Slow Factory Foundation and Swarovski with support from the United Nations to bring together scientists with designers to create innovative solutions for the fashion industry in three priority areas related sustainability (One X One, 2022):

- Circularity
- Equity-centred design
- Regenerative technologies.

As we move towards 2030, there will be an increasing movement towards collaborative consumption or sharing economy. Collaborative consumption is an economic model based on sharing, swapping, trading, or renting products and services, enabling access over ownership (Meghan et al., 2018). In the coming years, technology will provide new channels to connect users and owners, which will make sharing resources at scale cheaper and easier. Some garment companies have explored new product and service business models as part of the sharing economy. Fast fashion may be replaced by more clothes sharing. For example, new emerging rental models enable consumers to borrow items for a set time period, typically at the cost of 10–20% of an item's retail value. Over recent years, there have been many start-ups in the area including Girl Meets Dress in the UK; Chic by Choice in Europe and Glam Corner in Australia. In addition, there have been the launch of more niche ventures including:

Gwynnie Bee for plus-size fashion rental and Borrow For Your Bump for maternity wear rental (Pike, 2018). There has also been a number of apps launched to focus on the resale of luxury fashion products including The RealReal, Poshmark, Grailed (men's clothes) and Totspot (children's clothes).

FUTURE-READY FASHION DESIGNERS IN 2030

Future-ready designers will start to choose bio-based fabrics and dyes that are produced through less toxic processes. For example, Blond & Bieber, a German design studio, uses microalgae to dye fabrics. Some sustainable fashion designers might choose to de-materialise and de-carbonise by designing items to be distributed and worn locally, using local production and assembly models that incorporate locally grown or produced materials and employing a local work force. In 2030, future-ready fashion, clothing and apparel designers, developers and innovators will need to adapt to growing environmental pressures and become increasingly aware of the sustainability dimensions of design. There will be increasing product-related environmental pressures directly linked to global risks associated with climate change and resource scarcity. These pressures will collectively translate into increased environmental policy surrounding consumer products, growing requirements from customers and more eco-innovators that are developing sustainable solutions with lower environmental impacts and improved social performance across the supply networks.

NOTES

1 The authors use clothing as an equivalent for the term apparel in the chapter.
2 Wearable technologies are technologies (mobiles, watches and common eyeglasses are wearable technologies) and other devices (electronic sensing and actuation devices) originally made for medical and other engineering uses.

REFERENCES

Ananas Anam (2021) Available at: https://www.ananas-anam.com/products-2/
Bolt Threads (2022) Available at: https://boltthreads.com/
BBC (2021) https://www.bbc.co.uk/news/av/technology-56114512

Boer Group Recycling Solutions (2022) Available at: https://boergroup-recycling-solutions.com/projects/renewcell

Carmen Busquets (2018) 4 Reasons fashion is the second-largest polluter. [Online] https://www.carmenbusquets.com/journal/post/sustainable-fashion

Changing markets (2019) Dirty fashion disrupted leaders and laggards revealed. Available at: http://changingmarkets.org/wp-content/uploads/2019/12/CM_REPORT_FINAL_DIRTY_FASHION_DISRUPTED_LEADERS_AND_LAGGARDS_REVEALED.pdf

Charter & Cheng (2020) G20: *Accelerating the Transition to Global Circular Economy*, IAI, Italy G20 – to be published in 2021

Craghoppers (2022) https://www.craghoppers.com/

Desserto (2021) Available at: https://desserto.com.mx/

EC (2021) EU strategy for sustainable textiles, Available at: https://ec.europa.eu/info/law/better-regulation/have-your-say/initiatives/12822-EU-strategy-for-sustainable-textiles

Ellen Macarthur Foundation (2018) A new textiles economy: Redesigning fashion's future. [Online] https://www.ellenmacarthurfoundation.org/publications/a-new-textiles-economy-redesigning-fashions-future

Engelhardt, A. (2022) – World supply – highlights in upstream business, International Fiber Journal. Available at: https://fiberjournal.com/world-supply-highlights-in-upstream-business/

EON (2021) Available at: https://www.eongroup.co/platform

European Parliamentary Research Service (2020) What if fashion were good for the planet? https://www.europarl.europa.eu/thinktank/en/document/EPRS_ATA(2020)656296

European Investment Bank (2021) Sweden: EU backs Renewcell to boost circularity in the fashion industry, https://www.eib.org/en/press/all/2021-239-eu-backs-renewcell-to-boost-circularity-in-the-fashion-industry

Fashion for Good (2022) https://fashionforgood.com/about-us/

Franklin-Wallis, O. (2019) Stella McCartney is on a quest to save you from the fashion industry. [Online] Wired.co.uk. Available at: https://www.wired.co.uk/article/stella-mccartney-sustainable-fashion

Hendriksz, V. (2018) Sustainable textile innovations: Banana fibres. [online] https://fashionunited.uk/news/fashion/sustainable-textile-innovations-banana-fibre/2017082825623

Heralder, F. (2020) Will technology be the game-changer for rising transparency in the fashion supply chain? | Greenbiz (2021). Available at: https://www.greenbiz.com/article/will-technology-be-game-changer-rising-transparency-fashion-supply-chain-sponsored

HerMin (2023) [Online] https://www.hermin.com/

Kerr, J. and Landry, J. (2017). Pulse of the fashion industry. Global Fashion Agenda & The Boston Consulting Group

MaskFone (2022) Available at: https://maskfone.com

Meghan, O. et al. (2018) Eco-innovation of products: Case studies and policy lessons from EU Member States for a product policy framework that contributes to a circular economy https://ec.europa.eu/environment/ecoap/sites/default/files/documents/eio_report_2018.pdf

One X One (2022) https://onexone.earth/

Patagonia (2022) Why recycled? https://eu.patagonia.com/gb/en/why-recycle

Pickstone (2021) Commission to target global impact of 'fast fashion' in textiles strategy (2021). Available at: https://www.endseurope.com/article/1703837/commission-target-global-impact-fast-fashion-textiles-strategy

Pike, H. (2018) Will the 'sharing economy' work for fashion? The business of fashion [Online] https://www.businessoffashion.com/articles/fashion-tech/will-the-sharing-economy-work-for-fashion-rent-the-runway-rental

Preuss, S. (2017) Sustainable textile innovations: Lotus fibres, Fashionunited.uk. Available at: https://fashionunited.uk/news/business/sustainable-textile-innovations-lotus-fibres/2017060924784

Renewcell (2022) https://renewcell.com/

Samatoa Lotus Textiles (2021) Available at: https://samatoa.lotus-flower-fabric.com/about-us-and-the-lotus-flower-fabric/

Singtex (2022) https://www.singtex.com

Sustainable Apparel Coalition (2022) https://apparelcoalition.org

Sustainable Fashion (2022) Textile produced from Algae – Sustainable Fashion (2022). https://www.sustainablefashion.earth/type/recycling/textile-produced-from-algae/ TextileGenesis™ https://textilegenesis.com/; 30 Sustainable Fabrics For The Most Eco Friendly Fashion, https://www.sustainablejungle.com/sustainable-fashion/sustainable-fabrics

Teijin (2022) http://www.teijinfiber.com

Textiles Environment Design (2022) Chelsea college of art & design, London, http://tedresearch.net/media/files/Polyester_Recycling.pdf

The Fiber Year Consulting (2022) The Fiber Year 2022; world survey of textiles and nonwovens Available from: https://www.thefiberyear.com/home/

WEAR Sustain (2018) Project briefing documents [Online] http://wearsustain.eu/

Wikirateproject (2021) Chain React, https://wikirateproject.org/Corporate_Network_Mapping_ChainReact

ZOZO (2022) https://corp.zozo.com

29 Risky business: sustainable fashion through new technologies

Trevor Davis, Lucy E. Dunne and Elizabeth Bigger

INTRODUCTION

Advanced technologies, such as artificial intelligence (AI) and others under the umbrella term "Industry 4.0", can improve sustainability in the fashion industry. The Industry 4.0 concept was first used in 2011,[1] and continues to develop based on advances in foundational information technologies including AI, machine-to-machine communication, cloud computing and digital platforms (see Box 29.1 for an historical perspective). The cultural context of the fashion industry creates unique opportunities for technological innovation to increase sustainability. This chapter discusses the maturity of the tools for advancing the industry, the practical steps to manage risks and how to overcome barriers to rapid adoption.

Transitioning to Industry 4.0 is important for fast fashion brands in particular. Overproduction and high environmental footprints result from their mass production business models. Some fast fashion brands are producing up to half a billion garments a year, perhaps generating about 20,000 different styles a year (Kozlowski, 2020). Despite efforts within the industry and action by regulators, significant sustainability challenges remain. Designers and manufacturers are looking to advanced technology to find more sustainable designs, materials and manufacturing processes. New generation technologies can make the value chain more sustainable through adaptation, matching supply to actual demand and reducing overproduction.

DOI: 10.4324/9781003272878-37

Box 29.1

Evolution of Industry 4.0

The first industrial revolution, Industry 1.0, started in the 18th century with the textile industry moving from manual to machine methods. As steam power became common, many other industries followed suit.

Industry 2.0 in the late 19th and early 20th centuries was based on technological innovations including electrification, high-speed communication, extensive rail networks and production lines. Industry 2.0 brought about the rise of globalization as we know it today.

Industry 3.0 is often referred to as the digital revolution, with manual processes being translated to computers and the internet.

Industry 4.0 brings multiple information and communication technologies together to allow machines and computers to make decisions and change their behavior autonomously, or in collaboration with a human user.

In particular, rapid advances in AI are creating a new generation of 'smart' advanced garment tools (autonomous, interconnected and intelligent) across the entire fashion life-cycle. New business models (e.g. in secondary fashion markets and digital fashion) benefit directly from these innovations and digital transformation.

THE SUSTAINABILITY CHALLENGE

A wicked problem requiring clumsy solutions

Sustainability in the fashion industry is multi-faceted, spanning the full product life-cycle. The industry requires solutions that balance environmental concerns, social justice and value creation. Both supply- and demand-side change is needed. Defining the problems to be solved is complex, with contradictory facts, missing information, hidden interconnections and conflicting stakeholder goals.

The industry faces a classic 'Wicked Problem' (see Chapter 3) with no single, neat solution: multiple solutions are needed based on whole-system thinking, bringing together emerging technologies and manual fixes. These may initially appear clumsy or imperfect, but over time, they will improve as understanding and technology improve. However, this requires a structured approach to managing the risks of technology in the industry's cultural context and a willingness to collaborate with non-traditional partners (such as technology companies).

In other consumer industries (such as beauty), Industry 4.0 has led to innovative solutions to both consumption and supply challenges. However, multiple Industry 4.0 technologies are in a low state of readiness for mass adoption in fashion (e.g. lacking integrations with existing systems, availability of AI training data sets for specific fashion use cases). Despite this, they offer one of the most hopeful routes to a more sustainable fashion system.

New generation information technologies

As the fashion industry wakes up to the full potential of Industry 4.0, a distinct architectural pattern for interconnected, intelligent and autonomous systems is emerging based on five pillars (see Figure 29.1). The technology-set underpinning these pillars comprises:

- established foundational digital technologies (such as machine learning, robotics, 5G and digital twins[2]);
- emerging technologies (blockchains,[3] improved AI models such as GPT-3 from OpenAI[4] and quantum computing); and
- adjacent technologies (such as smarter agriculture and bio-fabrication).

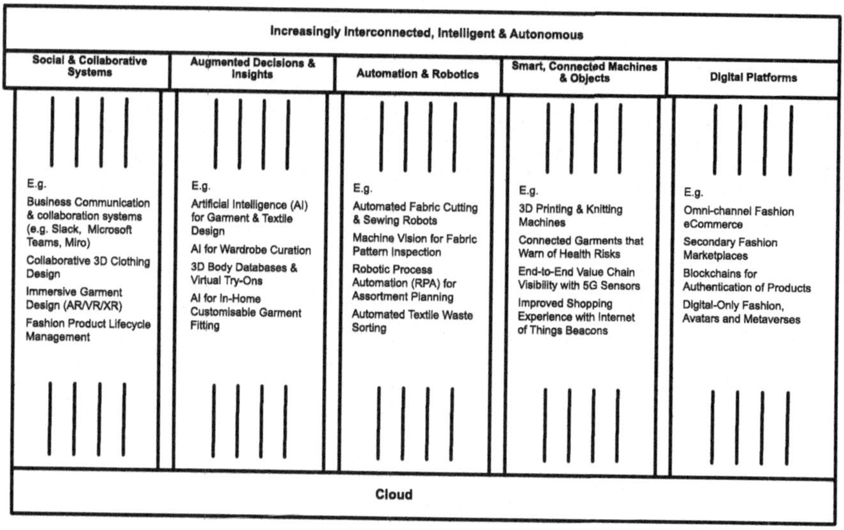

Social & Collaborative Systems	Augmented Decisions & Insights	Automation & Robotics	Smart, Connected Machines & Objects	Digital Platforms
E.g. Business Communication & collaboration systems (e.g. Slack, Microsoft Teams, Miro) Collaborative 3D Clothing Design Immersive Garment Design (AR/VR/XR) Fashion Product Lifecycle Management	E.g. Artificial Intelligence (AI) for Garment & Textile Design AI for Wardrobe Curation 3D Body Databases & Virtual Try-Ons AI for In-Home Customisable Garment Fitting	E.g. Automated Fabric Cutting & Sewing Robots Machine Vision for Fabric Pattern Inspection Robotic Process Automation (RPA) for Assortment Planning Automated Textile Waste Sorting	E.g. 3D Printing & Knitting Machines Connected Garments that Warn of Health Risks End-to-End Value Chain Visibility with 5G Sensors Improved Shopping Experience with Internet of Things Beacons	E.g. Omni-channel Fashion eCommerce Secondary Fashion Marketplaces Blockchains for Authentication of Products Digital-Only Fashion, Avatars and Metaverses

Increasingly Interconnected, Intelligent & Autonomous

Cloud

Figure 29.1 Five pillars that underpin Industry 4.0 in fashion

The literature dedicated to Industry 4.0 in fashion already contains a surprising number of sustainability benefits (see Figure 29.2).

As with other manufacturing industries, Industry 4.0 facilitates reduced energy consumption, de-carbonization and lower water usage. Examples include:

- advanced analytics for a clearer understanding of progress against environmental and social goals, and to improve resource efficiencies;
- computer vision to improve quality control, reduce waste during cutting and to improve color sorting for waste textile recycling;
- robotics to reduce waste from errors in manual processes such as pattern making, cutting and sewing; and
- additive manufacture (3D printing) of textiles from marine plastics as a substitute for virgin materials.

However, fashion also derives additional sustainability benefits from virtualization and digital transformation of the end-to-end value chain. Examples include optimization tools for designers, moving away from physical samples and digital-only garments for augmented realities and metaverses[5] (acknowledging that there can be hidden energy costs with digital systems).

Accurate status information about garments and accessories across their life-cycle can help with optimizing waste, recycling, repair and reuse. Less obvious is the potential for that data to reduce chemical and water usage in that life-cycle. Currently, textile manufacture uses over

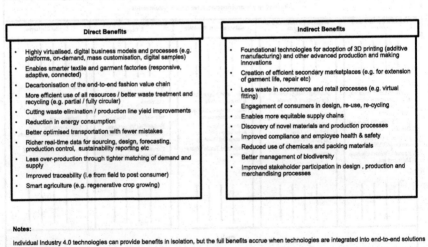

Direct Benefits	Indirect Benefits
• Highly virtualised. digital business models and processes (e.g. platforms, on-demand, mass customisation, digital samples) • Enables smarter textile and garment factories (responsive, adaptive, connected) • Decarbonisation of the end-to-end fashion value chain • More efficient use of all resources / better waste treatment and recycling (e.g. partial / fully circular) • Cutting waste elimination / production line yield improvements • Reduction in energy consumption • Better optimised transportation with fewer mistakes • Richer real-time data for sourcing, design, forecasting, production control, sustainability reporting etc • Less over-production through tighter matching of demand and supply • Improved traceability (i.e from field to post consumer) • Smart agriculture (e.g. regenerative crop growing)	• Foundational technologies for adoption of 3D printing (additive manufacturing) and other advanced production and making innovations • Creation of efficient secondary marketplaces (e.g. for extension of garment life, repair etc) • Less waste in ecommerce and retail processes (e.g. virtual fitting) • Engagement of consumers in design, re-use, re-cycling • Enables more equitable supply chains • Discovery of novel materials and production processes • Improved compliance and employee health & safety • Reduced use of chemicals and packing materials • Better management of biodiversity • Improved stakeholder participation in design , production and merchandising processes

Notes:

Individual Industry 4.0 technologies can provide benefits in isolation, but the full benefits accrue when technologies are integrated into end-to-end solutions

Figure 29.2 Examples of current direct and indirect sustainability benefits from Industry 4.0 in fashion

15,000 chemicals (Roos et al., 2019), and water consumption amounts to 79 trillion liters per annum (Niinimäki et al., 2020).

RE-IMAGINING INDUSTRY BUSINESS MODELS AND WORKFLOWS

A new direction of travel for the industry

Embracing advanced technology in itself doesn't promote sustainability. If Industry 4.0 technologies simply lead to increased over-production of garments at greater efficiency, then fashion sustainability problems will worsen. In contrast, technology supporting smaller-volume, quick-response and more customized production models can offer more effective support for material efficiency and circularity. Digital business models, perhaps, offer the greatest potential for improvement.

Efforts to improve sustainability in fashion remain fragmented and there are many initiatives (e.g. Better Cotton Initiative,[6] Make Fashion Circular[7]). Individual organizations promote different facets of sustainability throughout the product development process, supply chain and product life-cycle (e.g. reducing waste versus protecting nature). Consequently, results may end up being insubstantial or counterproductive. The industry needs a shared vision to guide overall efforts.

Figure 29.3 shows fashion industry approaches to sustainability based on two axes. The vertical axis progresses from lower to higher information intensity in the value chain. Horizontally, there is a shift from value being tightly coupled with creation of physical garments to less tightly coupled, as fewer new garments are manufactured (or digital garments increase).

The horizontal shift is important. Among the drivers of sustainability in the fashion industry, perhaps the sheer volume of clothing produced is the most impactful (see Box 29.2).

Both supply and demand-side solutions needed

Current application of Industry 4.0 is skewed toward the production part of the life-cycle (to be discussed later). Advanced garment tools[8] and data analytics have already become a driving force in the fashion industry. However, they often omit a full life-cycle environmental design analysis (Bigger, 2021). Most attempts in the industry to reduce waste occur at the marker making stage[9] and not during design. Yet design is where there is greater scope for waste reduction (McQuillan, 2020).

Box 29.2

Overconsumption and under-use

The United Nations Environment Program and the Ellen MacArthur Foundation reported that an estimated 100 billion new garments were produced annually as of 2019.

This is clearly too many. Several indicators point to most clothing produced never actually being used: due to waste in manufacturing, unsold stock, returned garments that never make it back into circulation and overconsumption/under-use by consumers.

Technology is vital in correcting this unsustainable course of travel for the fashion industry, by helping designers and manufacturers understand what individual consumers want, how to produce it efficiently without relying on high-volume batch processes. Also, advanced garment technology could ultimately divorce consumption of fashion from the volume of unique garments that make up the current approach.

Source: https//ellenmacarthurfoundation.org

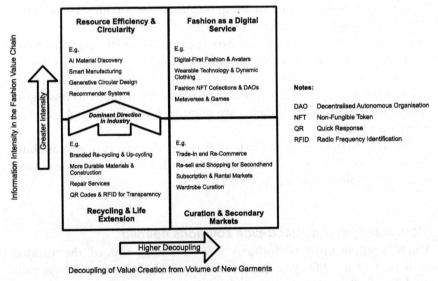

Figure 29.3 Framework for the future direction of the fashion industry

Some Industry 4.0 technologies address both supply and the demand-side challenges. For example, digital twins are used to support product development and marketing processes[10] as well as production.

Linking digital twins to sustainability data, such as embodied carbon, can help manufacturers make better decisions from concept to the end of the first garment life-cycle (e.g. identifying materials to be harvested for recycling or up-cycling).

Digital twins can also help reduce demand for new garments:

- if a digital twin travels with a garment throughout its life-cycle, consumers can use virtual try-on to make fewer, more targeted purchase decisions. Purchases of new items may be further reduced if consumers make better daily dressing decisions based on a digital representation of their home wardrobe (Dunne, 2021); and
- information about materials and construction linked to digital twins can also help consumers make better informed decisions about life extension and resale; and
- consumers may select a virtual garment based on the digital twin rather than a physical item.

Virtual- or mixed-reality clothing represent the more extreme future for fashion, where "clothing" exists more in the digital world than in the physical: purely virtual garments can be worn by the consumer or their avatars (e.g. in virtual photoshoots for social media and in games). However, there is insufficient information about the hidden energy and emissions impacts resulting from use of IT for these digital solutions (e.g. virtual garments have embedded carbon).

Industry 4.0 technologies, specifically AI, can also be effective in changing consumption behavior, for example, nudging shoppers toward more sustainable options. These tools also underpin digital platforms facilitating garment rental and re-use. This is a developing area, with current demand-side technologies focused on helping consumers navigate the complexity of the market: sorting and filtering options and supporting consumption decisions with environmental and social data.

Advances in machine and deep learning have dramatically improved the field of automated decision-support and recommendation systems for sustainability in fashion. These systems can help design waste out of the garment life-cycle and improve matching of clothing to wearers (and hence avoid production of unwanted or unused clothing). For designers, there are AI-based material selection tools that incorporate life-cycle assessments (LCA) for common textiles such as cotton, polyester and nylon.

The latest supply chain developments address waste by automating matching production and sourcing to real-time consumer brand and size preferences and optimizing assortments based on financial, environmental and social metrics. Rather than being programmed, such systems learn from patterns in demand and supply, as well as garment and outfit attributes in images and text annotation.

It is important to take all factors into account to ensure that innovations that appear to reduce negative impacts continue to do so at scale. Many initially thought digital music delivery would bring strong benefits for sustainability. However, a recent study showed that the music industry greenhouse gas (GHG) emissions footprint has grown because of the infrastructure needs of streaming versus vinyl, cassettes and compact discs (Brennan and Devine, 2019). A broad view of the impact of new technologies on environmental goals, from changes in individual behavior to disruption of entire markets, is critical in order to prevent any rebound effect (see earlier comment on the environmental footprint of virtual garments).

Information is key

Industry 4.0 technologies generate, collect and analyze a large volume and variety of data. The volume of sustainability data increases as more systems and components are connected (e.g. sensors for water consumption or drone data from cotton fields). Hence, the fashion industry's efforts toward achieving environmental and social goals must involve a change to ensure that it is managing information, knowledge and insight in the smartest ways possible.

The opportunity to make information-centric changes in planning, design, prediction and management processes to deliver sustainability goals increases as more advanced technology is infused into workflows. Opportunities include:

- evidence-backed designs supporting net-zero and other sustainability goals (this could include real-time information from wearables and smart garments);
- eliminating waste from failed product launches by predicting the right product assortments and volumes to produce;
- minimizing overproduction waste based on more intelligent demand signals from the marketplace (e.g. matching individual consumers with clothing that they will like, need and use);
- optimizing real or simulated fashion end-to-end value chains against multiple, often conflicting, financial, environmental and social goals (e.g. biodiversity gains versus rural employment); and
- reducing production of new garments through more effective utilization of the world's existing clothing resources, better traceability throughout the life-cycle and secondary markets.

Human–machine collaborations can leverage the strongest capabilities of human cognition (creativity, novelty, insight) and those of computation (rapid iteration, accessing and processing high volumes of data and information). As Industry 4.0 technologies become more common in fashion workflows, the interaction between human and machine intelligence becomes increasingly important. The integration of sophisticated decision-support and other smart tools into design and other processes in the fashion life-cycle remains an emerging area. A new tool or paradigm (such as AI for experimenting with a higher number of body fit points[11]) may require the designer to expand their process and formalize their design goals. To successfully improve sustainability, humans and machines need to work together seamlessly across the development, consumption and disposal/re-use life-cycle. This is illustrated for the case of generative design in Box 29.3.

Information-intensive interventions can also reduce overproduction and overconsumption and potentially waste, at different scales. For example:

- elements of a decision-support system to inform individual consumer choices can be used to nudge consumers to reduce their consumption of new clothing. They can also inform design workflows to

---

Box 29.3

Case study: human–machine collaboration

Generative design is a set of algorithm-driven processes which generate designs under given objectives and constraints. For generative design analysis of fashion, the algorithm considers multiple sustainable design objectives in parallel, such as textile waste, estimated microfiber and chemical effluent release rates and consumer care. The algorithm can evaluate far more objectives than an unaided human designer could.

Machines excel at such multi-objective optimization problems, while human creativity remains unmatched. The design objectives form the parameters which determine the fitness function of the optimization algorithm. Typically, machine-generated designs are numerous and include designs a human designer might not consider. Hence, the visual design analysis of fashion design versus sustainability impact occurs in real-time as a collaboration between the human designer and machine.

See Chapter 31 for further examples.

Box 29.4

Case study: human–machine collaboration

The sustainability benefits of Industry 4.0 technologies often depend on implementation decisions and infrastructure.

Take the example of a blockchain used to track garments in the supply chain and capture sustainability metrics. If that blockchain uses Proof of Work (PoW) consensus methods to verify each transaction, the carbon footprint can be very high. This is because PoW involves many people and powerful computers in "mining" (solving cryptographic puzzles) to authenticate each block on the blockchain.

However, if the Proof of Stake (PoS) method is used, the footprint is much lower. With PoS, there is a limited pool of validators or "forgers" with a cryptocurrency stake in which blocks they bet will be added next to the blockchain. When a block gets added, the validators get rewarded in proportion to their stake. The carbon footprint is much lower than with PoW.

In this blockchain scenario, smart contracts could complete 'batch' transactions (for a seasonal collection, for example) which lowers the footprint versus individual transactions per item. Similarly, the level of granularity involved in supply chain tracking and tracing also has an impact. There is more computation for authentication of all raw materials versus finished goods stock keeping units (SKUs). There is also potential physical waste involving identification choices such as QR codes on labels versus a physical tag fixed to the garment. Besides the carbon footprint of methods and algorithms involved, there is also the question of the electricity mix. A miner or forger in one country may consume energy from renewables and in another, from coal. The mix may even vary day to day. Little of this is obvious to people outside of the technology industry.

Blockchain presents an extreme case, but analogous arguments apply to machine and deep learning. Training a new computer vision model for classification of clothes consumes more energy than leveraging a pre-trained model. Deploying models in a modern, energy-efficient data center powered by renewables is clearly desirable, but requires expert due diligence from fashion businesses using these services.

make decisions about product development and manufacturing that lead to reduced GHG, water usage and so forth;

- if an in-home system understands enough about body/outfit relationships to combine garments into a successful outfit for a consumer, that same information can be used for entire customer segments or even at a national population level for sizing and fit systems that reduce the volume of textiles going to landfill; and
- AI models used to predict successful combinations of garments in outfits can also inform design decisions and set constraints on style options that will deliver against multiple sustainability goals within a larger garment ecosystem.

Importantly, information intensity, as well as decisions regarding systems and tools, also has an impact on the environmental footprint (see Box 29.4).

BARRIERS TO RE-INVENTING THE INDUSTRY

Managing risk

Any new technology brings risk. This could be risk in terms of an individual technology failing, or not working as intended when integrated into a system, or being commercially unattractive.

Figure 29.4 shows a modified version of the NASA Technology Readiness Level (TRL) scale (Davis, 2021).[12] This version brings in relevant

Description of Technology Risk Level (TRL)	TRL	Scope
Expansion and Proof of Success (e.g. Pre Initial Public Offering)	9	Commercially Viable Systems & Business Networks
	8	
Building Integrated Industry 4.0 Operational and Market Capabilities (e.g. Business Launched)	7	
	6	
Development & Validation of Industry 4.0 Technology and Business Model Components (e.g. Minimum Viable Prototype)	5	Individual Components or Complementarities (e.g. AI and Blockchain for Tracking Provenance)
	4	
Industry 4.0 Technology & Business Model Concept Development (Feasibility and Proof of Concept)	3	
	2	
Basic Technology & Market Exploration (Proof of Purpose)	1	

Figure 29.4 A Technology Readiness Scale modified for the fashion industry

Technology	TRL Score Across Creative Lifecycle			
	Inspiration	Creation	Making / Production	Experience / Consumption
Machine Learning, Deep Learning, Reinforcement Learning	4	6	7	8
Computer Vision	2	2	8	4
Robotics & Production Automation	3	6	8	1
Digital Twins	2	3	5	2
Robotic Process Automation	1	4	7	4
Augmented Reality / Virtual Reality / Mixed Reality	2	4	3	6
Simulation	2	8	6	5
Trusted Data & Analytics	1	3	9	6
5G / Edge Computing	1	2	4	3
Internet of Things / Machine to Machine Communication	1	3	8	7
Blockchains and Distributed Apps (DApps)	1	1	6	5
Additive Manufacturing (Incl. 3D Knitting & Similar)	4	7	7	2
Hybrid Clouds	8	9	8	9
Quantum Computing	1	2	2	1
Artificial General Intelligence	1	1	1	1
Bio-engineering / Bio-fabrication	1	2	4	1
4D Printing / Self Assembly	1	2	2	1
Computer-Aided Material and Process Discovery	3	2	2	2
Digital Self / Digital Clothing	5	4	4	4
Smart Farming	2	3	7	7
Autonomous Vehicles / Drones	2	1	6	6
Demand Shaping / Behavioural Nudging	4	4	1	6

Notes:
1. 243 individual fashion businesses' web sites evaluated
2. An initial scan of the web was performed using custom queries and an advanced research tool that can search multiple online sources in parallel). This identified potential Industry 4.0 users in fashion based on text phrases such as "artificial intelligence"
3. The initial scan was then run through a sequence of machine classifiers to identify the likely TRL
4. The final step was for a human researcher to validate the found set and construct the table.

Figure 29.5 A map of Technology Readiness by technology and stage in the creative life-cycle

elements from business models and venture capital. On this scale, a fashion business or start-up progresses from intellectual property creation to system development, then to business scale-up. Commercially viable systems and business networks only exist at level six and above.

Figure 29.5 shows the readiness scores for individual technologies in the fashion industry. This is based on an analysis of published statements about Industry 4.0 by fashion start-ups and larger businesses (Davis, 2021). On the vertical axis are technologies, including some of the latest ones such as blockchains, digital twins, quantum computing, bio-engineering and 4D printing. Horizontally, the stages in the fashion life-cycle exist. The numbers relate to TRL.

Applications in making and production dominate the cells classified as TRL six or higher (30% of the cells). Fifty percent of the cells are TRL three or less, with inspiration and ideation being the least ready stages of the life-cycle.

Managing TRL is an important competence that the fashion industry needs to develop, but most traditional players in the fashion industry are not technology experts. Therefore, it is difficult for them to understand the nuance of how feasible an innovation may be to implement in practice.

Advanced garment tool workflows[13] involve tools and methods from several disciplines. Multi-disciplinary working, co-design and collaboration, therefore, are central to the success of technology-enabled workflows. This can become problematic for quick implementation if there is no shared understanding of the risks and benefits. A TRL framework is useful in balancing the impact of a technology on sustainability versus practicality and risk. Broadening the base of the fashion industry to include technology experts will help. However, this may be a difficult transition to navigate because of the dominant culture of the industry.

Cultural resistance

While TRL is important to change-making in the fashion industry, an equally influential factor is socio-cultural readiness. Perhaps the analogous Societal Readiness Levels (SRL)[14] should complement TRL (Schraudner et al., 2020). Stakeholders need to buy into technology solutions as appropriate, or they may be impossible to deploy at sufficient scale to deliver sustainability benefits. Comparatively, the apparel industry lags in embracing new technologies, often favoring merchant-and designer-driven "gut-feel" over evidence-based decision-making. Also, the industry still relies extensively on manual labor practices, and many factories have old equipment, making any case for change complex.

Culturally, many view the hard problems in fashion (such as demand-supply matching, sizing and fit and predicting aesthetics) as "impossible" to address without subjective methods. However, machines can optimize decisions involving the interaction of many environmental, societal and financial objectives more efficiently and effectively than people. Designers (and factory owners) need to learn how to balance these technological innovations with their subjective evaluations.

Evolution of Industry 4.0

The ability of Industry 4.0 to support sustainability goals is developing as the technologies themselves continue to change. This is because of ongoing developments in cloud computing, pre-trained models[15] for AI, edge computing devices,[16] etc. Data sovereignty ideas, distributed ledgers and storage on blockchains offer the prospect of secure data decentralization coupled with greater transparency and security. This distributed paradigm shift also vastly increases the availability of data for AI models.

Decentralized infrastructures and platforms are creating Web 3.0 and will change Industry 4.0, too. In the future, businesses, individuals and machines in a network will implicitly trust interactions and data transfers. This removes the complexity and overhead of centralized governance, a major barrier in an industry with millions of freelancers, micro-, small- and medium-sized businesses. End-to-end sustainability reporting will likely improve significantly in this scenario.

At its most extreme, the next iteration of Industry 4.0 could lead to radical new business models. There are already early examples of businesses constructed from autonomous, decentralized multi-business global processes and fashion marketplaces based on self-sovereign data. The rise of non-fungible virtual fashion[17] is just the start (Tong, 2021).

Web 3.0 removes system integration barriers to expansion (e.g. a plethora of gatekeepers). Hence, businesses will be able to grow their operations to scale much faster than today. Likewise, the elimination of gatekeepers means that industry-wide adoption should happen more quickly. This acceleration can already be seen as blockchains are used to integrate many businesses in the cotton value chain to improve sustainability reporting and traceability from "crop to shop".[18]

CONCLUSIONS

The diverse, creative culture of the industry can be a barrier to the pursuit of technology innovation and digital transformation. The fashion industry needs a cultural shift towards:

- a common language in terms of standards and processes; and
- better ways of managing business and technology risk.

Individual technologies deliver sustainability benefits, but the full benefits of Industry 4.0 and its successors will come from integration of individual technologies into systems. This requires new collaborations among technology experts, fashion houses and consumers.

In conclusion, the industry has woken up to the potential benefits of Industry 4.0 technologies to address sustainability, but there are tough challenges to adoption:

- many Industry 4.0 solutions use unfamiliar concepts and language that betray their origins in engineered products, such as automobiles;

- extensive use of intelligent and automated systems raises tough societal concerns (e.g. privacy, employment); and
- there is a technology skills and knowledge gap within the industry alongside the cultural barriers discussed.

Ultimately, the industry needs to seize the opportunity of going through a social and technological revolution, much as it did in the 18th century. There are obvious benefits in terms of less overproduction and waste, greater emphasis on encouraging consumers to repair and re-use and re-shaping the industry in line with the UN sustainable development goals and new economic models.

NOTES

1 See https://blog.isa.org/what-is-industry-40.
2 See https://en.wikipedia.org/wiki/Digital_twin.
3 See https://en.wikipedia.org/wiki/Blockchain.
4 See https://en.wikipedia.org/wiki/GPT-3.
5 See https://www.gartner.com/en/articles/what-is-a-metaverse.
6 https://bettercotton.org.
7 https://pacecircular.org/make-fashion-circular.
8 Advanced garment tools (AGTs) include textile simulation, 3D body scans, 3D to 2D garment creation.
9 See http://www.apparel-merchandising.com/2012/05/marker-making-cutting-part-2.html.
10 Virtual garments reduce the number of physical samples and garments in the iterative development process, and in merchandising.
11 Historically, sizing and fit are assessed using human fit models. The combination of 3D body scanners and AI software can increase the number of fit points used to design a garment, reducing waste involved in sizing-related returns in retailing.
12 See https://en.wikipedia.org/wiki/Technology_readiness_level. Although the fashion context is different, the concept still applies with the most significant difference being the importance of market and commercial elements.
13 See https://en.wikipedia.org/wiki/Workflow.
14 An example is body scanning technology as a technical solution to poor clothing fit triggering a negative response because of privacy concerns.
15 Ready-to-use models trained on representative datasets. These can be fine-tuned or retrained with custom data (e.g. for waste sorting) quickly and with less energy consumption than generating a new model.
16 See https://en.wikipedia.org/wiki/Edge_computing.
17 See https://www.fashionlaw.co.uk/2022/01/18/non-fungible-token-licensing-what-are-the-commercial-legal-issues/.
18 Examples include https://unece.org/circular-economy/press/unece-and-fao-join-forces-cotton-traceability-connect-sustainable-rural and https://fashionforgood.com/our_news/successfully-tracing-organic-cotton-with-innovative-technologies/.

REFERENCES

Bigger, E. (15–21 March 2021) 'Generative garment design for circularity: Parametric patterns and transformative algorithms for enabling circular fashion design', *SUSTAINABLE INNOVATION 2021, 23rd International Conference*, Online, University for the Creative Arts/Centre for Sustainable Design.

Brennan, M. and Devine, K. (April 2019-last updated) *Music Streaming has a Far Worse Carbon Footprint than the Heyday of Records and CDs–New Findings*, The Conversation [Online]. Available at: https://theconversation.com/music-streaming-has-a-far-worse-carbon-footprint-than-the-heyday-of-records-and-cds-new-findings-114944 (Accessed: 20 December 2021).

Davis, T. (2021) Technology: Looking forwards and backwards for answers', *SUSTAINABLE INNOVATION 2021, 23rd International Conference*, University for the Creative Arts/Centre for Sustainable Design (Accessed: 16 March 2021).

Dunne, L. E. (2021) 'Management of the wardrobe system: An understudied & powerful influence on clothing waste', *SUSTAINABLE INNOVATION 2021, 23rd International Conference*, University for the Creative Arts/Centre for Sustainable Design (Accessed: 18 March 2021).

Kozlowski, A. (2020) 'Fashion's "sustainability" endeavors need to be about more than fabrics, recycling', *The Fashion Law*. Available at: https://www.thefashionlaw.com/fast-fashion-sustainability-is-about-more-than-the-fabrics/.

McQuillan, H. (2020) 'Digital 3D design as a tool for augmenting zero-waste fashion design practice', *International Journal of Fashion Design, Technology and Education*, 13, pp. 1–12. DOI: 10.1080/17543266.2020.1737248

Niinimäki, K., Peters, G., Dahlbo, H., Perry, P., Rissanen, T. and Gwilt, A. (2020) 'Author correction: The environmental price of fast fashion', *Nature Reviews Earth & Environment*, 1(5), pp. 278–278.

Roos, S., Jönsson, C., Posner, S., Arvidsson, R. and Svanström, M. (2019) 'An inventory framework for inclusion of textile chemicals in life cycle assessment', *The International Journal of Life Cycle Assessment*, 24(5), pp. 838–847.

Schraudner, M., Schroth, F., Millard, J., Jütting, M., Kaiser, S. and van der Graaf, S. (2020) 'Social innovation: The potential for technology development, rtos and industry (policy paper)'. Available: Fraunhofer. Available at: https://www.researchgate.net/publication/338855177_Social_innovation_the_potential_for_technology_development_rtos_and_industry_policy_paper.

Tong, A. (April 2021) 'Luxury fashion brands poised to join the NFT party', *Vogue Business* [Online]. Available: Condé Nast. Available at: https://www.voguebusiness.com/technology/luxury-fashion-brands-poised-to-join-the-nft-party (Accessed 23 December 2021).

30 Wearable tech, virtual fashion, and immersive technologies

Gözde Göncü-Berk and
Emily Rosa Shahaj

INTRODUCTION

Since the turn of the 21st century, humanity has witnessed many technological innovations in fashion, apparel, and textiles which have created entirely new product categories and brought new developments to all stages of the product life cycle. Wearable technology and virtual fashion represent two new product categories in the physical and digital realms of fashion. In this chapter, new opportunities and challenges for environmental sustainability emerging from the introduction of these new product categories in the marketplace are discussed. Focus is placed on textile-based wearable technologies, such as electronic textiles, smart clothing, virtual apparel, and textiles in digital social interactions and retailing; covering their implications for sustainability at all levels: from materials, production, and distribution to use and disposal.

WEARABLE TECHNOLOGY

Wearables are body-mounted technology that can come in the form of accessories and clothing. As a specific subgroup of wearable technology, smart clothing where electronic textiles (e-textiles) are the building blocks, can be distinguished from other wearables such as bracelets and watches. E-textiles could be fibers, yarns or fabrics with embedded

DOI: 10.4324/9781003272878-38

electronic functions that offer enhanced flexibility, stretchability, drapability, and breathability as well as aesthetic and customizability benefits compared with traditional electronics. They also offer the potential to detect and react to a wide range of data about the wearer due to their proximity to the whole body, as opposed to smart watches and wrist bands which are limited in scope. In addition, e-textiles have the potential not only to sense and monitor data, but also to act on the body with embedded actuation capabilities, such as promoting mechanical, electric, and thermal tactile stimuli.

Textile-based wearable technology products continue to grow in popularity and are expected to become more ubiquitous. While this does present an opportunity in innovation, we are also increasingly confronted with the potential long-term unintended consequences of revolutionary designs on the surrounding environmental systems and sustainability. Many problems have already emerged both in the textiles and the microelectronics industries. According to United Nations data, global e-waste is expected to reach 120 million tons per day by year 2050. Today, less than 20% of e-waste is formally recycled while 80% either ends up in landfill or in developing countries, exposing individuals to carcinogenic substances, such as mercury, lead, and cadmium, as well as contaminating soils and ground water (PACE, 2019). On the other hand, fashion industry accounts for up to 10% of global carbon dioxide output with an estimated 134 million tons of textiles waste a year by 2030 (Dottle & Gu, 2022). In addition to the waste problem, petroleum-derived synthetic fibers, such as polyester and rayon, dominate the textiles and fashion industries and are reported as the main microplastic pollutants found in ocean, fresh water, and land as a result of laundering practices. Within this context, the increasing popularity of e-textiles only compounds the issue, given the consumption of scarce raw materials and the difficult-to-recycle electronics built into the textiles.

Design, being tightly bound to production and consumption, plays a crucial role in the pursuit of a more sustainable environment. Sustainable design concepts for e-textiles and smart clothing could prioritize waste prevention (Köhler, 2013) and increase longevity during use-phase with dynamic aesthetics and by encouraging repairability through modularity.

Materials selection

E-textiles can be composed of many different components, including traditional fibers, like cotton or polyester, conductive yarns coated with silver or gold, steel or copper metallic yarns, optical fibers, conductive inks, wires, LEDs, batteries, plastic hardware, and many others. Large amounts of both electronic and textile waste can be expected if such wearable technologies become commonly mass-produced and mass-consumed (Köhler et al., 2011). Conductive textiles, in particular, contain scarce materials such as rare-earth elements, silver, and gold, which are difficult to recover once discarded (Köhler, 2013).

Selecting biodegradable and/or recyclable textiles and electronic materials is an important design consideration for sustainability. There are opportunities to reduce the consumption of primary resources by using recycled fibers and substituting traditional materials like aluminum and plastics in the storage of electronic components with eco-friendly textile materials. There has also been increased research and exploration in both academia and maker communities to incorporate biomaterials in e-textiles and develop bio-based smart textiles without the use of electronic components (Singh et al., 2012). Kombucha leather, a flexible bio-material made from cellulose nanofibrils spun by bacteria and yeast, has been explored as a biodegradable alternative to traditional textile in e-textile applications. Audrey Ng studied kombucha leather's self-adhesive features during the drying process to allow LEDs and conductive yarns to self-assemble between the two surfaces of kombucha (Ng, 2017). Similarly, mycelium leather bio-fabricated from the root structure of mushrooms was explored as a medium to incorporate electronic components (Lazaro Vasquez et al., 2020). Ecovative Design holds the patent for growing electrically conductive tissue consisting of a sheet of mycelium with a wiring pattern for an electrical circuit (Method of Growing Electrically Conductive Tissue, 2013). Biomaterials such as mycelium or kombucha offer the possibility of extracting electronic components for recycling as they biodegrade.

In addition, there has been recent research into the creation of smart textiles without the use of any electronic components. These include the electrically conductive cellulose yarns for machine-sewn electronic textiles (Darabi et al., 2020); bioactive silk-based inks screen printed on textiles that sense chemicals released by the body or environment and respond via color change (Guisy et al., 2020; Matzeu et al., 2020); and smart fabric that reacts to body heat and sweat based on the expansion and contraction behavior of an ancient bacteria embedded in its structure (Lacey, 2016).

Material integration

Existing e-waste recycling structures are not compatible with e-textiles. E-textiles create a new kind of waste that is hard to recycle at the end of the product lifetimes, due to the difficulties in separating electronics from textiles (McLaren, Hardy and Hughes-Riley, 2017). In addition, there is no governing body or regulation that oversees the design, manufacturing, and disposal of e-textiles as an individual product category. Making e-textiles easy to disassemble, and making materials recyclable once disassembled are the keys to future sustainability of these hybrid materials.

The integration mechanism of electronic components into textiles determines their ease of recyclability. Using textiles as a platform to carry electronic components in pocket-like structures or with fasteners increases recyclability, compared with when electrical properties are embedded into the textile structure by weaving, knitting, embroidering conductive threads, or using textile materials with inherent electronic functionality such as yarn transistors or photovoltaic fibers. For example, Embodisuit demonstrates electronic modules attached on clothing with snaps which allow easy disassembly (Brueckner & Freire, 2018), whereas the Google/Levi's Commuter Jacket demonstrates conductive yarns integrated into the fabric in the weaving process, which are not possible to extract from otherwise recyclable denim (Levi's & Google, 2017).

Product lifetime

Product lifetime can relate to physical durability as well as aesthetic durability. Cooper (2016) describes longevity as a product's active lifespan, considering user behavior and sociocultural influences, as well as its design and manufacturing processes. Issues of physical durability specific to e-textiles include repairability and washability and the lifetimes of electronic components and the technology (McLaren, Hardy and Hughes-Riley, 2017). It is possible that fibers wear out before electronic components, or the technology become outdated before the textiles are worn out. Therefore, the overall lifetime depends on the shortest-lived element in an e-textile structure (McLaren, Hardy and Hughes-Riley, 2017). For example, Google/Levi's Commuter Jacket can only withstand up to ten washes depending on the usage and wash conditions before it loses functionality of the touch-sensitive e-textile surface on the cuff. Sensoria smart running socks, which can monitor steps, calories, speed, and feet landing technique with knitted pressure sensors under the sole, display an example of how technological developments can make earlier versions of smart clothing obsolete. Sensoria smart running sock V1.0 came with a detachable hardware that grips the ankle and the next release V2.0 came with an entirely new hardware and an attachment system that would not fit the earlier socks.

Modularity is a design tool that can be effective in prolonging product longevity in all its aspects (Valentine et al., 2017). Electronic components contained in pockets or detachable units secured on textiles with snaps or Velcros enable separation of parts without damaging the fabric for washing, recycling, upcycling, repairing, refurbishment, and for transferring onto another textile piece. Labeling to indicate the presence and location of electronics in the clothing can also assist reparability and care (Valentine et al., 2017; Hardy, Wickenden & McLaren, 2020). In addition, Köhler (2013) highlights the potential for printing technology to print over faulty electrical transmission lines using conductive ink to repair textile-based wearable technologies.

An e-textile based product's aesthetic durability depends on the textile and clothing elements' relevance to the current fashion. Delaying aesthetic obsolescence and preventing waste could happen through the design of transformable and customizable smart clothing that can update its appearance through change in color, texture, pattern, or even form, and thereby reduce the need to constantly purchase an up-to-date item. Reactive dyes, electronic ink, and shape memory alloys are some technologies used in smart clothing that enable the appearance change capabilities (Göncü-Berk, 2019).

Energy source

Wearable technologies rely on an energy source such as lithium-ion batteries with limited life span. Even though lithium-ion batteries contain fewer toxic metals than other alkaline and lead-acid batteries that could contain toxic metals such as lead or cadmium, mining of lithium requires significant energy and water and has been accounted for unethical work conditions. In addition, it has been reported that the environmental footprint of lithium-ion battery recycling has not been studied in detail yet (Aalto University, 2021).

Research on energy-harvesting technologies address the issue of needing a continuous power supply to increase sustainability of wearable technologies. Integration of solar technology, also known as photovoltaic (PV) cells, into clothing could allow the wearer to harvest and use solar energy for other devices, while also solving the issue of power supply e-textiles (Smelik, Toussaint & Van Dongen, 2016).

VIRTUAL FASHION

Virtual fashion can be broadly defined as 3D, digitally represented apparel. Recent advancements have broadened its uptake and range of applications to include replacement of physical fashion in photos, improved shopping experiences, apparel for games, and made-to-order product visualizations. It is developing into three distinct categories: Virtual wear on photos, virtual product representation, and fashion for immersive technologies. Each of these is having its own impact on fashion sustainability to different effects. While some look to replace/ reduce the prominence of physical fashion, other developments in the form of marketing have served to promote consumption.

Virtual wear on photos

Virtual wear on photos largely aims to replace garments which are purchased for a single wear in photos on social media. Instead, the virtually represented garment is '3D-tailored' onto a photograph of the user. This technology aims to address the sustainability issues underlying in the fast fashion industry, whereby cheap garments are consumed exclusively for a photo and discarded thereafter.

Outfits for social media posts contribute to fashion's consumption problem. About 17% of U.K. shoppers aged 35–44 have bought clothing just to wear on social media with the intention of immediately returning it (Barclaycard, 2018). U.K. consumers expected to buy 50.3 million 'throwaway outfits' over the summer of 2019 (Censuswide, 2019). Virtual fashion for photos aims to replace the trend-driven fashion purchased by this audience. By replacing the once-worn garment with a virtual counterpart, virtual fashion fulfills the consumer desire for trend consumption and impulse purchase without the physical waste associated with manufacture, shipping, and disposal. It makes room for slower, more calculated purchase decisions with respect to physical clothing.

Does purchasing virtual garments for photos actually replace physical fashion purchases, or does it become an addition to physical buying behaviors? In the case of Farfetch's replacement of physical samples with digital versions for influencer marketing (McDowell, 2021), the impact is clear and defined: There was no need to manufacture and ship garments for these promotions. Whether this remains true for the average style blogger requires further research.

Virtual fashion representation

Virtual fashion is also used to depict and represent physical fashion, often in eCommerce. Seventy percent of consumers feel that finding clothes online which fit is difficult, often leading to returns (London, 2021). Eliminating a purchase which would be returned saves shipping emissions twice, wasted shipping materials, and potentially wasted product.

Virtual fashion simulations mimic fabric physics on a 3D human figure. It can reveal where the wearer of a physical equivalent would face tightness and realistically reveal undesirable fit and drape characteristics (CLO-SET, 2022). This provides potential buyers with a view of the item on a body which resembles their own, giving a more comprehensive understanding prior to purchase, thus potentially reducing the rate of returns for online orders (London, 2021).

Three-dimensional representation can enhance made-to-order products. Fashion brand Atacac uses virtual representation of their designs to showcase and sell their apparel online before producing a physical sample. This allows them to eliminate overproduction by only producing what has already been sold (Atacac, 2022). Similarly, RTFKT uses 3D representation for a primarily digital product. They primarily sell their NFT sneakers as digital 'proof of ownership' without physical ownership. The owner of any of their digital items can order a physical equivalent, but few actually do (RTFKT, 2021). Many owners instead wear the 3D versions in compatible virtual worlds. This allows consumption while saving physical manufacture and shipping.

Sustainability considerations in the area of virtual fashion representations include the concept of digital waste. While the impacts of physical manufacture and overproduction are reduced or eliminated, producing a 3D garment visualization still requires significant computing power and thus electricity: Approximately 4 kWh,[1] the equivalent of driving a Tesla Model S more than 20 km (Tesla).

Immersive technologies

Hardware advancements have led to more accessible virtual and mixed reality technology and created new opportunities for immersive interaction with fashion. These include mixed reality filters on social media, smart fit mirrors in stores, and virtual reality (VR) retail experiences. However, the sustainability benefits of these tactics are yet to be seen. As marketing tactics, they continue to facilitate physical consumption and generate digital waste. In the case of VR, they require the manufacture of specialized resource-intensive hardware. Fashion brands are exploring this for brand building and facilitating try-on: Already used by names including Gucci, Louis Vuitton, Burberry, Ralph Lauren, and Levi's, the technology is projected to grow to USD12.97 billion by 2028 (Globe Newswire). Immersive technologies as they are presently emerging streamline the consumer experience rather than accelerate fashion sustainability in any notable way.

Streamlining the consumer experience, however, is intended to facilitate immediate consumption. This returns us to the broader issue of needing to reduce fashion consumption to further sustainability. Instead, if brands intend to meaningfully embrace novel models to advance sustainability by reducing consumption by end-consumers while maintaining their bottom line, such immersive technologies could further these efforts. For example, brands could use such technology to display details about a garment's sourcing and environmental impact, its likelihood of trend obsolescence, or the evaluation of a database of the user's existing wardrobe to advice against buying a style or a type of garment already overrepresented. The perception that the brand cares about their consumers and the causes that are greater than themselves could foster brand loyalty and put companies in an optimal position as sentiments on brand responsibility evolve.

CONCLUSION

Sustainability is one of today's most complex and deeply systemic issues. How we approach the newly emerging industries of e-textiles, smart clothing, and virtual fashion will determine their future sustainability. As discussed throughout the chapter, they can become environmentally sustainable alternatives to traditional clothing and textiles if recyclability, disposal, and energy use impacts are addressed early enough before they come into the mainstream product lines. E-textiles with their unique capabilities could present a high level of personalization in their functions and appearance. On the other hand, combining electronics and textiles, which are both relatively short-lived mass consumer goods can intensify product obsolescence. Similarly, while virtual fashion can reduce excess physical consumption, its electricity consumption adds another dimension to their impact on the environment.

Wearable technology and virtual fashion are often situated within discourses of high technology and futurism. However, the global consumer market is already filled with countless iterations of novelty clothing and accessories with integrated light and/or sound technology or products that are not usually recognized as a form of e-textile, such as heated massage wraps or heated blankets that are not recyclable. There are also ancillary products associated with the development of virtual fashion. This includes the manufacturing of new computing equipment and electronic parts and accessories, VR headsets, electricity consumption, and the use of virtual fashion as a marketing tactic for increased physical fashion consumption. It is therefore urgent that we consider the comprehensive and long-term implications of new technological frontiers in fashion from all angles at a systematic level and direct them toward pro-sustainability uses rather than building tech for tech's or trends' sake, in order to afford the best chance of building an innovative and sustainable fashion industry of the future.

NOTE

1 From the author's own computational measurements in professional practice.

REFERENCES

Aalto University (2021) Is Battery Recycling Environmentally Friendly. Available at: https://www.eurekalert.org/news-releases/478406 (Accessed 12 April 2022).

Atacac (2022) 'Sustainability' Available at: https://atacac.com/sustainability (Accessed 23 January 2022).

Barclaycard (2018) 'Snap and Send Back' Available at: https://home.barclaycard/press-releases/2018/08/snap-and-send-back (Accessed 04 January 2021).

Brueckner, S. and Freire, R. (2018) 'Embodisuit: A wearable Platform for Embodied Knowledge' Proceedings of the Twelfth International Conference on Tangible, Embedded, and Embodied Interaction, pp. 542–548.

Censuswide (2019) 'The Fast Fashion Crisis' Available at: https://censuswide.com/censuswide-projects/barley-and-barnardos-the-fast-fashion-crisis-research/ (Accessed 23 May 2023).

CLO-SET (2022) 'About Us' Available at: https://style.clo-set.com/aboutus (Accessed 23 January 2022).

Cooper, T. (2016) 'The Significance of Product Longevity' In Cooper, T. (ed.). *Longer Lasting Products* (pp. 29–62). Routledge.

Darabi, S., Hummel, M. Rantasalo S., Rissanen, M., Månsson, I. O., Hilke, H. and Byungil Hwang, B. (2020) Green Conducting Cellulose Yarns for Machine-Sewn Electronic Textiles. *ACS Applied Materials & Interfaces*, 12, no. 50 (2020): 56403–56412.

Dottle, R. and Gu, J. (2022) The Global Glut of Clothing is an Environmental Crisis. *Bloomberg*. Available at: https://www.bloomberg.com/graphics/2022-fashion-industry-environmental-impact/ (Accessed: 12 April 2022)

Goncu-Berk, G. (2019) Smart Textiles and Clothing: An Opportunity or A Threat for Sustainability. *Proceedings of the Textile Intersections*. 14–19 September: London.

Hardy, D., Wickenden, R. and McLaren, A. (2020) Electronic Textile Reparability. *Journal of Cleaner Production*, 276: 124328.

Köhler, A. R. (2013) Challenges for Eco-Design of Emerging Technologies: The Case of Electronic Textiles. *Materials & Design*, 51: 51–60.

Köhler, A. R., Hilty, L. M. and Bakker, C. (2011) Prospective Impacts of Electronic Textiles on Recycling and Disposal. *Journal of Industrial Ecology*, 15, no. 4: 496–511.

Lazaro Vasquez, E. S., Wang, H. C. and Vega, K. (2020) Introducing the Sustainable Prototyping Life Cycle for Digital Fabrication to Designers. Proceedings of the 2020 ACM Designing Interactive Systems Conference, pp. 1301–1312.

Lacey, S. (2016) Biologic's Living Textile. Available at: https://arts.mit.edu/biologics-living-textile/ (Accessed: 23 March 2021).

Levi's & Google. (2017) Levi's Commuter Jacket with Jacquard by Google. Available at: https://atap.google.com/jacquard/about/ (Accessed: 13 February 2020).

London, L. (2021) 'Virtual Try-On is More Than a Pandemic Trend and These Brands Are Reaping the Rewards' In: Forbes 20–05–2021, Available at: https://www.forbes.com/sites/lelalondon/2021/05/20/virtual-try-on-is-more-than-a-pandemic-trendand-these-brands-are-reaping-the-rewards (Accessed: 23 January 2021).

McDowell, Maghan (2021) 'Influencers are wearing digital versions of physical clothes now.' In *Vogue Business* 21-09-2021, Available at: https://www.vogue-business.com/technology/influencers-are-wearing-digital-versions-of-physical-clothes-now (Accessed: 23 May 2023).

McLaren, A., Hardy, D. A. and Hughes-Riley, T. (2017) 'Electronic Textiles and Product Lifetimes: Exploring Design Strategies for Product Longevity'. In Bakker, C.A. and Mugge, R. (eds.), In *PLATE: Product Lifetimes and the Environment*, pp. 473–476. IOS Press: The Netherlands.

Method of Growing Electrically Conductive Tissue (2013) Available at: https://patents.google.com/patent/US20140097008A1/en (Accessed: 16 December 2020)

Ng, A. (2017) Grown Microbial 3D Fiber Art, Ava: Fusion of Traditional Art with Technology. Proceedings of the 2017 ACM International Symposium on Wearable Computers, ACM, 209–214.

PACE (2019) A New Circular Vision for Electronics. Available at: https://www3.weforum.org/docs/WEF_A_New_Circular_Vision_for_Electronics.pdf (Accessed: 12 April 2022).

RTFKT (2021) How it Works. Available at: https://rtfkt.com/forging (Accessed 14 November 2021).

Singh, A. V., Rahman, A., Kumar, S., Aditi, A. S., Galluzzi, M., Bovio, S., Barozzi, S., Montani, E. and Parazzoli, D. (2012) Bio-Inspired Approaches to Design Smart Fabrics. *Materials & Design* (1980–2015). 36: 829–839.

Smelik, A., Toussaint, L. and Van Dongen, P. (2016) Solar Fashion: An Embodied Approach to Wearable Technology. *International Journal of Fashion Studies*. 3, no. 2: 287–303.

Tesla (2022) 'European Union Energy Label' Available at: https://www.tesla.com/en_EU/support/european-union-energy-label (Accessed 25 March 2022).

Valentine, L., Ballie, J., Bletcher, J., Robertson, S. and Stevenson, F. (2017) Design Thinking for Textiles: Let's Make It Meaningful. *The Design Journal.* 20, no. sup1: S964–S976.

31 Fashion ex machina: human–machine collaboration to support sustainability through customized design and production

Elizabeth E. Bigger, Helga Ahrens-Wels and Hannah C. Kelbel

INTRODUCTION

The Latin phrase *deus ex machina* is a narrative plot device where an unsolvable problem is suddenly resolved by an unlikely occurrence (Britannica 2021). The fashion industry needs a device to radically change environmental problems from within. *Fashion ex machina*, translates to "fashion from the machine", a radical transition we propose relying on collaboration of humans and digital machines to pivot the industry's tragic environmental and biodiversity impact narrative toward solutions for the problems. Either human or machine processes alone may not be powerful enough to solve complex sustainability problems. We suggest however, building human and machine relationships can enable new design-to-production workflows with potential to contribute toward sustainability in the fashion sector.

Fashioning futures through machine and human collaboration is a complex process, but necessary to achieve sustainability within the fashion industry. Mass production volumes amount to more than 100

DOI: 10.4324/9781003272878-39

billion pieces of clothing per year (Greenpeace 2019). Additionally, it is projected that in 2030, we will see a 49% increase in climate change impacts, severe resource depletion and 47% increase in negative human health indicators directly resulting from current fashion industry production processes (Quantis 2018).

To render the fashion industry sustainable, garment value needs to increase and production volume needs to decrease. Production paradigms are shifting toward customization, on-demand and personalized fashion pipelines to address sustainability goals. Adding (1) customization and (2) collaboration with consumers changes fashion production models in a twofold manner: first, by changing cultural relationships the consumer has with products (bringing consumers closer to design and manufacture of items) and second, by changing from bulk production of products that may not be sold to on-demand production of products that have already been purchased. Existing design and manufacturing models are not able to support the speed, agility and complexity of personalized products. New processes are needed to encourage human and machine collaborations and increase value in garment production.

Agile systems that support the complexity required by personalization of products are becoming increasingly valuable (Lee & Xia, 2010). Interoperability and a new *lingua franca* can help broaden connections of global and local production networks and help achieve environmental sustainability goals. In this chapter, we outline challenges for transitioning to personalized production and present practical solutions to solve production transitions for sustainability. Two processes – Generative Garment Design for Sustainability and Adaptive Pattern Design – are presented with iterative workflows for increasing production agility. This chapter further discusses human–machine collaboration, increasing value over volume and systemic thinking for fashion production methodologies.

TRANSITIONS TOWARD SUSTAINABLE BESPOKE FASHION PRODUCTION

Factory transitions

Multiple influences are pushing manufacturers away from mass-production models toward methods that are better-suited to customization. Ever-shortening design and delivery schedules mean that producing high volumes and shipping globally is increasingly difficult. Global transport and coastal garment factories have begun to be upset by effects of

---

Box 31.1

Industry 5.0, Web 3.0 and blockchain smart contracts

Industry 5.0 places worker well-being at the center of production processes and uses new technologies to provide prosperity beyond jobs and growth while respecting planetary production limits (European Commission, 2020). This differs from Industry 4.0 that describes organizing production processes based on technology and devices autonomously communicating with each other along the value chain (European Parliament, 2016).

Web 3.0 is a phase of the World Wide Web based on blockchains, incorporating decentralization and token-based economics. Web 3.0 technologies help transfer power to communities and workforces via decentralization. Industry 5.0 and Web 3.0 work in tandem to reinforce transparency to build new production systems.

Blockchain transactions can be used to track trade of tokens from one entity to another. A token can be "fungible" (alterable), or a non-fungible token (NFT), which means it is immutable.

Digital assets are not typically stored on blockchain, but on the Interplanetary File System (IPFS), a decentralized and globally distributed file storage network. Smart contracts are programs stored on blockchains that can be used to execute specific actions, for example, a smart contract could be called upon to manage splitting royalties between multiple entities involved in creating an NFT.

Sources: European Commission and European Parliament

---

climate change from extreme weather events. Consequently, transitions to nearshoring production centers have begun, as manufacturing and factories transition toward distributed local production. Nearshoring (relocation of factories closer to consumers), in-store microfactories and localism, using local sewists for production, have become attractive solutions for supply chain issues.

Web 3.0 technologies together with Industry 5.0 strategies (see Box 31.1) provide low risk processes and decentralized production system opportunities. Reduced manufacturing and overhead footprints are needed to offset increasing investments into workforces, garments and new systems. Agile production systems involving human and machine collaborations throughout manufacturing processes, adapting as necessary, create smoother transitions for environmental and economic sustainability.

Emerging processes

Emerging production processes using Web 3.0 technologies challenge competition standards, workforce and consumer expectations. Small- and medium-sized enterprises are using new processes to engage consumers, exploiting niche categories for increased visibility and virtual consumer collaborations. Processes involving blockchain provide data verification and the exchange of value throughout manufacturing processes. Using smart contracts for splitting royalties between stakeholders in production processes transparently distributes economic gains. This visibility increases the value of each production step, and thus the focus toward the health and value of the corresponding garment worker. These emerging processes are resulting in new workflows. For example, in Figure 31.1, the IPFS digital fashion design-to-production workflow shows processes of design, pattern, virtual try-on and evaluation. If evaluation is satisfactory, two files are produced and stored: the interactive design and tech pack. Consumers then purchase files to be customized and sewn locally. Below the workflow is a reference of human, machine or human–machine visualizing emerging human and machine collaboration points. Emerging processes support the inevitability of an ever-shrinking workforce and added value of an upskilled garment worker. Challenges of upskilling workforces include addressing factory transitions and local workforce availability as well as the workforce relationship with emerging technologies. Working with emerging processes needs technical knowledge of blockchain and IPFS from each stakeholder's point of view. How stakeholders apply data outputs is key to unlocking actionable steps to reducing environmental resource depletion and biodiversity impact from utilizing emerging processes.

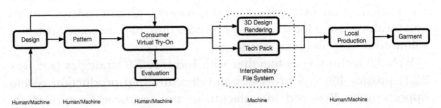

Figure 31.1 Interplanetary file system (ipfs) digital fashion production.
Adapted from Sync: The Phygital T-Shirt. A Test Case for Decentralized Fashion Customization Utilizing Blockchain Technology and Local Production (Bigger & Fraguada (2021). The NFT phygital t-shirt was stored on the Tezos blockchain in March 2021. Consumers who bought the interactive phygital t-shirt were sent another NFT in six sizing layouts, ready for digital textile printing and to be produced locally

HUMAN + MACHINE COLLABORATIONS FOR FASHION SUSTAINABILITY

Designing-in sustainability through human and machine collaborations

Production methods are important elements for improving sustaina-bility in fashion, but it is important to realize the critical impact that design activities have on downstream processes and effects. While 60% of effluents being from garment use phase (Laitala, Klepp & Henry 2018), decisions that create effluents can be traced back to the design stage where the majority of waste is determined (McQuillan 2020). Human–machine collaboration can transform design activities tech-nologically, but can also extend design activities to include consumers. Design-phase decisions affect impacts throughout the product life cycle. Consumer-phase decisions add intrinsic value, extending the garment lifespan. Agile production can facilitate design and consumer collabo-rations for decision-making toward enhanced sustainability.

Design collaborations for decision-making toward enhanced sustainability

Data-informed design could substantially alter a garment's ecological im-pact. Garment dimensions are complex parameters and changing them modifies fit, design and resulting wastes. A small change to garment's di-mension or pattern (such as adding a seam or decreasing flare) can have big impacts on pattern layout. These complex calculations are difficult for humans, but easily managed by machines. Personalization relies on co-cre-ation processes with consumers to alter the garment design to fit consumer needs whether in expression or fit. Artificial intelligence for virtual try-on, sizing and design augmentation can be programmed for continued learn-ing alongside human consumers who are also learning how to work with these systems to achieve desired results. The resulting personalized garment potentially has a larger impact on decreasing environmental footprints, as it fits better (both physically and in fashion expression). Personalization results in a longer lifecycle through extended use negating many of the causes of fashion waste, for example, by reducing consumption (Laitala et al., 2015). As studies have shown, a t-shirt used once and then discarded to a landfill has 100 times greater production-burden environmental im-pact than a t-shirt used 100 times before being discarded (Laitala et al. 2018). Most current personalization systems are focused on helping users customize aesthetics. However, computing can also help users navigate more complex parameters such as sustainability impacts of different design choices. Consumer personalization and sustainability goals evaluated using systems, including multi-objective optimization algorithms, can facilitate design compromises: for example, goals for decreasing effluent and microfiber release of a garment change requirements for textile finishing, dyes and fiber types. This could lead to garment design, fit and fashion compromises. Managing multiple sustainability goals in design is possible with human–machine collaboration, exploiting the machine's ability to calculate and manage data and the human's strengths in deciphering the societal needs of the design.

Consumer collaborations for decision-making toward enhanced sustainability

While mass-customization may rely on marketing data informing production, personalization and on-demand production rely on consumer collaboration. Integrating consumers into the production pipeline shifts some responsibility of design, fit and timing to the consumer. Successful consumer use of virtual try-on systems becomes crucial to product development processes. As seen in Figure 31.1, the virtual try-on stage can lead to an iterative collaboration between designer, consumer and machine, revisiting previous steps for further personalization, each time, consumer, designer and virtual try-on machine learning from each other. Consumers are also responsible for actualizing the garment's physical production. Sneaker design firm RTFKT's[1] NFTs could be used to redeem the physical shoe, but only one in 20 customers requested the physical shoe (Howcroft, 2021). The consumption of digital fashion among early adopters show a potential for decreasing physical production volumes and value shifting if digital footprints are taken into account. Producing or consuming digital fashion NFTs on proof-of-work (POW) blockchains uses irresponsible amounts of energy, while proof-of-stake (POS) uses minute energy (see Chapter 31 definitions). Understanding digital footprints of the multiple systems used in digital fashion is imperative for fashion brands and consumers in order to avoid increasing fashion's carbon footprint. Blockchains using POS systems layered on top of POW systems use similarly high amounts of energy as POW systems. Consumer knowledge building about system footprints is vital to creating sustainable consumer–machine collaborations.

Automation and social sustainability of manufacturing

In contrast to computer-aided design and data analysis, constructing garments historically involves a lot of human labor. In some areas of garment production, new technologies have reduced reliance on human labor, for example, knitted garments are able to be fully constructed using computerized knitting machines. Many factories have reduced workforces and transitioned to use automated knitting machines. Non-knit garments constructed via sewing machines are much more difficult to automate. Human hands possess a tactile ability to guide textiles, navigate intricate sewn details and immediately sense problems with a machine or textile. Over time, a sewist integrates machine knowledge, understanding any nuances when working together. A simple machine can be used to fabricate an infinite array of product shapes and construction techniques, with an infinite range of materials. By contrast, automating sewing processes often requires constraining designs to a limited variety of shapes, textile mechanics and construction operations. To build more agile machines that mimic human operators, humans must develop machines with abilities of sensing and reacting to touch, sight and sound. This is a large task, with much research required to address challenges of automating agile motor skills and tacit knowledge of experienced technicians.

Sustainability impacts of automation should be considered more broadly as well. Machine development frequently relies on an increase of efficiency and reduced labor costs which are typically goals for continuing mass production models. New goals for machine development and human collaboration should be considered for sustainable production processes. Slow production processes using human labor may increase cultural value of a garment, by emphasizing the human sewists' skills and understanding of textile subtleties. If production volume is to decrease, balanced goals for machine–human collaboration are necessary to alleviate possible future social and environmental sustainability problems. Two examples of collaboration with machines for agile production processes are demonstrated by Generative Garment Design analysis and Adaptive Pattern Design (Boxes 31.2 and 31.3).

Box 31.2

Generative garment design for sustainability

Generative garment design for sustainability uses genetic algorithms for inclusion of consumer and sustainable analytics, enabling design-phase multi-objective optimization where the majority of lifecycle waste is determined.

Generative design includes algorithm-driven design processes which generate designs under given objectives and constraints. For generative garment design analysis, multiple objectives are considered in parallel such as textile waste, microfiber and chemical effluent release rates and user care. Objectives form inputs of the fitness function of the genetic algorithm to optimize the minimization of negative environmental impact from the design. Generated designs are numerous and include designs a human designer may not have considered. Visual analysis of fashion design versus sustainability impact can occur in real time, machine or human designer able to review what is a more vital need for the climate.

The example of a jumpsuit was tested. Parametric pattern blocks were mathematically translated to the jumpsuit design using Grasshopper in Rhinoceros 3D software by Robert McNeel & Associates. Parametric garment patterns are a draft of a pattern's curves represented by functions and variables. Parameters of the garment pattern contain sizing systems, design, fit and sustainability data. To help manage the complex relationships between input parameters, evolutionary solver tool, Galapagos, was used to run a simple algorithm testing combined surface area of the design to minimize textile. The generative garment design process created 62 epochs with 50 generations in each, producing 3,101 design variations.

Source: Elizabeth Bigger

Box 31.3

Adaptive pattern design

Adaptive pattern design process investigates customized garment fit and decreasing waste through pattern design. The classic t-shirt is based on five pattern pieces, resulting in nine sewing steps. Thirty-six t-shirt sizes were analyzed regarding their similarities and differences. The neck width, shoulder width and half chest were identified as basic parameters. Utilizing these parameters, the alpha 36 sizes were reduced to six sizes.

The customization relies on two production steps, using both offshore and nearshore factories. The first step relies on offshore factories cutting t-shirt blanks to the dimension of the largest included size. All other sizes respectively fit within the maximum dimensions of the largest t-shirt blank. The sewing of shoulder seams, sleeves, neck tape and neck hole topstitching is completed. In the second production step, an on-demand model is followed only once the consumer buys the t-shirt. Consumer measurements are applied to the t-shirt blank and customized. Secondary sewing steps of closing sleeve seams, side seams and hems complete the customized process.

Cutting waste quantities were estimated from calculating adaptations of the t-shirt blank needed for the six different sizes. Additionally nearshoring the production processes creates the opportunity for the pattern adaptations to be completed by a local sewist.

Source: Ahrens-Wels & Koch, 2021

AGILE FASHION SYSTEM REQUIREMENTS

Iterative workflows for sustainable fashion systems

Agile processes with iterative workflows are a necessary part of sustainable fashion production systems. Humans creating systems use the machine's strength in algorithmic processes to achieve more sustainable outcomes of garments produced. The presented processes of Generative Garment Design and Adaptive Pattern Design have iterative workflows (Figures 31.2 and 31.3). Evaluation points and results are

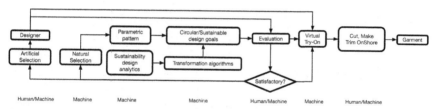

Figure 31.2 Generative garment design for sustainability workflow (Bigger 2021)

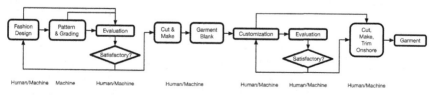

Figure 31.3 Adaptive pattern design workflow with the two cut and make customization process (Ahrens-Wels & Koch, 2021)

steps where processes can be repeated to yield better results. Generative Garment Design workflow progresses from evaluation results toward selection from the algorithm (natural selection) or selection by the designer (artificial selection). Adaptive Pattern Design can yield better results from both, design stage and the secondary customization step. The processes requires use of decision support tools wisely for analysis of fit and transitions to machine, which depend on reliable data. This requires knowledgeable consumers, technicians and robust data transfer systems. Maintaining healthy and ethical human–machine relationships in each step is necessary to create sustainable fashion workflows.

Interoperability and lingua franca

Fragmented global supply chains need a *lingua franca*, or common language, for interoperability of sustainable production. Interoperability, or computational systems' ability to share information between systems, is an opportunity for improved digital to physical garment production. A fashion language for systemic product development creates opportunities for proprietary algorithmic trade secrets for the next generation of fashion production. However, such a radical transition could catalyze sustainability by companies opting to openly share algorithmic developments. Companies could license another company's black box algorithms, allowing trade secret interoperability and collaboration. Further transparency could use open-source code, low code and no-code systems, contributing to future open agile production systems. Additionally democratizing garment creation and using no-code tools enhances co-creation between fashion stakeholders, local production and consumers. Optimization systems for sustainability can be shared for tackling environmental goals for both production and use phases of garments, benefiting many entities at one time. Agile production systems operate in real time, rather than supply chain sustainability assessments which may leave companies with smaller pocketbooks without manageable options for accessing production sustainability information. Global environmental standards need to be built into agile production systems in order for all companies to benefit and collaborate on global goals together.

Data generation from consumers needs to be addressed, as detailed data for personalization of garments is provided. Data privacy needs to be maintained, a challenge that can be addressed with federalized data management systems used in the medical field (Hite-Syed, 2021). In these systems, data stays at each place where it is generated and only derived measures (e.g. by applying machine-learning algorithms) are exchanged between partners. Nevertheless, humans should not become simply data points. Again, integrating humans with machines for collaborative development will help to create and support ethical systems.

Building sustainable bespoke local production

Addressing specific community needs in each region can build toward sustainable bespoke local production. A communique from the Alaska local assembly of The Union of Concerned Researchers in Fashion (UCRF), addressing a discussion of what a new production system for Alaska would need, acknowledged Alaska's limited resources and a population compelled to buy practical, well-functioning, good quality garments due to harsh weather conditions. Development of a local production system of micro mills with a community dividend model could both humanize producers and meet specific needs of the people of Alaska in a sustainable way (UCRF, 2021). Many communities may need to start from scratch reviewing resources, to address what will benefit regions and populations for long-term environmental sustainability. Other communities may need to evaluate repair and reuse of factories, machines and systems from the recent past. Emerging Web 3.0 processes, generative analysis and pattern adaptations support workflows for bespoke local production that can be completed with a laptop and home sewing machine.

CONCLUSION

The rise of fashioning with machines is proceeding, but it is up to humans to choose the desired relationships with emerging machines. Human creativity can alter how machines help produce and ultimately form uniquely positive partnerships for sustainability. *Fashion ex machina* collaborations have an opportunity to surprisingly shift fashion to a decentralized industry practicing sustainable bespoke local production. The foundations of Industry 5.0 fashion rely on four processes: focusing on humans in production, engaging with sustainable low risk Web 3.0 technologies, creating healthy human–machine collaborations and building inclusive interoperable systems for sustainable personalization. While the processes needed to achieve sustainability in fashion, environmentally and economically, are complex, we have only just begun to build the relationships needed to get there.

NOTE

1 https://rtfkt.com/.

REFERENCES

Ahrens-Wels, H., & Koch, H. 2021, "Sustainable Textile Production through Adapted Pattern Design.", Sustainable Innovation 2021, University for the Creative Arts Center for Sustainable Design, Epsom, Surrey, United Kingdom.
Bigger, E. 2021, 'Generative Garment Design for Circularity: Parametric Patterns and Transformative Algorithms for Enabling Circular Fashion Design.', Sustainable Innovation 2021, University for the Creative Arts Center for Sustainable Design, Epsom, Surrey, United Kingdom.
Bigger, E., & Fraguada, L. 2021, 'Sync: The Phygital T-Shirt. A Test Case for Decentralized Fashion Customization Utilizing Blockchain Technology & Local Production', The Sixth International Conference on Apparel Textiles & Fashion Design, Paris, France.
Britannica, T. Editors of Encyclopedia, 1998, "*deus ex machina.*" *Encyclopedia Britannica.*[Online] Available: https://www.britannica.com/art/deus-ex-machina [Accessed 15 December 2021].
European Commission, November 2020, "Industry 5.0: What This Approach Is Focused On, How It Will Be Achieved & How It Is Already Being Implemented." [Online] Available: https://ec.europa.eu/info/research-and-innovation/research-area/industrial-research-and-innovation/industry-50_en [Accessed 28 November 2021].
European Parliament, February 2016, "Policy Department A: Economic and Scientific Policy: Industry 4.0.", [Online] Available: https://www.europarl.europa.eu/FRegData/Fetudes/FSTUD/F2016/F570007/FIPOL_STU(2016)570007_EN.pdf [Accessed 30 March 2022]. Greenpeace, April 2019, "Konsumkollaps durch Fast Fashion-Greenpeace Greenwire." [Online]. Available: https://greenwire.greenpeace.de/system/files/2019-04/s01951_greenpeace_report_konsumkollaps_fast_fashion.pdf [Accessed 11 January 2021].
Hite-Syed, J. November 2021, "Healthcare Data Management: Understanding Interoperability, Integrity and Governance," [Online] Available: https://www.fedhealthit.com/2021/11/healthcare-data-management-understanding-interoperability-integrity-and-governance/ [Accessed 10 February 2022].
Howcroft, E. October 2021, "Crypto Fashion: Why People Pay Real Money For Virtual Clothes." [Online] Reuters. [Online] Available: https://www.reuters.com/business/finance/crypto-fashion-why-people-pay-real-money-virtual-clothes-2021-08-12/ [Accessed 15 October 2021].
Laitala, K., Boks, C., & Klepp, I. G. 2015, "Making Clothing Last: A Design Approach for Reducing the Environmental Impacts," *International Journal of Design*, vol. 9, no. 2, pp. 93–107. [Online] Available: https://oda.oslomet.no/oda-xmlui/bitstream/handle/10642/4920/1613-7733-2-PB.pdf?sequence=1&isAllowed=y> [Accessed 8 February 2022].
Laitala, K., Klepp, I., & Henry, B. 2018, "Does Use Matter? Comparison of Environmental Impacts of Clothing Based on Fiber Type.", *Sustainability*, 10(7), p.2524. Available at: http://dx.doi.org/10.3390/su10072524

Lee, G., & Xia, W. 2010, "Toward Agile: An Integrated Analysis of Quantitative & Qualitative Field Data on Software Development Agility," *MIS Quarterly*, vol. 34, no. 1, pp. 87–114. https://doi.org/10.2307/20721416.

McQuillan, H. 2020, "Digital 3D Design as a Tool for Augmenting Zero-Waste Fashion Design Practice", *International Journal of Fashion Design, Technology and Education*, vol. 13, no.1, pp. 89–100. DOI: 10.1080/17543266.2020.1737248

Quantis, 2018, "Environmental Impact of the Global Apparel and Footwear Industries Study", Quantis International, Zürich, Switzerland.

Union of Concerned Researchers in Fashion (UCRF), November 2021-last updated," Communiqué from Local Assembly Alaska" [Online]Available: https://concernedresearchers.org/communique-from-local-assembly-alaska/ [Accessed 18 December 2021].

32 Conclusion: progress, challenges and prospects

Martin Charter, Bernice Pan and Sandy Black

The COVID-19 pandemic of 2020–2021 exposed many cracks in the global Fashion System. This ranged from severe shortage and disruption in supply chains and logistics, to accelerated closure of bricks and mortar retail outlets and growth of 'everything online', to factory closures with worker's wages squeezed or unpaid and bankruptcies as demand dried up. In addition, the Russian-Ukrainian war that broke out in February 2022 has also highlighted the interconnectedness of global supply chains and markets from energy and raw materials supply to finished goods and market access e.g. if one cog ceases to work, the whole system draws to a halt or has to crisis manage and adjust to the 'new normal'. In addition, increased climate change risks and anxiety has started to emerge amongst young people in the decade of 2020s (Wu et al., 2020).

The fashion, clothing and textiles sector has a significant global footprint – economically, socially and environmentally. The economic worth is well understood but the significance of its carbon and waste impacts are only now starting to be recognised. Sitting at the heart of the sector is a financial model that rewards over-consumption and over-production driven by the emergence of fast fashion since the 1990s. The 'Wicked Problem' (Chapter 3) derived from a paradigm of 'growth, at all costs' to meet shareholder and retailer expectations, is driving poorer quality products, significant waste from 'cradle to grave', and water, air and chemical pollution at both agricultural and manufacturing levels in many countries. Endemic to this is the relentless pressure for profit maximisation which drives unfair wages and poor working practices and conditions which in many ways are no better than the

DOI: 10.4324/9781003272878-40

Victorian workhouses of 19th-Century England. The sector is not an early adopter of technology, with the use of manual labour for cutting, sewing and finishing processes being the norm. Whilst new Industry 4.0 technologies are starting to be adopted, they tend to be incorporated into manufacturing rather than the creative design, merchandise planning and product development phases. With cost of goods and per-garment profit margin at the heart of this industry, reducing fabric prices and labour costs is the top priority of brands and retailers. Therefore, many of the moral questions, and social and environmental impacts associated with the production and consumption of fashion and clothing get buried in the business economics. These issues range from altering the values of 'worth', 'need' and 'use', to enabling fast fashion amongst consumers and the systemic price cutting that forces manufacturers to put pressure on worker's pay in various tiers of supply chains. The sector suffers from a lack of availability and transparency of data and research on material sources and sustainability impacts, which means getting clarity over true social and environmental costs remains challenging.

Globally, there has been limited public policy pressure related to improvement of the sustainability performance in the fashion, clothing and textiles sector worldwide. However, this is changing in Europe with the European Commission's (EC) Circular Economy Action Plan 1.0 and 2.0 highlighting the sector as an area of forthcoming policy focus. This was reinforced by the launch of the EC Eco-design for Sustainable Products Regulation (ESPR) in March 2022 putting forward the EU Strategy for Sustainable and Circular Textiles.

Despite the increasing consumer awareness and desire for sustainability, many players in the sector are slow to take on board their broader responsibilities and accountability; selectively adopting sustainability initiatives – such as the many 'conscious collections' campaigns – that are backed up with little specificity or information to support claims. The marketing tactics used by many brands and retailers produce little to no sustainability improvement or impact reduction in the sector. This means that the sector lags far behind best practice in other sectors and leaves many brands and retailers open to a greenwashing backlash. There are now numerous sustainability initiatives in the sector across various regions that are fragmented and/or overlapping. It is also unclear who is engaging with these initiatives and what precise action is being taken, measured or monitored. Therefore, whilst legislation remains the most critical action required, a coherent and coordinated sector-wide approach must be urgently developed to spearhead a roadmap for the numerous stakeholders across the markets, supply chains and regions. For instance, the various national fashion councils and/or associations in key fashion capitals across the world could join forces to develop sustainable fashion standards and guidelines for both businesses and consumers. To move the sector forward, sustainability best practice in the fashion, clothing and textiles sector should also become a mandate and be prominently highlighted during seasonal fashion weeks, global trade shows and awards.

The growing sustainability consciousness in the fifth Green Consumer wave (see Introduction) that emerged in 2021–2022 and the legacy of the youth-led fourth wave before the pandemic, have contributed to an increased number of start-ups being launched in the sector where sustainability is part of the DNA of the businesses. New concepts, models, technology and investment are starting to flow into businesses with circularity dimensions, e.g. online reuse and repair platforms, new social enterprises and charities focused on repair or new material innovations. There is increased recognition of the high levels of waste at each stage of the value chain – pre- and post-consumption phase, with second-hand/pre-used garments gaining a new lease of life through the increased endorsement and channels for second-hand shopping.

A new circularity paradigm will emerge in the sector as more repair, reuse and recycling infrastructure is designed, implemented and invested in, particularly with the development and implementation of the forthcoming Extended Producer Responsibility (EPR) legislation in Europe. Innovation will also emerge in a range of areas from circular design to the sorting, separation, cleaning and processing of mixed materials for recycling and repurposing. The figure of 1% recycling of the global annual garment-textile output of some 100 billion units will be increasingly seen as a black mark for the sector.

Amongst the leading fashion and clothing brands and retailers, there have been high profile announcements as companies look to engage with the new sustainability paradigm in the sector. For example, the founder of Patagonia, Yvon Chouinard made a decision to make the Earth a shareholder by diverting profits into a trust to fight climate change, and Lululemon's founder announced the donation of US$75.8 million for nature preservation. The motivation for these announcements is not always clear, but it is calling out other industry players in the sector to take up their responsibilities and act. Significant commitments are also starting to be made by some brands and retailers, where the mandates and impacts will filter through the supply chains. For example, Burberry has announced its validation of carbon dioxide (CO_2) emission reduction commitments against Science Based Targets (SBTs) in 2022 (Wightman-Stone, 2022).

419

In the textiles space, Aquafil Group's innovation of Econyl, a 100% recycled and recyclable nylon generated entirely from fishing nets waste, is now being used by Prada amongst other global luxury heavyweights. Evrnu's newly launched NuCycl fibre engineered from discarded clothing is also starting to shift the dial at an industrial scale. Furthermore, there is increasing research and development into new plant-based materials and fibres as a substitutes for current options of polymer based products reliant on fossil fuel. A number of these innovations are now starting to be commercialised as highlighted in two of the book's chapters – see the Desserto case study in Chapter 10, and the examples of Circulose by Renewcell and Mylo® by Bolt Threads in Chapter 28.

The wide-ranging chapters making up *Accelerating Sustainability in Fashion, Clothing and Textiles* have demonstrated the importance of bringing together the numerous perspectives from different stakeholders in the fashion, clothing and textiles value chains to speed up the transition to sustainability in a realistic and scalable manner. The book provides a holistic overview of collaborative research and practice involving academia, clothing brands, consumers, manufacturers, local governments, and NGOs; addressing challenging and previously unaddressed issues whilst presenting solutions and prospects. It is evident that to accelerate change, progress must be made across many areas including innovation in business models and processes, materials and infrastructure, policy and education for net zero and a circular economy. Developing sustainability literacy and knowledge amongst consumers is essential, and educating future designers, industry professionals and business decision makers both in principles and practices of sustainable and circular design is crucial. The role of design and development is central to fashion, clothing and textiles and must be expanded from purely aesthetic, technical and financial considerations to encompass strategic thinking, with designers able to influence and advocate for fundamental sustainability changes both vertically and laterally throughout their organisations.

The future is inextricably linked to technological developments, which will be vital in facilitating many solutions to the 'Wicked Problem' of fashion. For example, AI generated consumer insights will enable more accurate forecasts for buying and procurement which can substantially help reduce or eliminate over-supply and subsequent clothing and textile waste. However, it is clear from the research and findings in this book that the dominating 'Fashion System' must pay more attention to incorporate the cultural dimensions and indigenous knowledge related to fashion, clothing and textiles inherent in many societies and regions, with a greater focus on the local and personal aspects of wearing, making, sharing and repairing clothes.

The Fashion System, that is, the entire fashion, clothing and textiles sector as well as the wider apparel sectors including accessories, footwear and leather goods sectors and beyond needs a fundamental reset. For real and accelerated change to take place, it is crucial for the sector to move from voluntary to legislated actions, where incentives and rewards for best practices are set up and penalties levied for the worst offenders. A 'carrot and stick' strategy needs to be adopted by government with enforcement. For example, calling out greenwashing without penalties and repercussions will not be effective, as 'hardnosed' industry players will simply make a judgement call should the claims serve their commercial purposes. It is essential that government not only engages with industry but also with wider societal and civic stakeholders. Campaigns and pressures to impact policy have increased, with the environment, social and governance (ESG) reporting gaining momentum across financial institutions and businesses sectors, but integrated action with specified criteria is required at all levels rapidly and coherently. New measures of quality products must be recognised by consumers through improved labelling by producers and retailers e.g. provenance of materials, and policymakers should reward industry leaders by introducing mandatory sustainability metrics and disclosures in financial reporting. Such change will be critical in transitioning the sector to sustainable practices that can be incrementally and continuously improved across all scales and sectors of businesses.

The fashion, clothing and textiles sector continues to face underlying issues of social injustice and inequity, but these are starting to be addressed not only by dedicated NGOs (such as Labour Behind the Label and Common Objective) and campaigns (including Fashion Revolution and #payupfashion) but also by policymakers. For example, the UK recently passed legislation on Modern Slavery to end malpractices in UK clothing manufacturing. Higher consumer demand for transparency throughout the value chain – from sourcing of raw materials and fibres (Tier 4 activities), and materials processing and textile manufacture (Tiers 2 and 3 activities) to the garment and product suppliers (Tier 1 activities) – means that traceability is becoming increasingly important, with more facilitation coming onstream through new digital systems. Some leading players have started to publish their sources and suppliers (see MUD Jeans case study in Chapter 13), and Fashion Revolution now ranks fashion businesses on its Transparency Index, based on the data businesses disclose.

Whilst sustainability progress demonstrated in the fashion, clothing and textile sector has been slow, the evidence presented in this volume gives strong indication that the journey has now begun albeit in its early days. However, what the sector now requires is the courage, candour and concerted efforts at every level of responsibility to confront its own negative impacts and start the first steps towards the structural changes.

The fundamental issue that global economies and societies need to address is the 'elephant in the room' namely, over-production and over-consumption in the sector. This 'Wicked Problem' needs to be addressed head-on by policymakers, industry, consumers and civil society. Leaving this to the industry to self-regulate has not worked, and there is a need for joined-up thinking, purpose and action, with a commitment by all stakeholders to change. Failure to tackle this quickly and directly will mean that commitments made in relation to the United Nations Fashion Industry Charter for Climate Action (FICCA) and the Sustainable Development Goals (SDGs) will not be met. More importantly, it means that the scale and force of the damage and depletion continuously done to the planet and people will pose intensifying risks to the future safety and wellbeing of all. Action is now required, if we are not to fail the youth and future generations.

On the positive side, the exceptionally powerful and agile sector that gathers the top creative, business, finance and technology minds amongst other talents and capabilities has historically weathered all crises and challenges to renew itself under times of pressure. Therefore, whilst time is running short, there is every reason to believe in a rapid transition to a new sustainability paradigm in the sector, once true commitments are made. The discourse for change now needs to move from the discussion table to positive action in order to mitigate the 'code red for humanity' warning issued by the UN Secretary-General following the Sixth Report of the Intergovernmental Panel on Climate Change (IPCC) in 2021.

REFERENCES

Wightman-Stone, D. 2022. Burberry receives SBTi approval for its net-zero emissions target. *FashionUnited*. Available at: https://fashionunited.uk/news/business/burberry-receives-sbti-approval-for-its-net-zero-emissions-target/2022081164599.

Wu, J, Snell, G, Samji, H. 2020. Climate anxiety in young people: A call to action. *The Lancet*. Published Online 9th September 2020. Available at: https://www.thelancet.com/pdfs/journals/lanplh/PIIS2542-5196(20)30223-0.pdf. https://doi.org/10.1016/ S2542–5196(20)30223-0.

Index

Note: **Bold** page numbers refer to tables; *Italic* page numbers refer to figures and page numbers followed by "n" denote endnotes.

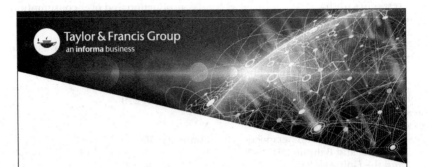

Printed in the United States
by Baker & Taylor Publisher Services